Edmc
50.00

BRAIN, BEHAVIOR, AND LEARNING IN LANGUAGE AND READING DISORDERS

CHALLENGES IN LANGUAGE AND LITERACY

Elaine R. Silliman and C. Addison Stone, Series Editors

Frame Work in Language and Literacy: How Theory Informs Practice
Judith Felson Duchan

Phonological Awareness: From Research to Practice
Gail T. Gillon

Handbook of Language and Literacy: Development and Disorders
C. Addison Stone, Elaine R. Silliman, Barbara J. Ehren, and Kenn Apel, Editors

Language and Literacy Learning in Schools
Elaine R. Silliman and Louise C. Wilkinson, Editors

Children's Comprehension Problems in Oral and Written Language: A Cognitive Perspective
Kate Cain and Jane Oakhill, Editors

Brain, Behavior, and Learning in Language and Reading Disorders
Maria Mody and Elaine R. Silliman, Editors

Brain, Behavior, and Learning in Language and Reading Disorders

Edited by

MARIA MODY and ELAINE R. SILLIMAN

Series Editor's Note by C. Addison Stone

THE GUILFORD PRESS
New York London

A Division of Guilford Publications, Inc.
72 Spring Street, New York, NY 10012
www.guilford.com

Printed in the United States of America

This book is printed on acid-free paper.

Last digit is print number: 9 8 7 6 5 4 3 2 1

Library of Congress Cataloging-in-Publication Data

Brain, Behavior, and Learning in Language and Reading Disorders / edited by Maria Mody and Elaine R. Silliman.
p. ; cm. — (Challenges in language and literacy)
Includes bibliographical references and index.
ISBN 978-1-59385-831-5 (hardcover : alk. paper)
1. Language disorders in children. 2. Language disorders. 3. Reading disability. 4. Neuropsychology. I. Mody, Maria. II. Silliman, Elaine R. III. Series.
[DNLM: 1. Language Disorders—therapy. 2. Child. 3. Learning Disorders—therapy. WL 340 L287596 2008]
RJ496.L35L3665 2008
618.92′855—dc22

2008010096

To my parents, who taught me to question
—M. M.

To Paul, whose patience makes all possible
—E. R. S.

About the Editors

Maria Mody, PhD, is a cognitive neuroscientist in the Department of Radiology at Massachusetts General Hospital and Harvard Medical School, Boston, specializing in developmental disorders of reading and language. She is a member of the faculty in the Health Sciences and Technology Program at the Massachusetts Institute of Technology in Cambridge, and also teaches in the Department of Communication Sciences and Disorders at Emerson College in Boston.

Dr. Mody uses a variety of neuroimaging methods, including functional magnetic resonance imaging, magnetoencephalography, and electroencephalography, to examine the relationship between spoken language and reading in normal and atypical development. Her work is supported by funding from the National Institutes of Health and the Mental Illness and Neuroscience Discovery Institute in Albuquerque, New Mexico. She is a past Associate Editor of the *Journal of Speech, Language, and Hearing Research,* and has published in a variety of journals, including *Neuropsychologia*, *Journal of Phonetics*, *Journal of Experimental Child Psychology*, and *NeuroImage*. Dr. Mody lectures widely, both nationally and internationally. Her work focuses on children with dyslexia, autism, and specific language impairment.

Elaine R. Silliman, PhD, is Professor of Communication Sciences and Disorders and Cognitive and Neural Sciences at the University of South Florida in Tampa, Florida. She is a Fellow of the American Speech–Language–Hearing Association (ASHA) and the International Academy for Research on Learning Disabilities. She also holds the Honors of the New York State Speech–Language–Hearing Association and the Distinguished Alumni

Achievement Award from the Graduate Center of the City University of New York.

Dr. Silliman is a past Editor of the ASHA journal *Language, Speech, and Hearing Services in Schools*. Her research has appeared in a wide variety of journals, including *Developmental Neuropsychology; Learning Disabilities Research and Practice; Language, Speech, and Hearing Services in Schools*; and the *American Journal of Speech–Language Pathology*. She also is the author or coauthor of 18 chapters and a coeditor of five books. Dr. Silliman's current research interests include the development of academic language proficiency in children who are struggling with reading, writing, and spelling, including monolingual English-speaking students with social dialect variations and bilingual (Spanish–English) students.

Series Editor's Note

I am pleased to present the sixth volume in The Guilford Press series *Challenges in Language and Literacy.* In their introduction to this volume, coeditors Maria Mody and Elaine Silliman characterize their goal as the production of a book that "stimulate[s] new thinking about development and disorders of language and reading." The book certainly does this; however, it does much more. Like the best edited volumes, the editors approached their endeavor with a clear purpose in mind, and they go beyond the simple presentation of recent work to provide a substantive contribution to the field.

In framing the book's purpose, the editors argue that progress in our understanding of typical and atypical development of oral and written language has been constrained by two related factors. First, theorists have failed to incorporate into their models the wide complexity and variations that exist within and across groups of people. Second, there has been little movement beyond the standard rhetoric of nature versus nurture toward a more dynamic view of cognitive–linguistic behavior. Consequently, the editors argue, "efforts to understand disorders of higher cognition, such as reading and language impairments, have become mired in oversimplistic localizationist accounts of brain–behavior relationships or theories of environmental constraints."

To build their case for a more nuanced understanding of language and literacy disorders, the editors have assembled a set of papers from prominent scholars that facilitates the integration of current knowledge from cognitive, neurolinguistic, and neuroimaging studies with analyses of differential response to experiential history and variation in outcome. The "big" argument evident in the editors' design for this book is the need to elaborate a theory of the dynamic interplay of experience and neurocognitive functioning in typical/atypical development. Included in this notion is the need to attend seriously to individual differences within the "typical" and "atypical" populations (e.g., varying developmental trajectories for late talkers) as we strive to develop a principled understanding of the dynamics involved in the development and treatment response of individuals with atypical language and literacy.

The editorial team brings a strong interdisciplinary background to the present project. Both editors are prominent authorities in speech–language pathology with particular expertise in developmental language and reading disabilities. In addition, they bring rich experience in cognitive behavior and neuroscience, particularly as applied to the study of the language–reading interface. The book's contributing authors are all recognized experts representing a range of disciplinary perspectives on language and literacy disabilities, including education, neuropsychology, developmental psychology, cognitive science, behavioral genetics, pediatrics, and speech–language pathology. Through thoughtful selection of authors and careful orchestration of the manuscript preparation process, the editors have created an unusually well-integrated edited volume. To further enhance this integration, the editors provide useful bridging introductions to the various sections, which highlight the common threads running through the chapters. In addition, the editors have contributed a capstone chapter of their own, which serves simultaneously as an encapsulation of major themes running through the volume and as a stimulating call for future work.

The present volume embodies many of the themes of the *Challenges in Language and Literacy* series of which it is a part. The aim of the series is to integrate interdisciplinary perspectives on language and literacy with empirically based programs and practices for promoting effective learning outcomes in diverse students. The series is based on the premise that oral and written language skills are functionally intertwined in individual development. Understanding the complexity of this relationship requires the collaborative contributions of scholars and practitioners from multiple disciplines. The series focuses on typical and atypical language and literacy development from the preschool years to young adulthood. Its goal is to provide informative, timely resources for a broad audience, including practitioners, academics, and students in the fields of language science and disorders, educational psychology, general education, special education, and learning disabilities.

I am confident that this book will do what we have in mind for the entire series, that is, stimulate the thinking and the practice of professionals devoted to the integration of work on language and literacy in myriad settings devoted to research and practice. The book is an important step forward in the integration of disciplinary perspectives on the acquisition of language and literacy.

C. ADDISON STONE

Contributors

Marnie E. Arkenberg, PhD, Department of Psychology, Carnegie Mellon University, Pittsburgh, Pennsylvania

Virginia W. Berninger, PhD, Department of Educational Psychology, University of Washington, Seattle, Washington

John T. Bruer, PhD, James S. McDonnell Foundation, St. Louis, Missouri

Brian Byrne, PhD, School of Behavioural, Cognitive, and Social Sciences, University of New England, Armidale, New South Wales, Australia

Julia L. Evans, PhD, School of Speech, Language, and Hearing Sciences, San Diego State University, San Diego, California

William Davis Gaillard, MD, Departments of Special Education and Psychology, Children's National Medical Center, Washington, DC

Jeffrey W. Gilger, PhD, College of Education, Purdue University, West Lafayette, Indiana

Jeffrey R. Gruen, MD, Department of Pediatrics, Yale University School of Medicine, New Haven, Connecticut

Donald W. Hine, PhD, School of Behavioural, Cognitive, and Social Sciences, University of New England, Armidale, New South Wales, Australia

Kathryn Kohnert, PhD, Department of Speech–Language–Hearing Sciences, University of Minnesota, Minneapolis, Minnesota

Maria Mody, PhD, Massachusetts General Hospital and Harvard Medical School, Boston, Massachusetts

Keith E. Nelson, PhD, Department of Psychology, Pennsylvania State University, University Park, Pennsylvania

Elizabeth Norlander, MS, CCC-SLP, Our Children's House, Grapevine, Texas

Andrew C. Papanicolaou, PhD, Department of Neurosurgery, University of Texas Medical School, Houston, Texas

Shirin Sarkari, PhD, University of Texas Health Sciences Center, Houston, Texas

Donald P. Shankweiler, PhD, Department of Psychology, University of Connecticut, Storrs, Connecticut

Bennett A. Shaywitz, MD, Departments of Pediatrics and Neurology, Yale University School of Medicine, New Haven, Connecticut

Sally E. Shaywitz, MD, Departments of Pediatrics and Neurology, Yale University School of Medicine, New Haven, Connecticut

Elaine R. Silliman, PhD, Department of Communication Sciences and Disorders, University of South Florida, Tampa, Florida

Panagiotis G. Simos, PhD, Department of Psychology, University of Crete, Crete, Greece

Anne van Kleeck, PhD, School of Behavioral and Brain Sciences, University of Texas at Dallas, Dallas, Texas

Deborah A. Weber, PhD, Children's National Medical Center, George Washington University School of Medicine, Washington, DC

Michael A. Wilkins, BS, College of Education, Purdue University, West Lafayette, Indiana

Jennifer Windsor, PhD, Department of Speech–Language–Hearing Sciences, University of Minnesota, Minneapolis, Minnesota

Contents

BRAIN, BEHAVIOR, AND LEARNING IN LANGUAGE AND READING DISORDERS

Part I

New Frameworks for Understanding Language Impairment and Reading Disorders

INTRODUCTION

The Nature of the Interactions between Brain, Behavior, and Experience

Framing Multiple Perspectives

MARIA MODY
ELAINE R. SILLIMAN

Over the years, there has been growing interest in the relative contributions of behavior, brain, and experience to the understanding of human cognition. Much less, however, is known about the interaction among these factors in cognitive development. Progress in this area has been hindered for two reasons. First, advances have been partly limited by a failure of the field to appreciate fully the complexity and variations within and across people. A second reason resides in the failure to move beyond the standard rhetoric of maturational accounts in critical period theory and the innateness hypothesis of nature versus nature to a more dynamic view of cognitive behavior. Consequently, efforts to understand disorders of higher cognition, such as reading and language impairments, have become mired in oversimplistic localizationist accounts of brain–behavior relationships or theories of environmental constraints.

Our purpose in this book is to stimulate new thinking about development and disorders of language and reading, and how to examine them. The first section presents three different perspectives highlighting the concepts of neurodevelopmental variation, emergentism, and critical period phenomena versus causal explanations that provide a new framework for examining language and reading disorders. At their core, these different perspectives pose a challenge to some basic assumptions in our investigation of brain–behavior relationships and articulate a need to rethink what constitutes normal and impaired learning profiles.

In Chapter 1, Gilger and Wilkins point out the errors of traditional approaches that have led researchers to focus on limited aspects of learning disabilities, resulting in an inability of research to explain the full continuum of behavioral and neurodevelopmental variations. The authors propose the use of the atypical brain development (ABD) model as a diagnostic framework for supplementing current approaches to the study of learning disabilities. According to the model, individual differences in behavior may be traced to variable brain structure and function, itself the result of the effects of genes and the environment on the learning brain. The ABD model describes the developmental variations of the brain and subsequent brain-based skills, encompassing phenomena at both ends of the ability continuum.

Recently, an emergentist account of language disorders in children appears to be gaining momentum. Emergentism stands in contrast to the symbolic representational nature of knowledge that originates in the environment or is hardwired at birth, as expressed by empiricists or nativists, respectively. In emergentism, novel coherent structure arises from the property of complex systems during a process known as "self-organization." In Chapter 2, Evans describes the emergentist perspective, with its roots in connectionism and dynamic systems theory, emphasizing that the emergent property of complex systems, such as language, is not reducible to its constituent parts. As Evans puts it, studies of typical and atypical language development need to move away from static, stage-like patterns in children's language trajectories toward an emergentist view of language development as a flexible and variable phenomenon. As such, language development is a process of the emergence of form, not specified in the genes or the environment. The chapter represents a thorough account of the application of emergentism to models of developmental and acquired disorders of language, with special reference to specific language impairment (SLI). At the core of the emergentist account is the important observation that a child's behavior at any point of time is a reflection of prior history and events, and can never be studied independently of the social context in which it was observed.

In the final chapter in this section, we come full circle to the notion of critical periods. Bruer provides in Chapter 3 a thoughtful review of the history and usefulness of critical periods in language learning, while cautioning against the conflation of critical period phenomena with causal explanations of the same. He then proceeds to dissect the popular maturational account of language acquisition and second language (L2) learning, citing evidence from a variety of studies involving L2 proficiency and foreign accent rating that were found to be inconsistent with a critical period theory for language. Bruer turns to the notion of entrenchment, which is an alternative to maturational accounts. The concept of entrenchment suggests that it may be the repeated exposure to the first language (L1) that makes it difficult to tune into L2 phonology, and not the closing of any neurobiologically sensitive period to phonetic distinctions per se. Support for the existence of critical period phenomena, but not of maturational accounts, provides a new framework for using critical period theory to examine issues in language learning as they relate to delays versus disorders in language and reading.

In conclusion, the chapters in this section highlight the importance of multiple perspectives. Practitioners and researchers alike are provided with new lenses to view and unravel the threads of behavior, brain, and learning that are central to our understanding of language impairment and reading disabilities.

1

Atypical Neurodevelopmental Variation as a Basis for Learning Disorders

JEFFREY W. GILGER
MICHAEL A. WILKINS

At times it seems as if those of us in the field of learning disabilities (LD) are like blind men looking at elephants: We are ostensibly studying the same pachyderm, yet we often come up with quite different impressions or highlight quite disparate facets. Indeed, the LD field is very broad in scope and diverse in disciplines. Because of this, there has been an abundance of intellectual creativity and fine science but, unfortunately, there has also been a lack of cohesion and perpetuating disagreements. Although the field of LD has made great progress over the years much is still unknown and some "knotty" issues in the field await resolution. For example, four of these issues revolve around "nosology" (i.e., the systemic classification of disorders) and include, among others: (1) arguments about LD categories; (2) disagreements about specific disorder criteria; (3) reconciliation of models that assume etiological and behavioral specificity of learning problems with findings of abundant comorbidity; and (4) changes in symptomology across the lifespan.

The purpose of this chapter is to stimulate some new thinking about LD, particularly the complexities and variations within and across people. This model is in reaction to a longstanding predilection in the LD field to use perspectives that are too narrowly focused to deal well with complexities such as those noted earlier. Over the years, traditional approaches have led many "blind men" to look upon only limited aspects of the LD animal, culminating in an inability to resolve the great variation that exists or explain the larger "beast" in its entirety. Although the findings of each study may be legitimate in their own right, there is a need for a model that can help us better understand and accommodate the multiple research messages that are available. Our proposal is that we need to combine current approaches with some new ways of thinking. This will allow us to appreciate fully the brain, which produces developmental LD, and the importance of viewing it as more than a simple reflection of its separate parts or domain specific symptoms.

The current chapter focuses on developmental reading disability (RD), or dyslexia, as an illustrative disorder. Reading disability is one of the more common LDs, and it has been well studied. In the next section we describe the phenotype of dyslexia and highlight some areas needing additional research. We then describe the concept of atypical brain development (ABD) as a "thinking tool" and discuss how it might supplement the current approaches and perspectives in the field.

OVERVIEW OF THE PHENOTYPE AND SYMPTOMOLOGY OF READING DISABILITIES

Definition

For our purposes, RD and dyslexia are essentially the same. "Dyslexia" is an older term derived from a medical model. Its use is avoided by some today because it was linked in the past with other symptoms, once believed to be etiologically related to dyslexia, such as right–left confusion, left-handedness, and reversal of letters and words (Orton, 1937; Fletcher, Lyon, Fuchs, & Barnes, 2007). However, these symptoms do not appear to be significantly related to dyslexia, as was once thought (Bishop, 1990; Bryden, MacManus, & Bulman-Fleming, 1994; Pennington, 1991).

RD is an unexpected difficulty learning to read (and/or spell) despite adequate intelligence and opportunity, and without demonstrable sensory, psychiatric, or neurological factors that explain the disorder (Lyon, Fletcher, & Barnes, 2003; Pennington, 1991). This definition, like that for many learning disorders, is largely exclusionary, in that other causes of reading problems must be ruled out (e.g., emotional problems). It is noteworthy that there has been a call for the field to define RD more in terms of inclusionary symptoms, although finite or "gold standard" criteria have yet to be accepted (Fletcher, Coulter, Reschly, & Vaughn, 2004).

The diagnosis of RD commonly requires a measured discrepancy between reading-related skills and the level of expected skills based on age or intelligence. Yet there is no universally accepted degree of deficit or discrepancy. For example, the U.S. federal definition of "learning disabilities" that is often used to establish eligibility for special education services specifies a discrepancy of at least 1 standard deviation (*SD*) between reading achievement and ability as measured, for example, by IQ (U.S. Office of Education, 1977). Other definitions have required more severe or weaker deficits in reading achievement, as related to age, grade, or IQ, and still others advocate dispensing with the required discrepancy all together (Fletcher et al., 2007; Pennington, 1991; Rutter & Yule, 1975).

One fairly well-accepted and research-based definition of RD was developed by a special task force of researchers and practitioners. This definition, formally adopted in 2002 by the International Dyslexia Association and the National Institutes of Health, reads:

> Dyslexia is a specific learning disability that is neurological in origin. It is characterized by difficulties with accurate and/or fluent word recognition and by poor spelling and decoding abilities. These difficulties typically result from a deficit in the phonological component of language that is often unexpected in relation to other cognitive abilities and the provision of effective classroom instruction. Secondary consequences may include problems in reading comprehension and reduced reading experience that can impede growth of vocabulary and background knowledge. (Lyon et al., 2003, p. 2)

Prevalence

The estimates of prevalence, of course, depends on the definition used, the age of the population, and the language or culture examined. For example, more children with reading problems are identified in grade 1 because of different rates of maturation. However, by grade 3, many of those children will have caught up with their peers in reading ability (Huston, 1992; Shaywitz, Escobar, Shaywitz, Fletcher, & Makuch, 1992; Fletcher et al., 2007; see Evans, Chapter 2, this volume, for an alternative perspective on catching up). This catch-up phenomenon may indicate an oversensitivity to tests at that age, instability of the disorder, and/or test–retest reliability problems (Huston, 1992; Shaywitz et al., 1992). These issues aside, common estimates of the prevalence of RD in English-speaking schoolchildren (grade 3 or beyond) have been 5 to 10% (Benton & Pearl, 1978; Keys, 1993; Fletcher et al., 2007).

Clinically referred populations' male:female sex ratios are generally 3:1 to 6:1, but this appears to be due mainly to biases in referral favoring males, which may in turn be due to cultural or severity issues. On the other hand, systematically ascertained populations, or populations that have had ascertainment biases controlled, typically yield a 1.3:1.7 male:female ratio

(DeFries & Alarcón, 1996; Raskind, 2001; Shaywitz, Shaywitz, Fletcher, & Escobar, 1990; Wadsworth, Olson, Pennington, & DeFries, 1992).[1]

Life Course

Although RD is generally considered to be a disorder of school-age children, there is evidence that perhaps some oral-language-based problems related to RD may be noted in the first few years of life (late speech onset, difficulties processing word sounds, etc.). Put another way, oral language problems prior to reading age are common in children who later develop RD (Catts, Fey, Zhang, & Tomblin, 1999; Lyytinen et al., 2004; see also van Kleeck and Littlewood, Chapter 10, this volume). Furthermore, the behavioral data are supported by brain imaging data. For instance, by age 3 months, the mismatch negativity (MMN), an evoked brain response (also called an event-related potential [ERP]) measuring acoustic–phonetic/phonological discrimination abilities was found to be significantly different (poorer) in infants at risk for RD compared to matched controls (Leppänen et al., 2002; Lyytinen et al., 2004).

Researchers have questioned whether dyslexia represents a "developmental lag." This would mean that children with RD actually read like younger, normal children but attain more age-appropriate reading ability at a later age. A lag hypothesis is different than a "disease" or "disorder" model, in which RD is seen as a deficit that is qualitatively different from normal reading skills, and that persists barring significant intervention. In fact, research indicates that reading weaknesses do persist into adulthood, and that there is a plateauing of reading skills in which skills gains decelerate (e.g., Bowen & Hynd, 1988; Bruck, 1990; Finucci, 1986; LaBuda & DeFries, 1988; Nopola-Hemmi et al., 2002; Scarborough, 1984; Shafrir & Siegel, 1994; Shaywitz et al., 1994). A number of these studies report ongoing reading problems or reading-related deficits in adults with RD histories, including phonological processing, selective auditory attention, naming, and short-term memory. Still, some adults compensate to some degree for their childhood reading problems (e.g., Felton, Naylor, & Wood, 1990; Gilger, Hanebuth, Smith, & Pennington, 1996; Lefly & Pennington, 1991; Pennington, 1991; Scarborough, 1984, 1989; Shaywitz et al., 1994, 2002).

Cognitive Basis of RD

With the assumption that RD is etiologically and phenotypically heterogeneous, a number of attempts have been made to define subtypes that might reflect pathogenic differences and/or be useful in treatment settings. However, subtype assignment may not be consistent within families or even within the same child over time, so subtype classifications appear at best to have more descriptive than etiological value (Pennington, 1991; Snowling, 1991; Stein, 2001; Wolff, 1999). It is clear that not all individuals with RD are the same, but it is unclear how and whether the behavioral profile differences among individuals with RD have any practical utility (Goldstein & Kennemer, 2005; Hallahan, Lloyd, Kauffman, Weiss, & Martinez, 2005; Pennington, 1991).

Pennington (1990) reviewed reading theories, some of which postulated a dual-processing route to reading acquisition and mastery that included phonology, orthography, and morphology. Over the past decade, the consensus has been that poor "phoneme awareness," the ability to understand and manipulate the basic sounds of language, was likely to be the primary deficit in reading. The predominance of phoneme awareness as the locus of an underlying deficit in RD did not mean that orthographic skills were normal, however. In the majority of readers with RD, both skills were in fact delayed (Castles & Coltheart, 1993).

Pennington (1999) and others have proposed a neural network design in which input is the visual image of the word, and output is the recognition and pronunciation of the word. A layered network was hypothesized to contain both phonological and orthographic levels. Network level interconnections are created through learning, such that the levels can work together in processing a word. If any of the interconnections are faulty or the input is degraded, or if there is too much reliance on one process at the expense of another, reading problems may result (Manis, Seidenberg, Doi, McBride-Change, & Petersen, 1996). More detailed cognitive models are reviewed by Ramus (2004a, 2004b) and Pind (1998). Although these theories help explain domain-specific difficulties in processing text, they do little toward understanding or accounting for the common associations found between RD and other disorders, and the processing–performance problems in domains other than reading-related abilities (various common comorbidities, soft neurological signs, occasional giftedness, etc.).

In summary, fully adequate models of reading acquisition and performance have not been determined (Pind, 1998), although phonological processing does appear to be the predominant deficit in RD. The contributions and interactions of auditory, visual, and other systems are now being assessed at neurological levels, and genetic studies are demonstrating that a single genetic locus can affect both orthographic and phonological phenotypes at once (Fisher et al., 1999; Gayán & Olson, 2003; Gayán et al., 1999; see Shaywitz, Gruen, & Shaywitz, Chapter 9, this volume).

RD and Other Learning Disorders

The commonly recognized LD types are displayed in Table 1.1. It is worth mentioning that what we say later about RD applies to these other disabili-

TABLE 1.1. Types of LD or Their Primary Symptoms and Behaviors

• Reading	• Activity level
• Attention	• Memory
• Motor coordination	• Social skills
• Mathematics	• Nonverbal abilities
• Spelling	• Language
• Writing	

ties as well. For instance, these LD types, like RD, are often studied, discussed, and treated as if they are separate and independent conditions, even though they are often associated, or comorbid, with other disorders, higher-order abilities or talents (i.e., twice exceptional individuals or those who are considered gifted and have LD disorder), and can show great interindividual variability in symptom characteristics.[2]

Finally, as in the case of RD, there is increasing evidence that many of the other LD types are truly developmental and commonly lead to continued difficulties throughout life (Goldstein & Kennemer, 2005; Scarborough, 1990; Shaywitz et al., 1994). And like RD, the LD types (e.g., math disorder) or behaviors (e.g., motor skills, attention) in Table 1.1 all show evidence of neurological and genetic roots, along with epigenetic and environmental processes (Gilger, Ho, Whipple, & Spitz, 2001; Pennington, 2002; Plomin & McClearn, 1993; Smith, Gilger, & Pennington, 2002).

THE CONCEPT OF ABD

The original conceptual framework behind the model of ABD was presented at the International Congress of Psychology (Lyytinen, 2000) and in a special issue of the journal *Developmental Neuropsychology* (Gilger & Kaplan, 2001; see also Gilger & Wise, 2004; Goldstein & Schwebach, 2004; Jeffries & Everatt, 2004; Kaplan, Dewey, Crawford, & Wilson, 2001; Kaplan & Gilger, 2001; Krueger & Markon, 2006; Lyon et al., 2003; Missiuna, Gaines, & Pollock, 2002; Rice & Brooks, 2004; Sonuga-Barke, 2003; Valtonen, Ahonen, Lyytinen, & Lyytinen, 2004). Originally conceptualized in terms of children and their early development, the ABD concept applies equally well throughout adulthood. In fact, there is a great need for theoretical and diagnostic frameworks for adults, in that there is little consensus on how to define or identify LD in this age group, and unique problems, such as assessment and tracking, transition, and LD expressions, are different for the older LD populations (Goldstein & Kennemer, 2005; Reiff, Gerber, & Ginsberg, 1993).

The ABD concept evolved primarily from thinking about the ecological validity of diagnostic categories. Issues were also raised by ongoing genetic and neurological research, especially in the area of RD that challenged the assumptions behind the concept of specific LD. The ABD approach was designed to provide some cohesion in ongoing research and to reconcile this research with the belief systems of many clinicians and educators who had extensive exposure to individuals with developmental problems, namely, that practitioners were becoming dissatisfied with the practical utility of dominant contemporary LD theories and guidelines.

ABD Fundamentals

There are three fundamental assumptions behind the ABD concept. By and large the validity of the first assumption is obvious. The second and third assumptions are also likely to be obvious, but some general references are provided (see Bartley, Jones, & Weinberger, 1997; Gilger, 1995; Pennington, 2002; Scerif & Karmiloff-Smith, 2005; Thompson et al., 2001; Thompson, Cannon, & Toga, 2002). The three assumptions are as follows:

1. The brain is the basis of behavior.
2. Individual differences in behavior are due to variable brain structure and function.
3. Ultimately, individual differences are the result of the complex effects of genes and the environment on the developing and learning brain. In fact, these processes are highly interactive (see Gilger & Wise, 2004).

It is important to realize that although the ABD concept is a neurological or neuropsychological model, it does not speak directly to how the brain is organized, or how specific areas or brain functions explain specific abilities, as do other "theories" or models (e.g., see Eden & Zeffiro, 1998; Hynd & Orbrzut, 1986; Lieberman, 1984; Luria, 1973; Pennington, 1991, 1999; Ramus, 2001; Rice & Brooks, 2004; Shaywitz et al., 1998). Again, the purpose of the ABD perspective is not to supplant these other models; rather, it supplies a frame of reference that is able to draw together these models and provide some externally valid coherence and understanding, as well as new directions for research.

ABD applies primarily to disorders that result from gene-regulated or gene-moderated developmental processes, and it does not apply to acquired disorders or disorders due mainly to adverse or teratogenic intrauterine environmental factors (Frith, 2001; Greenough, Black, & Wallace, 2002; Huttonlocher, 2002; Ramus, 2003, 2004a, b; see Note 2). The term "atypical" in ABD does not suggest dysfunction or damage. Instead, it is nonevaluative, encompassing phenomena at both ends of the ability continuum. It is not thereby invalidated by multiple, apparently disparate deficits in the same person, or by seeing people as having deficits and gifts at the same time. The term "development" in ABD accurately describes our current understanding: Developmental learning disorders are probably the result of prenatal and, to a lesser extent, postnatal brain growth and elaboration.

The application of the term ABD clearly contrasts that of the older, similar sounding term "minimal brain dysfunction," or MBD (Clements & Peters, 1962). MBD became an overly broad term employed to represent an ill-defined unitary syndrome for the categorization/diagnosis of a group of children (Satz & Fletcher, 1980). In contrast, ABD is meant to serve as a unifying concept regarding *etiology*, the expression of which is variable within and across individuals. As Gilger expressed it then (Gilger & Kaplan, 2001):

> ABD does not itself represent a specific disorder or syndrome and ABD does not pertain to brain injury, trauma, or disease in the classic medical sense. Rather, ABD is a concept that describes the developmental variation of the brain and subsequent brain-based skills on either side of the real or hypothetical norm. (p. 468)

ABD as Applied to RD

Dyslexia serves as a good illustrative disorder, in that it has been well researched with regard to epidemiology, definitions, genetics, and neurology/neuropsychology. Four aspects of RD fit well with the ABD model, and each of these is described below. Three of these aspects likely make ABD applicable to other types of LD as well, because LD research is beginning to show trends similar to those for RD. The fourth aspect, that RD is part of the "normal" range of reading and is not a *disease*, was always part of the ABD package (Gilger & Kaplan, 2001), but here we have chosen to make this point more salient.

Variants in the RD Profile: Comorbidity, Twice Exceptionality, and Cognitive Differences

One of the strongest arguments for supplementing current thinking about LD or RD per se with an ABD framework is the research that demonstrates the presence of a high degree of comorbidity, as well as intraindividual and interindividual variation in cognitive and behavioral profiles (Brody & Mills, 1997; Fuchs & Fuchs, 2002; Gilger & Kaplan, 2001; Kaplan et al., 2001; Pennington, 1999; Shapiro, Church, & Lewis, 2002). Therefore, in some proportion of cases the distinctions between disorders (RD, attention-deficit/hyperactivity disorder [ADHD], developmental coordination disorder, math disability, etc.) may be more artificial than real and may also muddle a complete understanding of the individual presenting a complicated symptom complex.

Data also indicate that RD (and other LD) can be significantly represented in gifted populations (e.g., Brody & Mills, 1997; Geschwind, 1982; Geschwind & Galaburda, 1987; Ruban & Reis, 2005). There exists a bit of folklore that giftedness is overrepresented in RD populations (e.g., Geschwind, 1982; Geschwind & Galaburda, 1987; West, 1999), but more research with better design and control is needed to address this belief properly. Nonetheless, the published rate for the twice exceptional child approximates .01 to .03, or even higher, when criteria are more lax (Ruban & Reis, 2005). Again, focusing on only the learning deficit in such individuals limits our understanding of their neurocognitive profile, the etiology of this profile, and what approaches to treatment may best be applied. Yet current theoretical approaches to the study and treatment of RD do not address twice exceptionality in any explicit or meaningful way. At best, contemporary thinking views RD and giftedness as separate and unrelated conditions that just happen to co-occur.

Given the common correlation of RD with other low- and high-end behavioral and cognitive traits, it would seem that maintaining a blanket approach, as if RD were a *completely* independent and domain-specific disorder, seems ill advised. Indeed, psychometric, genetic, and neurological research support at least some degree of nonindependence, often showing correlated cognitive abilities or cognitive factors, overlapping or multiple neurological substrates, and shared genes for phenotypes, brain morphology and brain function (e.g., Bartley et al., 1997; DeFries et al., 1979; LaBuda, DeFries, & Fulker, 1987; Olson, Forsberg, & Wise, 1994; Ramus, 2001, 2004a, b; Rice & Brooks, 2004; Sonuga-Barke, 2003; Thompson et al., 2001, 2002; Willcut et al., 2002; Wood & Flowers, 1999; Voeller, 1999).

Frequency of Comorbidity

As Gilger and Kaplan have argued elsewhere, the term "comorbidity" can be misleading, and the LD field might do well to apply it more carefully or abandon it altogether (Gilger & Kaplan, 2001; Kaplan et al., 2001). When the term "comorbidity" was transferred into the educational and mental health world, a missing element prevented its accurate application: the precise distinction between symptom and disease (or disorder). When an individual exhibits characteristics of dyslexia, memory problems, and motor skills deficits, it seems an open question whether that child is displaying comorbid unitary disorders or variable manifestations of a single underlying impairment, or several underlying impairments that may or may not be etiologically related. The co-occurrence of apparently disparate symptoms causes problems in both diagnosis and treatment, especially if they are on opposing ends of the continuum and, at the same time, complicates an understanding of etiology and interdependence (Bergman & Magnusson, 1997; Cloninger, 2002; Gilger et al., 1996; Gilger & Kaplan, 2001; Jeffries & Everatt, 2004; Kaplan et al., 2001; Lyytinen, Leinonen, Nikula, Aro, & Leiwo, 1995; Narhi & Ahonen, 1995; Sonuga-Barke, 2003).

One way to help relax the research and application "tensions" raised in this section is to view individuals with, say, RD, motor deficits, inattention, and intellectual gifts, as expressing symptoms produced by a diffusely atypical brain affecting multiple areas of behavior simultaneously. Thus, by evoking the concept of ABD, the problematic issues of symptom independence and comorbidity are ameliorated, in that attention is not overly focused on reading-related deficits, while neglecting the entire profile of neurocognitive strengths and weaknesses because they do not fit well into the preferred diagnostic scheme. These strengths and weaknesses, in an ABD perspective, are correlated etiologically because they derive from the same coherent and integrated organ—the brain.

Although we are recommending that RD not always be regarded as a trait of distinct and domain-specific origin and presentation, we *do not* believe that research into the etiology and manifestations of RD as a specialized category of LD should be discontinued. Quite the contrary, such research continues to refine the nosology, symptomatology, and treatments for this disorder in positive ways (Fletcher, Denton, Fuchs, & Vaughn, 2005; Fletcher, Shaywitz, & Shaywitz, 1999). We *do believe* that RD is a specific LD with its own neurological roots and processing components, but that it reflects developmental phenomena that are also reflected in many other facets of the individual brain in dyslexia. ABD explicitly reminds us that because there is variation within and between people in neurodevelopment, their symptoms, profiles, and developmental trajectories necessarily vary as well.

Etiological Variability in LD

It is a virtual certainty that genes play a significant role in RD-related symptoms or phenotypes and, therefore, logically, in the development of the brain that regulates RD-related symptoms (Gayán et al., 1999; Hannula-Jouppi et al., 2005; Meng et al., 2005; Pennington, 1997, 2002; Petryshen et al., 2001; Regehr & Kaplan, 1988; Smith et al., 2002). Tentative genes, or "susceptibility alleles," have been identified as contributors to RD risk (reviewed in Pennington, 2002; Smith & Gilger, 2007), and research indicates that the genes putting individuals at risk for RD do not necessarily correspond to specific or independent cognitive aspects of reading ability (Fisher et al., 1999, 2002; Gayán & Olson, 2003; Gayán et al., 1999; Grigorenko et al., 1997; Olson et al., 1994; Schulte-Körne, 2001; Smith et al., 2002). In other words, probably multiple heterogeneous effects of the RD-risk genes act alone or together to give rise to multiple profiles of reading-related skills (Frith, 2001; Gilger et al., 1996; Gilger & Kaplan, 2001; Ramus, 2001). In summary, research to date (pleiotropic effects) suggests that genes may affect multiple brain areas and contribute to the variance in learning in a complex manner rather than in a focused, singular, and direct manner, as predicted by single-gene–single-disorder models, or simple neural modularity models (e.g., Aaron, Joshi, & Ocker, 2004).

Even if we consider the effects of a single-gene variant for traits as complex as human learning, such a gene may yield multiple typical and atypical behaviors, especially if this gene is influential during the early stages of neural development and brain organization, or if it affects lower levels of neural organization upon which higher levels depend (Conn, 1992; Gerlai, 1996; Greenough et al., 2002; Huttonlocher, 2002; Luria, 1973; Rondi-Reig, Caston, Delhaye-Bouchaud, & Mariani, 1999; Scerif & Karmiloff-Smith, 2005). Relevant here is recent research reporting that genes on chromosomes 3 and 6 are linked to RD risk (Hannula-Jouppi et al., 2005; Meng et al., 2005). These genes are thought to be active in early neurodevelopment, such as neuronal migration. In one case (Meng et al., 2005), variants of the *DCDC2* gene on chromosome 6 were shown to cause migration errors, although it is not known whether these errors show up preferentially in the left hemisphere, as would be expected given anatomical and magnetic resonance imaging (MRI) studies of individuals with RD. A developmental gene that is important to cortical cell migration or connection, for instance, could possibly affect more than one brain area to varying degrees, thus having the potential to influence multiple behavioral areas (see further discussion on this topic in the next section). The discrimination of primary LD subtypes (RD vs. math disability vs. ADHD, etc.) on the basis of several distinct major genes, each influencing a different primary brain area, is not supported: The enormous co-occurrence of these conditions argues for at least some degree of multifocal action of the pertinent gene(s) and/or multifocal neurodevelopmental effects of single genes that originally operated on only specific brain areas (see also Marcus, 2004; Scerif & Karmiloff-Smith, 2005).

The Variable Neuroanatomy of Developmental LD

As we just mentioned, it is unlikely that there is a one-to-one correspondence between a single, finite brain area and type of developmental LD.

More likely would be a collection of specific brain areas, circuits, or systems that together place an individual at risk for a certain type of LD, but these systems do not operate in isolation from the rest of the brain and other functional circuits. The structural or activational anomalies in the brain of an individual with a LD are probably numerous, although they may be more heavily focused in one region or another (e.g., Scerif & Karmiloff-Smith, 2005; Shaywitz et al., 1998, 2002). Perhaps it is the area with the heavier focus that gives rise to a person's primary diagnosis, simply because it results in the most salient profile features.

According to this perspective, the symptoms exhibited by people (e.g., deficits in reading, math, spelling, motor skills, attention, or some combination of these) depend on two aspects: the relative amount of anomalous development in areas of the brain responsible for the primary symptoms (e.g., phonological awareness in RD), and the additional brain areas that are also affected (visual cortex, cerebellum, frontal lobes, etc.). Moreover, we expect a complete "whole-brain" study of an individual with RD or LD to show peaks and valleys in abilities, with the peak skills perhaps having compensatory powers for the valley skills.

While it may be an oversimplification, the ABD concept reminds us that *every individual's* interaction with the environment is a product of the neurodevelopmental variations he or she carries, and that a person's integrated and fully functioning brain is kind of an "average" of these variations across time. Within the same person, certain daily experiences may at times call upon aspects of brain functioning that tap his or her ABD at the low end (e.g., RD, when asked to read) or at the high end of the continuum (e.g., high spatial abilities, when asked to solve a puzzle).

Multiple atypical brain areas have in fact been demonstrated in RD populations. Beyond the most commonly cited language areas of the left hemisphere, studies have also indicated morphological and/or functional differences in the occipital, parietal, and frontal lobes, the cerebellum, corpus collosum, and cortical thickness, among others (see reviews in this chapter and in Démonet, Taylor, & Chaix, 2004; Mody, 2004; Pind, 1998; Smith et al., 2002; see also in this volume Weber & Gaillard, Chapter 6; Simos, Sarkari, & Papanicolaou, Chapter 7; Shaywitz, Gruen, & Shaywitz, Chapter 9). Thus, again, the brains of persons with dyslexia may be diffusely atypical. For this reason there remains some question as to the neurological specificity underlying RD. The absence of consensus on specificity may account for the large amount of correlated cognitive and behavioral traits typically observed in individuals with dyslexia, whether they be other disorders, giftedness, or a variety of subtle neuropsychological deficits.

This said, it is important to remember that not all genes have broad neurodevelopmental effects. Some have comparatively constrained or focused effects on the development of the brain. Neuroanatomical differences across species and similarities within species are largely driven by these genetic characteristics. Although brains can differ within humans, all "normal" brains have essentially the same structures in the same places, and these structures, or parts of these structures, are often built in a way that serves specialized purposes. Clearly, for example, the cerebellum is structurally and functionally different from the cortex. Similarly, portions of the temporal lobe seem prewired to acquire and to mediate spoken and written language. Therefore, it is not surprising that functional MRI (fMRI) studies show a characteristic, atypical left temporal lobe activation profile in dyslexia, and it is likely that some of the RD-risk genes appear to have effects primarily in this area of the brain. In this scenario we are still faced with the possibilities resulting from a diffusely atypical brain in individuals with RD.

In accord with the previous discussion, several of the *hypothetical situations* given in Table 1.2 suggest that even specialized genes can affect development in other areas of the brain, albeit in different or minimal ways (see also Conn, 1992; Gerlai, 1996; Greenough et al., 2002; Huttonlocher, 2002; Kolb & Whishaw, 1998; Luria, 1973; Marcus, 2004; Thompson et al., 2002; Toga & Thompson, 2005; Rondi-Reig et al., 1999; Scerif & Karmiloff-Smith, 2005).

RD Is Part of the Normal Continuum of Reading

A thorough discussion on this topic appears in Gilger et al. (1996). Briefly, RD does not appear to be a classic "disease." In the past there was some debate as to whether dyslexia actually existed as a separate learning disor-

TABLE 1.2. Hypothetical Secondary Effects of a Gene Specialized for Early Neurodevelopment in the Language and Other Areas of the Left Temporal Lobe

Left lobe deviations	Secondary effects
Atypical cortical cell migration	Atypical cell migration in analogous areas of the right hemisphere
Atypical development/function	Degraded communication and connections with other neurological units that hinder the operation of nets or systems for broader skills
Atypical connections and subsequent communications between this lobe and other lobes	Atypical development of other lobes because of poor or atypical stimulation
Atypical myelinization	Slow or degraded processing loops for information that include left temporal units

der from the continuum of normality, responsive to unique etiological factors (Fletcher, 1992; Pennington, 1991; Rutter & Yule, 1975; Siegel, 1989). Some researchers maintained that if dyslexia is etiologically distinct, it should produce a "hump" at the lower end of the otherwise continuous distribution of reading scores in children (Stevenson, 1988; Yule, Rutter, Berger, & Thompson, 1974), but several genetic and epidemiological studies did not detect such a hump (Gilger et al., 1996; Rodgers, 1983; Shaywitz et al., 1992).

Genetic research also suggests that RD is in fact part of the larger range of reading skills, and that it may represent the effects of the same etiological factors as normal reading ability (Gilger, Borecki, DeFries, & Pennington, 1994; Smith et al., 2002). It also appears that poor reading in children with below-average IQs, or in which there is no significant IQ–achievement discrepancy, is not qualitatively different from the poor reading of children with dyslexia (Fletcher, 1992; Lyon et al., 2003; Siegel, 1989). However, the heritability of dyslexia may be greater in a population selected for higher IQ (Wadsworth, Olson, Pennington, & DeFries, 2000), and the more severe the reading problem, the stronger some linkages on chromosome 6 may be (Fulker et al., 1991; Gayán et al., 1999; Knopik et al., 2002).

The normal continuum versus disease concept is also illustrated by a characteristic of RD that makes it unique compared to many of the other LDs. The RD concept was created by societal demands and were it not for the written alphabet would not otherwise exist. Reading itself was not instrumental to our development and survival as a species, although correlated traits may have been. Furthermore, oral language problems prior to reading age are common in children who later develop RD (e.g., poor oral language or spatial skills; Catts et al., 1999; Lyytinen et al., 2004). If reading ability were somehow indirectly influenced by selection pressures on some other trait, we might expect to see low-end reading abilities significantly represented in the population, just as we do (Geary, 1998). There might be some characteristic that on average is more prevalent in people now identified as having RD given that in our evolutionary past that characteristic gave them some advantage. What this advantage might have been is pure speculation. For example, progenitors of today's population with dyslexia may have had better interpersonal skills or spatial orientation abilities that gave them some sort of procreative edge (e.g., West, 1999).

That RD (or reading) was not under great selection pressures predicts that it does not reflect powerful effects of single genes or dominant genes. In contrast, the case may be different for an oral language disability or language ability in general (Gilger, 1995). It is possible that research will ultimately reveal specific links between "language genes" and "language brain structures" given how language evolved and how there are probably innate brain structures that are specialized to the neurocognitive needs for spoken language acquisition (Pinker, 1994). Although a person with a language disorder may display atypical brain development beyond the classic language areas, the genetic and neurological structure for language is probably more canalized (Marcus, 2004; Waddington, 1975) and prescribed than, for example, is the case for reading. Thus, it is more likely in the future that specific key genes will be found that strongly determine the development of specific brain areas important to language acquisition.

Research Supportive of the ABD Approach: Summary

In summary, the research basis for ABD as applied to RD suggests five findings:

1. There are multiple pathways by which abilities, such as reading, can be affected, and irregularities in one or all of these pathways may yield similar symptoms at the surface level. Although not all areas of the brain are involved in all tasks, these sorts of results should be expected given what we know about the complexity of the brain, especially for higher-order cognitive skills such as reading.
2. In part because of the complexity of reading, it is not likely that one common factor alone explains the majority of developmental RD cases in the population. Many factors, genetic and environmental, interact to create a tendency toward or away from developmental RD, as well as the variable expressivity of the underlying ABD responsible for the reading problems.
3. The ABD concept suggests that variation occurs first at the neurological level, within and between people in the population. Furthermore, this variation can lead to correlated symptoms or traits. The interpretation and identification of this variation depends on the level of analysis applied: from the level of the neuron or neurological structure to the level of neurological function and, at the most removed level, behavior (see discussion that follows and Figure 1.1).
4. Brain variation and ABD often go unnoticed in the laboratory unless the "whole brain" is assessed appropriately and with sensitive enough instruments. Similarly, the consequences of atypical brain development may go unnoticed in everyday life unless experience or life demands tap into the person's personal developmental peaks and/or valleys.
5. It is unlikely that there is a simple, one-to-one mapping of genes to brain structures or brain areas to cognitive abilities. This is especially true when the concerns are complex cognitive traits, the effects of developmental genes, and the development of cognitive abilities across the lifespan (Changeaux, 1985; Hahn, van Ness, & Maxwell, 1978; Johnson, Muna-

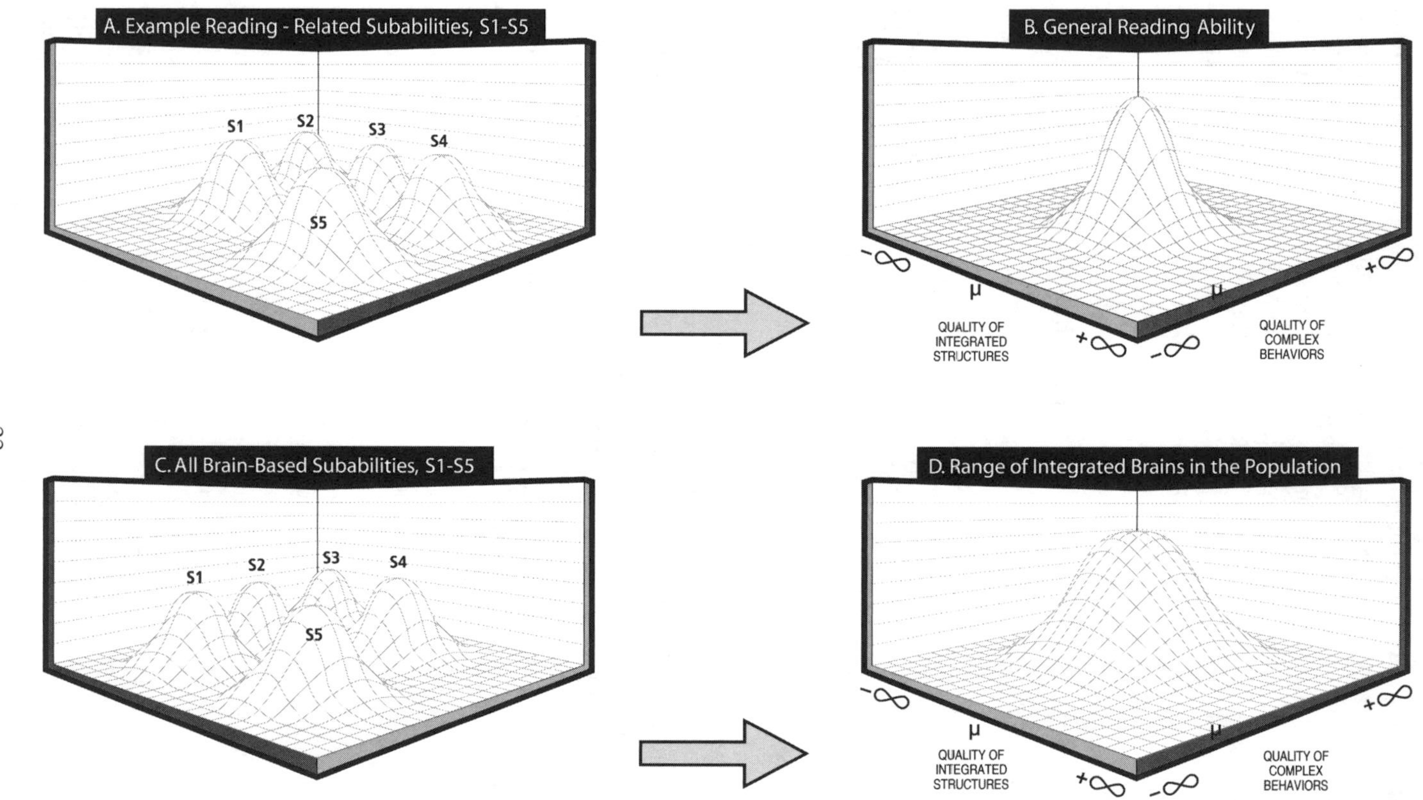

FIGURE 1.1. The ABD model. See text for explanation. ∞, infinity (– or +); μ, population mean.

kata, & Gilmore, 2002; Jones & Murray, 1991; Noctor, Flint, Weissman, Dammerman, & Kriegstein, 2001; Scerif & Karmiloff-Smith, 2005).

A Pictorial Summary of the ABD Concept

Figure 1.1 presents the way that the ABD model conceptualizes the role of individual and group differences in neurodevelopment and RD. For the sake of clarity and simplification, we assume that all distributions discussed are fairly normal (also see Note 2), and that we are referencing post-reading-age individuals. Of course, Figure 1.1 simplifies many complexities and confounds, and it is meant to serve only as a point for discussion.

According to the figure, reading ability depends on multiple brain-based subabilities (Figure 1.1A) that, in combination, average to yield the normal (multivariate) distribution of global reading ability in the population (Figure 1.1B). The range of these subabilities is due to variation in neurodevelopmental structures, all of which are influenced to some extent by genetics. It is hypothesized that structures correlate with internal brain function. In turn, function, correlates with measured behaviors. Because of the long line of neurological processes needed to produce a complex behavior, and because of measurement issues and other variables, structure and function are more strongly correlated than structure and external behavior, or function and external behavior. As predicted by a normal distribution, the smallest number of people will have brains with "superior" structure and concomitant "superior" reading ability, or "inferior" structures with "inferior" ability.

The characteristics of some of the structures, such as cell number and cortical layering or connectivity due to migrational effects, are set during the prenatal period. Other characteristics come from later brain elaborations, such as myelinization and neuronal connections due to learning. ABD recognizes that variation in these structures affects internal brain function, therefore affecting the external behavioral subabilities across and within people. It is primarily through these effects that we see variations in global reading scores that simply mirror average brain functioning for reading-related subabilities. These effects also lead to profiles of strengths and weaknesses within people for reading-related skills.[3]

Figure 1.1 further expands the example for reading to all brain-based cognitive skills. Again, ABD proposes within- and between-person variability in these structures and subsequent behaviors (Figure 1.1C). The average of the functional effects of these structures essentially yields a "continuum of integrated brains" and general cognitive ability in the population (Figure 1.1D). Thus, the average integrated brain represents the "mythical normal brain." But like the mean (μ) in a theoretical normalized z-distribution, the mythical normal brain probably exists less in reality than in imagination. Again, within-person variation in brain-based structures and abilities determines an individual's profile of strengths and weaknesses.

APPLICATIONS AND IMPLICATIONS OF THE ABD CONCEPT

The ABD concept is relevant to theory and practice, and should not be summarily dismissed as "stating the obvious" or being no better than the concept of "cerebral dysfunction" (Lyon et al., 2003). We have already pointed out how ABD is different from concepts of dysfunction and that the ABD concept, in our opinion, does more than state the obvious. The conceptual tool of the ABD model should be used in conjunction with other perspectives in the RD field. Recognition of the utility of the ABD concept does not require dispensing with efforts to differentiate LD categories or refine the category of RD. In fact, it is our hope that the implications of the ABD model will become part of the contemporary psychology of the LD field, sharing space with (not replacing) the more molecular approaches to research and treatment. We next outline seven benefits of thinking about ABD for basic research and practices.

Use a Whole-Brain Perspective

ABD as a concept strongly advocates for developmental and experimental studies of the whole brain. By this we mean that the commonplace methods of study that focus on distinct categories or the specific and microanalytical cognitive processing approaches to a behavior should be supplemented with an explicit awareness of the brain as a whole organ. An illustration of this point can be found in the typical neurogenetic study of children with RD, which typically assesses, then considers mainly verbal skills but not (for instance) motor coordination or attention. This approach has been common in the past, but the ABD model suggests expansion into realms other than verbal skills. Interestingly, when other, even nonlanguage areas of the RD brain are examined, they are often found to be atypical (reviewed in Mody, 2004).

The call for a broader approach is important, as is the recognition that the search for genes that influence learning abilities, LD, or specific cognitive processes is really a search for the genes that determine "atypical brain development" (Gilger, 1995; Gilger & Kaplan, 2001; Jones & Murray, 1991). We are looking for genes that underlie brain variation in the population, such that some people fare better or worse than others when it comes to learning. Consequently, future genetics research would be strengthened were it to include multiple measures of brain integrity and function, including, but not limited to, tests of general reading, word recognition, math, processing speed, motoric processes, attention, visual–spatial abilities, and so forth. Research employing a more limited phenotype may miss much of the complexity of an individual's skills.

Learning Ability Variation across the Continuum Can Be "Normal"

The ABD concept considers some "deficits" and "gifts" to be "normal" variation. One of the main tenets of the ABD approach is the existence of variation in brain structures, resulting in functional variation that can be identified at the behavioral level—sometimes as apparently unitary traits, such as RD or high spatial ability. But the compartmentalization of a collection of traits into supposedly independent categories may be misleading. Rather, the ABD concept suggests that such traits may also be viewed simultaneously as simple symptoms of brain variation, and that the best method for understanding etiology and treatment approaches is to *consider both the category and the broader presentation of traits as reflections of a variable brain*, or a diffusely atypical brain. We recommend that, with ABD as a sort of general perspective, more detailed and specific theories of brain–behavior relationships, networks, brain processing components, and so forth, can be tested and applied where valid (e.g., Eden & Zeffiro, 1998; Mody, 2004; Ramus, 2004a, b), thus expanding our understanding even further.

There is also an implication for educational and clinical practices. It is noteworthy that the ABD model recognizes that it may be perfectly normal to have both significant deficits and strengths in the same person. This is more than simple within-person ability variability. It means that one can literally have a child who cannot read, but who shows spectacular gifts in art or math, with both abilities reflecting different aspects of the same atypical brain development mechanism that may have been operating *in utero*. In other words, the factors (e.g., cell migration genes) causing ABD that yield reading deficits may be the same factors that yield a brain with a propensity for mathematical giftedness. This proposal needs research support (but see data and citations in Craggs, Sanchez, Kibby, Gilger, & Hynd (2006). Given the assumption that this sort of ABD is normal, we expect certain proportions of twice exceptional, but otherwise typical, people to be born every day, although they may go unnoticed.

Reminder: Behavioral Phenotypes Can Be Considered in Terms of Neurology

The concept of ABD helps us redefine behavioral phenotypes into terms dealing with their ultimate basis: the brain. This is important, because behavioral phenotypes often appears to be driving brain research rather than brain research driving phenotypes. Perhaps this is a necessary state of the art because our ability to view the brain *in situ* has only recently become possible (Kennedy, Haselgrove, & McInerney, 2003), and we still rely heavily on psychometric measures. However, along with the common methods of brain study, additional and unforeseen information may be obtained by approaching research from a bottom-up, alongside a top-down, methodology. Specifically, we suggest the need for large-scale multivariate analyses in which common brain areas that show up in atypical and typical behavioral phenotypes are sought, *as well as* concomitant studies that begin with brain imaging results, then look for their behavioral expression. Reconciliation of the findings from this sort of work is a first step toward a more fully developed and reliable picture of the brain, brain–behavior relationships, and individual variation in the population.

Developmental Models Are Important

ABD makes a general statement that a developmental perspective must be maintained when talking about genetic and neurological effects on learning or cognitive systems. At different points in time, the surface phenotype of, say, performance on a reading test may reflect genetic and environmental effects that occurred when the brain was just starting to form, and/or genetic and environmental effects on the brain that continue to affect reading throughout life. Certain aspects of brain development, such as cell migration and structural differentiation, occur very early, then more or less stop, and the key genes moderating these processes "turn off" or may assume other functions (Galaburda, 1992, 1993; Johnson et al., 2002; Greenough et al., 2002; Huttonlocher, 2002). This fact reminds us that when we look for genes that have affected brain structure and put a person at risk for RD, we may be looking for genes that are no longer active (Gilger, 1995).

Avoidance of One-Size-Fits-All Thinking

The ABD concept helps us to avoid single-etiology or one-size-fits-all schemes of thinking. It is again worth emphasizing that the ABD approach does not advocate against ongoing research or treatment approaches based on subtypes or diagnostic categories. Instead, we hope that the implications of ABD can be incorporated into these current models of study and treatment. The ABD concept should not be taken as anticategorization or antilabeling. Perhaps the ABD concept can best be thought of as a "thinking tool" that, when used conjointly with other tools, results in a more accurate etiological picture of behavior, with broader explanatory power.

Rather than employing one-size-fits-all thinking, the ABD concept emphasizes the complexity of the brain and brain–behavior relationships. Simple diagnostic schemes or treatments that focus on only one aspect of the symptoms of the atypical brain (e.g., phonemic awareness interventions) do not do justice to the underlying causes of what is observed at the surface. They increase the likelihood of treatment failure because of a limited focus on one behavioral category. Appreciating the complexities of within-person abilities not only has value in diagnostic and treatment domains but also has implications for prevention (see also Bergman & Magnusson, 1997; Shapiro et al., 2002).

Again, the ABD model suggests that risk for disorders is only part of the picture, and that potentialities for strengths might also be present at birth. In the future, with the likelihood of more molecular and chemical therapies, a focus on the whole brain or the entire person (at least philosophically) will have implications for the remediation of disorders. One implication is that interventions for a disorder might affect the positive potentialities in the person as well. When we treat one aspect of brain function, we likely affect other aspects at the same time, and such manipulations at the behavioral level may significantly change the life course of the individual in directions we cannot foresee. One example might be the use of some sort of radical *in utero* "gene replacement therapy" in an attempt to prevent anomalous brain development that might lead to RD. If such a treatment was applied, the brain would be modified toward avoiding RD, but the brain alterations might also ultimately affect other domains of skills (because these genes modify development in multiple brain areas, or the experience of not having a language problem may also modify neurology and personality as one ages, etc.).

Adults and People with Atypical Abilities in Multiple-Domain Disabilities

The ABD concept may be especially useful in understanding the child or adult who does not fit usual or simple diagnostic schemes. Individuals at all ages appear to have a variety of symptoms without clear etiology or coherence. These cases can be very confusing and frustrating to clinicians and educators, often requiring a huge amount of management effort, diagnostic tests, and failed treatments. Often such individuals do not receive appropriate treatments and, especially as children, may end up being placed in special programs that are better suited to other forms of LD when they have so many other ongoing issues.

Complexities are also likely to be seen in adults, because so many life experiences, skills, coping mechanisms, and learned behaviors decrease the clarity with which deficits are manifest (Goldstein & Kennemer, 2005). We have often seen persons with such a diffuse clinical picture exhibit traits spanning nonverbal LD, reading, coordination and math problems, social skills deficits, anxiety, ADHD, and so on, while exhibiting basically normal IQs and an ability to function fairly well with guidance and practice. Applying the suggestions of the ABD concept does not require that such individuals be diagnosed per se, but that they be recognized as having a diffusely atypical brain, of whatever etiology, that does not yield to simple classifications. Such individuals require broad-based assessments and treatments that focus on the many symptoms they exhibit, as well as the strengths they display.

Another point of particular relevance to adults is that symptoms can change significantly with age. By the time children with learning problems become teenagers or adults, often they have had multiple shifting diagnoses, none of which alone has done justice to their individual profiles. Having multiple diagnostic labels over the years is due to more than diagnostic unreliability; it may reflect a real change in the profile of symptoms given people's life experiences and brain maturation (see Ehri & Snowling, 2004; Rice & Brooks, 2004; Shaywitz et al., 1990).

Another advantage of thinking about adults in terms of the ABD conceptualization is that some of the pressures on children in our educational system, such as high-stakes testing, Individualized Education Plan (IEP) qualification, and so on, are not present for older age groups, although there is some need for classification to receive services (e.g., Americans with Disabilities Act, 1991). Consequently, treatments can be multifaceted at the start and dynamic, and address symptoms and profiles globally, without such a great demand for individual subtyping or categorization.

ABD's Diagnostic Utility

Finally, we are certainly not the first to question the value of diagnostic cat egories (e.g., Rapin, 2002). Yet there are many pressures to assign diagnoses to people, even while the concept of individual differences is being acknowledged, and it is possible that these pressures sometimes prevent thorough educational assessments of various skills (see also Berninger, Chapter 4, this volume). Recognition that children with ABD represent an enormously heterogeneous group at the neurological level can have important beneficial effects on educational assessment (and treatment) strategies. In our opinion, for educational purposes, children should be assessed for their individual strengths and needs, and treatment plans should be developed to address both. But there are often financial, cultural, and other pressures to distill a child's complex pattern of strengths and weaknesses into a few words describing a categorical diagnostic label, with all of its implications and myths. Whereas diagnoses tell us something important about the person and provide research-based information and guidance, the ABD concept emphasizes a thorough, broad-spectrum analysis of each individual, with the explicit aim to identify and track irregularities on *both* ends of the continuum.

We recognize that the financially driven pressure to categorize service funding is not likely to disappear quickly under any new conceptual framework. But there is good reason to believe that this pressure to categorize is more than financially driven, and only an open-minded reconsideration of the available data and approaches to research will allow a different perspective, leading to different therapeutic and diagnostic techniques. Today, for instance, there is a movement to initiate a multistep "three-tiered (response to intervention) model" in the schools (e.g., Fletcher et al., 2005; Vaughn & Fuchs, 2003). The focus of such models is not so much diagnosis per se as a careful assessment and tracking of a student with LD, and a responsive and evolving research-based remediation plan. In fact, at the first two levels of "intervention," a child need not necessarily be diagnosed as having a certain type of LD to receive services in the regular education classroom. Instead, the teacher and other professional staff identify a student struggling with reading in the regular curriculum, then initiate a form of intervention with monitoring. The teacher is supposed to modify his or her teaching methods according to how the student responds. This multilevel approach is just the beginning of some major changes to come in the LD field, and it fits in well with the ABD concept, in which diagnosis is less important and the focus on symptoms is key.

FINAL WORDS

The history of the study of developmental disorders is replete with debates between lumpers and splitters. "Lumpers" are people who develop large theories that tend to encompass many aspects of an issue; "splitters" tend to be more concrete, and attempt to categorize and subtype a phenomenon into smaller parts. What we propose is that in the area of LD, and RD in particular, both approaches can live side by side harmoniously.

It may be true, as Lyon et al. (2003) claim, that a broad concept such as ABD can be "overarching" and, consequently, not contribute to a field in which diagnostic specificity is often the goal. But we question whether such diagnostic specificity should be the sole goal given the fact that current diagnostic schemes seem partially to have failed to characterize the general population of people with learning disorders. We base this accusation of partial failure on the phenotypic, genetic, and neurological data reviewed in this chapter. We conclude that there is a bigger need and picture here—something beyond defining and redefining categories, while neglecting a much needed holistic approach to the person.

Our proposed approach of employing the concept of ABD does not presume to exclude the definition of a circumscribed phenotype; rather, it suggests that there is value in more broadly characterizing the skills sets of the individuals being studied. The coexistence of the lumping and splitting approaches likely offer an improved approach in both clinical and research applications, particularly with adults.

Figure 1.2 illustrates one way of thinking about ABD as a model and how it might work alongside other models. First, all neurological/neuropsychological research essentially deals with the atypical or typical brain, depending on its focus. Hence, for developmental disorders, we show in brackets that ABD can serve as the broader concept under which the more specialized research would fall. As the picture implies, the specialized type of research should not occur in isolation, but should take place in concert with the concepts of ABD. To put it succinctly, this figure highlights the fact that as researchers, clinicians, and teachers, we might do well to acknowledge the role of the whole brain, lest we lose sight of the forest for the trees.

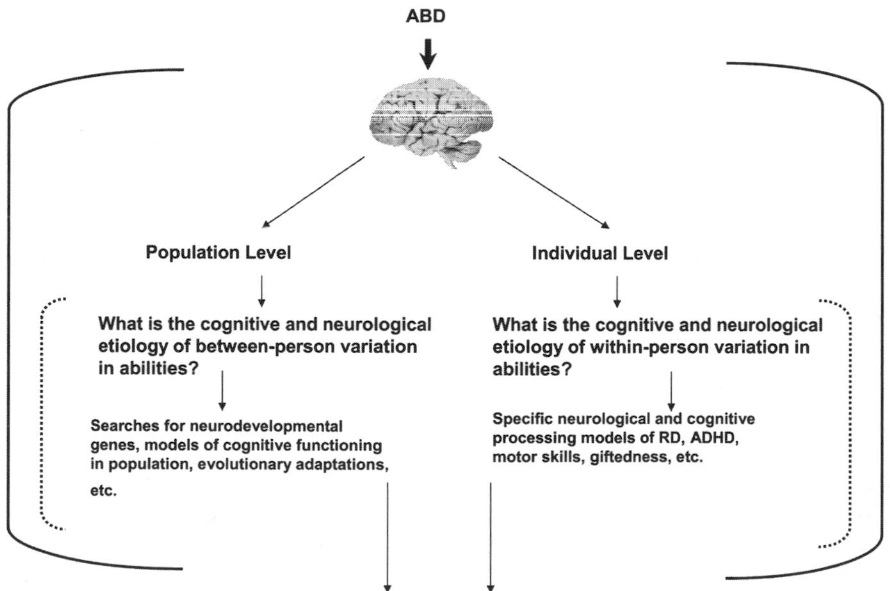

FIGURE 1.2. ABD as a collaborative model toward conceptualizing LD and inter-/intraindividual differences.

ACKNOWLEDGMENTS

The ideas for this chapter were presented at the 2004 annual meeting of the International Dyslexia Association, and some paraphrased portions of the text are based on prior publications (Smith & Gilger, 2007; Gilger & Kaplan, in press).

NOTES

1. Broader definitions of poor reading that do not require a significant discrepancy with nonreading abilities may yield prevalence rates as high as 20 to 30% (Berger, Yule, & Rutter, 1975; Eisenberg, 1978). In other linguistic populations in which written language is more phonetically consistent, such as Italian, the frequency of RD may be significantly lower (Paulesu et al., 2001).
2. In this chapter we are only dealing with nonsyndromic or developmental conditions. We are not concerned with extreme deviations in development related to some syndrome or those due to some specific genic or chromosomal aberration (Down syndrome, neurofibromatosis, etc.).
3. There are a number of levels of structures, from the very small and focal to the larger and more global. There are also structures that connect to other structures and are important for some behaviors and not others. Of course, some structures have major effects, whereas others have only minimal effects. Under a natural context, there are also neurochemical processes involved in learning and reading (e.g., Sabolek, Bunce, & Chrobak, 2004). These processes are important in memory formation, neuronal connection, cell-to-cell communication, and so on.

   In some ways, such as cell-to-cell communication, neurochemical processes that affect functioning may not necessarily seem structural. However, the production, utilization, and regulation of neurochemicals are due to neuronal microstructures that can also deviate from some hypothetical mean. All else being equal, variation in performance with concomitant effects on other systems (how well incoming information is processed, how well learning occurs, how well visual inputs get to and from the occipital lobe, etc.) may result to the extent that these systems and microstructures vary within or between people.

REFERENCES

Aaron, P. G., Joshi, M. R., & Ocker, E. S. (2004). Summoning up the spirits from the vast deep: LD and giftedness in historic persons. In T. Newman & R. Sternberg (Eds.), *Students with both gifts and learning disabilities* (pp. 199–234). New York: Kluwer Press.

Americans with Disabilities Act of 1990, Public Law 101-336. (1991).

Bartley, A. J., Jones, D. W., & Weinberger, D. R. (1997). Genetic variability of human brain size and cortical gyral patterns. *Brain, 120*, 257–269.

Benton, A. L., & Pearl, D. (Eds.). (1978). *Dyslexia: An appraisal of current knowledge*. New York: Oxford University Press.

Berger, M., Yule, W., & Rutter, M. (1975). Attainment and adjustment in two geopraphical areas: I. The prevalence of specific reading retardation. *British Journal of Psychiatry, 126*, 510–519.

Bergman, L. R., & Magnusson, D. (1997). A person-oriented approach in research on developmental psychopathology. *Development and Psychopathology, 9*, 291–319.

Bishop, D. V. M. (1990). *Handedness and developmental disorder.* Phildelphia: Lippincott.

Bowen, S. M., & Hynd, G. W. (1988). Do children outgrow deficits in selective auditory attention?: Evidence from dichotic listening in adults with learning disabilities. *Journal of Learning Disabilities, 21*, 623–631.

Brody, L. E., & Mills, C. J. (1997). Gifted children with learning disabilities: A review of the issues. *Journal of Learning Disabilities, 30*, 282–296.

Bruck, M. (1990). Word recognition skills of adults with childhood diagnoses of dyslexia. *Developmental Psychology, 26*, 439–454.

Bryden, M. P., MacManus, I. C., & Bulman-Fleming, M. B. (1994). Evaluating the empirical support for the Geschwind–Behan–Galaburda model of cerebral lateralization. *Brain and Cognition, 26*, 103–167.

Castles, A., & Coltheart, M. (1993). Varieties of developmental dyslexia. *Cognition, 47*, 149–180.

Catts, H., Fey, M., Zhang, X., & Tomblin, J. B. (1999). Language basis of reading and reading disabilities: Evidence from a longitudinal investigation. *Scientific Studies of Reading, 3*, 331–361.

Changeaux, J.-P. (1985). *Neuronal man*. New York: Oxford University Press.

Clements, S. G., & Peters, J. E. (1962). Minimal brain dysfunctions in the school-age child. *Archives of General Psychiatry, 6*, 185–197.

Cloninger, C. R. (2002). Implications of comorbidity for the classification of mental disorders: The need for a psychobiology of coherence. In M. Maj, W. Gaebel, J. J. Lopez-Ibor, & N. Sartorius (Eds.), *Psychiatric diagnosis and classification* (pp. 79–106). Chichester, UK: Wiley.

Conn, M. T. (Ed.). (1992). *Gene expression in neural tissue*. San Diego: Academic Press.

Craggs, J., Sanchez, J., Kibby, M., Gilger, J., & Hynd, G. (2006). Brain morphological and neuropsychological profiles of a family displaying superior nonverbal intelligence and dyslexia. *Cortex, 42*, 1107–1118.

DeFries, J., & Alarcón, M. (1996). Genetics of specific reading disability. *Mental Retardation and Developmental Disabilities Research Reviews, 2*, 39–47.

DeFries, J. C., Johnson, R. C., Kuse, A. R., McClearn, G. E., Polovina, J., Vandenberg, S. G., et al. (1979). Familial resemblance for specific cognitive abilities. *Behavioral Genetics, 9*, 23–43.

Démonet, J.-F., Taylor, M. J., & Chaix, Y. (2004). Developmental dyslexia. *Lancet, 363*, 1451–1460.

Eden, G. F., & Moats, L. (2002). The role of neuroscience in the remediation of students with dyslexia. *Nature Neuroscience, 5*, 1080–1084.

Eden, G. F., & Zeffiro, T. A. (1998). Neural systems affected in developmental dyslexia revealed by functional neuroimaging. *Neuron, 21*, 279–282.

Ehri, L. C., & Snowling, M. J. (2004). Developmental variation in word recognition. In C. A. Stone, E. R. Silliman, B. J. Ehren, & K. Apel (Eds.), *Handbook of language and literacy* (pp. 433–460). New York: Guilford Press.

Eisenberg, L. (1978). Definitions of dyslexia: Their consequences for research and policy. In A. L. Benton, & D. Pearl (Eds.), *Dyslexia* (pp. 29–42). New York: Oxford University Press.

Felton, R. H., Naylor, C. E., & Wood, F. B. (1990). Neuropsychological profile of adult dyslexics. *Brain Language, 39*, 485–497.

Finucci, J. M. (1986). Follow-up studies of developmental dyslexia and other learning disabilities. In S. D. Smith (Ed.), *Genetics and learning disabilities* (pp. 97–121). Philadelphia: Taylor & Francis.

Fisher, S. E., Francks, C., Marlow, A. J., MacPhie, I. L., Newbury, D. F., Cardon, L. R., et al. (2002). Independent genome-wide scans identify a chromosome 18 quantitative-trait locus influencing dyslexia. *Nature Genetics, 30*, 86–91.

Fisher, S. E., Marlow, A. J., Lamb, J., Maestrini, E., Williams, D. F., Richardson, A. J., et al. (1999). A quantitative-trait locus on chromosome 6p influences different aspects of developmental dyslexia. *American Journal of Human Genetics, 64*, 146–156.

Fletcher, J. M. (1992). The validity of distinguishing children with language and learning disabilities according to discrepancies with IQ: Introduction to the special series. *Journal of Learning Disabilities, 25*, 546–548.

Fletcher, J. M., Coulter, W. A., Reschly, D. J., & Vaughn, S. (2004). Alternative approaches to the definition and identification of learning disabilities: Some questions and answers. *Annals of Dyslexia, 54*, 304–331.

Fletcher, J. M., Denton, C. A., Fuchs, L., & Vaughn, S. R. (2005). Multi-tiered reading instruction: Linking general education and special education. In S. O. Richardson & J. W. Gilger (Eds.), *Research-based education and intervention: What we need to know.* Baltimore: The International Dyslexia Association.

Fletcher, J. M., Lyon, G. R., Fuchs, L. S., & Barnes, M. A. (2007). *Learning disabilities: From identification to intervention.* New York: Guilford Press.

Fletcher, J. M., Shaywitz, S. E., & Shaywitz, B. A. (1999). Comorbidity of learning and attention disorders: Separate but equal. *Pediatric Clinics of North America, 46*(5), 885–897.

Frith, U. (2001). What framework should we use for understanding developmental disorders? *Developmental Neuropsychology, 20*(2), 555–563.

Fuchs, L. S., & Fuchs, D. (2002). Mathematical problem-solving profiles of students with mathematics disabilities with and without comorbid reading disabilities. *Journal of Learning Disabilities, 35*, 564–574.

Fulker, D. W., Cardon, L. R., DeFries, J. C., Kimberling, W. J., Pennington, B. F., & Smith, S. D. (1991). Multiple regression analysis of sib-pair data on reading to detect quantitative trait loci. *Reading and Writing: An Interdisciplinary Journal, 3*, 299–313.

Galaburda, A. M. (1992). Neurology of developmental dyslexia. *Current Opinion in Neurology and Neurosurgery, 5*, 71–76.

Galaburda, A. M. (1993). Neurology of developmental dyslexia. *Current Opinion in Neurobiology, 3*, 237–242.

Gayán, J., & Olson, R. K. (2003). Genetic and environmental influences on individual differences in printed word recognition. *Journal of Experimental Child Psychology, 84*(2), 97–123.

Gayán, J., Smith, S. D., Cherny, S. S., Cardon, L. R., Fulker, D. W., Brower, A. M., et al. (1999). Quantitative-trait locus for specific language and reading deficits on chromosome 6p. *American Journal of Human Genetics, 64*, 157–164.

Geary, D. (1998). *Male, female: The evolution of human sex differences*. Washington, DC: American Psychological Association.

Gerlai, R. (1996). Gene-targeting studies of mammalian behavior: Is it the mutation or the background genotype? *Trends in Neuroscience, 19*, 177–181.

Geschwind, N. (1982). Why Orton was right [The Orton Dyslexia Society Reprint No. 98]. *Annals of Dyslexia, 32*, 13–30.

Geschwind, N., & Galaburda, A. M. (1987). *Cerebral lateralization: Biological mechanisms, associations and pathology*. Cambridge, MA: MIT Press.

Gilger, J. W. (1995). Behavioral genetics: Concepts for research in language and language disabilities. *Journal of Speech, Language, and Hearing Research, 38*, 1126–1142.

Gilger, J. W., Borecki, I., DeFries, J. C., & Pennington, B. F. (1994). Commingling and segregation analysis of reading performance in families of normal reading probands. *Behavioral Genetics, 24*, 345–355.

Gilger, J. W., Hanebuth, E., Smith, S. D., & Pennington, B. F. (1996). Differential risk for developmental reading disorders in the offspring of compensated versus noncompensated parents. *Reading and Writing: An Interdisciplinary Journal, 8*, 407–417.

Gilger, J. W., Ho, H., Whipple, A., & Spitz, R. (2001). Genotype–environment correlations for language-related abilities: Implications for typical and atypical learners. *Journal Of Learning Disabilities, 34*, 492–502.

Gilger, J. W., & Kaplan, B. J. (2001). The neuropsychology of dyslexia: The concept of atypical brain development. *Developmental Neuropsychology, 20*, 465–481.

Gilger, J. W., & Kaplan, B. J. (in press). Atypical brain development in learning disorders. In L. E. Wolf, H. I. Schreiber, & J. Wasserstein (Eds.), *Adult learning disorders: Contemporary Issues*. New York: Psychology Press.

Gilger, J. W., & Wise, S. E. (2004). Genetic correlates of language and literacy impairments. In C. Addison Stone, E. R. Silliman, B. J. Ehren, & K. Apel (Eds.), *Handbook of language and literacy development and disorders* (pp. 25–48). New York: Guilford Press.

Goldstein, S., & Kennemer, K. (2005). Learning disabilities. In S. Goldstein & C. R. Reynolds (Eds.), *Handbook of neurodevelopmental and genetic disorders in adults* (pp. 91–114). New York: Guilford Press.

Goldstein, S., & Schwebach, A. J. (2004). The comorbidity of pervasive developmental disorder and attention deficit hyperactivity disorder: Results of a retrospective chart review. *Journal of Autism and Developmental Disorders, 34*(3), 329–339.

Greenough, W. T., Black, J. E., & Wallace, C. S. (2002). Experience and brain development. In M. H. Johnson, Y. Munakata, & R. O. Gilmore (Eds.), *Brain development and cognition: A reader* (pp. 186–216). Boston, MA: Blackwell.

Grigorenko, E. L., Wood, F. B., Meyer, M. S., Hart, L. A., Speed, W. C., Shuster, A., et al. (1997). Susceptibility loci for distinct components of developmental dyslexia on chromosomes 6 and 15. *American Journal of Human Genetics, 60*, 27–39.

Hahn, W. E., van Ness, J., & Maxwell, I. H. (1978). Complex population of mRNA sequences in large polydenylylated nuclear RNA molecules. *Proceedings of the National Academy of Science USA, 75*, 5544–5547.

Hallahan, D. P., Lloyd, J. W., Kauffman, J. M., Weiss, M. P., & Martinez, E. A. (2005). *Learning disabilities: Foundations, characteristics, and effective teaching* (3rd ed.). Boston: Allyn & Bacon.

Hannula-Jouppi, K., Kaminen-Ahola, N., Taipale, M., Eklund, R., Nopola-Hemmi, J., Kääriänen, H., et al. (2005). The axon guidance receptor gene ROBO1 is a candidate gene for developmental dyslexia. *PLoS Genetics, 1*(4), e50.

Huston, A. M. (1992). Letter. *New England Journal of Medicine, 327*, 280.

Huttonlocher, P. R. (2002). *Neural plasticity: The effects of the environment on the development of the cerebral cortex*. Cambridge, MA: Harvard University Press.

Hynd, G. W., & Orbrzut, J. E. (1986). Exceptionality: Historical antecedents and present positions. In R. Brown & C. Reynolds (Eds.), *Psychological perspectives on childhood exceptionality: A handbook* (pp. 3–27). New York: Wiley.

Jeffries, S., & Everatt, J. (2004). Working memory: Its role in dyslexia and other specific learning difficulties. *Dyslexia, 10*, 196–214.

Johnson, M. H., Munakata, Y., & Gilmore, R. O. (2002). *Brain development and cognition: A reader*. Boston, MA: Blackwell.

Jones, P., & Murray, R. M. (1991). The genetics of schizophrenia is the genetics of neurodevelopment. *British Journal of Psychiatry, 158*, 615–623.

Kaplan, B. J., & Gilger, J. W. (2001). The concept of atypical brain development for clinicians who work with developmental learning disabilities. In P. Fadjukoff, T. Ahonen, & H. Lyytinen (Eds.), *Learning disabilities, from research to practise*. Jyvaskyla, Finland: Niilo Mäki Institute.

Kaplan, B. J., Dewey, D. M., Crawford, S. G., & Wilson, B. N. (2001). The term comorbidity is of questionable value in reference to developmental disorders: Data and theory. *Journal of Learning Disabilities, 34*, 555–565.

Kennedy, D. N., Haselgrove, C., & McInerney, S. (2003), MRI-based morphometric analysis of typical and typical brain development. *Mental Retardation and Developmental Disabilities Research Reviews, 9*, 155–160.

Keys, M. P. (1993). The pediatrician's role in reading disorders. *Journal of Pediatric Ophthalmology and Strabismus, 40*, 869–879.

Knopik, V. S., Smith, S. D., Cardon, L., Pennington, B., Gayàn, J., Olson, R. K., et al. (2002). Differential genetic etiology of reading component processes as a function of IQ. *Behavior Genetics, 32*, 181–198.

Kolb, B., & Whishaw, I. Q. (1998). Brain plasticity and behavior. *Annual Review of Psychology, 49*, 43–64.

Krueger, R. F., & Markon, K. E. (2006). Reinterpreting comorbidity: A model-based approach to understanding and classifying psychopathology. *Annual Review of Clinical Psychology, 2*, 111–133.

LaBuda, M. C., & DeFries, J. C. (1988). Cognitive abilities in children with reading disabilities and controls: A follow-up study. *Journal of Learning Disabilities, 21*(9), 562–566.

LaBuda, M. C., DeFries, J. C., & Fulker, D. W. (1987). Genetic and environmental covariance structures among WISC-R subtests: A twin study. *Intelligence, 11*, 233–244.

Lefly, D. L., & Pennington, B. F. (1991). Spelling errors and reading fluency in compensated adult dyslexics. *Annals of Dyslexia, 41*, 143–162.

Leppänen, P. H. T., Richardson, U., Pihko, E., Eklund, K. M., Guttorm, T. K., Aro, M., et al. (2002). Brain responses to changes in speech sound durations differ between infants with and without familial risk for dyslexia. *Developmental Neuropsychology, 22*, 407–422.

Lieberman, P. (1984). *The Biology and evolution of language*. Cambridge, MA: Harvard University Press.

Luria, A. R. (1973). *The working brain*. Baltimore: Penguin.

Lyon, G. R., Fletcher, J. M., & Barnes, M. C. (2003). Learning disabilities. In E. J. Mash & R. Barkley (Eds.), *Child psychopathology* (2nd ed., pp. 520–558). New York: Guilford Press.

Lyon, G. R., Shaywitz, S. G., & Shaywitz, B. A. (2003). A definition of dyslexia. *Annals of Dyslexia, 53*(1), 1–4.

Lyytinen, H. (Chair). (2000, July). *The neuropsychology of dyslexia* (with R. Olson, J. Stein, G. Hynd, J. Gilger, B. Kaplan, & U. Frith). Presented at the 27th International Congress of Psychology, Stockholm, Sweden.

Lyytinen, H., Aro, M., Elklund, K., Erskine, J., Guttorm, T. K., Laakso, M.-L., et al. (2004). The development of children at familial risk for dyslexia: Birth to early school age. *Annals of Dyslexia, 54*, 184–220.

Lyytinen, H., Leinonen, M., Nikula, M., Aro, M., & Leiwo, M. (1995). In search of the core features of dyslexia: Observations concerning dyslexia in the highly orthographic regular Finnish language. In V. W. Beringer (Ed.), *The varieties of orthographic knowledge II: Relationships to phonology, reading, and writing*. Dordrecht: Kluwer.

Manis, F., Seidenberg, M. S., Doi, L., McBride-Change, C., & Petersen, A. (1996). On the basis of two subtypes of developmental dyslexia. *Cognition, 58*, 157–195.

Marcus, G. (2004). *The birth of the mind: How a tiny number of genes creates the complexities of human thought*. New York: Basic Books.

Meng, H., Smith, S. D., Hager, K., Held, M., Liu, J., Olson, R. K., et al. (2005). *DCDC2* is associated with reading disability and modulates neuronal development in the brain. *Proceedings of the National Academy of Sciences USA, 102*(47), 17053–17058.

Missiuna, C., Gaines, B. R., & Pollock, N. (2002). Recognizing and referring children at risk for developmental coordination disorder: Role of the speech–language pathologist. *Journal of Speech–Language Pathology and Audiology, 26*(4), 172–179.

Mody, M. (2004). Neurobiological correlates of language and reading impairments. In C. A. Stone, E. R. Silliman, B. J. Ehren, & K. Apel (Eds.), *Handbook of language and literacy development and disorders* (pp. 49–72). New York: Guilford Press.

Nopola-Hemmi, J., Myllyluoma, B., Voutilainen, A., Leinonen, S., Kere, J., & Ahonen, T. (2002). Familial dyslexia: Neurocognitive and genetic correlation in a large Finnish family. *Developmental Medicine and Child Neurology, 44*(9), 580–586.

Narhi, V., & Ahonen, T. (1995). Reading disability with or without attention deficit hyperactivity disorder": Do attentional problems make a difference? *Developmental Neuropsychology, 11*, 337–350.

Noctor, S. C., Flint, A. C., Weissman, T. A., Dammerman, R. S., & Kriegstein, A. R. (2001). Neurons derived from radial glial cells establish radial units in neocortex. *Nature, 409*, 714–720.

Olson, R. K., Forsberg, H., & Wise, B. (1994). Genes, environment, and the development of orthographic skills. In V. W. Berninger (Ed.), *The varieties of orthographic knowledge I: Theoretical and developmental issues* (pp. 27–71). Dordrecht: Kluwer Academic.

Orton, S. (1937). *Reading, writing and speech problems in children.* New York: Norton.

Paulesu, E., Démonet, J.-F. Fazio, F., McCrory, E., Chanolne, V., Brunswick, N., et al. (2001). Dyslexia: Cultural diversity and biological unity. *Science, 291*, 2165–2167.

Pennington, B. F. (1990). Annotation: The genetics of dyslexia. *Journal of Child Psychology and Psychiatry, and Allied Disciplines, 31*(2), 193–201.

Pennington, B. F. (1991). *Diagnosing learning disorders: A neuropsychological framework.* New York: Guilford Press.

Pennington, B. F. (1997). Using genetics to dissect cognition. *American Journal of Human Genetics, 60*, 13–16.

Pennington, B. F. (1999). Dyslexia as a neurodevelopmental disorder. In H. Tager-Flusberg (Ed.), *Neurodevelopmental disorders* (pp. 307–330). Cambridge, MA: MIT Press.

Pennington, B. F. (2002). Genes and brain: Individual differences and human universals. In M. H. Johnson, Y. Munakata, & R. O. Gilmore (2002), *Brain Development and Cognition: A Reader* (pp. 494–508). Blackwell Publishers.

Petryshen, T. L., Kaplan, B. J., Liu, M. F., Schmill de French, N., Tobias, R., Hughes, M. L., et al. (2001). Evidence for a susceptibility locus (DYX4) on chromosome 6q influencing phonological coding dyslexia. *American Journal of Medical Genetics: B. Neuropsychiatric Genetics, 105*, 507–517.

Pind, J. (1998). Advances in dyslexia research. *Trends in Cognitive Sciences, 2*(1), pp. 1–2.

Pinker, S. (1994). *The language instinct: How the mind creates language.* New York: Morrow.

Plomin, R., & McClearn, G. E. (Eds.). (1993). *Nature, nurture and psychology.* Washington, DC: American Psychological Association.

Ramus, F. (2001). Dyslexia: Talk of two theories. *Nature, 412*, 393–395.

Ramus, F. (2003). Developmental dyslexia: Specific phonological deficit ro general sensorimotor dysfunction? *Current Opinion in Neurobiology, 13*, 1–7.

Ramus, F. (2004a). Should neuroconstructivism guide developmental research? *Trends in Cognitive Sciences, 8*(3), 100–101.

Ramus, F. (2004b). The neural basis of reading acquisition. In M. S. Gazzaniga (Ed.),

The cognitive neurosciences (3rd ed., pp. 815–824). Cambridge, MA: MIT Press.

Rapin, I. (2002). Diagnostic dilemmas in developmental disabilities: Fuzzy margins at the edges of normality: An essay prompted by Thomas Sowell's new book: *The Einstein Syndrome. Journal of Autism and Developmental Disorders, 32*, 49–57.

Raskind, W. H. (2001). Current understanding of the genetic basis of reading and spelling disability. *Learning Disability Quarterly, 24*, 141–157.

Regehr, S., & Kaplan, B. J. (1988). Reading disability with motor problems may be an inherited subtype. *Pediatrics, 82*, 204–210.

Reiff, H. B., Gerber, P. J., & Ginsberg, R. (1993). Definitions of learning disabilities from adults with learning disabilities: The insiders' perspective. *Learning Disability Quarterly, 16*, 214–225.

Rice, M., & Brooks, G. (2004). *Developmental dyslexia in adults: a research review.* London: National Research and Developmental Centre for Adult Literacy and Numeracy.

Rodgers, B. (1983). The identification and prevalence of specific reading retardation. *British Journal of Educational Psychology, 53*, 369–373.

Rondi-Reig, L., Caston, J., Delhaye-Bouchaud, N., & Mariani, J. (1999). Cerebellar functions: A behavioral neurogenetics perspective. In B. Jones & P. Mormede (Eds.), *Neurobehavioral genetics: Methods and applications* (pp. 201–216). New York: CRC Press.

Ruban, L. M., & Reis, S. M. (2005). Identification and assessment of gifted students with learning disabilities. *Theory Into Practice, 44*(2), 115–124.

Rutter, M., & Yule, W. (1975). The concept of specific reading retardation. *Journal of Child Psychology and Psychiatry, and Allied Disciplines, 16*(3), 181–197.

Sabolek, H. R., Bunce, J. G., & Chrobak, J. J. (2004). Intraseptal tacrine can enhance memory in cognitively impaired young rats. *Neuroreport, 15*(1), 181–183.

Satz, P., & Fletcher, J. M. (1980). Minimal brain dysfunctions: An appraisal of research concepts and methods. In H. Rie & E. Rie (Eds.), *Handbook of minimal brain dysfunctions: A critical view* (pp. 669–715). New York: Wiley Interscience.

Scarborough, H. S. (1984). Continuity between childhood dyslexia and adult reading. *British Journal of Psychology, 75*(3), 329–348.

Scarborough, H. S. (1989). Prediction of reading disability from familial and individual differences. *Journal of Educational Psychology, 81*, 101–108.

Scarborough, H. S. (1990). Very early language deficits in dyslexic children. *Child Devopment, 61*, 1728–1743.

Scerif, G., & Karmiloff-Smith, A. (2005). The dawn of cognitive genetics?: Crucial developmental caveats. *Trends in Cognitive Sciences, 9*(3), 126–135.

Schulte-Körne, G. (2001). Genetics of reading and spelling disorder. *Journal of Child Psychology and Psychiatry, and Allied Disciplines, 42*(8), 985–997.

Shafrir, U., & Siegel, L. S. (1994). Subtypes of learning disabilities in adolescents and adults. *Journal of Learning Disabilities, 27*, 123–134.

Shapiro, B., Church, R. P., & Lewis, M. E. B. (2002). Specific learning disabilities. In M. Batshaw (Ed.), *Children with disabilities* (pp. 417–442). Baltimore: Brookes.

Shaywitz, S. E., Escobar, M. D., Shaywitz, B. A., Fletcher, J. M., & Makuch, R.

(1992). Evidence that dyslexia may represent the lower tail of a normal distribution of reading ability in dyslexia. *New England Journal of Medicine, 326*, 145–150.

Shaywitz, B. A., Pugh, K. R., Constable, R. T., Shaywitz, S. E., Bronen, R. A., Fulbright, R. K., et al. (1994). Localization of semantic processing using functional magnetic resonance imaging. *Human Brain Mapping, 2*(3), 149–158.

Shaywitz, S. E., Shaywitz, B. A., Fletcher, J. M., & Escobar, M. D. (1990). Prevalence of reading disability in boys and girls: Results of the Connecticut Longitudinal Study. *Journal of the American Medical Association, 264*, 998–1002.

Shaywitz, S. E., Shaywitz, B. A., Pugh, K. R., Fulbright, R. K., Constable, R. T., Mencl, W. E., et al. (1998). Functional disruption in the organization of the brain for reading in dyslexia. *Proceedings of the National Academy of Science USA, 95*(5), 2636–2641.

Shaywitz, B. A., Shaywitz, S. E., Pugh, K. R., Mencl, W. E., Fulbright, R. K., Skudlarski, P., et al. (2002). Disruption of posterior brain systems for reading in children with developmental dyslexia. *Biological Psychiatry, 52*(2), 101–110.

Siegel, L. S. (1989). IQ is irrelevant to the definition of learning disabilities. *Journal of Learning Disabilities, 24*(1), 48–64.

Smith, S. D., & Gilger, J. W. (2007). Dyslexia and related learning disorders. In D. L. Rimoin, J. M. Connor, R. E. Pyeritz, & B. R. Korf (Eds.), *Principles and practice of medical genetics* (4th ed., pp. 2548–2568). Philadelphia: Churchill Livingstone/Elsevier.

Smith, S. D., Gilger, J. W., & Pennington, B. F. (2002). Dyslexia and other language/hearing disorders. In D. Rimoin, J. Connors, & R. Pyeritz (Eds.), *Emory and Rimoin's principles and practices in medical genetics* (5th ed., Vol. 3, pp. 2827–2865). New York: Churchill Livingstone.

Snowling, M. J. (1991). Developmental reading disorders. *Journal of Child Psychology and Psychiatry and Allied Disciplines, 32*, 49–77.

Sonuga-Barke, E. J. S. (2003). On the intersection between ADHD and DCD: The DAMP hypothesis. *Child and Adolescent Mental Health, 8*, 114–116.

Stein, J. (2001). The magnocellular theory of developmental dyslexia. *Dyslexia, 7*, 12–36.

Stevenson, J. (1988). Which aspects of reading ability show a hump in their distribution? *Applied Cognitive Psychology, 2*, 77–85.

Thompson, P. M., Cannon, T. D., Narr, K. L., Erp, T. v., Poutanen, V.-P., Huttunen, M., et al. (2001). Genetic influences on brain structure. *Nature Neuroscience, 4*(12), 1253–1258.

Thompson, P. M., Cannon, T. D., & Toga, A. W. (2002). Mapping genetic influences on human brain structure. *Annals of Medicine, 34*, 523–536.

Toga, A. W., & Thompson, P. M. (2005). Genetics of brain structure and intelligence. *Annual Review of Neuroscience, 28*, 1–23.

U.S. Office of Education. (1977, December 29). Assistance to states for education of handicapped children: Procedures for evaluating specific learning disabilities. *Federal Register, 42*(250), 65082–65085.

Valtonen, R., Ahonen, T., Lyytinen, P., & Lyytinen, H. (2004). Co-occurrence of developmental delays in a screening study of 4-year-old Finnish children. *Developmental Medicine and Child Neurology, 46*, 436–443.

Vaughn, S., & Fuchs, L. S. (2003). Redefining learning disabilities as inadequate response to instruction: The promise and potential problems. *Learning Disabilities Research and Practice, 18*, 137–146.

Voeller, K. (1999). Neurological factors underlying the comorbidity of attentional dysfunction and dyslexia. In D. Duane (Ed.), *Reading and attention disorders: Neurobiological correlates* (pp. 185–211). Timonium, MD: York Press.

Waddington, C. H. (1975). *The evolution of an evolutionist*. Edinburgh: Edinburgh University Press.

Wadsworth, S. J., Olson, R. K., Pennington, B. E., & DeFries, J. C. (1992). Differential genetic etiology of reading disability as a function of IQ. *Journal of Learning Disabilities, 33*, 192–199.

Wadsworth, S. J., Olson, R. K., Pennington, B. F., & DeFries, J. C. (2000). Differential genetic etiology of reading disability as a function of IQ. *Journal of Learning Disabilities, 33*(2), 192–199.

West, T. G. (1999). The abilities of those with reading disabilities: Focusing on the talents of people with dyslexia. In D. D. Duane (Ed.), *Reading and attention disorders: Neurobiological correlates* (pp. 213–241). Baltimore: York Press.

Willcutt, E. G., Pennington, B. F., Smith, S. D., Cardon, L. R., Gayán, J., Knopik, V. S., et al. (2002). Quantitative trait locus for reading disability on chromosome 6p is pleiotropic for attention deficit hyperactivity disorder. *American Journal of Medical Genetics: B. Neuropsychiatric Genetics, 114*, 260–268.

Wolff, P. H. (1999). A candidate phenotype for familial dyslexia. *European Child and Adolescent Psychiatry, 8*(Suppl. 3), 21–27.

Wood, F., & Flowers, L. (1999). Functional neuroanatomy of dyslexic subtypes. In D. Duane (Ed.), *Reading and attention disorders: Neurobiological correlates* (pp. 129–160). Timonium, MD: York Press.

Yule, W., Rutter, M., Berger, M., & Thompson, J. (1974). Over and under achievement in reading: Distribution in the general population. *British Journal of Educational Psychology, 44*, 1–12.

2

Emergentism and Language Impairment in Children

It's All About Change

JULIA L. EVANS

Since the late 1950s, cognitivism has been a dominant theoretical framework in both psychology and linguistics. "Cognitivism," using the computer as its predominant metaphor, is the belief that human knowledge resides in symbolic representations that stand for events in the world. "Knowledge" is viewed as discrete, abstract, mental symbols that are operated on by a set of internal rules or algorithms. The metaphor of the digital computer has had a strong influence on child language researchers' focus on *how* language is acquired. In addition, child language researchers find themselves in the midst of a longstanding debate between empiricism and nativism regarding the fundamental nature of knowledge and how it is acquired.

"Empiricism" has its foundations in work by Aristotle, Hume, and Locke. It is the belief that knowledge originates in the environment and comes into the mind or brain through the senses. The brain is believed to have little innate ability, and what is learned occurs through interactions with the environment. "Nativism" comes from the work of Plato, Kant, and Descartes, and is the belief that fundamental aspects of knowledge are hardwired at birth, and experience operates by filling in preexisting categories and by selecting, activating, and triggering latent mental states. Few child language researchers are strict adherents of either empiricism or nativism, however. Most take a perspective that merges the two camps and view learning as having a central role in language development, but only within the constraints of the biology of the human system. This combined view is known as the "interactionist perspective." There is a third theoretical account that goes beyond the interactionism, empiricist, and nativist perspectives; it is sometimes referred to as "emergentism."

Emergentism has its roots in neural networks and connectionism, dynamic systems theory, the study of complex systems, and artificial intelligence. Key concepts underlying emergentism are that (1) features or forms not previously manifested by the system can arise spontaneously (e.g., radical novelty); (2) self-organized states that emerge in a system are themselves integrated wholes that maintain their form over some specific period of time (e.g., coherence); (3) there is some property of "wholeness" inherent in these novel, self-organized states—that there is a global or macro "level" of behavior (e.g., the whole is greater than the sum of the parts); and (4) self-organization. A foundational concept in emergentism is that novel, coherent structure arises from the properties of complex systems during a process known as "self-organization," and these novel structures emerge for reasons that cannot be discovered by studying the individual components of a system. Thus, this emergent property of complex systems is not reducible to the system's constituent elements.

In this chapter, I outline the emergentist perspective, including work in connectionism and dynamic systems theory, with the goal of laying the groundwork for thinking about an emergentist account of language disorders in children. The version of connectionism presented in this chapter was developed by researchers such as Elizabeth Bates, Jeff Elman, Mark Johnson, Annette Karmiloff-Smith, Brian MacWhinney, Jay McClelland, Mark Seidenberg, Yuko Munikata and Randy O'Reilly. The branch of dynamic systems theory presented in this chapter has its roots in Haken's theory of synergetics and Waddington's epigenetic landscape, which researchers such as Esther Thelen, Linda Smith, Lisa Gershkoff-Stowe, Gregor Schöner, John Spencer, and Larissa Samuelson have extended to the study of language and cognitive development.

COGNITIVISM, NATIVISM, AND LANGUAGE IMPAIRMENTS IN CHILDREN

Nativist Explanations (or Accounts) of Language Impairment

Whereas both nativist and empiricist approaches view knowledge as abstract symbolic structures, nativism assumes that the human brain contains specific knowledge about these abstract symbols, and that this knowledge is species-specific. With respect to language acquisition, nativist approaches view the process as unfolding in strict adherence to a maturational schedule governed by a specific genetic program (e.g., Wexler, 2003).

Arguments that provide support for the idea that these language forms must be innate include the following:

1. Language is simply too complex for a child to learn without some prior knowledge regarding its structure.
2. Language acquisition occurs so rapidly and effortlessly that there must be innate language structures that are hardwired in the brain.
3. Languages across the world have many more structural commonalities and similarities in surface form than could occur simply by chance, which is evidence for innate language universals.
4. The knowledge a child must acquire in language acquisition far outstrips the information available in the environment and is also evidence for some sort of a priori language knowledge (Chomsky, 1965, 1986, 1988; Gold, 1967).

Universal Grammar: Standard Linguistic Theory

A fundamental problem for a nativist account of language development, however, is the issue of "learnability." How does the child actually go about learning his or her native language? Before being able to address this question, one must first outline the nature of the language the child must actually learn. Standard linguistic theory would argue that the child begins the language learning process with "universal grammar"—a set of linguistic principles that comprise the system in the brain that is the basis for human language. Aspects of languages that are not specified in the UG, such as pronunciation differences, are set by experience. This process is called "parameter setting" (Pinker, 1984). Thus, acquisition is the movement along a trajectory from not knowing to knowing grammar. The goal for language development researchers is to characterize this parameter setting process. Specifically, researchers must answer four questions:

1. Do children have linguistic systems that conform to the principles of UG?
2. Do children show evidence, with development, of setting the parameters of their native language?
3. How do children go about setting these parameters, and, finally, with respect to children with language disorders?
4. Is there evidence that children with language disorders have set the parameters incorrectly?

Standard Linguistic Theory and Language Impairment

These questions have guided the study of language disorders in children as well, where it has been argued that impaired representations, specific to the grammatical system, are the cause of the language disorder (Clahsen, 1989; Gopnik & Crago, 1991; Rice, 1996; Ullman & Gopnik, 1999; van der Lely, Rosen, & McClelland, 1998). Nativism views children with language disorders as missing certain aspects of the grammar or failing in some way to be guided by innate capacities to set the parameters that are specific to their language. If one starts from the assumption that language development is guided by genetic instructions that specify the basic contents and form of the grammar, it also makes sense to ask to what extent the language disorders in children are the result of missing or defective specifications of the contents, categories, or rules that constitute the universal grammar (Clahsen, 1989; Gopnik & Crago, 1991; Rice, 1996; van der Lely et al., 1998).

Although associated impairments in cognitive processing, attention, and reading are present in children who meet the criteria for specific language impairment (SLI; Leonard, 1998), the focus from a nativist approach is exclusively on the grammatical knowledge of children with language disorders. For example, Rice and colleagues (Rice, 1996, 2003; Rice & Warren, 2004; Rice & Wexler, 1996) offer an account of the grammatical deficits in SLI known as the "extended optional infinitive" account, in which the parameters for marking tense are believed to be set later in children with SLI compared to their peers. In contrast, van der Lely and colleagues argue that a subgroup of children with SLI have a primary deficit in the computational grammatical system itself, and propose that at least a subgroup of children with language impairments, while sharing many grammatical inflectional characteristics of other children, have a primary and disproportionate grammatical impairment—grammatical SLI (G-SLI; van der Lely, 2003; van der Lely et al., 1998; van der Lely & Stollwerk, 1996).

If one starts with the assumption that linguistic universals are specified within the genetic code, it also makes sense to ask to what extent impaired grammars themselves represent possible candidate phenotypes. Rice and colleagues have argued that deficits in the ability to mark verb tense in children with SLI is evidence of an immature stage of a relatively discrete inherited grammatical ability, a genetic grammatical marker for SLI (Rice & Wexler, 1996; Rice, Wexler, & Redmond, 1999). Alternatively, van der Lely and colleagues argue that G-SLI is consistent with an autosomal (non-sex-linked) dominant inheritance (van der Lely & Stollwerck, 1996).

Information-Processing Explanations (or Accounts) of Language Impairment

While much of the research framed within the nativist–empiricist debate has focused on nativist accounts of language disorders in children, a second line of work has been influenced more directly by the cognitivists' metaphor of the computer as a model of human intelligence—the idea that digital computation in its essential essence was so similar to that of human intelligence that human processing should be viewed as computations on symbolic representations (for detailed discussion, see Verela, Thomson, & Rosch, 1996). The shift away from behaviorism and toward the computer metaphor of human cognition enabled cognitive scientists to replace the "black box" of the 1950s and 1960s behaviorist era with the idea of the human information processor or central processing unit (CPU). The computer provided a powerful mechanical model of thought, specifically, that intelligence comprises computations on symbolic entities. Thus, cognitive processing was seen as the manipulation of "mental representations," discrete static structures that were physically realized in the form of a symbolic code in the brain, as they are in a computer. Information was believed to be *processed* through a serial set of stages from input to output. This work was believed to be done by devices or structures that encode the rules, like the program in a computer.

Concepts inherent in this metaphor include the speed at which symbols can be manipulated and the capacity available to the system at each step in the processing sequence. "Knowledge" is still viewed as abstract symbols that stand for meaning; however, from the cognitivist perspective, the emphasis is not on the nature of this abstract symbolic knowledge, but on the cognitive operations that manipulate and transform these symbols. Like actual computer programs, cognitivism views mental transformations as discrete, effectively instantaneous, sequential codes, in which one set of codes takes symbolic representations as input and computes symbolic representations as output that then serves as the input in the next step of processing.

Processing Capacity of Working Memory

CPU speed and size of memory have been translated directly in models of human cognition into concepts such as processing speed and working memory capacity. Questions confronting researchers taking an information-processing account of language and cognition include whether there is a single working memory capacity or multiple modality-specific, distinct capacities; whether there are systemwide constraints on these abilities; and what actually constitutes capacity (Fodor, 1983; Just & Carpenter, 1992; Kail &

Salthouse, 1994; MacDonald & Christiansen, 1992). Although the details of processing capacity models vary, they all start with the assumptions that individuals have a fixed pool of operational resources available to perform computations and that, when computational demands exceed available resources, both the processing and storage of information will be degraded (Chi, 1976, 1977; Chi & Gallagher, 1982).[1]

The mind-as-computer metaphor has been extended to the study of children with language impairments as well. If one sees language as symbols that are manipulated by cognitive processing mechanisms, it makes sense to focus on speed and capacity as possible candidate mechanisms that may be impaired in children with language disorders. Researchers who investigate processing capacity in children with language disorders have looked at whether processing demands exceed the capacity of children with language disorders more quickly than that of typically developing peers across a range of verbal and nonverbal tasks, such as sentence comprehension, and phonological and verbal working memory tasks (Bishop, 1992; Dollaghan & Campbell, 1998; Ellis Weismer, Evans, & Hesketh, 1999; Gillam, Cowan, & Marler, 1998; Montgomery, 2000; see also Berninger, Chapter 4, this volume). They have also looked at whether verbal processing capacity has high specificity and sensitivity in the identification of children with SLI (e.g., Dollaghan & Campbell, 1998; Ellis Weismer & Thordardottir, 2002).

Speed of Processing in SLI

Speed-of-processing accounts assume that an individual has a maximum rate at which he or she can execute elementary cognitive operations (Kail & Salthouse, 1994). This rate limit is considered a processing resource in the sense that it is believed to be finite. The faster cognitive operations can be performed, the better the resulting level of cognitive performance. According to the "generalized slowing hypothesis" of language disorders, children differ in the degree of slowing, but not in the locus of slowing (Kail, 1994). Reaction times for children with language disorders are significantly slower than typically developing controls across a range of linguistic and nonlinguistic tasks, such as scanning short-term memory, word naming, sentence comprehension, mental rotation, and signal detection tasks (e.g., Miller, Kail, Leonard, & Tomblin, 2001; Montgomery, 2000).

One problem with a straight-processing-speed account of language disorders, however, is that it is not clear whether children with language disorders are processing each successive step in a cognitive task more slowly by a constant proportion (e.g., Kail, 1994), whether cognitive processes are slowed but speed of sensory motor processing is not, or whether there is a progressive increase in the proportion of slowing with each successive information-processing step (cf. Windsor & Hwang, 1999).

Problems with Cognitivism, Nativism, and the Mind-as-Computer Metaphor

The Dualism Problem

The mind-as-computer metaphor is an excellent model to study both the abstract symbolic universal aspects of language development, and capacity and speed of processing; however, questions remain that are problematic for the study of language disorders in children. One problem is a dualism that is created when one thinks of language as abstract, stable, mental structures that reside in memory and are time-independent (e.g., language competence) versus the manipulation of these symbolic structures in real-time (e.g., real-time performance). This dualism, in the same way that the full range of a computer program's processing power is never manifested in each individual operation, means that a speaker's language competence may never be fully realized during language performance.

This foundational distinction between competence and performance sets researchers and practitioners up to disregard data that may be crucial to understanding language disorders. Specifically, focusing on competence means excluding not only performance "mishaps," such as false starts, hesitations, and errors, but also more central aspects of linguistic performance, such as real-time language performance. This sets researchers up to view language competence as being independent of the perceptual and motor systems employed in language use, the memory capacities that limit the complexity of utterances that can be produced or understood, and the reasoning capacities used in comprehension. It also sets researchers and practitioners up to exclude systematically information about the statistical and probabilistic aspects of language—such as the fact that *that* is used more often than *than*, or that the word *the* is followed more often by a noun than by a verb—that is not seen as relevant to the characterization of the child's linguistic "competence."

This dualism between competence and performance also creates vexing questions (e.g., Where does competence reside?) If language competence is genetic, as Chomsky argued (1986), how is it specified in the genetic code? If one assumes that the linguistic code resides in the genes, one ends up in an inevitable logic trap—trying to define what turns on the genes or decides which information stays or goes (Oyama, 1985). What is processing capacity and where does it reside? What determines individual differences in the size of capacity and processing speed? And finally, why do some tasks exceed an individual's processing capacity, whereas others do not?

Variability May Be Key

By starting from a competence–performance distinction, researchers and clinicians attempt to control the noisy, messy "stuff" of real-time language in the experimental conditions and/or assessment contexts in which children are observed. Often this is done to an extreme and even artificial degree in the attempt to "discover" a child's underlying language competence. But what if the very noisy, messy vagaries of real-time language use are the key to understanding language development and disorders? What would it mean to bring the variability of real-time language performance to the forefront? How could we view variability as the focus of research instead of variance in the data or noise in the system? (See also Gilger & Wilkins, Chapter 1, this volume, for a related discussion on reading disability.)

A cognitivist perspective makes it difficult to bring together, under one theoretical rubric, disparate aspects of the language profiles in children with SLI that include (1) the global, stable characteristics of disorder, in which deficits in one or more language subsystems (e.g., syntax, morphology, semantics, or pragmatics) vary along continua such as degrees of severity and the degree to which comprehension, production, or both are involved (cf. Leonard, 1998); and (2) the variable and inconsistent characteristics of children's language use, such as the use of verb tense knowledge in probe tasks designed to elicit the specific target but not in naturalistic conversational contexts, or the marking of past tense for high-frequency verbs but not low-frequency verbs (e.g., Dromi, 2003; Marchman, Wulfeck, & Ellis Weismer, 1999), or the categorical perception deficits observed in children with SLI in synthesized speech testing but *no* evidence of such deficits in the *same* children tested with real-speech stimuli (Coady, Kluender, & Evans, 2005; Coady, Evans, Mainela-Arnold, & Kluender 2007).

Starting from the assumption that language development is the acquisition of abstract symbols also makes it difficult to think about the developmental process itself as a causal factor in the disorder. Accounts of language disorders in children predominantly rely on static, steady-state descriptions of the deficit profile at a single point in developmental time (Karmiloff-Smith, 1997). However, developmental studies show that both neural localization and neural specialization for biologically important functions, such as language, take place gradually over time (Johnson, 1999; Neville, 1991). To work from a static "snapshot" view of the disorder at only one point in developmental time creates an incongruity in which, by definition, the language disorder co-occurs in the context of intact intelligence—and in the case of nativists' accounts—intact cognition, motor skills, working memory, and attention. To believe that a child could have an impairment in a high-level cognitive function such as language, while retaining normal functioning of all other aspects of the neurocognitive developmental system, requires that a model of neurological developmental must compensate for, and overcome early deficits in all other areas except language, which, although statistically possible is, in reality, highly unlikely (Thomas & Karmiloff-Smith, 2002).

Whereas large-scale epidemiological studies have gone a long way in contributing to our knowledge of the changes in the language profiles of children with SLI (Bishop & Clarkson, 2003; Tomblin et al., 1997), to date the mechanism of development in SLI remains largely obscured. No one would argue that cognitive and language processes unfold continuously and simultaneously in real time. However, an account of the global deficit profile exhibited by children with language disorders, as well as an explanation of changes in this language processing profile both moment to moment *and* over developmental time, requires a different starting point. At the heart of this problem is *change over time*—specifically, a theoretical framework that allows one to view language development and real-time language processing as the same phenomenon, differing only in the time scale in which they are observed.

A Fundamental Shift

A truly developmental approach to the study of language and cognitive impairments in children requires a fundamental shift in thinking; Karmiloff-Smith (1997) argues that what is needed is "(1) a recognition that plasticity is the *rule*, not simply a specialized response to injury, (2) the inclusion of the dynamics of development at multiple levels, (3) a recognition that specialization within some brain regions is the *product* of development rather than its starting point, (4) a focus not only on the end state but on how the child progressively develops to the end state, and (5) an in-depth analysis of the different processes by which seemingly normal surface behavior can be produced by a brain that has developed differently from the outset (p. 514)."

Studies of typical and atypical language development are shifting away from the focus on the static, globally ordered, stage-like patterns in children's language, toward an emergentist view of language development as a flexible, transient, variable phenomenon. From this alternative perspective, language development is not the acquisition of abstract rules, but is instead the *emergence* of language forms in real *time*. From this perspective, the changes seen in children's language abilities over months and years are the same as changes seen in moment-to-moment, *real-time* language "processing." This shift in focus highlights the nature of the interaction between the constraints in the child and the language-learning environment, and the patterns that arise as a result of this interaction from an emergentist perspective.

EMERGENTISM

Emergentist accounts of language development start from the assumption that language is softly assembled, unfolding in *real time* as a process of continuous, simultaneous changes in the interactions between the environment, the body, and the nervous system of the child—with *change over time* being foundational (Elman, 1995, 2003; Elman et al., 1996; Port & van Gelder, 1995). The focus is on the learning mechanisms that account for the interaction between the biological constraints that the child brings to the process and the extant language-learning environment, with the goal of constructing models that are devoid of hardwired circuitry.

Shifting one's focus to think about language and cognition as emerging states is not easy. Bates and MacWhinney (1989) have used the examples of the shape of a soap bubble and the shape of the honeycomb in a beehive as ways to begin thinking about emergent properties of complex systems (Bates & MacWhinney, 1989). The shape of a soap bubble does not come from the specific properties of the soap. It arises because the sphere is the only possible solution to achieve maximum volume with minimum surface. Thus, the shape of the soap bubble is not explainable by an understanding of the properties of the soap or the water, no matter how detailed and precise the description. Similarly, the honeycomb in a beehive takes a hexagonal form not because the hexagonal form is preprogrammed into the genetic code of the bee, nor because of the properties of the wax or the honey. The hexagonal form spontaneously emerges as the result of packing circles together. It is the self-organization of the properties of the complex system of the bees, the honey, and the wax. The hexagonal form cannot be discovered, however, by breaking the system back down into these individual components, no matter how detailed the study. "Grammar" is a self-organization of the properties of meaning, memory, perception, motor, and speech systems (Bates & MacWhinney, 1989). Thus, the *form* of human language emerges in the same way as the *form* of the honeycomb. It is specified neither in the genes nor in the environment, nor is it the simple additive outcome of each of these.

Emergetism views developmental outcomes as the spontaneous emergence of more complex forms of behavior due to the influence of properties of the multiple heterogeneous parts of the system that results in coherent, complex patterned behavior. This processes is formally known as "self-organization." It occurs without prespecification from internal rules or genetic code. Rather, development is truly self-organizing, because it occurs through the recursive interactions of the components of the system. This process depends upon the organism itself and the constraints on the organism from the environment in which the organism resides. This self-organization results in the emergence of novel, complex forms of behavior. Thus, developmental scientists, working within this perspective, see language development as a process of emergence of form as opposed to growth or acquisition (see Lewis, 2000).

A second assumption of emergentism is one of continuity—the idea that this process of self-organization is both continuous in time, and across multiple levels and multiple time scales. Specifically, developmental processes are viewed as being both nested and coupled across different time scales, where *time* is viewed as a critical part of the equation (Corbetta & Thelen, 1996; Fogel & Thelen, 1987; Gershkoff-Stowe & Thelen, 2004; Kelso, Ding, & Schöner, 1986; Muchisky, Gershkoff-Stowe, Cole, & Thelen, 1996; Smith & Thelen, 1993; Thelen, 1989; Thelen, Corbetta, & Spencer, 1996; Thelen & Fischer, 1982; Thelen, Schöner, Scheier, & Smith, 2001; Thelen & Smith, 1994; Thelen & Ulrich, 1991).

Most emergent accounts of language and cognitive development can be grouped broadly into connectionist models and dynamic systems theory. Although there are differences between the two approaches, there are also fundamental similarities. Neither connectionist nor dynamic systems theories adhere to the view that human cognition is commensurate with symbolic representations. Both approaches view cognition as an emergent process grounded in lower, simpler, nonsymbolic processes. Both view language as softly assembled, unfolding in *real time* as a process of continuous, simultaneous changes in the interactions among the environment, the body, and the nervous system—with *time* being fundamental (Elman, 2003; Port & van Gelder, 1995). Both focus on the self-organizing property of complex systems as the mechanism that underlies language development.

The focus of dynamic systems theories and connectionism approaches differ fundamentally with respect to the issue of embodiment and mental representations, however. Dynamic systems theory assumes a fully embodied mind, in which the sensorimotor level of cognition is the foundational basis of higher cognition, placing in the forefront the study perception and action rather than mental processes. In contrast, developmental work in connectionism has focused on understanding the internal changes in mental representations over development. For example, connectionist models show how learning networks mirror the nonlinear nature of development. Fundamental to connectionist models is the idea of graded representations—as opposed to the "all-or-none" representations of nativism—in which differing strength of representations emerge behaviorally over time, resulting in what looks like distinct "stages" in development.

Connectionism and SLI

Computational models are well known as tools for investigating mechanisms of change in cognitive and language development. In typical development, the focus of connectionist models is on the emergence of complex behavior (see Elman et al., 1996; O'Reilly & Munakata, 2000; Rumelhart & McClelland, 1986; Rumelhart, McClelland, & Group, 1986). Using principles of neuroscience and computer simulations, connectionist accounts of language development demonstrate that seemingly rule-governed language forms emerge spontaneously from locally distributed information (e.g., Elman et al., 1996). What the child brings to the process of language development, from the connectionist perspective, is neurological in nature and constrains the child's processing of information in the language-learning environment. These constraints include neurons with different structures found in different parts of the brain, with different firing thresholds and refractory periods.

In connectionist models, the classic, innately determined symbolic grammars are represented in a distributed manner through local connections that vary in degree of connection weights—the microcircuitry of the brain. Connectionist models show that the seemingly distinct "modular" aspects of language emerge from the intrinsic properties of language input—the classic example being the regular and irregular forms of English past tense (e.g., *jumped* vs. *went*)—in which seemingly distinct language forms actually arise from the distributional features of the verbs themselves, such as differences in their frequency in the language, their phonological form, semantic classification, or whether they are regular or irregular verbs in English (e.g., Plunkett & Marchman, 1993; Rumelhart & McClelland, 1986).

Connectionist models of developmental disorders emphasize the developmental processes and start from the assumption that the adult modular structure of language is not present at birth, but is the outcome of the developmental processes itself (Karmiloff-Smith, 1997). While domain-specific accounts of SLI contend that genetically determined cognitive mechanisms could uniquely subserve specialized cognitive functions, such as grammar, connectionist accounts of language impairments in children argue that domain general mechanisms underlie specialized functions that are not unique to any one function, but become specialized with the developmental process and specific environmental interactions. Moreover, Karmiloff-Smith (1998) contends that any genetic deficit affecting cognitive functioning is likely to result from a cascade of subtle deficits rather than a single, higher level one, with different cognitive disorders lying on a continuum rather than being truly specific.

Acquired disorders, such as aphasia, have been simulated in neural network models using posttraining manipulations of the network. In contrast, pretraining manipulations of network models, including (1) changing the number of hidden units in the initial network architecture, (2) decreasing the number of hidden units, (3) altering the similarity structure in the input, (4) constraining learning (by using weight decay), (5) eliminating connection weights, and (6) eliminating intermediary layers of units, have been used for models of developmental disorders, including autism (Cohen, 1994; Gustafsson, 1997), developmental dyslexia (Harm & Seidenberg, 1998), SLI (Hoeffner & McClelland, 1992), the development of morphology (Plunkett & Marchman, 1993), and language development in Williams syndrome (Karmiloff-Smith, 1998).

Connectionist models have been extended to the study of children with SLI and to date have focused predominantly on how perceptual deficits, specifically, the inability to use phonological information, in turn lead to poorer than expected syntactic comprehension and acquisition of grammatical morphology (Hoeffner & McClelland, 1993; Joanisse & Seidenberg, 2003). These connectionist models have allowed for investigations of both the distinction between delay and disorder and the interaction between impairments in different parts of the language system (e.g., the lexicon and the grammar). Although there are experimental data that indicate children with SLI have deficits in both speech perception and comprehension of certain types of syntactic relationships, including bound pronouns, reflexives, and reversible passives, deficits in the comprehension of syntax have not been directly linked to deficits in phonological processing or auditory perceptual skills.

Joanisse and Seidenberg (2003), starting with this speech perception data, used a connectionist model to investigate the hypothesis that speech processing deficits seen in SLI could interfere with children's ability to comprehend key aspects of grammar. In their connectionist model, anaphoric resolution (e.g., "The man was driving to the store and the boy went with *him* or *her*") was represented by recognition of the semantics of the correct antecedent (e.g., *the man*) when a bound pronoun (e.g., *him*) was the input. Joanisse and Seidenberg trained the neural network on distorted phonological inputs by using Gaussian noise, which resulted in the model being exposed to slightly different phonological forms of the word at each epoch.[2] The model exhibited marked difficulty resolving these bound anaphoric referents. Importantly, the model was able to perform other aspects of sentence comprehension, such as correctly comprehending gender information inherent in the pronouns, as well as being able to resolve some of the anaphoric pronoun references. These outcomes indicated that the pattern of deficits exhibited by the model, similar to the impaired performance seen in children with SLI, was *graded* (i.e., 70% correct), in contrast to the complete absence of anaphoric referring abilities. The perceptual deficits simulated in this model are consistent with data suggesting that children with SLI are working with degraded, imperfect, or incomplete phonological representations of phonemes and words (Coady et al., 2005; Chiat, 2001). The Joanisse and Seidenberg (2003) model also shows that the network is in fact *impaired*, not delayed, in its ability to resolve reflexive contrasts, in contrast to it simply taking more training trials to reach correct performance, as would be predicted by a simple quantitative delay.

There are several advantages to using connectionist models to study language disorders in children. First, connectionist models allow one to investigate relationships between disparate aspects of clinical profiles within the *same* model. The models provide a means of understanding how difficulties in the initial conditions in developmental language trajectories can result in profound, and seemingly disparate, impairments at much higher cognitive levels later in development. Second, connectionist models can account for "imperfect" or partial performance (e.g., 70% correct). Third, connectionist models provide a framework to study self-organization in development, whereby structure emerges in a representational system in response to the system's dynamic interactions with its environment. Finally, connectionist models provide a powerful way to explore how deviations in self-organization resulting from changes in the initial constraints result in the emergence of atypical language abilities, such as those found in SLI and other developmental disorders (Mareschal & Shultz, 1996; Thomas & Karmiloff-Smith, 2002).

Dynamic Systems Theory and Language Impairments in Children

Although connectionist models focus on how rule-like patterns in language (e.g., grammar) can be represented as patterns of distributed weights in the brain that emerge in real time, fundamental to a dynamic systems approach is the time-dependent characterization of the state of a complex system at any moment in time. Dynamic systems theory not only derives from advances in the study of complex, nonlinear, dynamic systems in physics and mathematics but also follows from a longstanding tradition of systems thinking in biology and psychology. The term "dynamic systems" refers both to complex, nonlinear systems that change over time and to the formal class of mathematical equations used to describe these systems.

The foundational principle in dynamic systems is *change* in the behavior of a complex system, in particular, the trajectory of behavioral states of a system across different time scales. A defining property of development from dynamic systems theory is the spontaneous occurrence of increasingly complex, novel forms of behavior and the idea of dissonance and *stability* and *instability*. Stability in the context of dynamic systems theory is the "persistence of behavioral or neural states in the face of systematic or random perturbations" (Spencer & Schöner, 2003, p. 394). Although achieving behavioral stability is critical in development, so is the need for flexibility and dissolution of old behavioral states. For novel, more complex forms to emerge, stable patterns must become unstable for change to occur. This instability itself allows the components of the system to reorganize in novel ways. *Variability* is not "noise" in the system, from a dynamic systems perspective, but is the actual mechanism of change in development (Gershkoff-Stowe & Thelen, 2004).

Similar to connectionism, dynamic systems theory is a broad theoretical approach with many models and research programs. For example, van der Maas and colleagues have extended specific aspects of the mathematics of complex systems known as "catastrophe theory," showing that complex systems will suddenly shift into different organizational states, and that these discontinuous jumps in development can be formally predicted (van der Maas, 1998; van der Maas & Molenaar, 1992). Although this work is not discussed in detail in this chapter, it has significance for the study of the developmental trajectory of children with language disorders. Specifically, van der Maas and Molenaar's work shows that the emergence of new language behaviors is marked by a sudden increase in behavioral instability, such as the simultaneous use of multiple language forms from different stages in development (e.g., "I RUNDED, I RANDED, I ran from the doggie!"), and slower reaction times for processing of novel information.

A second dynamic systems approach to the study of language development is van Geert's use of ecological growth models (van Geert, 1991, 1993, 1994, 1998). In this work, van Geert extends mathematical models of dynamic systems, developed originally to study the ebb and flow of animal populations and the impact of competing resources on ecosystems, to the study of language growth within a framework of competing cognitive resources. Van Geert's work shows how one can model trade-offs between the competing demands of different levels of language, such as the competition between lexical and syntactic growth in children's language development.

The most well developed dynamic systems approach to the study of language and cognitive development is the work pioneered by Thelen, Smith, and colleagues (e.g., Thelen & Smith, 1994). This work derives from synergetics and its principles of self-organization of complex systems (Haken, 1983). Synergetics focuses on the most striking feature of biological systems—the emergence of behavior at the macroscopic level, behavior that does not exist at the level of the individual components of the system (Haken, 1993; Nicolis & Priogogine, 1989). This is known as "pattern complexity," in which the collective impact of the aggregation of interconnected components of the system is greater than the sum of the individual parts. This relationship between the components of a system is viewed as a synergetic one, in which components are temporally assembled in a functional, task-specific manner when under the influence of some external variable (Haken, 1996; Kelso, 1984; Kelso, Ding, et al., 1986; Kelso, Scholz, & Schöner, 1986). By definition, complex systems comprise many individual elements and, under certain conditions, these elements, instead of acting independently, begin to act collectively. When a system self-organizes in this manner, it settles into one of a range of behavioral modes as a function of the interaction between the intrinsic properties of the system. These different self-organized states are known as "attractors." Of particular interest in dynamic systems is how these behavioral attractor states change over time.

Biological systems are open systems that maintain behavioral states that are far from equilibrium. They maintain these states with a continuous flux of energy into the system. Because these behavioral states or attractors are always softly assumed from the interactions with the external environment, changes in external context influences the patterns that emerge, as well as the stability of these patterns. The underlying attractor landscape changes over time in response to this input to the system, with attractors becoming more or less stable, and more or less responsive to external perturbations. From a dynamic systems perspective, the accumulated effect of repeated, real-time, ordered states gives rise to the emergence of new collective behavioral states and the disappearance of developmentally older states—what is traditionally called "learning" (Haken, 1996). These self-organized states of the system are more or less stable and coherent with development, and are a direct reflection of the underlying architecture of an individual's representational multiattractor landscape (van der Maas, 1998).

Because principles of complexity hold across all levels of the system, the "heuristic" value of the approach taken by Thelen and colleagues is that the same principles can be extended to discussions of all conventional "stages" in children's language development. Development, in dynamic systems theory, is the emergence of "softly assembled" patterns from the interaction between the intrinsic dynamics of the child and external conditions. Thelen and Smith (1994) argue that development is the emergence and dissolution of behavioral attractors, and that it is input from the environment that alters the underlying attractor landscape, which then results in the emergence of new behavioral states.[3] Importantly, at points in development that traditionally have been viewed as being "between developmental stages," emerging states are less stable and more vulnerable to changes in external demands. As the underlying attractor landscape changes, attractors become more or less stable, and more or less responsive to changes in external control parameters. Thus, the relative variability of a system's behavior around a mean state is not error variance, but a measure of the stability of that system and the states in which it resides.

From this view of dynamic systems theory, knowledge is embodied; it is derived from, and inextricably bound to, actions and perceptions—specifically, that cognition emerges from bodily interactions with the world. From this perspective, cognition depends on the kinds of experiences that come from having a body with particular perceptual and motor capabilities that are "inseparably linked and that together form the matrix within which reasoning, memory, emotion, language, and all other aspects of mental life are meshed" (Thelen et al., p. 1). Thus, from a dynamic systems perspective, cognition is behavior that is softly assembled, unfolding in *real time* as a process of the continuous, simultaneous changes in the interactions between the environment, the body, and the nervous system (Port & van Gelder, 1995).

The emphasis of Thelen, Smith, and colleagues' approach is on how children's prior learning influences current learning—the "developmental language trajectory." Their work demonstrates that at any point in time, children's behavior is the instantaneous, functional self-organization of the child's system within the constraints of the immediate environment. This emergence of language is a reflection of not only the intrinsic dynamics of the child but also the child's entire language-learning history, current preferred communicative states, and the extrinsic dynamics of the immediate communicative context (Corbetta & Thelen, 1996; Fischer, Rotenberg, Bullock, & Raya, 1993; Smith & Thelen, 1993; Thelen & Ulrich, 1991).

Dynamic systems theory provides a framework to interpret patterns of variability and instability in the language "competence" of children with language disorders. From a dynamic systems perspective, we would expect that the developmentally older, more stable developmental language states are less vulnerable to context demands, whereas newer, emerging language states would be unstable and more vulnerable to external perturbations. In particular, more preferred attractor states would be energetically more efficient and require less energy to maintain compared with less preferred attractors (Hoyt & Taylor, 1981; McMahon, 1984; Thelen & Smith, 1994). With respect to language in particular, there would be an associated energy with any given attractor that corresponds to the precision of that attractor. If one thinks of the learning, representation, and processing of all aspects of language (e.g., speech, words, and grammar) as attractors that emerge over time, then the strength of the attractor changes over time as a direct result of frequency of input from the environment. With respect to children with language impairments, we would expect to find that variability and instability in language processing are more clear-cut for low- compared to high-frequency forms of language. Specifically, we would predict that speech and accuracy of language processing would be greater for high-frequency words, grammatical forms, semantic concepts, and even cognitive problem-solving tasks in the environment than for those having lower frequency of occurrence. This is precisely what we see in children with SLI, who process high- versus low-frequency aspects of language faster and more accurately, including accurate marking of verb tense for high-frequency versus low-frequency verbs (Marchman et al., 1999), faster word naming speed for high- compared to low-frequency words (Leonard, Nippold, Kail, & Hale, 1983), and even better working memory recall of high- compared to low-frequency words on working memory tasks (Mainlea-Arnold & Evans, 2005).

The study of variability and instability in the comprehension abilities of children with SLI is one area in which the dynamic systems theory framework has been employed directly. In typically developing children, prior to full-sentence comprehension, we see reliance on comprehension strategies, and there is a developmental order to the comprehension strategies used by young children. One strategy young children use is known as a "probable event strategy," in which toddlers choose the most *probable location* or *action* in their interpretation of sentences. At this stage in development, toddlers choose the animate object when presented with two objects, one animate and the other inanimate (e.g., a dog, a ball) and are asked to pick the one doing the action (e.g., "Show me the ball is chasing the dog"). Around ages 3–4 years, for English-speaking children, we see the emergence of the ability to use syntax to comprehend sentences through the use of word order cues such as first noun as agent. So, for the same sentence, "Show me the ball is chasing the dog," a 4-year-old now chooses the *ball* instead of the *dog*.

In children with and without language disorders, however, we see a great deal of variability in "apparent" comprehension of these syntactic constructions, in which children's knowledge is highly sensitive to changes in experimental condition. Thus, children show comprehension of syntactic constructions, but simply by changing the experimental context, this "knowledge" suddenly seems to disappear. For example, Strohner and Nelson (1974) observed that typically developing 4-year-olds, when asked to act out their understanding of equally probable sentences (e.g., "The girl feeds the baby" or "The baby feeds the girl"), relied exclusively on word order strategies when choosing the first noun as agent. When the same children were asked instead to point to a picture of their answer, for the same sentence constructions, their "first noun as agent" comprehension strategy disappeared, and they switched to using a probable event strategy.

Similarly, van der Lely and Harris (1990) observed that children with language impairments correctly comprehended a range of canonical (subject–verb–object [SVO]; *the girl pushes the boy*) and noncanonical (object–verb–subject [OVS]; *the boy is pushed by the girl*) constructions in an enactment paradigm using toys, but these same children did not show comprehension of these same constructions when a picture-pointing response paradigm was used. Why would children with SLI show knowledge of noncanonical constructions when asked to act out their response, but not show evidence of comprehending these same constructions when asked to point to a picture? Do these children comprehend noncanonical constructions or not?

From a dynamic systems perspective, we would predict that a child has a multiple, overlapping comprehension strategy states at any given point in time in development, some that are newly emerging and more vulnerable to external perturbations, and others that are developmentally older and more stable. One would also expect, then, that newly emerging strategies would be less efficient, require more energy to maintain, and be more sensitive to external demands than developmentally older strategies.

In a study framed within a dynamic systems perspective, we asked whether the reliance on animacy is a developmentally older, more stable comprehension strategy in children with language disorders as compared to the ability to use word order cues (Evans, 2002). In prior work, we observed that some children with SLI relied heavily on the use of animacy cues, as opposed to word order cues, to determine the agent of SVO, OSV, and verb–ojbect–subject (VOS) sentence forms (Evans & MacWhinney, 1999). From a dynamic systems approach, we predicted that children with SLI who showed emerging evidence of word order comprehension strategies would be more vulnerable to changes in external demands than would children with SLI who showed no evidence of emerging word order strategies. In other words, we asked whether we could intentionally make children appear variable in their comprehension knowledge. Specifically, could we shift children into and out of different comprehension states by changes in external demands, but, importantly, would the children shift into the older, more stable animacy comprehension state with increased demands? Thus, using principles from dynamic systems theory, we assumed that the comprehension state of the child with SLI is a reflection of (1) the child's prior developmental history, (2) the child's current state, and (3) the external demands on the child in that moment in time. But, more importantly, we predicted that newly emerging word order comprehension strategies would be vulnerable in children with language impairments.

Two groups of children with SLI, ages 7–9 years, were identified for the study. One group of children with SLI showed evidence of being in a development transition in which their ability to use word order to determine the agent of a sentence was just *emerging*. Specifically, these children chose the first noun as agent in sentences that comprised highly salient nouns and where both word order and animacy cues supported a choice of first noun as agent (e.g., *the dog chases the ball*). When presented with sentences in which animacy cues were not present (e.g., *the chair hugs the ball*), however, these children did not reliably choose the correct agent.

The second group of children with SLI, also ages 7–9 years, only used animacy comprehension strategies characteristic of younger typically developing children, choosing the animate noun as the agent regardless of its position in the sentence (e.g., *the ball chases the cat* vs. *the cat chases the ball*). The children were asked to determine the agent in sentences in which word order and animacy cues were in competition with each other. In the first condition the children simply pointed to the picture of the animal or object they thought was doing the action. In the second condition, children pressed a button that corresponded to the picture of the animal or object. The pointing condition was designed to provide the lowest cognitive demands, by using the oldest most salient means of communication for these children (e.g., pointing). The button pushing condition, in contrast, was designed to be a less frequently occurring response state that required the children to connect mentally the corresponding button to their picture of choice.

For the first group of children with SLI, those who appeared to show evidence of emerging word order knowledge, we could shift them into and out of two completely different comprehension profiles, simply by changing the response paradigm from picture pointing to button pressing. In the picture-pointing condition, these children with SLI looked like typical peers, using word order cues to choose the first noun as agent. However, in the button-pressing condition, these *same* children suddenly looked like the other group of children with SLI, and only picked the animate noun when it was available, but guessed when both nouns were either animate or inanimate (e.g., *the horse hugs the cow; the comb kisses the chair*).

In this study, we used a dynamic systems approach in which external conditions were *intentionally* altered to induce variability in performance in children with language impairments, which suggested that the underlying language attractor states for children with SLI are not sufficiently strong to override these perturbations to the system. Why should performance of these children shift in this manner? From a dynamic systems theory perspective, newly emerging attractors are less efficient, less stable, and more effortful to maintain than developmentally older strategies; thus, the different experimental conditions were more or less effortful for the two groups of children, with some response modes being more stable, thereby allowing the children to maintain less stable, newly emerging comprehension states.

It has been argued that SLI is secondary to limitations in processing capacity (cf. Bishop, 1992; Leonard, 1998). These limited processing accounts are grounded in more general theories of cognitive processing that share a basic set of assumptions: (1) that individuals have a limited capacity for processing information, and (2) given this fixed pool of operational resources available to perform symbolic computations, when computational demands exceed available resources, processing and storage of information are degraded (e.g., Just & Carpenter, 1992; Salthouse, 2000; Shiffrin, 1993). Studies of cognitive capacity limitations in children with SLI indicate that these children may have slower rates of processing and/or less efficient access to information (for a detailed review, see Leonard, 1998). Clearly, the question arises: Are the differences in performance seen across the pointing and button-pressing conditions for both groups of children with SLI a reflection of processing limitations or weak comprehension attractor states that are more vulnerable to changes in external processing demands?

In other language domains, it has been suggested that the processing deficits seen in children with SLI result in the inability to generate "strong" central representations of the language forms in question (e.g., Edwards & Lahey, 1999; Stark & Heinz, 1996a, 1996b). For example, Leonard (1998) has argued that processing capacity limitations, in the form of slower speed of processing, result in bound morphology being incompletely processed and weakly represented for children with SLI. He suggests that the weakly represented nature of grammatical morphology makes it disproportionately more vulnerable to increases in processing demands compared to other aspects of the children's language.

If, as Haken (1996) argues, "learning" in biological systems is synonymous with changes in the underlying attractor landscape resulting from input to the system, and an intrinsic property of children with SLI is slower, less efficient processing of the language input, then the underlying attractor landscapes of children with SLI may be qualitatively different from those of typically developing children. Specifically, aspects of the language input that are slower, less efficiently processed in children with SLI may be weakly represented, and may require more energy to maintain compared to well-represented aspects of the language system, making these forms more vulnerable to increases in external processing demands.

With respect to this study in particular, this would suggest that the changes in performance seen across the pointing and button-pressing conditions indicate that comprehension strategies in both groups of children with SLI may be weakly represented, require more energy to maintain, and be more vulnerable to the demands of the button-pressing condition. From a dynamical systems perspective, then, intrinsic limitations in processing capacity in children with SLI not only affect real-time language processing when task demands exceed a child's processing capacity, but also have a continuous impact on shaping, or failing to shape, the underlying representation of language for the child with SLI throughout his or her lifetime.

From a dynamic systems account, the variability seen in the performance of children with SLI may be the result of newly emerging strategies that are more vulnerable to changes in external conditions compared to developmentally older states, in which children with SLI have shallower attractor states that are more vulnerable to external perturbations compared to their typically developing peers. Only when experimental methods are used that specifically attempt to shift children with SLI into and out of different performance states will the nature of their language representations be revealed.

Several points are important about the study of language disorders in children from a dynamical systems perspective. First, by starting with the assumption that the behavior of the child at any given point in time is a reflection of that child's prior language learning history, his or her current underlying language attractor landscape, and external demands on his or her system *at that moment in time*, we can account for much of the variability we see in the abilities of children with language disorders. Moreover, these findings lead to the prediction that newly emerging skills in children with SLI will be more vulnerable to external processing demands, and when external demands reach a critical threshold, we will see these children shifting back into developmentally older, more stable language states—a prediction that can be tested directly.

Importantly, this means that children's behavior can never be studied independent of the context in which it was observed—be it an experimental condition or an assessment context. In terms of language assessment, this has important methodological implications. For example, a common method of studying language development is to collect a spontaneous language sample during examiner–child or parent–child dyadic interactions, then analyze the child's language in detail. However, if the child's behavior at any point in time emerges in response to external conditions, then there is no point at which a children's language *competence* can be studied independent of the social context within which the data are collected. Thus, from a dynamic systems theory perspective, there is no language competence to be studied. The language that emerges from any assessment context, or spontaneous interaction is unique to that child under that set of constraints at that moment in time, and is always and only performance.

How does one do any kind of language assessment? What does it mean to have a language disorder? If one starts from the assumption that the language abilities that emerge are a reflection of the child's intrinsic dynamics, prior language learning history, current preferred states, and the extrinsic dynamics of the immediate context, one definition of "unimpaired language" is greater behavioral stability and less sensitivity to external contextual demands and/or changes in the child's current state. But don't all children show instability in language behaviors at some point in their development? The answer would be "yes," but the key question here is, at what point in time developmentally? Whereas the typically developing child may show more instability when using novel, unfamiliar vocabulary, but not when using highly familiar vocabulary, the same-age child with a language disorder may show the same level of instability as the typical child when using highly familiar vocabulary.

We would not only expect the language profiles of the children with a language disorder to be sensitive to changes in assessment context, but a dynamic systems approach would also predict that moment-to-moment changes across communicative context (e.g., gym class vs. history) or even a change in the same communicative context at different points in time (e.g., history class at 9 A.M. vs. history at 3 P.M.) would result in the emergence of different language behavioral states. We would also expect children with a language disorder to show greater sensitivity to increased processing demands during standardized testing than their unimpaired peers. But one might ask, isn't this a flaw in the standardized assessment measure? From an emergentist perspective, the answer would be "no." It is this *change* in language behavior that emerges from the properties of the child's system in the context of the properties of the assessment that would be the focus of assessment from an emergentist perspective. We would expect to see different patterns of change in children with and without language disorders. Specifically, and importantly, one could not "qualify" a typically developing child without a language disorder for services by placing him or her under increased processing demands when being tested, because the child's language behavior would remain fairly stable and constant. In contrast, the child with a language disorder would be shifted easily into a disorder state—this being the very definition of a language disorder from an emergentist account. It is the behavior that emerges for the child with language impairment. Thus, by intentionally shifting the child with a language disorder into and out of different language states, one can begin to see aspects of the child's language system that are more or less stable.

CONCLUSION

Cognitivist and nativist approaches to the study of language impairments in children provide little guidance for an integrated account of real-time language processing and the longer time frame of language development. With emergentist approaches, however, moment-to-moment language processing and the longer time course of development are the same phenomenon viewed at differing time scales. Online language processing is the spontaneous self-organization of the system as it moves into and out of different meaning attractors, whereas language development is the change in this *same* underlying attractor language landscape over a longer time span.

There is no distinction between "competence" and "performance" in an emergentist approach. Instead, language is always and only performance within context. Importantly,

> even though some preferred states of the system will be so stable that they may 'look' like they are the result of symbolic rules, or stages in development, the stability of the child's multi-attractor language landscape is a function of the child-in-context, always. In other words, development looks stage-like only because in the immediate assembly of the activity within context, certain patterns are strongly preferred. (Thelen, 1995, p. 77)

Emergentism is the study of self-organized, emerging patterns of complex systems. Its strength is its focus on the simultaneous stability and the variability of emerging language abilities of the child at any given moment in time, providing a set of assumptions about how language is organized and changes over time. It also provides an approach to unlock the nature of these patterns empirically as they change in real time, as well as a framework to integrate the study of development from the neurophysiology of embodied representations to intentional communication within the communicative context. Importantly, it is at points of instability and variability—the noisy, messy, unpredictable points in the emergence of language—that the underlying dynamics of the emergence of language in children with language impairments are revealed. By not holding experimental conditions *constant*, but intentionally *changing* experimental conditions in clearly specified ways, both practitioners and researchers will be able to understand more fully not only the nature of the impairment at any given point in time in development but also the process of the emergence of language in these children over time.

Emergentism provides an ecologically viable approach to the integration of diagnostic assessment models and intervention approaches. Traditionally, assessment has focused on determining those aspects of the language system that may be missing in the child with SLI, but the actual aspects of intervention have remained poorly specified. Often clinicians who incorporate assessment measures developed within a nativist framework that focus on characterizing missing aspects of the child's grammar are then forced to switch to different theoretical views that emphasize *learning*, such as behaviorist models, during intervention. An emergentist approach to clinical intervention would view instability and variability in a child's language skills as newly emerging states, and intervention would focus on the strengthening of these language states through changes in external contextual demands.

NOTES

1. This separation between the CPU and memory brings with it a concept known as the "von Neumann bottleneck"—that the data transfer rate between the CPU and memory is very small in comparison with the amount of memory a computer has. In modern machines, this transfer rate (also know as the "bandwidth") is also very small in comparison with the rate at which the CPU can process information. Under some circumstances (when the CPU is required to perform minimal processing on large amounts of data), this gives rise to a serious limitation in overall effective processing speed. The CPU is continuously forced to wait for vital data to be transferred to or from memory. As CPU speed and memory size have increased much faster than the bandwidth between the two, the bottleneck has become more and more of a problem.
2. A step in the training process of an artificial neural network.
3. "Environment," from this perspective, includes the child's physical world: the visual and auditory stimuli; the physical characteristics and affordances of the objects, humans, and animals in the child's world.

REFERENCES

Bates, E., & MacWhinney, B. (1989). Functionalism and the competition model. In B. MacWhinney & E. Bates (Eds.), *The crosslinguistic study of sentence processing*. New York: Cambridge University Press.

Bishop, D. V. M. (1992). Biological bases of specific language impairment (developmental aphasia). In I. Kostovic, S. Knezevic (Eds.), *Neurodevelopment, aging and cognition* (pp. 253–271). Cambridge, MA: Birkhäuser.

Bishop, D. V. M., & Clarkson, B. (2003). Written language as a window into residual language deficits: A study of children with persistent and residual speech and language impairments. *Cortex, 39*, 215–223.

Chi, M. T. H. (1976). Short-term memory limitations in children: Capacity or processing deficits? *Memory and Cognition, 23*, 266–281.

Chi, M. T. H. (1977). Age differences in the speed of processing: A critique. *Developmental Psychology, 13*, 543–544.

Chi, M. T. H., & Gallagher, J. D. (1982). Speed of processing: A developmental source of limitation. *Topics in Learning and Learning Disorders, 2*, 23–32.

Chiat, S. (2001). Mapping theories of developmental language impairment: Premises, predictions and evidence. *Language and Cognitive Processes, 16*, 113–142.

Chomsky, N. (1965). *Aspects of the theory of syntax*. Cambridge, MA: MIT Press.

Chomsky, N. (1986). *Knowledge of language: Its nature, origins and use*. New York: Praeger.

Chomsky, N. (1988). *Language and the problems of knowledge*. Cambridge, MA: MIT Press.

Clahsen, H. (1989). The grammatical characterization of developmental dysphasia. *Linguistics, 27*, 897–920.

Coady, J., Evans, J. L., Mainela Arnold, E., & Kluender, K. (2007). Children with specific language impairments perceive speech most categorically when tokens are natural and meaningful. *Journal of Speech, Language, and Hearing Research, 50*, 41–57.

Coady, J. A., Kluender, K. R., & Evans, J. L. (2005). Categorical perception of speech by children with specific language impairments. *Journal of Speech, Language, and Hearing Research, 48*, 944–959.

Cohen, I. L. (1994). An artificial neural network analogue of learning in autism. *Biological Psychiatry, 36*(1) 5–20.

Corbetta, D., & Thelen, E. (1996). The developmental origins of bimanual coordination: A dynamic systems perspective. *Journal of Experimental Psychology: Human Perception and Performance, 22*, 502–522.

Dollaghan, C., & Campbell, T. (1998). Nonword repetition and child language impairment. *Journal of Speech, Language, and Hearing Research, 41*, 1136–1146.

Dromi, E. (2003). Different methodologies yield incongruous results: A study of the spontaneous use of verb forms in Hebrew. In Y. Levy & J. Schaeffer (Eds.), *Language competence across populations: Toward a definition of specific language impairments* (pp. 273–290). Mahwah, NJ: Erlbaum.

Edwards, J., & Lahey, V. H. (1998). Nonword repetitions of children with specific language impairment: Exploration of some explanations for their inaccuracies. *Applied Psycholinguistics, 19*, 279–309.

Ellis Weismer, S., Evans, J., & Hesketh, L. (1999). An examination of verbal working memory capacity in children with specific language impairment. *Journal of Speech, Language, and Hearing Research, 42*, 1249–1260.

Ellis Weismer, S., & Thordardottir, E. (2002). Cognition and language. In P. Accarod, A. Capute, & B. Rogers (Eds.), *Disorders of language development* (pp. 21–37). Timonium, MD: York Press.

Elman, J. (1995). Language as a dynamical system. In R. F. Port & T. van Gelder (Eds.), *Mind as motion*. Cambridge, MA: MIT Press.

Elman, J. (2003). Development: It's about time. *Developmental Science, 6*(4), 430–433.

Elman, J., Bates, E., Johnson, M., Karmiloff-Smith, A., Parisi, D., & Plunkett, K. (1996). *Rethinking innateness: A connectionist perspective on development.* Cambridge, MA: MIT Press.

Evans, J., & MacWhinney, B. (1999). Sentence Processing strategies in children with expressive and expressive-receptive specific language impairments. *International Journal of Language and Communication Disorders, 34*(2), 117–134.

Evans, J. L. (2002). Variability in comprehension strategy use in children with specific language impairments: A dynamical systems account. *International Journal of Language and Communication Disorders, 47*, 95–116.

Fischer, K. W., Rotenberg, E. J., Bullock, D. H., Raya, P. (1993). The dynamics of competence: How context contributes directly to skill. In R. H. Wozniak & K. W. Fischer, (Eds.), *Development in context: Acting and thinking in specific environments* (pp. 93–117). Hillsdale, NJ: Erlbaum.

Fodor, J. A. (1983). *Modularity of mind.* Cambridge, MA: MIT Press.

Fogel, A., & Thelen, E. (1987). Development of early expressive and communicative action: Reinterpreting the evidence from a dynamic systems perspective. *Developmental Psychology, 23*(6), 747–761.

Gershkoff-Stowe, L., & Thelen, E. (2004). U-shaped changes in behavior: A dynamic systems approach. *Journal of Cognition and Development, 5*(1), 11–36.

Gillam, R., Cowan, N., & Marler, J. (1998). Information processing by school-age children with specific language impairment: Evidence from a modality effect paradigm. *Journal of Speech, Language and Hearing Research, 41*, 913–926.

Gold, E. M. (1967). Language indentification in the limit. *Information and Control, 10*, 447–474.

Gopnik, M., & Crago, M. (1991). Familial aggregation of a developmental language disorder. *Cognition, 39*, 1–50.

Gustafsson, L. (1997). Inadequate cortical feature maps: A neural circuit theory of autism. *Biological Psychiatry, 42*, 1138–1147.

Haken, H. (1983). *Synergetics, an introduction.* New York: Springer-Verlag.

Haken, H. (1993). *Advance synergetics: Instability hierarchies of self-organizing systems and devices.* New York: Springer-Verlag.

Haken, H. (1996). *Principles of brain functioning: A synergetic approach to brain activity, behavior and cognition.* Berlin: Springer-Verlag.

Harm, M. W., & Seidenberg, M. S. (1998). Phonology, reading acquisition, and dyslexia: Insights from connectionism models. *Psychological Review.*

Hoeffner, J. H., & McClelland, J. L. (1993). Can a perceptual processing deficit explain the impairment of inflectional morphology in developmental dysphasia?: A computational investigation. In E. V. Clark (Ed.), *Proceedings of the 25th Child Language Research Forum.* Palo Alto, CA: Stanford University Press.

Hoyt, D. F., & Taylor, C. R. (1981). Gait and the energetics of locomotion in horses. *Nature, 292*, 239–240.

Joanisse, M., & Seidenberg, M. (2003). Phonology and syntax in specific language impairment: Evidence from a connectionist model. *Brain and Language, 86*, 40–56.

Johnson, M. (1999). Cortical plasticity in normal and abnormal cognitive development: Evidence and working hypothesis. *Development and Psychopathology, 11*, 419–437.

Just, M. A., & Carpenter, P. A. (1992). A capacity theory of comprehension: Individual differences in working memory. *Psychological Review, 99*, 1–28.

Kail, R. (1994). A method for studying the generalized slowing hypothesis in children with specific language impairment. *Journal of Speech and Hearing Research, 37*, 418–421.

Kail, R., & Salthouse, T. A. (1994). Processing speed as a mental capacity. *Acta Psychologica, 86*, 199–225.

Karmiloff-Smith, A. (1997) Crucial differences between developmental cognitive neuroscience and adult neuropsychology. *Developmental Neuropsychology, 13*, 513–524.

Karmiloff-Smith, A. (1998). Development itself is the key to understanding developmental disorders. *Trends in Cognitive Sciences, 2*(10), 389–398.

Kelso, J. A. S. (1984). Phase transitions and critical behavior in human bimanual coordination. *American Journal of Physiology: Regulatory, Integrative, and Comparative Physiology, 15*, R1000–R1004.

Kelso, J. A. S., Ding, M., & Schöner, G. (1986). Dynamic pattern formation: A tutorial. In L. B. Smith & E. Thelen (Eds.), *A dynamic systems approach to development: Applications* (pp. 13–50). Boston: MIT Press.

Kelso, J. A. S., Scholz, J. P., & Schöner, G. (1986). Non-equilibrium phase transitions in coordinated biological motion: Critical fluctuations. *Physic Letters A, 118*, 279–284.

Leonard, L. B. (1998). *Children with specific language impairment.* Cambridge, MA: MIT Press.

Leonard, L. B., Nippold, M. A., Kail, R., & Hale, C. A. (1983). Picture naming in language-impaired children. *Journal of Speech and Hearing Research, 26*, 609–615.

Lewis, M. D. (2000). The promise of dynamic systems approaches for an integrated account of human development. *Child Development, 71*(1), 36–43.

MacDonald, M. C., & Christiansen, M. H. (1992). Reassessing working memory: Comment on Just and Carpenter and Waters and Caplan. *Psychological Review, 109*, 35–54.

Mainela-Arnold, E., & Evans, J. L. (2005). Beyond capacity limitations: Determinants of word recall performance on verbal working memory span tasks in children with SLI. *Journal of Speech Language, and Hearing Research, 48*, 897–909.

Marchman, V., Wulfeck, B., & Ellis Weismer, S. (1999). Morphological productivity in children with normal language and SLI: A study of the English past tense. *Journal of Speech, Language, and Hearing Research*, 42, 206–219.

Mareschal, D., & Shultz, T. R. (1996) Generative connectionist networks and constructivist cognitive development. *Cognitive Development, 11*, 571–603.

McMahon, T. A. (1984). *Muscles, reflexes, and locomotion.* Princeton, NJ: Princeton University Press.

Miller, C., Kail, R., Leonard, L., & Tomblin, B. (2001). Speed of processing in children with specific language impairment. *Journal of Speech, Language, and Hearing Research, 44*, 416–433.

Montgomery, J. W. (2000). Relation of working memory to off-line and real-time sentence processing in children with specific language impairment. *Applied Psycholinguistics, 21*, 117–148.

Muchisky, M., Gershkoff-Stowe, L., Cole, E., & Thelen, E. (Eds.). (1996). *The epigenetic landscape revisited: A dynamic interpretation* (Vol. 10). Westport, CT: Greenwood.

Neville, H. J. (1991). Neurology of cognitive and language processing: Effects of early experience. In K. R. Gibson & A. C. Peterson (Eds.), *Brain maturation and cognitive development: Comparative and cross-cultural perspectives: Foundation of human behavior* (pp. 355–380). New York: Aldine de Gruyter.

Nicolis, G., & Prigogine, I. (1989). *Complexity in natureA An introduction.* New York: Freeman.

O'Reilly, R. C., & Munakata, Y. (2000). *Computational explorations in cognitive neuroscience: Understanding the mind by simulating the brain.* Cambridge, MA: MIT Press.

Oyama, S. (1985). *The ontogeny of information: Developmental systems and evolution*. Cambridge, MA: Cambridge University Press.

Pinker, S. (1984). *Language learnability and language development*. Cambridge, MA: Harvard University Press.

Plunkett, K., & Marchman, V. (1993). From rote learning to system building: Acquiring verb morphology in children and connectionist nets. *Cognition, 48*(1), 21–69.

Port, R. F., & van Gelder, T. (1995). *Mind as motion*. Cambridge, MA: MIT Press.

Rice, M. L. (Ed.). (1996). *Toward a genetics of language*. Mahwah, NJ: Erlbaum.

Rice, M. L. (2003). Unified model of specific and general language delay: Grammatical tense as a clinical marker of unexpected variation. In Y. Levy & J. Schaeffer (Eds.), *Language competence across populations: Toward a definition of specific language impairments* (pp. 63–94). Mahwah, NJ: Erlbaum.

Rice, M. L., & Warren, S. F. (Eds.). (2004). *Developmental language disorders: From phenotypes to etiologies*. Mahwah, NJ: Erlbaum.

Rice, M. L., & Wexler, K. (1996). A phenotype of specific language impairment: Extended optional infinitives. In M. L. Rice (Ed.), *Toward a genetics of language*. Mahwah, NJ: Erlbaum.

Rice, M., Wexler, K., & Redmond, S.M. (1999).Grammaticality judgments of an extended optional infinitive grammar: Evidence from English-speaking children with specific language impairment. *Journal of Speech, Language, and Hearing Research, 42*: 943–961.

Rumelhart, D. E., & McClelland, R. J. (1986). On learning the past tenses of English verbs. In R. J. McClelland & D. E. Rumelhart (Eds.), *Parallel distributed processing: Explorations in the microstructure of cognition* (Vol. II). Cambridge, MA: MIT Press.

Rumelhart, D. E., McClelland, R. J., & Group, T. P. R. (1986). *Parallel distributed processing: Explorations in the microstructure of cognition*. (Vol. I). Cambridge, MA: MIT Press.

Salthouse, T.A. (2000). Aging and measures of processing speed. *Biological Psychology, 54*, 35–54.

Shiffrin, R. M. (1993). Short-term memory: A brief commentary. *Memory and Cognition, 21*(2), 193–197.

Smith, L. B., & Thelen, E. (Eds.). (1993). *A dynamic systems approach to development: Applications*. Cambridge, MA: MIT Press.

Spencer, J., & Schöner, G. (2003). Bridging the representational gap in the dynamic systems approach to development. *Developmental Science,* 6(4), 392–412.

Stark, R., & Heinz, J. (1996a). Perception of stop consonants in children with expressive and receptive-expressive language impairments. *Journal of Speech, Language, and Hearing Research, 39*, 676–686.

Stark, R., & Heinz, J. (1996b). Vowel perception in children with and without language impairment. *Journal of Speech Language and Hearing Research, 39*, 860–869.

Strohner, H., & Nelson, K. (1974). The young child's development of sentence comprehension: Influence of event probability, nonverbal context, syntactic form and strategies. *Child Development, 45*, 567–576.

Thelen, E. (1989). Self-organization in developmental processes: Can systems approaches work? In M. Gunnar & E. Thelen (Eds.), *Systems and development: The Minnesota Symposia on Child Psychology* (Vol. 22, pp. 77–117). Hillsdale, NJ: Erlbaum.

Thelen, E. (1995). Time-scale dynamics and the development of an embodied cognition. In R. F. Port & T. van Gelder (Eds.), *Mind in motion*. Cambridge, MA: MIT Press.

Thelen, E., Corbetta, D., & Spencer, J. (1996). The development of reaching during the first year: The role of movement speed. *Journal of Experimental Psychology: Human Perception and Performance, 22*, 1059–1076.

Thelen, E., & Fischer, D. M. (1982). Newborn stepping: An explanation for a "disappearing reflex." *Developmental Psychology, 18*, 760–770.

Thelen, E., Schöner, G., Scheier, C., & Smith, L. B. (2001). The dynamics of embodiment: A field theory of infant perseverative reaching. *Behavioral and Brain Sciences, 24*, 1–86.

Thelen, E., & Smith, L. B. (1994). *A dynamic systems approach to the development of cognition and action*. Cambridge, MA: MIT Press.

Thelen, E., & Ulrich, B. D. (1991). Hidden skills: A dynamical systems analysis of treadmill stepping during the first year. *Monographs of the Society for Research in Child Development, 56*(1, Serial No. 233).

Thomas, M. S. C., & Karmiloff-Smith, A. (2002). Are developmental disorders like cases of adult brain damage?: Implications from connectionist modeling. *Behavioral and Brain Sciences, 25*, 727–788.

Tomblin, B., Records, N. L., Buckwalter, P. R., Zhang, X., Smith, E., & O'Brien, M. (1997). Prevalence of specific language impairment in kindergarten children. *Journal of Speech, Language, and Hearing Research, 40*, 1245–1260.

Ullman, M., & Gopnik, M. (1999). The production of inflectional morphology in hereditary specific language impairment. *Applied Psycholinguistics, 20*, 51–117.

van der Lely, H. K. J. (2003). Do heterogeneous deficits require heterogeneous theories?: SLI subgroups and the RDDR hypothesis. In Y. Levy & J. Schaeffer (Eds.), *Language competence across populations: Toward a definition of specific language impairments* (pp. 109–134). Mahwah, NJ: Erlbaum.

van der Lely, H. K. J., & Harris, M. (1990). Comprehension of reversible sentences in specifically language-impaired children. *Journal of Speech and Hearing Disorders, 55*, 101–117.

van der Lely, H. K. J., Rosen, S., & McClelland, A. (1998). Evidence for a grammar-specific deficit in children. *Current Biology, 8*, 1253–1258.

van der Lely, H. K. J., & Stollwerk, L. (1996). A grammatical specific language impairment in children: An autosomal dominant inheritance? *Brain and Language, 52*, 484–504.

van der Maas, H. L. J. (1998). The dynamical and statistical properties of cognitive strategies: Relations between strategies, attractors, and latent classes. In K. M. Newell & P. C. M. Molenaar (Eds.), *Applications of nonlinear dynamics to developmental process modeling* (pp. 161–176). Mahwah, NJ: Erlbaum.

van der Maas, H. L. J., & Molenaar, P. C. (1992). Stage-wise cognitive development: An application of catastrophe theory. *Psychological Review, 99*, 395–417.

van Geert, P. (1991). A dynamic systems model of cognitive and language growth. *Psychological Review, 98*, 3–53.

van Geert, P. (1993). A dynamic systems model of cognitive growth: Competition and support under limited resources conditions. In L. Smith & E. Thelen (Eds.), *A dynamic systems approach to development: Applications*. Cambridge, MA: MIT Press.

van Geert, P. (1994). *Dynamic systems of development*. London: Harvester Wheatsheaf.

van Geert, P. (1998). A dynamic systems model of cognitive and language growth. *Psychological Review, 98*(1), 3–53.

Verela, F. J., Thompson, E., & Rosch, E. (1996). *The embodied mind*. Cambridge, MA: MIT Press.

Wexler, K. (2003). Lenneberg's dream: Learning, normal language development, and specific language impairments. In Y. Levy & J. Schaeffer (Eds.), *Language competence across populations: Toward a definition of specific language impairments* (pp. 11–46). Mahwah, NJ: Erlbaum.

Windsor, J., & Hwang, M. (1999). Test of generalized slowing hypothesis in specific language impairment. *Journal of Speech, Language, and Hearing Research, 42*, 1205–1218.

3

Critical Periods in Second-Language Learning

Distinguishing Phenomena from Explanations

JOHN T. BRUER

Bialystok and Hakuta (1994) introduced their chapter on the existence and significance of critical periods for second-language acquisition (L2A) with the observation that in this, as in other scientific debates, there is a danger of conflating descriptions of a phenomenon with an explanation of the phenomenon. Here I expand on Bialystok and Hakuta's insight by presenting and applying two distinctions that have been prominent in discussions of critical periods in imprinting. The first distinction is exactly that of Bialystok and Hakuta: There is a difference between establishing the existence of a critical period phenomenon and providing a causal theory that might account for such a phenomenon. The second distinction is one that has had a long history in the imprinting literature. There are (at least) two general types of theories to explain critical-period phenomena. What I call "maturational" theories posit endogenous causes for the opening and closing of critical periods. These contrast with "learning" theories that posit exogenous causes for a least the closure of a critical period.

When one applies these distinctions to L2A, one first sees that, most likely for historical reasons, maturational theories dominate the field. Indeed it appears that in the L2A literature, "critical periods" are defined as requiring a maturational explanation. Assimilating a maturational etiology into the definition of a critical-period concept can obscure what the force of arguments, pro and con, on critical periods are about. Most arguments against critical periods in L2A intend to show that the maturational hypothesis is untenable. These arguments, however, do not refute the maturational hypothesis; rather, their force is to show that critical period phenomena do not exist, so there is nothing to explain. In addition, theorists who develop alternative explanations for critical period phenomena sometimes conclude that these explanations render the critical-period concept theoretically uninteresting.

Analyzing the L2A critical-period debate from the perspective of the phenomenon–explanation distinction has implications for research, and possibly for practice, However, most importantly, this analysis suggests that the status of critical-period phenomena in L2A research is considerably different than that of critical periods in research areas such as imprinting, birdsong learning, and development of the visual system.

Note that what I focus on here is what Bateson (1979) characterized as the "general idea" of a critical-period phenomenon: A person's traits and behavior can be more strongly influenced at one point in development than at others. In the spirit of Bateson's general idea, then, I include under the critical-period concept all related concepts, such as sensitive period, optimal period, susceptible period, vulnerable point, and so forth.

I should add that this chapter is not, and could not be, an exhaustive review of the critical-period literature, even for L2A, viewed from the phenomenon versus explanation perspective. I present the historical background for the distinctions and illustrate various forms of argument, pro and con, for critical periods in L2A, against this historical background. For these reasons, I concentrate on argument types using selected, but prominent and representative examples, from the literature.

CRITICAL-PERIOD PHENOMENA: THE DESCRIPTIVE TASK

Over the past 30 years, numerous researchers and commentators on the critical period concept have upheld the importance of distinguishing between critical-period phenomena—descriptions of critical periods—and hypotheses that explain why, or how, such phenomena occur. Connolly (1972) observed that to speak of a critical period is to describe certain temporal characteristics of a developmental phenomenon. Critical periods, he claimed, could serve as useful empirical generalizations, but once such generalizations were established, the task of discovering the causal mechanisms that generated the phenomenon remained. Oyama (1979), Bateson (1979, 1983), and Bateson and Hinde (1987) also argued that the term "critical period" is properly considered a descriptive term. It describes a period within the life span of heightened sensitivity or responsiveness to certain kinds of stimuli. It is this pattern of responsiveness that requires explanation in terms of underlying causal processes. Colombo (1982) upheld this distinction and pointed out that critical-period research confined to specifying the temporal boundaries of critical periods constitutes a strictly descriptive task. It is only by looking for the underlying causes that critical-period research becomes an explanatory endeavor. Bornstein (1987) listed 17 structural characteristics, such as onset, offset, and peak sensitivity, that descriptively characterize critical periods. He distinguished between establishing these defining characteristics and providing causal theories of critical-period phenomena, and observed that explanatory accounts of critical periods may derive from biology, information theory, learning theory, or theories of cognitive development.

Thus, there is a history of distinguishing *critical-period phenomena* from causal explanations of critical-period phenomena. A study must satisfy numerous discussions of the methodological criteria to provide unambiguous evidence for the existence of a critical-period phenomenon (Bateson, 1979; Bateson & Hinde, 1987; Bialystok & Hakuta, 1994; Bornstein, 1987; Bruer, 2001; Colombo, 1982). Again, in the spirit of Bateson's general idea, to establish the existence of a critical period one must expose organisms to the same stimuli at different ages, control the duration of the experience, control for confounding variables, and measure the organisms' responses to the stimuli. Such an experiment yields a curve that shows response to the stimuli as a function of age. Response is higher—that is, the organism is more sensitive to the stimuli (or their absence)—during the critical period. In L2A studies, the stimuli are linguistic, and the response that varies with age is a measure of second language (L2) grammatical performance or non-native L2 accent. For brevity, I call this experimental result that describes the critical-period phenomenon in L2A the "behavioral function."

DISTINGUISHING EXPLANATORY THEORIES: ENDOGENOUS VERSUS EXOGENOUS CAUSES

Once the existence of a critical-period phenomenon has been experimentally established, there remains the second distinct task of providing a causal explanation for the behavioral function. Bateson (1979) noted that numerous distinct causal hypotheses might explain the same observed behavioral function. To elucidate how different hypotheses might explain the same observed outcomes, Bateson introduced an analogy: Think of the developing organism as a train traveling on a one-way journey from Conception Station to Ultimate Terminal. The train's passenger coaches are divided into windowed compartments. Each compartment and its occupants represent a behavioral system. The compartment windows are opaque. So, a compartment's occupants can be influenced by the passing scenery only when the compartment's windows are open. If we have established the existence of a critical-period phenomenon, one place to look for a causal explanation is to inquire about the mechanism that operates the windows and how open versus closed windows might affect the passengers. Bateson offered two train analogies that suggest possible answers to this question.

Train 1: Maturational Theories That Posit Endogenous Causes

Suppose the mechanism that opens and closes compartment windows is regulated by an onboard clock. According to this model, windows open and close as a function of how long the train has been traveling from Conception. Train 1 is the clock, or maturational, model of a critical period. This model maintains that the onset and offset of critical periods is regulated by intrinsic, endogenous causes that arise during biological development, or maturation, independent of any exogenous input.

Train 2: Learning Theories That Posit Exogenous Causes

Suppose again that windows in different compartments of the train open at different points on the journey. But now suppose that once a window opens at a particular stage in the journey, it never shuts until the train stops running. On this model, according to Bateson, critical periods appear to end not because windows shut, but because of changes to the compartment occupants caused by exogenous events; occupants learn from the passing scenery. According to this learning model, although maturational events might cause the onset of the critical period, the critical period appears to end not because of endogenous, maturational changes originating from within the organism, but because of exogenous causes. Experience, or learning, plays a causal role in the apparent close of a critical period. The critical period appears to close because, after a time, passengers have learned all they can, or all they need, from the trackside scenery, not because maturation turns off the learning mechanisms.

THE HISTORICAL CONTEXT FOR THE TRAIN ANALOGY

The current paradigmatic example of a critical period, following the pioneering work of Hubel and Wiesel (1970), is the development of ocular dominance columns in visual cortex. However, Bateson's discussion of critical periods occurred within the context of imprinting. Indeed, Bateson suggested that the notion of a critical period for imprinting was the source of the concept for both research in birdsong learning and the influence of experience on the development of the visual system.

Lorenz's papers on imprinting (Lorenz, 1937, 1957) introduced the critical-period concept into behavioral science. Lorenz, like earlier ethologists, had observed that for some bird species, within a few hours of hatching, the hatchlings imprint on, and subsequently follow, the first moving object they see. If they do not encounter a moving object during these first few hours, imprinting does not occur. In natural situations, the first moving objects a young bird sees are the hen and its siblings. Lorenz was keen to establish that imprinting was a unique type of learning process, one that was different from the associative learning then studied by psychologists. Lorenz identified features of imprinting that distinguished it from associative learning. Among these features were, first, that imprinting occurred only during a critical period, unlike associative learning that could occur at any point in the life cycle; and, second, that imprinting, unlike associative learning, was permanent or irreversible. According to Lorenz, maturational changes, independent of experience, opened and closed the critical period for imprinting; that is, Lorenz proposed a Train 1 theory to explain the imprinting phenomenon.

Although the existence of imprinting as a phenomenon was not questioned, over the next 35 years, Lorenz's strong claims about the uniqueness, criticality, and irreversibility of filial imprinting did not withstand experimental test. By the 1970s, Hess (1973) was among the very few ethologists who still advanced Lorenz's strong maturational account of filial imprinting. Even Hess had modified his view from a strict maturational account to a genetic account (Hess, 1959). He maintained that the genetic program provided a topological ordering of events in the maturational sequence, but the rate of progression through this sequence could be affected by experience. The genetic program provides an ordered sequence rather than a railroad timetable of developmental events. Although the sequence of critical periods is universal in the development of a species, Hess argued, critical periods do not always open and close at the same ages in all individuals. Individual differences arise (within limits) based on genetic endowment and experience. In Hess's modified maturational theory, exogenous factors had some influence on the timing of critical periods, but endogenous factors predominated. For this reason, it remained a Train 1, maturational account.

Bateson's Train 2 model was an attempt to characterize an alternative theoretical model to explain the imprinting phenomenon. He claimed it provided the best theoretical account for the mechanism underlying the phenomenon. In particular, studies had shown that under some experimental conditions, imprinting could be reversed after the ostensible close of the critical period (Salzen & Meyer, 1968). The Train 2 analogy allowed for this reversal: "If this analogy can be pressed just a little further, it looks as though the occupants can, under certain circumstances, be persuaded to study strange things outside the train later in the journey, and when they do so, they are influenced by what they see" (Bateson, 1979, p. 475). This allowed him to argue that although behavioral systems might be shaped by early experience, the learning mechanisms that shape these systems might remain operative throughout the life of the organism. This allows for the possibility, as Bateson wrote in a later article (Bateson & Hinde, 1987), that although certain forms of behavior are *normally* dependent on early experience, *sometimes* these forms of behavior can nonetheless be changed later in life.

THE DOMINANCE OF MATURATIONAL THEORIES IN LANGUAGE ACQUISITION

Historical Background

The predominant view in language acquisition research has been that critical-period phenomena occur and are best explained by theories that posit endogenous, maturational causes for the opening and closing of critical periods. The dominance of Train 1 models in L2A is due in part to the historical context in which the critical-period hypothesis for language acquisition was first articulated.

Lenneberg (1967) provided the first extended argument that language acquisition was subject to critical-period constraints. At that time, the prevailing critical-period paradigm was imprinting, not visual acuity. Hubel and Wiesel's (1970) article on critical periods in the development of the cat visual system had not yet appeared. In fact, Lenneberg made only one, critical citation of Hubel and Wiesel's (1962, 1963) work, expressing concern that neurophysiologists' preoccupation with recording from single cells might cause brain scientists to neglect the equally important insight that the brain might encode experiences as temporal patterns over cell ensembles.

There are numerous parallels between the programs of Lorenz and Lenneberg. Just as Lorenz was committed to the development of a biology of behavior, Lenneberg was committed to the development of a biology of language. Like Lorenz, Lenneberg was interested in a species-specific behavior, human language. Like Lorenz, Lenneberg believed that the development of species-specific behaviors should be thought of in analogy with organ development in embryogenesis. Lenneberg thought of cognitive functions as physiological functions that developed the same way tissues and organs do in ontogeny. Similar to Lorenz, Lenneberg observed how his biological theory of language was related to then-current thinking in genetics. Just as Lorenz spoke of external stimuli that released innate action patterns (e.g., moving objects release following behavior in hatchlings), Lenneberg spoke of the infant's linguistic experience as a releaser that activated innate language skills and behaviors. Lenneberg's examples of other critical periods included imprinting, specifically, age-limited emergence of behavior in mammals, citing Hess (1962), Hinde (1961), Lorenz (1958), and Thorpe (1961), along with work on socialization in dogs (Scott, 1963) and attachment in humans (Bowlby, 1953). It is not surprising, then, that Lenneberg, like Lorenz, espoused a Train 1 maturational account of critical periods in language acquisition. He hypothesized that the critical period for first-language acquisition began around age 2 years and ended at puberty. It was his view, which as since been shown to be untenable, that the critical period drew to a close when lateralization of brain function was complete. Lenneberg (1967) did not explicitly address the issue of critical periods for L2 acquisition (Johnson & Newport, 1989).

Assimilation of Maturational Causes to the Critical-Period Concept

Some readers may be surprised to learn that explanations other than maturational accounts have been advanced for critical-period phenomena. They might be further surprised to learn that Train 2–type explanations for critical-period phenomena were developed to account for the *reversibility* of critical-period phenomena. For many, critical-period phenomena are considered to be irreversible by definition (e.g., see Hess, 1973).

In Oyama's 1979 analysis of the critical-period concept, she argued that the concept had suffered from "definitional assimilation," which occurs when two formerly independent characteristics of a concept are assumed to be logically related. For example, Lorenz claimed that imprinting was subject to critical-period constraints and that the effects of imprinting were irreversible. Over time, Oyama pointed out, these two independent characteristics of imprinting were assimilated into the critical-period concept, so that that any phenomenon subject to critical-period constraints was also assumed to be irreversible. In other words, the critical-period concept was assumed to entail irreversibility.

Within the debate about critical periods for L2A, it would appear that another definitional assimilation has occurred. In the L2A area, critical-period hypotheses explain critical-period phenomena (that are assumed to be irreversible), but in addition it is assumed that the critical-period concept entails the existence of endogenous, maturational causes for the close of critical periods. It has become definitional, at least in the L2A literature, that critical-period phenomena require maturational explanations.

For example, the Birdsong (1999) book contains six contributed chapters, three pro and three con, on the critical-period hypothesis for L2A. In that volume, both proponents and critics state the hypothesis in terms of maturational constraints. For example, critical-period proponents Eubank and Gregg (1999) stated that a critical period in a domain involves the ability to form and maintain neural connections relevant to the domain, during, but not after, a period that is determined by innate, genetically constrained mechanisms. The critics Bialystok and Hakuta (1999) characterized the critical-period hypothesis as a causal explanation for age-dependent L2A, because variance in L2 achievement is attributed to maturational changes in the brain. Snow (1987), another critic, claimed that the critical-period hypothesis for L2A entails, among other things, that the existence and timing of the critical period is controlled by biological maturation. Many of these discussion cite Long (1990), Patkowski (1990), and Scovel (1969, 1988) as providing canonical definitions of critical periods in L2A. All these authors assume that a maturational etiology is definitional of the L2A critical-period hypothesis. Critical periods entail maturational explanations.

Definitions of the critical-period concept that assimilate maturational etiology are also found in Johnson and Newport (1989) and Newport, Bavelier, and Neville (2001). Johnson and Newport (1989) define a "critical period" as changes over maturation in the ability to learn. Newport et al. (2001) identify the key feature of a critical period as a peak period of plasticity, occurring at a maturationally defined time, followed by reduced plasticity.

One might view this talk of definitional assimilation as a mere exercise in logic chopping and semantics. However, first the exercise has the benefit of making us aware that there are logically consistent alternatives to viewing critical periods as necessarily irreversible and as arising from maturational constraints. Second, it has the benefit of making explicit what the L2A critical-period debate is about. In particular, it allows us to see the force and point of skeptical arguments in the L2A literature. As mentioned earlier, it is beyond the scope of this review to address all such arguments, so I address types of arguments offered by prominent parties to this debate. At this point, I do not intend to comment on their soundness and validity. I am more interested in the form of these arguments.

WHAT IS THE CRITICAL PERIOD FOR L2A DEBATE ABOUT?

If one assimilates the necessity of a maturational explanation in the definition of the critical-period concept, then one can give a succinct formulation of the critical-period hypothesis in L2A and see what is at issue in the debate. The definition must include conditions the behavioral function must satisfy if a critical-period phenomenon exists and further specify that the behavioral function arises from maturational causes. Johnson and Newport (1989) also clearly stated criteria that the behavioral function must satisfy if a critical-period phenomenon exists. So what is at issue in the debate is the following claim: A critical period for L2A requires (1) that there be a *nonlinear* behavioral function of L2 proficiency (as determined by grasp of grammatical knowledge or accent) with age over the lifespan; (2) that the function show a consistent decline over age for those exposed to the language before the end of the favored learning period, followed by a leveling off in performance for those exposed after the close of the favored learning period; (3) that there be no systematic relation of L2 performance to age of exposure for those exposed after the close of the favored learning period; and (4) that the opening and closing of the favored learning period be due to endogenous, maturational changes in the learner. In this definition, the first three criteria on the behavioral function must be present to establish the existence of a critical-period phenomenon; the fourth criterion requires that the phenomenon arise out of maturational constraints.

Anti-critical-period hypothesis arguments are of two types. The first type of argument attempts to show that the behavioral function does not satisfy one or more of conditions 1 through 3. The second type of argument grants that although conditions 1–3 may be satisfied, condition 4 is not established, or that there exist alternatives to condition 4 that are equally consistent with the behavioral function.

Arguments That Conditions 1 and 2 Are Not Satisfied

Condition 1 requires that the behavioral function be nonlinear. If the function were linear with age, then inability to acquire L2 at later ages could be explained as the result of general decrease in ability to learn with age that is found with other learning tasks, such as paired-associate learning. Condition 2 specifies the type of nonlinearity required for a critical period. There must be a critical point in the function, such that before this critical point, age is negatively but significantly correlated with L2 proficiency, but after which L2 proficiency is consistently lower and not significantly correlated with age of first exposure to L2. If the behavioral function is shown to be a linear violating criterion (condition 1), then it follows that condition 2, cannot be satisfied either. Below are several prominent examples of this argument type.

Bialystok and Hakuta (1999) argued that the minimal requirement to reject a null hypothesis of no critical period is to establish the existence of a discontinuity or nonlinearity in the age of acquisition–L2 proficiency function. Based on a large-scale study of native Chinese and Spanish speakers using 1990 census data, Bialystok and Hakuta (1999) and Hakuta, Bialystok, and Wiley (2003) showed that self-reported English proficiency is best described as a linear function of age of first exposure to L2 across the lifespan. Flege, Munro, and MacKay (1995) showed that foreign accent ratings decrease linearly with age of arrival, in violation of condition 1, and that the behavioral function for age of arrival (AOA) shows no discontinuity at any AOA, in violation of condition 2. Flege, Yeni-Komshian, and Liu (1999) found that a linear function best fits data on the relation between AOA in the United States and foreign accent rating in a population of 240 Korean–English bilinguals. They concluded that this linearity is inconsistent with the existence of a critical period for L2 phonetics acquisition.

Arguments That Condition 3 Is Not Satisfied

Condition 3 states that for individuals exposed to an L2 after the close of the critical period, there is no systematic relationship between age of exposure and eventual L2 proficiency. Condition 3 is usually stated for populations. The condition is deemed satisfied if there is no significant correlation between age of exposure and eventual L2 proficiency, if age of exposure occurs after the critical-period age identified under condition 2.

Bongaerts (1999), reviewing his own and others' work, argued against a particularly strong version of the maturational hypothesis for L2 phonology as stated by Scovel (1988): Late L2 learners (after age 12 years) fail to acquire native-like pronunciation because brain maturation causes basic language-learning abilities to be irreversibly lost at onset of puberty. Bongaerts argued that if such a biological barrier exists, then it should be impossible for adult learners to acquire native accents in L2. Bongaerts reported three studies of carefully screened, highly successful adult L2 learners. He found that a significant proportion of these individuals achieved native-like performance in an L2, even though they began L2 learning after the close of the purported critical period. Although Bongaerts granted that his findings represent exceptional cases, he nevertheless argued that his results provide evidence that there is no absolute biological barrier at puberty that prevents acquisition of a native accent in L2 for a late learner. His argument shows that there are exceptions to condition 3.

Birdsong (1992) made a similar argument for L2 grammar acquisition. In a group of 20 adult English speakers who had resided in France for at least 3 years, 15 participants approached native speaker norms, and 6 were within the range of performance showed by native controls. Birdsong also found that L2 proficiency in these subjects was predicted by the age of arrival in France, implying that age of exposure is significantly associated with L2 attainment. In his review of the literature, Birdsong (1999) noted that in studies of special, restricted populations, rates of native-like L2 proficiency in adult learners range from 5 to 25% and cannot be dismissed as statistical outliers. Again, this argument shows that there may be individual exceptions to condition 3. However, these arguments turn on an assumption of strong biological impossibility, which allows few, if any, exceptions. Exceptions can occur in a population of late L2 learners, where condition 3 still holds for the entire population.

Bialystok and Hakuta's (1994) argument that condition 3 is not satisfied is more in line with how the condition is usually formulated and evaluated. Taking the critical period to end at age 15, Johnson and Newport (1989) found a significant correlation precritical period ($r = -.87$) and a nonsignificant correlation postcritical period ($r = -.16$) for acquisition of L2 morphosyntax. Bialystok and Hakuta (1994) found that if one replots the Johnson and Newport (1989) data, one observes an apparent discontinuity in the behavioral function at age 20 rather than age 15. If one calculates the correlation coefficients between age of first exposure and grammar score test both pre- and post-age 20, there is a significant correlation between age and proficiency for both groups. So, at an age past the purported critical period, proficiency in L2 is still associated with age of exposure, violating condition 3. Oyama (1976) also showed that age of first exposure was predictive of eventual L2 accent even when first exposure occurs after the close of the critical period.

Flege et al. (1999) tested condition 3 explicitly. They employed a pre- versus postcritical-period test in a study of 240 native-speaking Korean participants who differed in age of arrival into an English-speaking environment. For both accent and morphosyntax, Flege et al. found significant correlations between L2 proficiency and age of first exposure for those first exposed both before and after the purported close of the critical period, in violation of condition 3.

Arguments That Challenge Condition 4

Critics whose arguments challenge condition 4 grant that there are instances in L2A when the first three conditions on a critical period are satisfied. Arguments over the status of condition 4 are of two kinds. The first type of challenge has it roots in the methodological problem of confounded independent variables. The first three conditions specify the behavioral function in terms of age. Condition 4 assumes that age is a relatively pure proxy variable for maturation; however, these critics point out, age is also correlated with numerous other nonbiological, nonmaturational variables. For example, age is also correlated with nonbiological variables, such as education, work experience, and relative use of first language (L1) versus L2. The second type of argument points to empirical evidence that suggests maturational hypotheses cannot account for critical-period phenomena.

Problems with Confounds

Flege et al. (1999) provided an example of how issues of statistically confounded independent variables enter into arguments that challenge condition 4. This study is particularly interesting, because it employed three different tests of the critical-period hypothesis for L2 accent and morphosyntactic knowledge. Tests of linearity of the behavioral function and a pre- versus postcritical-age test provided tests of conditions 1–3. Their third test, the matched subgroup analysis, attempted to control for variables that may be confounded with AOA in the L2 environment. Flege et al. formed subgroups of study participants that differed in AOA but were matched on other independent variables confounded with AOA. If there is a significant difference on the dependent variable (here, either foreign accent rating or morphosyntax score) between the matched subgroups, then AOA can be considered the cause of that difference. If there is no significant difference, then AOA per se does not have a causal influence on the dependent variable, and there would be no support for an age-dependent critical period and a maturational explanation of the behavioral function.

In the Flege et al. (1999) study, the results of the first two tests provided mixed support for the critical-period hypothesis. For accent, they found a linear function with age and both pre- and postcritical-age correlations in L2 scores with AOA. For morphosyntax, they found a nonlinearity in the function at around age 12, but, again, found both pre- and postcritical-age correlations with morphosyntactic knowledge. However, the authors argue, because of possible statistical confounds with AOA, these tests are not definitive. For this reason, they judged the matched subsample test as definitive. When they formed matched subgroups in which each group differed only in AOA, they found a significant relation between AOA and foreign accent rating, but no significant relation between AOA and grammatical knowledge score. They concluded that the matched subgroup analysis, which controls for statistical confounds between AOA and the other dependent variables, supports the existence of a critical-period phenomenon for L2 phonetics acquisition but not for acquisition of grammatical knowledge. Apparent differences in grammatical proficiency commonly attributed to AOA arise from the influence of variables confounded with AOA, such as amount of formal education received in L2 and age-dependent patterns of L1 versus L2 use. Therefore, condition 4 is not satisfied for L2 grammar acquisition because there is no fundamental age-dependent behavioral function for grammar acquisition. However, L2 phonology acquisition would appear to be consistent with condition 4.

However, consistency is a very weak constraint. In this case, the Flege et al. (1999) argument indicates that although it is possible that the behavioral function for L2 phonology acquisition has a maturational etiology, other explanations are also possible, explanations that take age as a proxy for some other, nonmaturational variable. For example, instead of interpreting age as a proxy measure for biological maturation, one could take age as a proxy for the state of development of the L1 phonological system. Flege et al. hypothesized that *ceteris paribus*, the more strongly developed the L1 phonological system when L2 learning begins, the more strongly L1 phonology influences L2 phonology acquisition. Age-related changes in L2 pronunciation would then be caused by the interaction between the L1 and L2 phonological systems; that is, the relation of age to degree of foreign accent may be the result of prior language and linguistic experience, not brain maturation. Thus, they propose a Train 2 model of the critical-period phenomenon for L2 phonology acquisition that distinguishes between critical-period phenomena and explanations of critical-period phenomena.

Seidenberg and Zevin (2006) provide another interesting example of an anti-critical-period argument that focuses on condition 4. They argue that connectionist models can provide an explanation for critical-period phenomena that call into question what they call the "standard view" of critical periods: Neurobiological developments on a strict maturational timetable limit language learning capacity. Seidenberg and Zevin do not deny the existence of critical-period phenomena, nor do they explicitly attack any of the first three conditions in the previous definition that ensure the presence of a critical-period phenomenon. According to Seidenberg and Zevin, an adequate connectionist model should account for the following behavioral phenomena that characterize language learning: (1) There is early rapid learning of L1; (2) there is a gradual decrease in language-learning ability over the lifespan; (3) there are differences in learning ability over the lifespan for different components of language (semantics, phonology, grammar); and (4) both the timing of exposure to a L2 and structural relations between L1 and L2 affect L2 acquisition. Given these conditions on an adequate connectionist model, Seidenberg and Zevin would seem to agree that there is some age-dependent learning phenomenon with respect to L2A that requires explanation.

However, Seidenberg and Zevin (2006) reject maturational explanations. They argue that the behavioral function arises as a result of "entrenchment," a property that characterizes learning in a connectionist network. Learning in a connectionist network occurs via adjustment to weights connecting network nodes. Feedback adjusts these weights. When a network has learned a task, activations in the network are close to the desired values. Exposure to additional stimuli patterns, for example, from the same language, then produces only small error signals. Thus, it becomes difficult to adjust weights any further, unless input to the network is radically altered. In this way, learning a task causes the network to become less plastic. Seidenberg and Zevin claim that whereas endogenous causes may open the critical period for language learning, entrenchment—the loss of network plasticity caused by successfully learning a task—makes subsequent learning more difficult. As for L2 acquisition beyond the L1 critical period, they point out that the typical learning situation is one in which L2 is acquired later in life, and L1 and L2 linguistic experiences are interleaved as L2 learning is underway. Under such learning conditions, critical-period phenomena in L2 acquisition arise because network weights that are highly favorable for processing L1, and that are still being reinforced by L1 during L2 learning, are unfavorable for learning L2.

Observed behavioral phenomena surrounding L2A, they argue, can be explained in terms of a theory of learning that specifies what is learned, how well it is learned, when it is learned, and how learning one system (e.g., L1) affects subsequent learning (e.g., L2). One need not appeal to endogenous biological developments within the organism that follow a strict maturational timetable to explain these behavioral phenomena. Entrenchment provides a more general and parsimonious explanation of the observed phenomena.

However, the prevailing trend in L2A studies to assimilate a maturational etiology into the critical period concept results in Seidenberg and Zevin (2006) possibly underestimating the interest and implications of their conclusion. They reason as follows: If entrenchment explains the behavioral phenomenon, then maturational hypotheses are superfluous, condition 4 is not fulfilled, and critical periods for L2A do not exist. They conclude, then, that there is *no* critical period for language acquisition in any theoretically interesting sense. There are merely learning phenomena that result from entrenchment. A more interesting statement of their conclusion—one that observes the distinction between phenomenon and explanation—would be to say that critical-period phenomena exist and require explanation, but that entrenchment provides an alternative theoretical account of these phenomena. We can maintain that behavioral functions satisfying conditions 1–3 exist *and* offer alternative, Train 1 or Train 2, accounts of these phenomena. Maturational explanations are not the only things that render critical-period phenomena theoretically interesting.

Recent publications by Allison Doupe, and Patricia Kuhl and her colleagues provide another example of a skeptical argument that focuses on condition 4. Their argument complements those made by Flege et al. (1999) and Seidenberg and Zevin (2006) by adding an appeal to empirical evidence into the mix. Kuhl and Doupe (1999) reviewed research on birdsong learning and speech acquisition in humans, both areas in which learning is believed to be constrained by critical periods. Unlike many of the advocates and critics of critical periods in L2A, who assume that critical periods require a maturational explanation, Kuhl and Doupe offered a theory-neutral characterization of a critical period that follows in the general spirit of Bateson: A critical period for acquiring a behavior is a specific phase in an organism's life cycle, during which there is enhanced sensitivity to a specific type of behavior-relevant experience, or to its absence. They acknowledge that for both birdsong and speech, critical-period phenomena exist. However, they expressed reservations about what they call the "classical" [my maturational] critical-period hypothesis, according to which critical periods close because of endogenous, neurological changes that occur during development. A review of the birdsong and speech literatures, they argue, suggests that the classical, maturational critical-period hypothesis is not consistent with the more complex picture emerging in these fields (see also Seidenberg & Zevin [2006] for a discussion of the implications of birdsong research for language acquisition studies). Converging evidence suggests that learning and experience, not endogenous factors, have a causal role in closing critical periods.

In Kuhl's (2004) view, initial phonetic learning emerges according to a maturational timetable between ages 7 and 11 months. Then, linguistic stimuli in the child's environment tune the relevant neural networks. Given no change in the input stimuli, entrenchment occurs; the network becomes stable and efficiently processes native-language speech sounds, at the cost of an increasing inability to process non-native speech sounds. A main theme in Kuhl's research has been that infants' phonetic discrimination is initially language-universal, but discrimination for non-native phonemes (i.e., phonemes that do not occur in their early linguistic environment) declines by the end of the first year. She and her colleagues (Kuhl, Conboy, Padden, Nelson, & Pruit, in press) found that among infants (average age 7.4 months), living in monolingual English-speaking homes, ability to discriminate English language contrasts increases as their ability to discriminate non-English (Mandarin) contrasts decreases. Thus, she hypothesizes, for L2 learning that occurs after L1 acquisition, the L1 networks act as a filter through which L2 stimuli must pass, and this filter is not tuned to L2 phonology. Previous L1 learning, not biological maturation, gives the appearance that the critical period closes.

WHAT ARE THE IMPLICATIONS?

What is the force of these arguments, and what are the implications? The anti-critical-period arguments reviewed here are of two general forms. Some arguments attempt to establish that purported critical periods for grammar or phonetics acquisition in L2 do not satisfy at least one of the first three conditions. Other arguments focus on condition 4, arguing in general that chronological age and age of first exposure to L2 are not clean proxy variables for maturation, and that other correlates of age provide more parsimonious explanations of critical-period phenomena. I discuss these argument types in reverse order, beginning with those that target condition 4, and concluding with those that target the "phenomenal" conditions 1–3.

Force and Implications of Arguments Challenging Condition 4

The broadest implication of arguments that focus on condition 4 is that they provide consistency arguments. They establish, first of all, that it is not conceptually incoherent to claim that critical-period phenomena exist, but that these phenomena need not be explained by maturational theories. Second, the arguments suggest alternative explanations for critical-period phenomena that appear to be consistent with existing data. In the preceding examples, Flege, Kuhl and Doupe, and Seidenberg and Zevin all acknowledge the existence of a critical period for phonology acquisition and present alternative, learning-based theories to explain the behavioral functions. Other variables, such as level of L1 proficiency at onset of L2 learning, amount of formal education in L2, and relative use of L1 versus L2 during L2 learning, can generate explanations other than maturational ones for empirically established behavioral functions. For L2A, as with imprinting, these arguments remind us that Train 2 explanations are viable theoretical alternatives to Train 1 explanations not only for imprinting but also for L2A.

As noted earlier, however, consistency is a weak constraint. Consistency only implies that these alternative explanations are possible explanations, just as the maturational hypothesis is a possible explanation. Note also in the examples discussed here that Flege et al. (1999) and Seidenberg and Zevin (2006) expressed their preferences for alternative, Train 2 accounts of L2A critical periods. These preferences, at least in the articles reviewed here, are not based on new empirical evidence. Kuhl and Doupe (1999) do introduce empirical data to support their critique of condition 4. However, their argument does assume that critical periods in birdsong learning provide a useful model for contemplating mechanisms that generate critical-period phenomena in speech acquisition. Kuhl's infant study (2004), although of considerable theoretical interest and importance, at this point establish only that data on infant phonology acquisition are consistent with a Train 2 theory.

Critiques of condition 4 have their most significant implication if we think of them as preludes to further research. Alternative theoretical accounts consistent with the behavioral data generate new hypotheses and experiments, both pro and con maturational accounts. New data force investigators on both sides of the debate to refine further and test their hypotheses more rigorously. This should be particularly invigorating for the field of L2A research, which, since Lenneberg (1967) the field has revolved around maturational accounts.

Generally critiques of condition 4 spawn Train 2 theories. Another implication of Train 2 theories, and the reason Bateson (1979) was partial to them, is that in addition to giving an adequate account of critical-period phenomena, such theories could reconcile the existence of critical-period phenomena with the efficacy of later experience in changing the preferences or behaviors acquired during the critical period, thus reconciling the view that the young might be especially susceptible to particular experiences at particular times in development, with the view that, given appropriate experiences, adults can be rehabilitated. Train 2 theories allow for the possibility that critical-period effects might be reversible via reactivation of dormant, not atrophied, learning mechanisms. As Bateson said, under "certain circumstances," occupants of the train could be persuaded to learn from the appearance of "strange things" that appeared along the train route later in the journey. The point of the Train 2 model, and the essence of Bateson's argument, is that although the characteristics of a behavioral system, such as imprinting or language learning, might appear to be determined at a particular stage in development, given normal experiences, this does not mean that the mechanisms generating those behaviors cease operating at that stage of development. The mechanisms generating those behaviors, like the windows on the train compartments, can remain open throughout life.

Learning theories of critical-period phenomena encourage us to identify what special circumstances are required to reactivate dormant learning mechanisms. Let us take the connectionist view as an example. Successful learning causes entrenchment, which blocks or inhibits later learning. However, the effects of entrenchment can be overcome, if input to the organism is altered, according to Kuhl (2004), or radically changed, as Seidenberg and Zevin (2006) stated. The interesting research question then becomes: How much or in what ways does input—the trackside scenery—have to change to reactivate dormant learning mechanisms?

This research question will have different answers depending on the specific critical-period phenomenon in which one is interested. Snow (1987) has argued against the existence of maturational accounts of critical period for phonology acquisition, on the grounds that adults and children, after the apparent close of the critical period for L1 phonology acquisition, are able to acquire new accents and dialects when they move to a different dialect region. If children and adults can learn the new phonological contrasts of a dialect, then this suggests that the input to their language systems need not be all that radically different to reactivate phonological learning mechanisms. As another example, studies, also from a connectionist perspective, have shown that adult Japanese-language speakers can be trained to achieve native-like identification of the English /l/ versus /r/ contrast. This research suggests that the input to adult language learners must be different from that heard in normal speech contexts. Artificial stimuli must be presented in a graded sequence for such learning to occur (McClelland, Fiez, & McCandliss, 2002). Although artificial stimuli are needed, it is surprising how rapidly Japanese adults can learn the discrimination given appropriate input. Three 20-minute training sessions are sufficient for Japanese adults to show evidence of learning the English /l/ versus /r/ distinction.

These are only two examples of "certain circumstances." If there are critical-period phenomena and Train 2 theories explain them, then research that focuses on identifying the special circumstances under which language-learning mechanisms are reactivated is an enterprise that could have both theoretical and practical significance. Train 2 theories would encourage us to think about what kinds of experiences and instruction can facilitate L2 learning in later life, rather than thinking only about how early L2 learning must begin.

In this same vein, although not an anti–condition 4 argument, Bongaerts (1999) and Birdsong (1999) showed that select adult learners *can* acquire native-like proficiency in an L2. Although these exceptional cases provide weak evidence against maturational accounts, they do point to other "certain circumstances," or rather "certain individuals," worthy of further investigation. What about these certain individuals allows them to acquire native fluency at an advanced age? Is it due to biological variation? Do these people exploit special learning skills or make better use of prevalent learning skills? Are they more adept at transferring L1 knowledge to L2? Can we make their learning strategies explicit and incorporate them into language-learning curricula?

Implications of Arguments Attacking Conditions 1–3

The anti-critical-period arguments that focus on conditions 1–3 all have a common form. First, the authors of the critiques state that they intend to provide an argument against the "critical-period hypothesis" for L2A. They assume and state that this hypothesis entails a maturational explanation for a critical-period phenomenon. These arguments then proceed by producing data that result in a behavioral function that violates one of the first three conditions on the shape of the behavioral function required to establish the presence of a critical-period phenomenon. For example, the resulting behavioral function is linear with age and demonstrates neither discontinuities at claimed or plausible critical points nor a significant statistical dependence between age of first exposure to L2 and eventual L2 grammatical or phonological proficiency, even when the age of first exposure is greater than the purported age of closure for the critical period.

Although the intended target of these arguments is the maturational hypothesis for L2A, their direct targets are the existence of critical-period phenomena per se. If these arguments are sound and valid, then they show not that the maturational hypothesis is false, but that there is no critical period phenomenon that requires explanation. These arguments render the maturational hypothesis not false, but vacuous, as it would render vacuous any alternative Train 2 explanation of a nonexistent phenomenon. One might think that observing the phenomenon–explanation distinction in these cases yields a rather trivial conclusion, but these arguments have a broader implication for debates about critical periods in L2A.

Newport et al. (2001) argued, in defense of the maturational hypothesis and the existence of critical period phenomena that anti-critical-period arguments focusing on conditions 1–3 acquire what strength they have by making unrealistic claims about the temporal characteristics of critical periods, that is, about the criteria the behavioral function must meet to establish the existence of a critical-period phenomenon. For example, Newport et al. stated that critical-period skeptics maintain that a critical period must have an abrupt end, occur at a well-defined and consistent age, and, for language at least, be related to the onset of puberty. However, in the arguments reviewed here (with the exception of Bongaerts [1999]), it would appear that the critics did not use unreasonable, arbitrary criteria to specify the behavioral function; rather, these critics appear to employ criteria taken from, or at least consistent with, the criteria presented in the L2A critical-period *locus classicus*, Johnson and Newport (1989). Furthermore, these criteria are restated in Newport et al. (2001). In addition, puberty is taken as the marker for the end of the critical period for L2A in numerous behavioral and neuroscientific studies of language acquisition (e.g., see Kim, Relkin, Lee, & Hirsch, 1997; Newman, Bavelier, Corina, Jezzard, & Neville, 2002; Weber-Fox & Neville, 1999; Pallier et al., 2003; Perani et al., 1998).

Newport et al.'s (2001) overall strategy is to argue that evidence in favor of the existence of critical-period phenomena in L2A is no different, or worse, than the evidence for the existence of critical-period phenomena in other research areas. However, given the presence and prevalence of arguments whose purpose is to show that there are no critical-period phenomena associated with L2A that require explanation, this would appear to be a questionable strategy for a defense. In light of these arguments attacking conditions 1–3, it is difficult to maintain that the status of critical periods within language acquisition is no different than that of critical periods for imprinting, development of the visual system, or birdsong learning. In these latter areas, there is no debate about whether critical-period phenomena occur. The scientific debate in these areas is over causal mechanisms that might best explain acknowledged critical-period phenomena.

One challenge to the L2A research community is to attempt to resolve the debate over the existence of relevant critical-period phenomena. Some of the impediments to resolving this debate arise from methodological difficulties in conducting critical-period experiments. For language, it would be particularly important to specify as clearly as possible the specific language function in question. Are semantics, phonology, and syntax sufficiently precise specifications of function, or should one instead specify functions as defined by theoretical constructs within phonology and syntax? Also, in reading the L2A critical-period literature, one is overwhelmed by the variety and incommensurability of data collected, as well as the variety of tests used to operationalize criteria that characterize the behavioral function. Flege et al. (1999) provided an instructive example of how different tests for critical-period phenomena (linearity, pre- and post-critical-period tests, and matched-subgroup analyses) provide different answers to the question of whether critical periods for L2 grammar and phonology acquisition exist. It would appear that a lot of careful descriptive work, using universally accepted descriptive categories, remains to be done for critical-period phenomena in L2A.

CONCLUSION

I began this chapter with Bialystok and Hakuta's (1994) observation that in L2A, as in other research areas, there is a danger of confusing descriptions of phenomena with explanations of those phenomena. I hope to have convinced readers that this distinction is an important one. It is a distinction that has roots in the history of critical-period research and that, rather than being observed in L2A research, has been assimilated into the critical-period concept itself. Maintaining the distinction allows us to view the L2A debate from a different perspective and consider arguments, pro and con, in a different light.

Bialystok and Hakuta (1999) elaborated on their original insight by appealing to the example of Ptolemaic versus heliocentric theories of planetary motion. They observed that overthrowing Ptolemy's theory required 14 centuries, and that part of what was required to complete this scientific revolution was the ability to step away from the observable data and to imagine alternative explanations. Criticisms of condition 4 lead to Train 2 models of critical-period phenomena, which provide such alternatives.

However, as we have seen, a second problem with critical periods for L2A does not occur at the theoretical level. We can also illustrate this problem with an analogy to observational astronomy. The challenge for observational astronomy was to explain the irregular wandering of planets against a background of the fixed stars. The Ptolemaic system posited epicycles to explain this phenomenon; the Copernican system posited a heliocentric universe. The problem within L2A is that there is no agreement on what phenomena require explanation. L2A researchers are in a situation like that of the observational astronomers who could not agree on whether the planets wander.

A BOTTOM LINE FOR PRACTITIONERS

What might practitioners take away from this rather abstract, theoretical, philosophical discussion? First, I hope it helps practitioners who attempt to apply research to language instruction or rehabilitation better understand the issues involved in debates within the research community about critical periods and L2A. They should be aware that research on critical periods has a long history, and that there is considerable disagreement within the research community about both whether and which critical periods exist, and how best to explain these phenomena. Practitioners should be wary of overly simplified presentations of this research and equally wary of claims that the research may have direct, straightforward applications to practice.

Practitioners might also be advised that interpreting critical periods too strongly as universal, biologically determined, and irreversible under all circumstances can be counterproductive. The best example here is the application of neurobiological research on critical periods in the development of the visual system to patient treatment in ophthalmology. Strong interpretations of critical-period research contributed to the widespread practice of not providing therapeutic interventions to correct amblyopia in patients older than 6 years—the age at which the relevant critical period was assumed to close. Recent research has shown that a substantial percentage of such patients older than age 6 benefit from therapy (Mintz-Hunter & Fernandez, 2000; Pediatric Eye Disease Investigator Group, 2005). The challenge for ophthalmologists becomes how to provide the best therapy possible given a patient's age and not to infer from overly simplified presentations of visual science that therapy is ineffective. Thus, despite decades of L2A critical-period research, the challenge is to provide the best possible instruction to language learners, whatever their age.

The area that practitioners might most usefully follow is research on the "certain circumstances" that allow for native-like proficiency in late L2 learners. Those involved in the L2A debate all agree that such circumstances exist, and making those circumstances explicit should provide a research basis for designing more effective curricula and instructional regimens.

Finally, in evaluating the relevance of research for teaching, practitioners should reflect on whether a certain result from critical-period research has practical implications for instruction or only theoretical interest for neuroscience or psychology. How does one tell the difference? Appealing to the phenomenon–explanation distinction might again help us tell the difference. In their daily work, practitioners are confronted by critical-period phenomena. The challenge is to find instructional methods that make the behavioral functions as linear as possible. No matter which theory of critical-period phenomena eventually prevails, we have seen research examples that have the potential to address instructional issues. It is research that attempts to identify those "certain circumstances" that facilitates native-like proficiency for late L2 learners. Connectionist models that reject maturational accounts can lead to insights about how language stimuli might be refined and sequenced to overcome entrenchment, as in the case of Japanese adults learning to make the English /l/ versus /r/ distinction. Theorists who hold to maturational accounts acknowledge that there are "certain individuals" who can acquire native-like proficiency in adulthood. Making their learning strategies explicit and using these strategies, if possible, to design instruction should certainly contribute to making the L2A behavioral functions less nonlinear with age.

REFERENCES

Bateson, P. (1979). How do sensitive periods arise and what are they for? *Animal Behaviour, 27*, 470–486.

Bateson, P. (1983). Sensitive periods in behavioral development. *Archives of Disease in Childhood, 58*(2), 85–86.

Bateson, P., & Hinde, R. A. (1987). Developmental changes in sensitivity to experience. In M. H. Bornstein (Ed.), *Sensitive period in development: Interdisciplinary perspectives* (pp. 19–34). Hillsdale, NJ: Erlbaum.

Bialystok, E., & Hakuta, K. (1994). *In other words: The science and psychology of second-language acquisition.* New York: Basic Books.

Bialystok, E., & Hakuta, J. (1999). Confounded age: Linguistic and cognitive factors in age differences for second language acquisition. In D. Birdsong (Ed.), *Second language acquisition and the critical period hypothesis* (pp. 161–181). Mahwah, NJ: Erlbaum.

Birdsong, D. (1992). Ultimate attainment in second language acquisition. *Language, 68*, 706–755.

Birdsong, D. (1999). Whys and why nots of the CPH-L2A. In D. Birdsong (Ed.), *Second language acquisition and the critical period hypothesis* (pp. 1–22). Mahwah, NJ: Erlbaum.

Bongaerts, T. (1999). Ultimate attainment in L2 pronunciation: The case of advanced late L2 learners. In D. Birdsong (Ed.), *Second language acquisition and the critical period hypothesis* (pp. 135–159). Mahwah, NJ: Erlbaum.

Bornstein, M. H. (1987). Sensitive periods in development: Definition, existence, utility, and meaning. In *Sensitive periods in development: Interdisciplinary perspectives* (pp. 3–110). Hillsdale, NJ: Erlbaum.

Bowlby, J. (1953). Critical phases in the development of social responses in man and other animals. In J. M. Tanner (Ed.), *Prospects in psychiatric research: The proceedings of the Oxford Conference of the Mental Health Fund* (pp. 80–85). Oxford, UK: Blackwell.

Bruer, J. T. (2001). A critical and sensitive period primer. In D. B. Bailey, J. T. Bruer, F. J. Symons, & J. Lichtman (Eds.), *Critical thinking about critical periods* (pp. 3–26). Baltimore: Brookes.

Colombo, J. (1982). The critical period concept: Research methodology and theoretical issues. *Psychological Bulletin, 91*(2), 260–275.

Connolly, K. (1972). Learning and the concept of critical periods in infancy. *Developmental Medicine and Child Neurology, 14*(6), 705–714.

Eubank, L., & Gregg, K. R. (1999). Critical periods and (second) language acquisition: Divide et impera. In D. Birdsong (Ed.), *Second language acquisition and the critical period hypothesis* (pp. 65–99). Mahwah, NJ: Erlbaum.

Flege, J. E., Munro, I. A. R., & MacKay, I. (1995). Factors affecting degree of perceived foreign accent in a second language. *Journal of the Acoustical Society of America, 97*, 3125–3134.

Flege, J. E., Yeni-Komshian G. H., & Liu, S. (1999). Age constraints on second language learning. *Journal of Memory and Language, 41*, 78–104.

Hakuta, K., Bialystok, E., & Wiley, E. (2003). Critical evidence: A test of the critical-period hypothesis for second-language acquisition. *Psychological Science, 14*(1), 31–38.

Hess, E. H. (1959). Imprinting. *Science, 130*(3368), 133–141.

Hess, E. H. (1962). Ethology: an approach toward the complete analysis of behavior. In R. W. Galanter, E. H. Hess, & G. Mandler (Eds.), *New directions in psychology* (pp. 159–199). New York: Holt, Rinehart & Winston.

Hess, E. H. (1973). *Imprinting: Early experience and the developmental psychobiology of attachment*. New York: Von Nostrand Reinhold.

Hinde, R. A. (1961). The establishment of the parent–offspring relation in birds, with some mammalian analogies. In W. H. Thorpe & O. L. Zangwill (Eds.), *Current problems in animal behavior* (pp. 175–193). Cambridge, UK: Cambridge University Press.

Hubel, D. H., & Wiesel, T. N. (1962). Receptive field, binocular interaction and functional architecture in the cat's visual cortex. *Journal of Physiology, 160*, 106–154.

Hubel, D. H., & Wiesel, T. N. (1963). Receptive fields of cells in striate cortex of very young, essentially inexperienced kittens. *Journal of Neurophysiology, 26*, 994–1002.

Hubel, D. H., & Wiesel, T. N. (1970). The period of susceptibility to the physiological effects of unilateral eye closure in kittens. *Journal of Physiology, 206*, 419–436.

Johnson, J. S., & Newport, E. L. (1989). Critical period effects in second language learning: The influence of maturational state on the acquisition of English as a second language. *Cognitive Psychology, 21*, 60–99.

Kim, H. S. K., Relkin N. R., Lee, K. M., & Hirsch J. (1997). Distinct cortical areas associated with native and second languages. *Nature, 388*, 171–174.

Kuhl, P. K. (2004). Early language aAcquisition: Cracking the speech code. *Nature Reviews Neuroscience, 5*, 831–843.

Kuhl, P. K., Conboy, B., Padden, D., Nelson, T., & Pruitt J. (in press). Early speech perception and later language development: Implications for the "critical period."

Kuhl, P., & Doupe, A. (1999). Birdsong and human speech. *Annual Review of Neuroscience, 22*, 567–631.

Lenneberg, E. (1967). *Biological foundations of language*. New York: Wiley.

Long, M. H. (1990). Maturational constraints on language development. *Studies in Second Language Acquisition, 12*, 251–285.

Lorenz, K. (1937). The companion in the bird's world. *Auk, 64*, 245–273.

Lorenze, K. (1957). Companionship in bird life. In C. H. Schiller (Ed.), *Instinctive behavior: The development of a modern concept* (pp. 83–128). New York: International Universities Press.

Lorenz, K. Z. (1958). The evolution of behavior. *Scientific American, 119*(6), 67–78.

McClelland, J. L., Fiez, J. A., & McCandliss, B. D. (2002). Teaching the /r/–/l/ discrimination to Japanese adults: Behavioral and neural aspects. *Physiology and Behavior, 77*(4–5), 657–662.

Mintz-Hunter, H. A., & Fernandez, K. M. (2000). Successful amblyopia treatment initiated after age 7 years. *Archives of Ophthalmology, 118*, 1535–1541.

Newman, A. J., Bavelier, D., Corina, D., Jezzard, P., & Neville, H. J. (2002). A critical period for right hemisphere recruitment in American sign language processing. *Nature Neuroscience, 5*(1), 76–80.

Newport, E. L., Bavelier, D., & Neville, H. J. (2001). Critical thinking about critical periods: Perspectives on a critical period for language acquisition. In E. Dupoux (Ed.), *Language, brain, and cognitive development: Essays in honor of Jacques Mehler* (pp. 481–502). Cambridge, MA: MIT Press.

Oyama, S. (1976). A sensitive period for the acquisition of syntax in a second language. *Journal of Psycholinguistic Research, 5*, 261–285.

Oyama, S. (1979). The concept of the sensitive period. *Merrill–Palmer Quarterly, 25*(2), 83–103.

Pallier, C., Dehaene, S., Poline, J. B., LeBihan, D., Argenti, A. M., Dupoux, E., et al. (2003). Brain imaging of language plasticity in adopted adults: Can a second language replace the first? *Cerebral Cortex, 13*(2), 155–161.

Patkowski, M. S. (1990). Age and accent in a second language: A reply to James Emil Flege. *Applied Linguistics, 11*, 73–89.

Pediatric Eye Disease Investigator Group. (2005). Randomized trial of treatment of amblyopia in children aged 7 to 17 years. *Archives of Ophthalmology, 123*, 437–447.

Perani, D. Dupoux, E., Paulesu, E., Sebastain Galles, N., Dupoux, E., Dehaene, S., et al. (1998). The bilingual brain: Proficiency and age of acquisition of the second language. *Brain, 121*, 1841–1852.

Salzen, E. A., & Meyer, C. C. (1968). Reversibility of imprinting. *Journal of Comparative Physiology and Psychology, 66*, 269–275.

Scott, J. P. (1963). The process of primary socialization in canine and human infants. *Monograph of the Society for Research in Child Development, 28*(1), 1–47.

Scovel, T. (1969). Foreign accents, language acquisition, and cerebral dominance. *Language Learning, 19*, 245–253.

Scovel, T. (1988). *A time to speak: A psycholinguistic inquiry into the critical period for human speech*. Rowley, MA: Newbury House.

Seidenberg, M. S., & Zevin, J. D. (2006). Connectionist models in developmental cognitive neuroscience: Critical periods and the paradox of success. In Y. Munakata & M. Johnson (Eds.), *Attention and performance: Vol. 21. Processes of change in brain and cognitive development* (pp. 585–612). Oxford, UK: Oxford University Press.

Snow, C. (1987). Relevance of the notion of a critical period to language acquisition. In M. H. Bornstein (Ed.), *Sensitive periods in development: Interdisciplinary perspectives* (pp. 183–210). Hillsdale, NJ: Erlbaum.

Thorpe, W. H. (1961). Sensitive periods in the learning of animals and men: A study of imprinting with special reference to the induction of cyclic behavior. In W. H. Thorpe & O. L. Zangwill (Eds.), *Current problems in animal behavior* (pp. 194–224). Cambridge, UK: Cambridge University Press.

Weber-Fox, C. M., & Neville, H. J. (1999). Functional neural subsystems are differentially affected by delays in second language immersion: ERP and behavioral evidence in bilinguals. In D. Birdsong (Ed.), *Second language acquisition and the critical period hypothesis* (pp. 23–38). Mahwah, NJ: Erlbaum.

Yeni-Komshian, G., Flege, J. E., & Liu, H. (1997). Pronunciation proficiency in L1 and L2 among Korean–English bilinguals: The effect of age of arrival in the U.S. *Journal of the Acoustical Society of America, 102(A)*, 3139.

Part II

Brain–Behavior Relationships

INTRODUCTION

The Language–Reading Interface

Associations and Dissociations within an Atypically Developing System

MARIA MODY
ELAINE R. SILLIMAN

The previous section presented interesting new ways of conceptualizing differences between normal and atypical development in reading and language. This section provides a comprehensive overview of a number of behavioral and neurobiological approaches to operationalizing these differences. A striking feature of the research reported here is its collaborative and cross-disciplinary nature. The authors have paved the way for a scientific understanding of reading and language disorders by investigating brain–behavior relationships under well-controlled experimental conditions, guided by clinically relevant questions. In navigating through these exciting findings, three observations become apparent: (1) the significance of individual differences in the cognitive architecture on which language and reading build from the very outset; (2) the limitations of traditional norm-referenced measures of literacy and language; and (3) the need to examine the brain in terms of structural and functional networks to understand its role in processing, organization, and reorganization.

In Chapter 4, Berninger draws on two decades of programmatic research on written language disabilities. The findings support the existence of writing disorders, both with and without a concomitant reading disorder, as well as a role for working memory in conjunction with executive functions. In Chapter 5, Windsor and Kohnert build on this view with a slightly different twist. They call for the use of general cognitive fundamentals such as memory and processing speed as measures of the integrity of the underlying language learning system rather than traditional measures of language and reading abilities per se. The authors contend that insofar as language is part of a broader cognitive network, proficiency with which information is processed and/or manipulated in memory is likely to prove more insightful about an individual's true underlying oral language capability. It is worth noting, though, that studies using traditional linguistic measures do increasingly incorporate age- and performance-matched controls in their paradigms to tease out general from more specific linguistic processing effects.

In the three chapters that follow, Weber and Gaillard; Simos, Sarkari, and Papanicolaou; and Shaywitz, Gruen, and Shaywitz (Chapters, 6, 7, and 8, respectively) provide an extensive review of neuroimaging studies of language and reading in normally developing individuals and populations with impairments such as dyslexia, specific language impairment, and autism. Results from functional magnetic resonance imaging (fMRI), magnetoencephalography (MEG), and electroencephalography (EEG) reported with children as young as 6 years of age demonstrate a left-hemisphere-distributed pattern of language activation similar to that found in adults, though less consolidated and with a tendency to be more bilateral. Additionally, across all imaging modalities, oral language and reading tasks appear to engage a common network of anterior and posterior brain areas in the left hemisphere, incorporating inferior frontal, posterior superior, and middle temporal and occipitotemporal areas. The identification of a neurobiological signature of a disorder has the additional requirement that the task be ecologically valid; that is, the task must be capable of eliciting a response that can stand as objective proof of the impaired function. As such, the selection of the task used and the reproducibility of its effects play a critical role in the search for neurobiological markers, especially for subtypes in reading and language disorders. Insofar as findings appear to support a phonological account of reading disability, neuroimaging tasks appear to have successfully used a variety of phonological tasks to distinguish good from poor readers, to identify compensatory systems in older dyslexics, and to determine the plasticity of the reading-related neural circuitry. The reliability of the brain-behavior relationships established using these tasks has also proven useful in isolating genetic markers of dyslexia.

In the final chapter (Chapter 9), Byrne, Shankweiler, and Hine review the characteristics of young children at genetic risk for reading difficulties, and the early interventions to help them. Through large-scale studies, these authors have shown that preschool children at risk are compromised in their phonological processing abilities. Surprisingly, this deficit does not appear to be in the quality of their phonological representations, but in the children's slower retrieval or activation of the phonological code. Additionally, aspects of phonological processing linked to reading growth in school-age children were found to be influenced by genes prior to the onset of formal reading instruction. Thus, some children start school with a genetic burden. However, the authors do not take this as reason for discouragement but as a challenge to practitioners and researchers to continue to find better ways to teach literacy.

In conclusion, the integration of behavioral, phenotypic, and neuroimaging research holds tremendous promise for moving the field in the direction of new hypotheses and interventions.

4

Defining and Differentiating Dysgraphia, Dyslexia, and Language Learning Disability within a Working Memory Model

VIRGINIA W. BERNINGER

This three-part chapter draws on 17 years of research on assessment, instruction, and development of typical and disabled writing, and over a decade of programmatic research on the biological basis (genetic and neurological), assessment, and treatment of specific learning disabilities influencing acquisition of written language. My perspectives are based on my background in experimental (developmental psycholinguistics, cognitive psychology, and neuropsychology specialization) and clinical (developmental and learning disabilities specialization) psychology, teaching experience, and collaborations with speech and language scientist–practitioners. In the first part, which is based on researcher-defined inclusion criteria for early intervention studies, data are reported to show that some written language disabilities are writing-specific, whereas others involve both writing and reading, and some reading disabilities involve only word reading, whereas others involve both word reading and reading comprehension. In addition, results reported from studies of children with reading disabilities in middle childhood show that reading disabilities differ in the nature of the selective oral language impairment associated with them. Children with dyslexia have selective impairment in phonological awareness, but those with language learning disabilities have selective impairment in phonological, morphological (especially derivational suffixes), and syntactic awareness.

In the second part, which is based on a family genetics studies, dyslexia, which is both a reading and spelling disorder, is characterized within a working memory architecture that includes three main components: (1) word storage in phonological, orthographic, and morphological code format; (2) a time-sensitive phonological loop for integrating verbal and visual codes in oral or written word learning; and (3) an executive system that inhibits irrelevant codes and regulates switching between orthographic and phonological codes. The widely supported phonological core deficit is attributable to deficits in the phonological processes of each of these working memory components, and the frequently observed fluency problems are attributable to inefficiencies in the temporal coordination of the components of working memory.

In the third part, dysgraphia, dyslexia, and language learning disability (LLD) are differentiated, respectively, on the basis of the codes that store words in working memory during processing: orthographic; orthographic + phonological; or orthographic + phonological + morphological/syntactical. A conceptual analysis of what a Verbal IQ assesses is offered to explain why many individuals with LLD typically do not meet IQ-discrepancy criteria for learning disability or criteria for primary language or communication disability, but nevertheless require and deserve treatment of combined oral and written language problems. The chapter ends with a call for greater cross-disciplinary talk and collaboration between psychologists and speech and language specialists.

INTRODUCTION

Neither researchers nor practitioners have been careful in defining whom they are studying within the population with written language disabilities, which may include reading and/or writing difficulties. Studies of reading disabilities often use samples of convenience, which may have referral biases related to the professional group most involved in qualifying these samples for services in the schools (e.g., psychologists or speech and language pathologists). Schools are more concerned with whether a student qualifies for special education than in characterizing the nature of a written language learning disability. In an era in which science-based reading instruction (SBRI) is emphasized, it is equally important to emphasize science-based diagnostic practices that have *definitional precision* in describing who is being studied and to whom the results of treatment studies can be generalized.

DESCRIBING PROFILES OF EARLY WRITTEN LANGUAGE DIFFICULTIES

Writing-Specific versus Combined Writing and Reading Problems

Currently the field of literacy is reading-centric and phonological-centric. Insufficient attention is being devoted to writing skills—handwriting, spelling, and composition—and related written language skills, such as orthographic coding (Abbott & Berninger, 1993). As shown in Table 4.1, three large-scale studies that ascertained children on the basis of researcher criteria for specific writing problems showed that specific writing problems, independent of specific reading problems, may exist. Table 4.1 values are based on the percentage of the final sample of children who met research criteria for writing problems after whole schools at given grade levels were screened with a battery designed by the research team. These criteria changed from study to study in Table 4.1 but always involved significantly low performance for grade level on target writing measures—handwriting, spelling, and compositional fluency.

For the first study, the target writing skill was ability to produce legible, automatic alphabet letters. For the second study, it was ability to spell dictated words. For the third study, it was speed of writing sentences with three provided words. Table 4.1 summarizes the percentages of children with writing problems who definitely had only the specific writing problem, those who probably had only a writing problem (i.e., their reading skills were not sufficiently low to meet criteria for a reading problem), and children who had both reading (met research criteria for impaired accuracy and/or rate of oral reading of single words, pseudowords, or passages) and

TABLE 4.1. Percent of Children with Writing-Only Problems (No Reading Problems) and Combined Writing and Reading Problems in Early Intervention Studies for Writing

	Definitely writing only	Probably writing only	Also met criteria for reading[a]
Study 1 (*N* = 144)	38.9%	20.8%	40.3%
Study 2 (*N* = 128)	33.6%	19.5%	46.9%
Study 3 (*N* = 96)	53.1%	16.6%	30.2%

Note. N = total number of participants in each study. Study 1: handwriting, first graders—Berninger et al. (1997); criteria were impaired legibility and automaticity of alphabet letter writing. Study 2: spelling, second graders—Berninger, Vaughan, et al. (1998); criteria were impaired written spelling. Study 3: compositional fluency, third graders—Berninger, Vaughan, et al. (2002); criteria were impaired compositional fluency.

[a] Used the same criteria as for dyslexia or reading skills as in our family genetics study: accuracy and/or rate of oral reading of real words or pseudowords or passages.

writing problems. Table 4.1 data show that about 33–50% had only writing problems, about 20% probably had only writing problems, and about 40% had both reading and writing problems. Clearly, there are students who are at-risk in writing only, but there are also children at risk in both reading and writing.

Decoding-Only versus Decoding + Reading Comprehension Problems

In a 2-year longitudinal intervention study, even when students were selected on the basis of researcher criteria for being at-risk readers, not all selected students exhibited the same profile of relative strengths and weaknesses in reading. In the first year of the study, first graders whose word reading and/or decoding skills fell on average below the 15th percentile but whose Wechsler Intelligence Scale for Children (WISC 3; Wechsler, 1991) oral vocabulary score was at least in the low-average range were identified and randomly assigned to treatment or control groups (Berninger et al., 2000). After 24 lessons (twice a week over a 4-month period), half the children performed at or above grade level (the faster responders) and half still had not reached grade level (the slower responders). In the second year of the study, follow-up testing assessed word reading and comprehension skills at the beginning and end of second grade for both the faster and slower responders, and the slower responders were given additional early reading intervention at the beginning of second grade. The faster responders maintained their gains in word reading and decoding at the beginning and end of second grade; the slower responders maintained their initial gains and, after a second dose of early intervention, reached, on average, the average range for grade on word reading and decoding skills (Berninger, Abbott, et al., 2002). In both the first and second years, the early reading intervention emphasized phonological and orthographic awareness, the automatic alphabet principle, and transfer of orthographic–phonological correspondences to word reading, fluency, and comprehension close in time within the same lesson to facilitate connections across levels of language in working memory.

Reading profiles were analyzed, with a focus on individuals who exhibited a large difference between word reading (out of context) and reading comprehension, both at the beginning and end of second grade. The average difference between reading comprehension and word reading, or word reading and comprehension, for each kind of profile within both the faster responders and the slower responders is reported in Table 4.2. In the most frequent profile among the faster responders, reading comprehension scores were markedly higher than word reading scores. In the most frequent profile among the slower responders, reading comprehension scores

TABLE 4.2. Stronger Reading Comprehension Than Word Reading[a] and Stronger Word Reading Than Reading Comprehension[b]

			Average difference[e]		Average difference[e]
Faster responders (N = 64, year 1)					
Text[c] > Word[d]	46%	Beginning second grade	11.5	End second grade	14.0
Word[d] > Text[c]	29%	Beginning second grade	14.2	End second grade	16.7
Slower responders (N = 64, year 1)					
Word[d] > Text[c]	60%	Beginning second grade	19.6	End second grade	23.3
Text[c] > Word[d]	13%	Beginning second grade	27.3	End second grade	28.7

Note. Based on 75% with consistent profile at beginning and end of second grade.

[a] Tended to be the faster responders in first grade, the first year of the intervention study, who maintained their gains at the beginning and end of second grade.

[b] Tended to be the slower responders in first grade who required additional intervention at the beginning of second grade but maintained their gains at the end of second grade.

[c] Gates–McGinitie Reading Comprehension test.

[d] Woodcock Reading Mastery Test—Revised (WRMT-R) Word Identification.

[e] Average difference in standard scores transformed to a scale of M = 100, SD = 15.

were markedly lower than those for word reading, which were also low. This association between rate of responding to early intervention and strength versus weakness in reading comprehension compared to word reading skill was statistically significant. However, within the total sample about 25% of the children did not fit either of these profiles or show the same profile at the beginning and end of second grade.

These four classes of response to instruction were observed in response to the same reading instruction that included all the components recommended by the National Reading Panel (2000), therefore suggesting that individual differences in students will mediate response to intervention. The first class within the faster responders in Table 4.2 represents children who are mildly at-risk for word reading and decoding, have strong comprehension skills, and respond quickly in improving their word reading and decoding. The second class within the faster responders represents children who responded quickly in improving their word reading and decoding but had persisting relative weaknesses in reading comprehension (Oakhill & Yuill, 1996). The first class within the slower responders represents the group of children with not only word reading but also reading comprehension problems. The fourth class within the slower responders represents children with persisting relative weaknesses in word reading, but typically their reading comprehension was not impaired following intervention for decoding written words. Both research and special education samples in schools may have differing mixes of these four classes of profiles in response to early intervention. If either the first or last group in Table 4.2 is overrepresented, researchers and educational professionals may erroneously conclude that all reading disabilities can be prevented and eliminated with early intervention targeted at word reading and decoding skills. In contrast, the second and third classes require explicit instruction in reading comprehension. Collectively, these results point to the need for better assessment to determine who struggles in reading, and to pinpoint the skills in children's individual profiles that have diagnostic significance and may require specialized instruction in the current and later grades. For comparable findings, see Catts, Adoph, and Weismer (2006).

Relationship between Oral Language and Written Language Problems

Because we collect extensive data on developmental and educational history in all our studies, we have discovered that some children with written language disabilities have a history of problems in learning oral language in the preschool years, whereas others do not (Berninger & O'Donnell, 2004). Longitudinal studies have shown that some oral language problems in the preschool years may persist in the school years and put children at risk for reading and writing problems, or they may resolve (Catts & Kamhi, 2005). However, our data suggest that whereas some of the oral language problems may resolve in terms of production during contextualized conversation, so that children no longer qualify for language and communication services, the oral language problems may not have fully resolved at the metalinguistic level, and their diagnosis may require formal testing. Our evidence to date suggests that those whose difficulties surface during the preschool years are more likely to have pervasive metalinguistic problems in phonological, morphological, and syntactic awareness that interferes with their ability to (1) use decontextualized oral language to understand teachers' instructional language, (2) learn written language, and (3) self-regulate, that is, verbally mediate, the learning process across the academic curriculum. In contrast, children who showed no difficulty in oral language during the preschool years and whose first signs of difficulty in learning written language occurred when letters were introduced, for example, in kindergarten, are more likely to have problems only in phonological awareness. In the third part of this chapter, the implications of these differences in the relationship of oral language and written language are considered for differential diagnosis and treatment of LLD and dyslexia.

UNDERSTANDING WRITTEN LANGUAGE DISABILITIES WITHIN A WORKING MEMORY MODEL

First, recent advances in understanding verbal working memory are reviewed. Next, the debate about whether dyslexia is the result of a phono logical core deficit or a fluency deficit is reconciled within a working memory model. Finally, the findings of the family genetics study that investigated the phenotypic expression of written language disability with a focus on dyslexia are summarized and discussed in reference to this new working memory model.

Recent Advances in Verbal Working Memory Theory

The concept of working memory, first proposed by Miller, Galanter, and Pribram (1960), was operationalized by Baddeley and colleagues (e.g., Baddeley, 1986; Hitch & Baddeley, 1976) as a unitary system with a phonological or visual–spatial storage unit, an articulatory loop for maintaining information in the temporary storage unit, and the central executive. As research studies increased in methodological sophistication and new evidence mounted, this early view was substantially revised, with a redirection of focus of the storage unit to the multiple components in working memory, integration of those components with each other and long-term memory, and structural relationships among the components (Baddeley, 2002). Early models emphasized the span limitations of phonological short-term memory, but current models allow for other kinds of storage, including an episodic buffer for novel stimuli and other kinds of verbal coding, such as orthographic, for the written word. The articulatory loop, originally thought to maintain information in temporary phonological stores through overt speech and rehearsal, is now referred to as a "phonological loop," and is thought to rely on internal, as well as overt, vocalization processes to guide the learning of new words. The central executive's capacity limitations are no longer thought to be due to limited span length or work space size, but rather to limited or inefficient attentional resources for maintaining task-relevant information and inhibiting task-irrelevant information. Efficiency of working memory is related to (1) inhibition (Gunter, Wagner, & Friederici, 2003), which operates on memory at both encoding and retrieval (Ribaupierre, 2002); (2) processing speed of the various components of working memory; and (3) executive functions that manage the component operations singly and in coordination with each other. Temporal coordination of the multiple processes in working memory influences its overall efficiency (Fuster, 1997).

Reconciling Phonological Core and Working Memory Deficits

The phonological core deficit has been a leading contender in psychological research explaining the etiology of dyslexia (e.g., Morris et al., 1998; Stanovich & Siegel, 1994; Wagner & Torgesen, 1987). However, Swanson (2000) proposed that impaired working memory or executive functions may also explain this developmental disorder. Each of three main components of verbal working memory—storage, time-sensitive phonological loop, and executive functions—may contribute to understanding dyslexia (Smith-Spark, Fisk, Fawcett, & Nicolson, 2003) (see Figure 4.1).

Storage

Brain imaging evidence shows that words may be stored in three different formats, which are referred to as "word forms" rather than word codes, each with distinct neural signatures, as well as common patterns of neural activation: a phonological word form (sound pattern for the whole word), a morphological word form (word parts conveying meaning and grammar beyond the semantic features of word stems), and an orthographic word form (all the letters in the spelling of the written or visible word; Richards, Aylward, Berninger, et al., 2006; Richards et al., 2005; Richards, Aylward, Raskind, et al., 2006). Some of these studies were done with adults and found evidence for (1) semantic, phonological, and orthographic working memory (Crosson et al., 1999); and (2) phonological word forms (McCrory, Frith, & Brunswick, & Price, 2000) and orthographic word forms (Cohen et al., 2002). Other studies were done with children and reported evidence for (1) phonological and morphological word forms (Aylward et al., 2003), and (2) orthographic, morphological, and phonological word forms (Richards et al., 2005; Richards, Aylward, Berninger, et al., 2006; Richards, Aylward, Raskind, et al., 2006). In our brain imaging studies, children performed both morphological word tasks and control semantic tasks, so that brain activation specific to the morphological word form, apart from processing semantic features, could be assessed.

Phonological Loop

This time-limited component (Kail, 1984) is specialized for three functions during acquisition of listening and speaking (Baddeley, Gathercole, & Papagno, 1998): (1) learning new spoken words by storing novel sound patterns in the episodic buffer until they are consolidated into a more permanent representation; (2) representing and accessing the sound patterns of

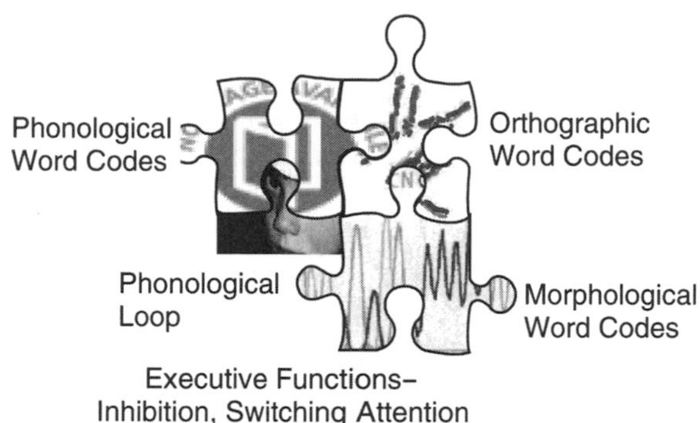

FIGURE 4.1. Working memory architecture. Adapted from Richards, Aylward, Raskind, et al. (2006). Copyright 2006 by Taylor & Francis (*http://www.informaworld.com*). Adapted by permission.

familiar words; and (3) learning morphology and syntax. Because the episodic buffer is uniquely designed as a multimodal coding system that serves as an interface between systems using different kinds of codes and works closely with the central executive (Baddeley et al., 1998), it is also uniquely designed for learning to read, which requires coordination of the new orthographic word forms with the existing phonological word forms already in long-term memory, while both word forms are held in temporally constrained working memory long enough for the connections to be forged.

Executive Support for Language

The early working conceptualization of the supervisory attentional system (Norman & Shallice, 1986) for regulating switching attention (mental set) as tasks changed (Towse, Hitch, & Hutton, 2000) has been replaced with an executive control module that serves a constellation of executive functions (Towse, 1998). These are not restricted to attention regulation and include inhibiting, mental set shifting, self-monitoring, and updating (Miyake et al., 2000). In some theoretical accounts, working memory supports executive functions, whereas in others, like the one presented here, executive functions are a component of the working memory system. In the brain, neither the executive function nor working memory system is likely to be fully modular; the brain regions that participate in the neural networks supporting executive function and working memory are likely to interact with each other in different ways depending on an individual's neurological, developmental, and educational history, and the task at hand.

Applying the Model to Understanding Dyslexia

Our recent family genetics study (Berninger et al., 2006) reconciled the competing phonological deficit and working memory deficit theories of dyslexia. Each working memory component involves a phonological subcomponent. For storage of word forms, one storage unit is specialized for phonological word forms. For the phonological loop, the novel or familiar phonological word forms are named overtly or covertly in the process of coordinating them with the new visual objects or orthographic word forms. For the executive support for language, the control processes regulate inhibition of phonological or orthographic codes when they are irrelevant, and rapid switching among phonological and orthographic word codes. If any of these components is impaired, overall working memory is inefficient, because the components cannot work in concert. The net effect may be a reading fluency problem, which is often observed in persons with dyslexia after they manage to learn phonological decoding.

We used criteria comparable to the current definition of "dyslexia" recommended by the International Dyslexia Association (Lyon, Shaywitz, & Shaywitz, 2003) to identify children who qualified their families for participation in the multigenerational genetics study: unexpected impairment in accuracy and/or rate of oral reading real words, pseudowords, passages or written spelling, that fell at least one standard deviation below prorated Verbal IQ and below the population mean. We also required a prorated Verbal IQ (WISC 3 Comprehension Factor; Wechsler, 1991) of at least 90 to ensure that it fell within the top 75 percent of the population that is less likely to have reading problems related to other neurogenetic disorders affecting development and learning. For the 122 children in this recent study, 200 of their biological parents also showed indicators of dyslexia. Whether we used absolute criteria relative to the population mean or relative criteria in reference to Verbal IQ, both children (mean age 11) and adults showed severe impairment in the three working memory components—phonological word-form storage, time-sensitive phonological loop, and executive functions involving inhibition or attention switching between phonological and orthographic processes. Our aggregation, segregation, and chromosome linkage studies also showed a genetic basis for phonological word storage (Hsu, Wijsman, Berninger, Thomson, & Raskind, 2002; Wijsman et al., 2000), time-sensitive phonological loop (Chapman, Igo, Thomson, Berninger, & Wijsman, 2003; Raskind et al., 2005), and executive or attention functions (Hsu et al., 2002).

Structural equation modeling (Bentler & Wu, 2000) was used to model the structural relationships among the three components of working memory—storage, phonological loop, and executive function. The phonological word factor was assessed with four measures that require temporary storage of spoken words, while sound patterns in them are analyzed. The orthographic word factor was assessed with three measures that require temporary storage of written words, while spelling patterns in them are analyzed. The morphological word factor was assessed with four measures that require temporary storage of words presented both orally and visually, while the morpheme patterns ("derivational" suffixes in them that signal meaning and grammar) are analyzed. The phonological loop factor was assessed with two timed tasks that required multimodal coding (orthographic and phonological codes) and overt articulation of phonological word forms (naming). The executive function factor was assessed with two Stroop measures that require naming ink color (inhibition) or switching between naming ink color and naming words (inhibition/switching), and two rapid automatic switching (RAS) measures that require naming of alternating stimuli (letters and numbers, or colors, letters, and numbers) to assess mental set shifting. See Berninger et al. (2006) for details.

A single phonological word factor was not used for two reasons. First, prior research had shown that the orthographic word factor accounted for unique variance not explained by phonological word factor in reading and spelling words in typically developing children (Abbott & Berninger, 1993; Berninger, Cartwright, Yates, Swanson, & Abbott, 1994; Berninger, Yates, & Lester, 1991; Nagy, Berninger, & Abbott, 2006), at-risk readers (Nagy, Berninger, Abbott, Vaughan, & Vermeulen, 2003), and children and adults with dyslexia (Berninger, Abbott, Thomson, Raskind, 2001). Second, prior research with fourth to sixth graders showed that instruction directed to awareness of morphological word forms and their parts was more effective than instruction directed to awareness of phonological word forms and their parts in:

- Improving the rate of phonological decoding (translating orthographic word form into phonological word form) on a behavioral measure (Berninger et al., 2003).
- Improving neural efficiency during a phonological judgment during functional magnetic resonance spectroscopy (fMRS) scanning (Richards et al., 2002).
- Increasing blood-oxygenation-level-dependent (BOLD) activation on group maps for a phoneme mapping task (Aylward et al., 2003) during functional magnetic resonance imaging (fMRI) scanning on the right (parietal–occipital junction) and the left (occipital gyrus, superior parietal and occipital gyrus, and precentral gyrus) (Berninger, Nagy, et al., 2002).
- Increasing BOLD activation on group maps for a morpheme mapping task (Aylward et al., 2003) during fMRI scanning on the right (occipital gyrus, inferior parietal lobule and angular gyrus, middle

frontal gyrus, supramarginal gyrus, and gyrus medialis) and on the left (fusiform gyrus, parietal–occipital regions, superior parietal gyrus, and superior frontal gyrus) (Berninger, Nagy, et al., 2002).

The structural equation modeling results (Berninger et al., 2006) showed that for children, first-order phonological, orthographic, and morphological factors uniquely predicted 11 reading and writing outcomes, but for adults, a second-order factor based on the interrelationships among the three first-order word factors uniquely predicted the same reading and writing outcomes. These behavioral findings converged with prior brain imaging and treatment evidence to support *triple word form theory* (Berninger, Abbott, Billingsley, & Nagy, 2001; Berninger & Richards, 2002; Richards, Aylward, Raskind, et al., 2006), according to which distinct, spatially separated neural signatures for the phonological, morphological, and orthographic word forms are coordinated at a given point in real time in the brain and over the course of development. In children, phonological loop and executive support could be modeled as separate factors in the structural models, but in adults they could be modeled only as combined factors, consistent with Baddeley et al.'s (1998) claim that the executive system plays a role in regulating the phonological loop during learning, but not necessarily after mastery has occurred.

Is Dyslexia Just Poor Reading at the Lower Tail of Normal Distribution?

For both children and adults with dyslexia, individual differences occurred relative to which of the three working memory components or three word form factors fell outside the normal range, defined as 1 1/3 standard deviations or more below the mean (Berninger et al., 2006). Of the 122 children, only about 12% (N = 15) did not fall outside the normal range on any working memory components; for children, the working memory component that most often fell outside the normal range was executive function, followed by phonological loop, with phonological word factor occurring least often. Of the 200 adults, 42% (N = 84) did not fall outside the normal range on any working memory component, but the rest did; the working memory component that most often fell outside the normal range was executive functions, followed by phonological loop, with phonological word factor occurring least often.

Of the children, about one-third did not fall outside the normal range on any word factor (N = 41), but the rest did. Overall for children, the orthographic factor was most likely to fall outside the normal range, followed by the morphological word factor, with phonological word factor least likely to do so. Of the 200 adults, over half were not outside the normal range in any word factor ($N = 135$), but the rest were. Overall for adults, phonological word factor fell outside the normal range most often, followed by morphological word factor, with orthographic word factor least often. Adults may be more impaired in phonological word factor, because they have been out of school longer than their children, who likely receive intensive phonological decoding training, one of the most widely accepted treatments for dyslexia. A genetic vulnerability may be treatable but show some degree of regression if the individual is not given booster treatment from time to time.

Taken together, these results suggest that typically dyslexia is *not* simply a matter of an individual reading at the lower limit of the normal range; rather, it is a qualitatively different reading because one or more working memory components fall outside the normal range, thus impairing efficiency and fluency of reading and/or writing.

Is There a Single Cause or Effective Treatment for Dyslexia?

Multifaceted Behavioral Expression

Dyslexia is a heterogeneous disorder (e.g., Chapman et al., 2004; Raskind et al., 2005). Nevertheless, dyslexia appears to be a predictable *constellation* of impairments within which the heterogeneity expresses itself. At one level of analysis, this constellation comprises the verbal working memory components. At another level, the variable expression may be related to a variety of factors rather than to a single factor. The controversy about whether sensory or motor deficits, which may occur in some individuals with dyslexia, cause dyslexia can be reconciled within Fuster's (1997) model of working memory that emphasizes the links between internal working memory, and incoming sensory and outgoing motor systems that have more direct contact with the external environment. Visual sensory (e.g., Eden, Stein, Wood, & Wood, 1994) or fast visual motion deficits (e.g., Eden et al., 1996) may interfere with development of normal orthographic coding (e.g., Sperling, Lu, Manis, & Seidenberg, 2005) in some individuals. Auditory sensory deficits early in speech processing may also contribute to phonological processing downstream (e.g., Manis et al., 1997) in some individuals.

Others have precise timing impairments (Bowers & Wolf, 1993), detected on tasks requiring hand (Wolff, Cohen, & Drake, 1984; Wolff, Michel, Ovrut, & Drake, 1990) or mouth (Berninger, Nielsen, Abbott, Wijsman, & Raskind, 2008) function, that result in inefficient working memory. According to Fuster (1997), two sources of temporal coordination in working memory work in conjunction with the inhibitory mechanisms of the frontal supervisory attention system to regulate suppression of irrelevant external and internal stimuli. The first is achieved through cross-temporal contingencies between the sensory system, organized in bottom-up fashion in the posterior brain, and the motor system, organized in top-down fashion in the front of the brain. The second is through a mechanism that coordinates subcortical and cortical temporal contingencies. Breznitz (2002) reported the first evidence that deficits in the timing of the auditory–phonological, visual–orthographic, and phonological–orthographic mapping processes may cause dyslexia. This evidence is consistent with fMRI functional connectivity findings for phoneme mapping in word reading: Fathers with and without dyslexia, all of whom had children with dyslexia, differed in temporal coordination of frontal executive regions, connections between these frontal regions and word form regions in the back of the brain, and subcortical (cerebellar)–cortical connections (Stanberry et al., 2006).

Instructional Deficits

Although students with dyslexia are most likely to become compensated dyslexics if given appropriate instruction, it is unlikely that instructional variables alone completely explain the etiology of dyslexia, because other students learn to read in response to the same instruction. Pseudoword reading, which requires executive coordination of the three word forms within temporally constrained verbal working-memory, is reliably impaired in compensated adults with dyslexia who struggled earlier with reading (Berninger et al., 2006). Phonological vulnerabilities in working memory may surface again across the lifespan. The story of the new vicar who, when stressed with the challenges of a new career and congregation, began reversing and transposing sounds in his speech (Dahl, 1991) illustrates this genetic vulnerability that may not disappear permanently even in individuals who receive appropriate early intervention in reading.

Developmental Issues

The signs of dyslexia and instructional needs of people with dyslexia may change across schooling as curricular tasks change. Initially students struggle with phonological decoding, but later they may experience reading fluency problems when expected to read more and longer texts. As the words in texts become increasingly longer, students also need explicit instruction in morphology (Carlisle, 2000). Later, as the written assignments increase in length and complexity, problems in spelling and organization of written text that may become evident respond to explicit instruction in transcription (handwriting legibility and automaticity, and keyboard fluency), spelling, and composition (e.g., Berninger, Winn, et al., 2007; Berninger & Hidi, 2006), if provided. Regrettably many schools dismiss students with dyslexia from special education once they learn to read and do not provide ongoing explicit instruction in writing, until writing skills are adequately developed for successful completion of written assignments throughout the grades. These students need more than accommodations on high-stakes test in writing: They also need continuing explicit, systematic writing instruction to express themselves at age-appropriate levels in language by hand, just as those with expressive oral language problems need therapy until they can express themselves in age-appropriate oral language by mouth. (See Berninger, 2006). Regardless of the stage of schooling, students with dyslexia require orchestrated instructional components that are not only explicit but also carefully timed. Just like the orchestra conductor who must coordinate the timing of the various musicians (and their instruments), the teacher must coordinate the timing of the relevant instructional components to assist the learners, who must coordinate their mental processes in time. This teaching task is difficult for teachers, as is the learning task for students, because, as already shown, some of the relevant processes are outside the normal range. This unevenness of necessary components of a functional system is the fundamental problem to be overcome in teaching people with dyslexia (Berninger, 2001).

Summary of Educational Treatment Issues

It is unfortunate that the movement to replace whole language that emphasizes semantics, with a narrow approach to literacy instruction that may overemphasize phonology, may have *left the students with dyslexia behind*. Not all their problems are related to phonology or even reading. Individuals with this biological disorder require systematic, explicit, specialized instruction in the phonological, orthographic, and morphological aspects of written word learning, the phonological loop that guides verbal learning in working memory, and executive functions (especially inhibition and switching attention) geared to the grade-appropriate curriculum requirements in reading and writing throughout their schooling, so that they do not read and write at levels substantially below their measured verbal intelligence (Berninger, Abbott, Thomson et al., 2001, 2006; Berninger, 2006).

DIFFERENTIATING SPECIFIC WRITTEN LANGUAGE LEARNING DISABILITIES

Dysgraphia, dyslexia, and LLD, all disorders that affect written language during the school-age years, may be understood within the context of verbal working memory. The verbal working memory system allows literacy goals to be achieved using oral and written language codes stored in working memory and language processing operating in temporary working memory, which draws on incoming information from the environment stored in short-term memory and existing information stored in long-term memory. Evidence to date shows a common orthographic coding deficit in dysgraphia, dyslexia, and LLD that explains why students with each of these specific writing disabilities experience difficulty in producing written words and often word parts—alphabet letters (see Figure 4.2). Evidence to date also shows a common phonological coding deficit in dyslexia and LLD; in addition, students with LLD experience difficulty in morphological and syntactic awareness (see Figure 4.2). The pervasive metalinguistic awareness problems affecting both oral and written language of students with LLD, which is the only disability associated with oral language problems during the preschool years, may interfere with their listening comprehension, reading comprehension, and written expression. For example, the syntax of the written compositions of students with LLD may be shorter in length and have more agrammatical constructions (e.g., Scott, 2002) than those of students with dysgraphia or dyslexia, which is more likely to be full of misspellings. In this section I compare dysgraphia and dyslexia first and then dyslexia and LLD. Criteria for differential diagnosis are offered for dysgraphia, dyslexia, and LLD. A conceptual analysis of how the cognitive–linguistic bridges may be breaking down in LLD is offered for clues to effective treatment.

Comparing Dysgraphia and Dyslexia

"Dysgraphia" results when the mapping process within verbal working memory is inefficient in *only one direction—from phonological to orthographic words and parts*—impairing spelling and possibly handwriting (producing letters in response to their name). "Dyslexia" results when there is inefficiency in the mapping process within verbal working memory in *two directions—from orthographic to phonological words and parts* (impairing oral reading) and *from phonological to orthographic words and parts* (impairing spelling). For people with dyslexia and those with dysgraphia, mapping problems interfere with formation of the "autonomous orthographic lexicon": precise, word-specific spellings (including letters not corresponding to phonemes) that can be accessed automatically. Dysgraphia is associated with inefficiencies in the time-limited "graphomotor loop" (Abbott & Berninger, 1993; Berninger, Nielsen, et al., 2008) that coordinates the internal orthographic word codes and phonological–orthographic maps with writing acts in the external environment. In contrast, dyslexia is associated with inefficiencies in the time-limited "phonological loop" (Amtmann, Abbott, & Berninger, 2006) that coordinates internal phono-

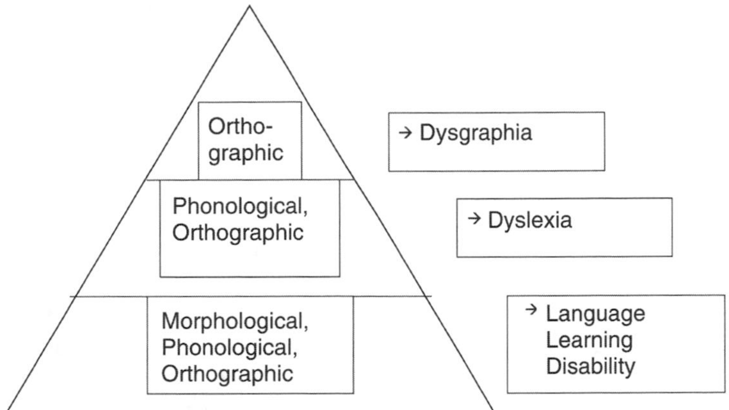

FIGURE 4.2. Relationship between word form deficit and diagnosis. From *Process Assessment of the Learner—Second Edition*. Copyright © 2007 by NCS Pearson, Inc. Reproduced with permission. All rights reserved.

logical word codes and orthographic–phonological maps with speaking acts in the external environment during oral reading. The executive functions most likely to be impaired in dysgraphia are planning and reviewing (updating), revising functions (Berninger, Vaughan, et al., 2002), and supervisory attention for motor output (Berninger, 2004); the executive functions most likely to be impaired in dyslexia are inhibition and switching attention (Berninger et al., 2006).

Dysgraphics have also been left behind with the reauthorization of Individuals with Disabilities Education Act (IDEA), which has not given sufficient explicit attention to the need for early assessment and identification, and treatment of writing in students at risk for writing, and not only reading, disabilities, or to scientifically supported differential diagnosis in students with persisting problems with written language. See Berninger and O'Donnell (2004) and Berninger (2004, 2006) for additional information on differential diagnosis of dysgraphia and dyslexia.

Comparing Dyslexia and LLD

Not all reading problems are dyslexia. School-age children whose overall development falls outside the normal range in all or two or more of these developmental domains—cognition and memory, receptive and expressive language, gross and fine motor skills, attention and executive function, and social–emotional function—or who have sustained an injury or disease in the brain or are a substance abuse baby or have neurogenetic disorders such as fragile *X*, Down or Williams syndrome, are likely to have reading problems too. However, the etiology, most effective treatment, and prognosis are unlikely to be the same as for individuals with either developmental dyslexia or LLD (Berninger, 2006).

IQ–Achievement Discrepancy Is Relevant to Diagnosing Dyslexia

Verbal IQ is a better predictor of reading achievement than Performance IQ or Full Scale IQ (Greenblatt, Mattis, & Trad, 1990; Vellutino, Scanlon, & Tanzman, 1991). The genetic basis of dyslexia is associated with higher IQs (Wadsworth, DeFries, Stevensen, Gilger, & Pennington, 1992). Some have argued, therefore, that IQ should no longer be assessed, and that reading disability can be assessed solely on the basis of low reading achievement or slow response to reading instruction. Another approach, for which there is research support, considers the developmental profile in which low reading achievement occurs, screens to determine who is likely to benefit from early intervention, implements early intervention, monitors response to intervention, and conducts comprehensive psychological and language assessment to identify the nature of the written language disability (e.g., persisting problems in individuals in the third and fourth classes of slower responders in Table 4.2).

In the case of dyslexia, the specific problems in reading occur despite strengths in the skills assessed by the Verbal IQ scale. Consider what a Verbal IQ test really measures (see Figure 4.3). Each of the subtests below requires use of the executive system in verbal working memory to search structures in the cognitive system, operate on that information, and then express the outcome of that operation in units of decontextualized oral language: Ability to use "decontextualized" language (outside the conversational context) is the best predictor of school transition and achievement (Snow, Cancino, Gonzales, & Shriberg, 1989).

- *Vocabulary*, which is the best correlate of overall IQ (scholastic aptitude), requires access to concepts in semantic memory signaled by a single spoken word and translation of these concepts into verbal explanations that hold across many contexts in which that word is encountered.
- *Information*, which assesses representative background knowledge in semantic memory that children bring to the task of learning to read and write, requires that children use executive functions for controlled searches to retrieve that information from long-term memory.
- *Similarities*, which assesses commonality between concepts, requires that children search through concepts in semantic memory signaled by two discrete words, determine how they are alike (not different), and explain verbally how they are alike.

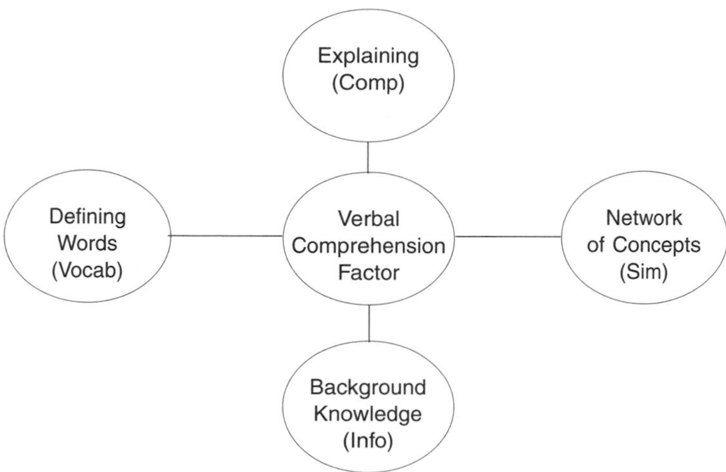

FIGURE 4.3. Processes assessed by WISC 3 prorated Verbal IQ or Verbal Comprehension factor. Info, reproducing background knowledge in long-term memory; Sim, abstracting the patterns of similarity among concepts in semantic memory; Vocab, using language to explain word meaning based on concepts in semantic memory organized in long-term memory in semantic association networks or feature-based categories; Comp, explaining background knowledge about the everyday world in long-term memory.

- *Comprehension*, which assesses practical understanding of the real world, requires access to episodic memory of everyday experience in the real world and provision of verbal explanations that reflect ability to interpret real-world experience.

Children with dyslexia who score high on these measures but low on word decoding skills may need different kinds of instructional activities than those who do not show such a discrepancy. For example, students with dyslexia may benefit from focused instruction on interrelationships among phonological, orthographic, and morphological cues in written words, and how these interrelationships can be applied to written word decoding and spelling.

IQ–Achievement Discrepancy Is Not Relevant to Diagnosing LLD

The term "language learning disability" has been used to refer to various difficulties with learning oral language (e.g., Wallach & Butler, 1994; Butler & Silliman, 2002). In this section I explain how LLD can be operationalized in a way that is useful in multidisciplinary assessment and treatment planning. LLD is characterized by initial difficulty in learning oral language during the preschool years that may resolve sufficiently at the production level, so that affected students no longer qualify for language and communication services during the school-age years, even if they have residual, pervasive problems in metalinguistic awareness and semantic access that interfere with their acquiring reading and writing, and using language to learn academic content subjects. Nor do such students qualify under the category of learning disabilities, because the same processes that contribute to their language learning problems tend to lower their Verbal IQ scores and reduce the probability that they will show a discrepancy between written language achievement and Verbal IQ or Full Scale IQ scores.

In the process of trying to understand how children who met our research criteria for dyslexia differed from children who clearly had reading problems but did not show a discrepancy between Verbal IQ and reading or writing achievement, we observed that they had preschool histories of LLD and current severe impairment (sometimes 3–5 *SD*s below the mean) on multiple measures of morphological and syntactic awareness tasks used in our research (morphological and syntactic measures described in Berninger et al., 2006; Nagy et al., 2003, 2006; Clinical Evaluation of Language Fundamentals, fourth edition [CELF-4] Sentence Formulation) but not necessarily on the production tasks or in conversation. In contrast, of the 122 children with dyslexia in the phenotyping study I discussed earlier, only five children scored below the mean—1 1/3 *SD* in syntactic awareness—and then only on one measure. Furthermore, children with LLD had severe reading comprehension problems, whereas the children with dyslexia did not, once they received explicit decoding instruction. Children with LLD responded more quickly than those with dyslexia to phonics instruction in improving their pseudoword reading but had greater persisting problems in reading real words than did those with dyslexia.

LLD and dyslexia share common phonological deficits (e.g., Bishop & Snowling, 2004). Dyslexia has associated strengths in semantic processing (Snowling, 2005), but LLD does not (Berninger & O'Donnell, 2004). The listening and reading comprehension problems of LLD are not necessarily solely the result of faulty language or cognition, but possibly also are the result of difficulty in building bridges across the language and cognitive systems, as I explain later in the chapter. Dyslexia and LLD also may have different underlying genetic mechanisms (Raskind, 2001) and neuroanatomical signatures (Leonard, 2001). Early reports of structural brain differences between good readers and those with dyslexia were based on samples that are better characterized as having LLD (impaired reading comprehension and word reading) rather than dyslexia (specific to word decoding and related oral reading skills with spared comprehension; e.g., Leonard, 2001).

Proposed Differential Diagnosis of Dysgraphia, Dyslexia, and LLD

We have found the following research-supported definitions useful in diagnosing specific learning disabilities that affect written language acquisition:

- *Dysgraphia*: Low handwriting legibility and automaticity and/or Verbal IQ–spelling achievement discrepancy + associated processing deficits in orthographic awareness, graphomotor planning, and/or rapid automatic naming (Berninger, 2004).
- *Dyslexia*: Verbal IQ–reading/spelling achievement discrepancy + associated processing deficits in phonological awareness, orthographic awareness, and/or rapid automatic naming (Berninger, Abbott, Thomson, et al., 2001, 2006).
- *LLD*: Low reading achievement (word reading and reading comprehension) in a profile in which Performance IQ is at least in the normal range, Verbal IQ and reading achievement are not significantly different, and the Verbal IQ holds clues to reasons the child is having difficulty creating the language–cognition connections I introduced earlier and elaborate on later in this chapter. Also, associated processing deficits in phonological, orthographic, and morphological/syntactic awareness, and/or rapid automatic naming (Berninger & O'Donnell, 2004).

Children with LLD may also be left behind unless comprehensive and appropriate assessment is required to evaluate whether their linguistic awareness (phonological, morphological, and syntactic), semantic memory, and attention–executive abilities may be interfering with the efficiency of their verbal working memory and their ability to build bridges between language and cognition to support using language to learn and behave. Exclusive use of response to intervention is inadequate to identify children with LLD whose problems and treatment include but also transcend reading and writing instruction: (1) word reading, and oral and written vocabulary learning; (2) morphological and syntactic awareness, listening and reading comprehension, and semantic access; (3) understanding and attending to teachers' instructional language; (4) using language to verbally mediate academic learning across the curriculum and to self-regulate strategies involved in learning to learn; and/or (5) using language to self-regulate behavior. These problems are most likely to be identified and treated appropriately if they are diagnosed through comprehensive, multidisciplinary assessment by a team that includes speech and language specialists, and psychologists who translate their assessment results into instructional approaches that classroom teachers can implement effectively.

Understanding Instructional Needs in LLD

The reasons why students with learning disabilities may not show scores discrepant with IQ may be relevant to treatment planning and progress monitoring. In the spirit of cross-disciplinary collaboration, I offer theoretical explanations for LLD based on the perspectives of cognitive psychology, developmental psycholinguistics, and neuropsychology. These build upon the model of verbal working memory discussed throughout this chapter, and assume that language is not acquired through a single acquisition device but develops through reciprocal *nature–nurture interactions* that include genetic and neurodevelopmental factors, *and* environmental experiences with language users. It also assumes that, through these interactions, one system develops for learning language and another develops for using language to learn and to manage the learning process, including but not restricted to scholastic learning. LLD may result from impairment in any or all of the following working memory components, each of which could be included in the treatment plan, in addition to explicit instruction in reading and writing: (1) mapping across levels of language (e.g., morphology to syntax first in aural and oral language, and later in written language); (2) linking sequentially accumulating word forms to the syntactic structures of the language; and/or (3) building bridges between the language system and the cognitive system in semantic memory. I now discuss each of the three proposed mechanisms for creating language–cognition connections.

Building Bridges across Levels of the Language System

Children who have difficulty building bridges between morphology and syntax are likely to have difficulty in comprehending and constructing aural or written language. Morphology contributes directly to oral vocabulary and reading comprehension processes in at-risk readers (Nagy et al., 2003; Stahl & Nagy, 2005) and normal readers (Nagy et al., 2006). Problems of students with LLD in listening comprehension may be more evident if their ability to understand the instructional language of the teacher, which is decontextualized language, is assessed rather than if their ability to understand conversation, which is highly contextualized, is assessed. Instruction should help students with LLD create bridges between word-level morphology (derivational suffixes that mark part of speech) and syntax, and to apply this bridging knowledge to text-level listening or reading comprehension. For example, students with LLD can be given base words and asked to add suffixes to change the base word from nouns into adjectives or verbs, or to change verbs into nouns or adverbs, then to use each of the words—original and transformed—in sentences they create.

Creating Structures for Temporally Accumulating Word Forms

Initially, the language learning mechanism *maps* single spoken words onto concrete, perceptually salient objects in the environment (e.g., *mommy*) and eventually abstract concepts (e.g., *fun*). Language learning capability improves as verbal working memory increases its temporal–spatial storage capability beyond maps for single words at a time to sets of sequential words glued simultaneously together in "syntactic structures" (e.g., by naming actors [*daddy*] and actions [*run*], using adjectives to describe objects and their properties or relationships [*cake yummy*; *toy mine*], and naming topics and making comments about them [e.g., "TV I like"]). Eventually sophisticated structures that flag main (independent) and auxiliary (dependent) clauses, and interrupted main clauses (embedded clauses) are acquired. In the process, the syntactic structures that evolve, which coregister words in time and space, allow language (a code for integrating sensory–perceptual, motor, and cognitive functions) to participate in a variety of functional systems, including those for using language to learn and verbally mediate self-regulation of the learning process, and to behave by verbally mediating self-regulation of interactions with the social and physical environment.

During the preschool years, children whose working memory does not support effortless development of syntax, or whose problems in learning syntax interfere with the development of an efficient working memory system, may have difficulty with listening comprehension and behavioral regulation. During their school years, they may have all those problems, as well as reading comprehension and written expression problems. In addition, they may have problems in using language to (1) understand teacher talk during instruction, (2) acquire declarative knowledge from the content of the curriculum, (3) acquire procedures for oral reading and spelling of words, (4) self-regulate their academic learning to complete assignments, (5) self-regulate the translation of thought to expression in writing, and (6) self-regulate their behavior in and out of school. Instructional activities that may help students with LLD improve the syntactic structures for holding serial, accumulating words in working memory include the following:

- Unscrambling words to create grammatically acceptable sentences.
- Choosing glue words (prepositions, pronouns, conjunctions, and articles) to form links between content words to create grammatically acceptable sentences.
- Creating sentences of increasing length from Jabberwocky words (nonword bases with real English derivational suffixes or structure words, as in Lewis Carroll's *Alice in Wonderland*).

Building Bridges between Language and Cognitive Systems

The representational structures of the language system and the cognitive system differ and complicate the creation of bridges between language and cognition (cross talk between layers of mind; Minsky, 1986). Language is organized around levels that are hierarchical, in that lower levels can be subsumed under higher levels. As explained in Stahl and Nagy (2005), language may only become unitized after written language is acquired, and words may be discrete units in written language but not necessarily in cognition or spoken language. Literate listeners impose discrete words and hierarchical levels of language on the continuous auditory signals. In contrast, cognition has formats for storage and processing that are not necessarily leveled, hierarchical, or discrete:

- One format is based on interactions with the environment, is stored in episodic memory (e.g., Tulving, 2002), and consists of sequential, real-life episodes, as in narrative or snapshot exposures that affect overall word frequency in the language (e.g., Stahl & Nagy, 2005).
- Another format is conceptual, is stored in semantic association networks, and consists of nodes and connections (verbal and nonverbal) with varying strengths of associations that communicate via spreading activation (e.g., Anderson & Bower, 1973).
- Another format is categorical, is stored in semantic memory, consists of prototypical and differentiating features, and has flexible organization in that exemplars may belong to different categories depending on context (e.g., Rosch & Mervis, 1975).
- Another format is schematic (e.g., Anderson, 1984; Barlett, 1932), is stored in semantic memory, and consists of organizing schemes for components and their interrelationships.
- Another format is dimensional, is stored in quantitative memory, and consists of values along a continuum (e.g., degree of temperature, ranging from very hot to very cold) (e.g., Clark & Clark, 1977).

Consequently, the connections between language and cognition in semantic memory are structurally and functionally complex. The morphological word form may play a special role in bridging language and cognition. The base word may activate semantic features in concepts in the cognitive system, while the derivational suffixes mark the syntactic features of parts of speech in the language system. Thus, the morphological word form builds a bridge between language and cognition, and has a special advantage, in that it relates directly to comprehension in a way that the phonological and orthographic word forms alone do not (see Nagy, in press;

Nagy et al., 2003, 2006). "Polysemy," which is accessing multiple meanings from the same phonological word form, may be an index of how well the language–cognitive connections are developed in semantic memory (see Stahl & Nagy, 2005). Some computational models for understanding the brain compare phonological and orthographic processing directly with semantic processing, without the intervening morphological word form (e.g., Crosson et al., 1999; connectionist models of reading), which may provide a reasonable account of beginning reading. However, teaching morphological awareness is critical for skilled reading, because it is the bridge between the word-form map and the syntactic comprehension processes underlying discourse understanding.

The semantic system is neither purely language nor purely cognition. Semantic memory is a bridge through which two mental worlds—language and cognition—communicate. Children may have semantic weaknesses because of underlying problems in (1) language, (2) cognition, (3) the interface between the two systems (e.g., retrieving the linguistic word that goes with the cognitive concept in semantic memory), and/or (4) all of these. As a result, they may experience difficulty not only in decoding unknown words by integrating orthographic, phonological, and morphological word forms but also in reading familiar words by accessing their meaning in semantic memory, and in constructing meaning during the reading comprehension process and in constructing sentence syntax during the composing process. To the extent that professionals can pinpoint the source of semantic weakness they may be better able to teach children with LLD to read and write efficiently.

SUMMARY AND CONCLUDING REMARKS

We need to be ever mindful of whom we serve and how *multiple disciplines* can contribute to overcoming written language disabilities. Effective treatment of specific learning disabilities requires more than purchasing commercially available tests or instructional materials, or implementing a legal code that is driven by compliance rather than best professional practices. It also requires knowledgeable professionals to implement services. That knowledge includes a deep understanding of current scientific research on (1) how language, memory, cognition, attention, sensory, and motor systems in the learner's brain/mind mediate response to instruction; and how (2) language is used to learn and behave as students interact with the teacher and other students in the learning environment. The professionals in school settings who have the most *scientific disciplinary training* in the relevant knowledge are speech and language specialists, and psychologists. I hope that the potential contribution of these professionals, who have the requisite training to assess which students are struggling with written or oral language learning and why, will not be stifled as states create their own legal code for implementing the reauthorization of IDEA. Working collaboratively, speech and language specialists and psychologists can offer diagnostic and treatment services in schools that are driven by the most current scientific and professional knowledge, based on research on language, cognition, learning, instruction, and brain, to determine who struggles in learning to read and why, and point to what is likely needed to overcome those struggles.

ACKNOWLEDGMENTS

Grant Nos. P50 33812 and HD25858 from the National Institute of Child Health and Human Development (NICHD) supported the research discussed in this chapter. I thank the principal investigators (Drs. Wendy Raskind, Todd Richards, and Robert Abbott), coinvestigators (Dr. William Nagy and the late William Winn), and research coordinators (Dr. Kathy Nielsen and Ms. Patricia Stock) in the University of Washington Multidisciplinary Learning Center (UW LDC); and co-investigators (Drs. Robert Abbott, Janine Jones, Dagmar Amtmann, William Nagy, and the late William Winn) and research coordinators (Shirley Shimada and Katherine Vaughan) on Literacy Trek, a longitudinal study of writing, reading, and writing–reading connections, for their contributions to the research discussed in this chapter. I also thank Charles MacArthur and Tana Shuy for stimulating discussion that led to Table 4.1 analyses.

REFERENCES

Abbott, R., & Berninger, V. (1993). Structural equation modeling of relationships among developmental skills and writing skills in primary and intermediate grade writers. *Journal of Educational Psychology, 85*(3), 478–508.

Amtmann, D., Abbott, R., & Berninger, V. (2006). Mixture growth models for RAN and RAS row by row: Insight into the reading system at work over time. *Reading and Writing: An Interdisciplinary Journal, 20*, 85–813.

Anderson, J. R., & Bower, G. R. (1973). *Human associative memory.* Washington DC: Winston.

Anderson, R. C. (1986). Role of the reader's schema in comprehension, learning, and memory. In R. C. Anderson, J. Osborne, & R. J. Tierney (Eds.), *Learning to read in American schools*. Hillsdale, NJ: Erlbaum.

Aylward, E., Richards, T., Berninger, V., Nagy, W., Field, K., Grimme, A., et al. (2003). Instructional treatment associated with changes in brain activation in children with dyslexia. *Neurology, 61*, 212–219.

Baddeley, A. (1986). *Working memory.* London: Oxford University Press.

Baddeley, A. (2002). Is working memory still working? *European Psychologist, 7*, 85–97.

Baddeley, A., Gathercole, S., & Papagno, C. (1998). The phonological loop as a language learning device. *Psychological Review, 105*, 158–173.

Bartlett, F. C. (1932). *Remembering*. Cambridge, UK: Cambridge University Press.

Bentler, P., & Wu, E. (2000). *EQS program*. Los Angeles: Multivariate Software.

Berninger, V. (2001). Understanding the lexia in dyslexia. *Annals of Dyslexia, 51*, 23–48.

Berninger, V. (2004). Understanding the graphia in dysgraphia. In D. Dewey & D. Tupper (Eds.), *Developmental motor disorders: A neuropsychological perspective* (pp. 328–350). New York: Guilford Press.

Berninger, V. (2006). A developmental approach to learning disabilities. In I. Siegel & A. Renninger (Eds.), *Handbook of child psychology: Vol. IV. Child psychology and practice* (pp. 420–452). New York: Wiley.

Berninger, V. (2007). *Process assessment of the learner—second edition: Diagnostics for reading and writing (PAL-II Reading and Writing)*. San Antonio, TX: Harcourt Assessment.

Berninger, V., Abbott, R., Billingsley, F., & Nagy, W. (2001). Processes underlying timing and fluency: Efficiency, automaticity, coordination, and morphological awareness. In M. Wolf (Ed.), *Dyslexia, fluency, and the brain* (pp. 383–414). Baltimore: York Press.

Berninger, V., Abbott, R., Brooksher, R., Lemos, Z., Ogier, S., Zook, D., et al. (2000). A connectionist approach to making the predictability of English orthography explicit to at-risk beginning readers: Evidence for alternative, effective strategies. *Developmental Neuropsychology, 17*, 241–271.

Berninger, V., Abbott, R., Thomson, J., & Raskind, W. (2001). Language phenotype for reading and writing disability: A family approach. *Scientific Studies in Reading, 5*, 59–105.

Berninger, V., Abbott, R., Thomson, J., Wagner, R., Swanson, H. L., Wijsman, E., et al. (2006). Modeling developmental phonological core deficits within a working-memory architecture in children and adults with developmental dyslexia. *Scientific Studies in Reading, 10*, 165–198.

Berninger, V., Abbott, R., Vermeulen, K., Ogier, S., Brooksher, R., Zook, D., et al. (2002). Comparison of faster and slower responders to early intervention in reading: Differentiating features of their language profiles. *Learning Disability Quarterly, 25*, 59–76.

Berninger, V., Cartwright, A., Yates, C., Swanson, H. L., & Abbott, R. (1994). Developmental skills related to writing and reading acquisition in the intermediate grades: Shared and unique variance. *Reading and Writing: An Interdisciplinary Journal, 6*, 161–196.

Berninger, V., & Hidi, S. (2006). Mark Twain's writers' workshop: A nature–nurture perspective in motivating students with learning disabilities to compose. In S. Hidi & P. Boscolo (Eds.), *Motivation in writing* (pp. 159–179). Amsterdam: Elsevier.

Berninger, V., Nagy, W., Carlisle, J., Aylward, E., Richards, T., Thomson, J., et al. (2002, June). *Added value of morphology treatment for dyslexics in grades 4 to 6: Behavioral and brain evidence*. Presented at the National Dyslexia Research Foundation Meeting in Hawaii.

Berninger, V., Nagy, W., Carlisle, J., Thomson, J., Hoffer, D., Abbott, S., et al. (2003).

Effective treatment for dyslexics in grades 4 to 6. In B. Foorman (Ed.), *Preventing and remediating reading difficulties: Bringing science to scale* (pp. 382–417). Timonium, MD: York Press.

Berninger, V., Nielsen, K., Abbott, R., Wijsman, E., & Raskind, W. (2008). Writing problems in developmental dyslexia: Under-identified and under-treated. *Journal of School Psychology, 46*, 1–21.

Berninger, V., & O'Donnell, L. (2004). Research-supported differential diagnosis of specific learning disabilities. In A. Prifitera, D. Saklofske, L. Weiss, & E. Rolfhus (Eds.), *WISC-IV: Clinical use and interpretation* (pp. 189–233). San Diego: Academic Press.

Berninger, V., & Richards, T. (2002). *Brain literacy for educators and psychologists*. San Diego: Academic Press.

Berninger, V., Vaughan, K., Abbott, R., Abbott, S., Rogan, L., Brooks, A., et al. (1997). Treatment of handwriting problems in beginning writing: Transfer from handwriting to composition. *Journal of Educational Psychology, 89*, 652–666.

Berninger, V., Vaughan, K., Abbott, R., Begay, K., Byrd, K., Curtin, G., et al. (2002). Teaching spelling and composition alone and together: Implications for the simple view of writing. *Journal of Educational Psychology, 94*, 291–304.

Berninger, V., Vaughan, K., Abbott, R., Brooks, A., Abbott, S., Reed, E., Rogan, L., & Graham, S. (1998). Early intervention for spelling problems: Teaching spelling units of varying size within a multiple connections framework. *Journal of Educational Psychology, 90*, 587–605.

Berninger, V., Winn, W., Stock, P., Abbott, R., Eschen, K., Lovitt, D., et al. (2007). Tier 3 treatment of writing disorders in students with dyslexia. *Reading and Writing: An Interdisciplinary Journal*, Springer Online. May 15, 2007.

Berninger, V., Yates, C., & Lester, K. (1991). Multiple orthographic codes in acquisition of reading and writing skills. *Reading and Writing: An Interdisciplinary Journal, 3*, 115–149.

Bishop, D. V. M., & Snowling, M. J. (2004). Developmental dyslexia and specific language impairment: Same or different? *Psychological Bulletin, 130*, 858–886.

Bowers, P., & Wolf, M. (1993). Theoretical links between naming speed, precise timing mechanisms, and orthographic skill in dyslexia. *Reading and Writing: An International Journal, 5*, 69–85.

Breznitz, Z. (2002). Asynchrony of visual–orthographic and auditory–phonological word recognition processes: An underlying factor in dyslexia. *Journal of Reading and Writing, 15*, 15–42.

Butler, K., & Silliman, E. (Eds.). (2002). *Speaking, reading, and writing in children with language learning disabilities*. Mahwah, NJ: Erlbaum.

Carlisle, J. (2000). Awareness of the structure and meaning of morphologically complex words: Impact on reading. *Reading and Writing: An Interdisciplinary Journal, 12*, 169–190.

Catts, H., Adoph, S., & Weismer, S. (2006). Language deficits in poor comprehenders: A case for the simple view of reading. *Journal of Speech, Language, and Hearing Research, 49*, 278–293.

Catts, H., & Kamhi, A. (Eds.). (2005). *The connections between language and reading disabilities*. Mahwah, NJ: Erlbaum.

Chapman, N., Igo, R., Thomson, J., Matsushita, M., Brkanac, Z., Hotzman, T., et al.

(2004). Linkage analyses of four regions previously implicated in dyslexia: Confirmation of a locus on chromosome 15q. *American Journal of Medical Genetics: B. Neuropsychiatric Genetics, 131*, 67–75.

Chapman, N., Raskind, W., Thomson, J., Berninger, V., & Wijsman, E. (2003). Segregation analysis of phenotypic components of learning disabilities.II. Phonological decoding. *American Journal of Medical Genetics: B. Neuropsychiatric Genetics, 121*, 60–70.

Clark, H., & Clark, E. (1977). *Psychology and language*. New York: Harcourt Brace Jovanovich.

Cohen, L., Lehéricy, S., Chocon, F., Lemer, C., Rivaud, S., & Dehaene, S. (2002). Language-specific tuning of visual cortex?: Functional properties of the visual word form area. *Brain, 125*, 1054–1069.

Crosson, B., Rao, S., Woodley. S., Rosen, A., Bobholz, J., Mayer, A., et al. (1999). Mapping of semantic, phonological, and orthographic verbal working memory in normal adults with functional magnetic resonance imaging. *Neuropsychology, 13*, 171–187.

Dahl, R. (1991). *The Vicar of Nibbleswicke*. London: Random Century Group.

Eden, G., Stein, J., Wood, H., & Wood, F. (1994). Differences in eye movements and reading problems in reading disabled and normal children. *Vision Research, 34*, 1345–1358.

Eden, G., VanMeter, J., Rumsey, J., Maisog, J., Woods, R., & Zeffiro, T. (1996). Abnormal processing of visual motion in dyslexia revealed by functional brain imaging. *Nature, 382*, 66–69.

Fuster, J. (1997). *The prefrontal cortex: Anatomy, physiology, and neuropsychology of the frontal lobes* (3rd ed., pp. 209–252). New York: Raven.

Greenblatt, E., Mattis, S., & Trad, P. (1990). Nature and prevalence of learning disabilities in a child psychiatric population. *Developmental Neuropsychology, 6*, 71–83.

Gunter, T., Wagner, S., & Friederici, A. (2003). Working memory and lexical ambiguity resolution as revealed by ERPS: A difficult case for activation theories. *Journal of Cognitive Neuroscience, 15*, 643–657.

Hitch, G.J., & Baddeley, A. (1976). Verbal reasoning and working memory. *Quarterly Journal of Experimental Psychology, 28*, 603–621.

Hsu, L., Wijsman, E., Berninger, V., Thomson, J., & Raskind, W. (2002). Familial aggregation of dyslexia phenotypes: Paired correlated measures. *American Journal of Medical Genetics: B. Neuropsychiatric Genetics, 114*, 471–478.

Kail, R. (1984). *The development of memory in children* (2nd ed.). New York: Freeman.

Leonard, C. (2001). Imaging brain structure in children: Differentiating language disability and reading disability. *Learning Disability Quarterly, 24*, 158–176.

Lyon, G. R., Shaywitz, S., & Shaywitz, B. (2003). A definition of dyslexia. *Annals of Dyslexia, 53*, 1–14.

Manis, F., McBride-Chang, C., Seidenberg, M., Keating, P., Doi, L., Munson, B., et al. (1997). Are speech perception deficits associated with developmental dyslexia? *Journal of Experimental Child Psychology, 66*, 211–235.

McCrory, E., Frith, U., Brunswick, N., & Price, C. (2000). Abnormal functional activation during a simple word repetition task: A PET study of adult dyslexics. *Journal of Cognitive Neuroscience, 12*, 753–762.

Miller, G. A., Galanter, E., & Pribram, K. H. (1960). *Plans and the structure of behavior.* New York: Holt, Rinehart & Winston.

Minsky, M. (1986). *Societies of mind.* New York: Simon & Schuster.

Miyake, A., Friedman, N., Emerson, M., Witzki, A., Howerter, A., & Wager, T. (2000). The unity and diversity of executive functions and their contributions to complex "frontal lobe" tasks: A latent variable analysis. *Cognitive Psychology, 41*, 49–100.

Morris, R., Stuebing, K., Fletcher, J., Shaywitz, S., Lyon, G. R., Shakweiler, D., et al. (1998). Subtypes of reading disability: Variability around a phonological core. *Journal of Educational Psychology, 90*, 347–373.

Nagy, W. (2006). Metalinguistic awareness and the vocabulary–comprehension connection. In R. K. Wagner, A. Muse, & K. Tannenbaum (Eds.), *Vocabulary acquisition and its implications for reading comprehension* New York: Guilford Press.

Nagy, W., Berninger, V., & Abbott, R. (2006). Contributions of morphology beyond phonology to literacy outcomes of upper elementary and middle school students. *Journal of Educational Psychology, 98*, 134–147.

Nagy, W., Berninger, V., Abbott, R., Vaughan, K., & Vermeulen, K. (2003). Relationship of morphology and other language skills to literacy skills in at-risk second graders and at-risk fourth grade writers. *Journal of Educational Psychology, 95*, 730–742.

National Reading Panel. (2000, April). *Teaching children to read: An evidence-based assessment of the scientific research literature on reading and its implications for reading instruction.* Washington, DC: National Institute of Child Health and Human Development.

Norman, D. A., & Shallice, T. (1986). Attention to action: Willed and automatic control of behaviour. In R. Davidson, G. Schwarts, & D. Shapiro (Eds.), *Consciousness and self-regulation: Advances in research and theory* (Vol. 4, pp. 1–18). New York: Plenum Press.

Oakhill, J., & Yuill, N. (1996). Higher order factors in comprehension disability: Processes and and remediation. In C. Cornoldi & J. Oakhill (Eds.), *Reading comprehension difficulties: Processes and intervention* (pp. 69–92). Mahwah, NJ: Erlbaum.

Raskind, W. (2001). Current understanding of the genetic basis of reading and spelling disability. *Learning Disability Quarterly, 24*, 141–157.

Raskind, W., Hsu, L., Thomson, J., Berninger, V., & Wijsman, E. (2000). Family aggregation of dyslexic phenotypes. *Behavior Genetics, 30*, 385–396.

Raskind, W., Igo, R., Chapman, N., Berninger, V., Thomson, J., Matsushita, M., et al. (2005). A genome scan in multigenerational families with dyslexia: Identification of a novel locus on chromosome 2q that contributes to phonological decoding efficiency. *Molecular Psychiatry, 10*(7), 699–711.

Ribaupierre, A. (2002). Working memory and attentional processes across the life span. In P. Graf & N. Ohta (Eds.), *Lifespan development of human memory* (pp. 59–80). Cambridge, MA: MIT Press.

Richards, T., Aylward, E., Berninger, V., Field, K., Parsons, A., Richards, A., et al. (2006). Individual fMRI activation in orthographic mapping and morpheme mapping after orthographic or morphological spelling treatment in child dyslexics. *Journal of Neurolinguistics, 19*, 56–86.

Richards, T., Aylward, E., Berninger, V., Winn, W., Stock, S., Wagner, R., et al. (2007). fMRI activation in children with dyslexia during pseudoword aural repeat and visual decode. *Neuropsychology, 21*, 732–747.

Richards, T., Aylward, E., Raskind, W., Abbott, R., Field, K., Parsons, A., et al. (2006). Converging evidence for triple word form theory in child dyslexics. *Developmental Neuropsychology, 30*, 547–589.

Richards, T., Berninger, V., Aylward, E., Richards, A., Thomson, J., Nagy, W., et al. (2002). Reproducibility of proton MR spectroscopic imaging (PEPSI): Comparison of dyslexic and normal reading children and effects of treatment on brain lactate levels during language tasks. *American Journal of Neuroradiology, 23*, 1678–1685.

Richards, T., Berninger, V., Nagy, W., Parsons, A., Field, K., & Richards, A. (2005). Dynamic assessment of child dyslexics' brain response to alternative spelling treatments. *Educational and Child Psychology, 22*(2), 62–80.

Rosch, E., & Mervis, C. B. (1975). Family resemblances: Studies in the internal structure of categories. *Cognitive Psychology, 7*, 573–605.

Scott, C. (2002). A fork in the road less traveled: Writing intervention based on language profile. In K. Butler & E. Silliman (Eds.), *Speaking, reading, and writing in children with language learning disabilities*. Mahwah, NJ: Erlbaum.

Semel, E., Wiiig, E. H., & Secord, W. A. (2003). *Clinical evaluation of language fundamentals* (4th ed.). San Antonio, TX: Pearson.

Smith-Spark, J., Fisk, J., Fawcett, A., & Nicolson, R. (2003). Investigating the central executive in adult dyslexics: Evidence from the phonological and visuospatial working memory performance. *European Journal of Cognitive Neuropsychology, 15*, 567–587.

Snow, C., Cancino, H., Gonzales, P., & Shriberg, E. (1989). Giving formal definitions: An oral language correlate of school literacy. In D. Bloome (Ed.), *Literacy in classrooms* (pp. 233–249). Norwood, NJ: Ablex.

Snowling, M. (2005). Literacy outcomes for children with oral language impairments: Developmental interactions between language skills and learning to read. In H. Catts & A. Kamhi (Eds.), *The connections between language and reading disabilities*. Mahwah, NJ: Erlbaum.

Sperling, A., Lu, Z., Manis, F., & Seidenberg, M. (2005). Deficits in perceptual noise exclusion in developmental dyslexia. *Nature Neuroscience, 8*, 862–863.

Stahl, S., & Nagy, W. (2005). *Teaching word meaning*. Mahwah, NJ: Erlbaum.

Stanberry, L., Richards, T., Berninger, V., Nandy, R., Aylward, E., Maravilla, K., et al. (2006). Low frequency signal changes reflect differences in functional connectivity between good readers and dyslexics during continuous phoneme mapping. *Magnetic Resonance Imaging, 24*, 217–229.

Stanovich, K. E., & Siegel, L. S. (1994). Phenotypic performance profile of children with reading disabilities: A regression-based test of the phonological-core variable-difference model. *Journal of Educational Psychology, 86*, 24–53.

Swanson, H. L. (2000). Working memory, short-term memory, speech rate, word recognition and reading comprehension in learning disabled readers: Does the executive system have a role? *Intelligence, 28*, 1–30.

Towse, J. (1998). On random generation and the central executive of working memory. *British Journal of Psychology, 89*, 77–101.

Towse, J., Hitch, G., & Hutton, U. (2000). A reevaluation of working memory capacity in children. *Journal of Memory and Language, 39*, 195–217.

Tulving, E. (2002). Episodic memory: From mind to brain. *Annual Review of Psychology, 53*, 1–25.

Vellutino, F., Scanlon, D., & Tanzman, M. (1991). Bridging the gap between cognitive and neuropsychological conceptualizations of reading disabilities. *Learning and Individual Differences, 3*, 181–203.

Wadsworth, S., DeFries, J., Stevenson, J., Gilger, J., & Pennington, B. (1992). Gender ratios among reading-disabled children and their siblings as a function of parental impairment. *Journal of Child Psychology and Psychiatry, 33*, 1229–1239.

Wagner, R., & Torgesen, J. (1987). The nature of phonological processing and its causal role in the acquisition of reading skills. *Psychological Bulletin, 101*, 192–212.

Wallach, G., & Butler, K. (Eds.). (1994). *Language learning disabilities in school-age children and adolescents: Some principles and applications* (2nd ed.). New York: Maxwell Macmillan International.

Wechsler, D. (1991). *Wechsler Intelligence Scale for Children, third edition* (WISC 3). San Antonio, TX: Harcourt Assessment.

Wijsman, E., Peterson, D., Leutenegger, A., Thomson, J., Goddard, K., Hsu, L., et al. (2000). Segregation analysis of phenotypic components of learning disabilities: I. Nonword memory and digit span. *American Journal of Human Genetics, 67*, 631–646.

Wolff, P., Cohen, C., & Drake, C. (1984). Impaired motor timing control in specific reading retardation. *Neuropsychologia, 22*, 587–600.

Wolff, P., Michel, G., Ovrut, M., & Drake, C. (1990). Rate and timing precision of motor coordination in developmental dyslexia. *Developmental Psychology, 26*, 349–359.

5

Processing Measures of Cognitive–Linguistic Interactions for Children with Language Impairment and Reading Disabilities

JENNIFER WINDSOR
KATHRYN KOHNERT

There is a large, heterogeneous population of children who show a primary language impairment (typically referred to as LI or as specific language impairment [SLI]) that is not secondary to conditions such as hearing loss, mental retardation, neurological insult, or environmental differences or deprivation (Tomblin et al., 1997). Children with LI conventionally have been defined by both the inclusionary behavioral criterion of language deficits relative to chronological-age peers and exclusionary criteria (typical nonverbal intelligence, hearing, and social–emotional abilities). A parallel population of children with reading disabilities (RD) is often identified by the same type of discrepancy between an observable deficit in reading performance and otherwise meeting chronological-age expectations. Although this discrepancy-based approach to identifying LI and RD has acknowledged theoretical and methodological problems (Fletcher, Foorman, Shaywitz, & Shaywitz, 1999), there is strong evidence that the populations of children with spoken language difficulties and reading disabilities overlap, and that children with LI are at high risk for a later diagnosis of RD (Catts, Fey, Tomblin, & Zhang, 2002). Whether or not LI and RD are distinct entities, the theoretical explanations of performance in both groups are increasingly very similar, and invoke similar underlying cognitive–linguistic mechanisms (Bishop & Snowling, 2004; Snowling, Bishop, & Stothard, 2000).

This chapter provides an overview of an approach to investigating spoken language that emphasizes cognitive fundamentals, such as memory and processing speed, rather than cumulative experience with language or literacy. Although our focus is on children with a primary diagnosis of LI, we also address children with a primary diagnosis of RD, using RD as a broad term for children with below-average reading skills in their native language. Our overall goal is twofold: to explore a theoretical model of language performance, and to identify assessment measures consistent with this framework that may facilitate identification of LI and RD in diverse groups of language learners. We first outline traditional, experience-dependent language measures and make the argument for alternative cognitive–linguistic processing approaches to spoken language. In contrast to a traditional approach that emphasizes language knowledge or competence, a cognitive-linguistic processing approach emphasizes two perspectives: first, that language, rather than being independent, is part of and interacts with a broader cognitive system, including both attention and preattentive perceptual processes; and second, that the proficiency with which information is manipulated or processed is likely to provide more insight about the nature of underlying capability than static performance measures, which may be influenced heavily by acquired knowledge.

Next, we introduce the notion that cognitive–linguistic processing measures may be manipulated to be more or less reliant on language or learner experience; that is, rather than viewing language tasks and nonlinguistic tasks as representing separate categories of homogeneous skills, we take the perspective that task demands vary within and across these conventional categories depending on information-processing complexity of the task and learner experience. This section is followed by a summary of our recent research on cognitive–linguistic processing tasks administered to children with and without LI, which in turn is followed by a final discussion of the theoretical and educational value of a cognitive–linguistic approach to examining spoken and written language development and breakdown.

CONTRASTING EXPERIENCE-DEPENDENT LANGUAGE AND LITERACY MEASURES WITH COGNITIVE–LINGUISTIC PROCESSING MEASURES

Experience-Dependent Measures

By definition, a child with LI or RD performs below chronological-age peers with similar experiences on many spoken language and literacy tasks.

The typical approach to characterizing LI or RD is to examine spoken language performance or reading achievement, whether through norm-referenced tests, criterion-referenced probes, or language samples. At first blush, to assess spoken language accuracy or developmental progress toward knowledge in the final adult state, measures of receptive and expressive semantics, syntax, phonology, and conversation are the obvious courses to pursue in better defining the nature of spoken language development and impairment. Similarly, performance measures of accuracy and fluency in word identification, passage comprehension, and discourse monitoring are natural areas to pursue in informing research on RD.

However, at least three factors speak against an exclusive focus on these types of language and literacy measures as the only informative markers of spoken and written language breakdowns. First, the most salient performance characteristics of language change across development, with toddlers at risk for LI or RD showing low vocabulary skills, preschoolers (in some languages) showing less frequent use of obligatory verb morphology, and school-age children manifesting poor discourse and literacy skills (Leonard, 1998). Thus, an array of performance measures is needed to be sensitive to language across development, and across LI and RD subgroups. Second, the specific characteristics of the language(s) to be learned are an important determining factor in the presenting performance of LI and RD. For example, the verb morphology deficits observed in English-speaking children are less evident in children with LI who learn highly inflected languages such as Italian or Hebrew (Dromi, Leonard, & Shteiman, 1993).

Third, and of key interest here, traditional language performance measures are heavily experience-dependent and rely to a great extent on both a child's opportunities or experiences in the test language or text and his or her developmental progress. Performance may be confounded by exposure to a particular language; educational, social, and cultural opportunities; and world experience (Kan & Kohnert, 2005; Kohnert, Windsor, & Yim, 2006; Peña, Bedore, & Zlatic-Giunta, 2002). As such, experience-dependent language measures may not be effective, for instance, in separating monolingual children with LI or RD from typically developing age peers from culturally and linguistically diverse backgrounds, including second-language learners (Håkansson & Nettelbladt, 1996; Paradis, Crago, Genesee, & Rice, 2003; Windsor & Kohnert, 2004).

Cognitive–Linguistic Processing Measures

An alternative to traditional, experience-dependent measures to characterize language breakdown is to investigate the processing of basic information, that is, the mental operations used to perceive, encode, manipulate, and respond to some type of stimulus. Processing-dependent tasks attempt to measure the integrity of the underlying language learning or cognitive processing system rather than language abilities or knowledge per se. For example, whereas children's accuracy on a traditional measure, such as an English vocabulary test, reflects their acquired vocabulary knowledge, it also reflects their exposure to and experience with English. On the other hand, children's performance on a language-based processing measure, such as a rapid automatic naming task with familiar objects, reflects the speed and accuracy with which children can process phonological and lexical representations that underlie vocabulary performance and reading fluency, and deemphasizes language-specific developmental expectations of acquired knowledge.

As a general starting point to guide our research on cognitive–linguistic processing, we have drawn on MacDonald and Christiansen's (2002) connectionist view of the cognitive system. In this framework, individual differences in typical adult language performance emerge from a biological processing system interacting with differential language and social experiences. Biological constraints are limits that are part of the cognitive system or "architecture" underlying language use. The central biological constraint is the precision of phonological representations developed from spoken and written input. Specifically, it is argued that because of individual differences in the integrity of phonological representations, there are individual differences in phonological activation during language comprehension tasks. A second biological constraint identified by MacDonald and Christiansen is the computational processing speed at which the brain carries out perceptual–motor and higher-level cognitive processing. Again, the proposal is that individual variation in processing speed or efficiency ultimately affects language performance.

Experiential constraints, which also vary among individuals, are limits derived from the extent of exposure to language. The central experiential factors proposed by MacDonald and Christiansen (2002) are the joint forces of frequency of occurrence of particular linguistic patterns (e.g., regular vs. irregular words) and the similarity to other patterns in the language input. Of particular interest to MacDonald and Christiansen is that some individuals have greater language experience because they read more than others. Greater experience is presumed to lead to more robust mappings between individuals' language input and their language performance or output. The overall amount of exposure an individual has is proposed to drive different interactions among input pattern frequency and similarity (or "regularity"); that is, individuals with high exposure may show what appear to be qualitatively different outputs than those of individuals with low exposure, because of the effects of different frequency–regularity interactions—rather than because of individual differences in the memory capacity to manipulate linguistic material. Indeed, a distinctive feature of MacDonald and Christiansen's approach is the argument that the traditionally important concept of verbal working memory capacity is not needed as a separate explanatory heuristic for language use; rather, it is simply one measure of individuals' language processing; that is, that the interaction of biological constraints (especially precision of phonological representations and processing speed) and experiential constraints (pattern frequency and regularity) alone is sufficient to explain individual differences in language performance. (See Caplan and Waters [2002] and Just and Varma [2002] for responses to this specific aspect of MacDonald and Christiansen's proposal.)

Although the MacDonald and Christiansen (2002) approach does not focus on LI and RD, we have started with this basic framework to explore the idea that LI and RD may be considered instances of extreme variation in typical biological constraints, perhaps mediated through a salient genetic contribution (Bishop, 2001). Children who are gifted in language or reading would be another example of variation in biological constraints. On the other hand, the performance of children at risk for poor language–reading performance in a given language because of low language exposure, such as some typical children's performance in a second language, children in impoverished home literacy environments, children raised in institutions with few direct caretakers, and other poor or rich experiential circumstances, may be thought of as instances of extreme variation in language or social experiences.

Some research on LI and RD emphasizes either biological constraints, such as processing speed and phonological representation or coding across populations (e.g., Swanson, Saez, Gerber, & Leafsteadt, 2004) or emphasizes a specific experiential factor, such as intensive instruction in phonological skills (e.g., Vellutino, Scanlon, & Sipay, 1997). In contrast, our interpretation of the MacDonald and Christiansen (2002) framework may give us a unique vantage point from which to consider the balanced and interactive relation between the breakdown of general cognitive mechanisms in LI and RD, *and* experiential factors in influencing overall language and reading abilities. Of particular interest here as an example of differences in exposure and experience, we have focused on the skills of typical children learning a second language. To our knowledge, this is the first application of MacDonald and Christiansen's framework to children. Although we have framed our research within the specific constructs proposed by MacDonald and Christiansen, other, similar developmental frameworks (e.g., Tomasello, 2003) that emphasize the social environment in which language is learned in conjunction with development and maturation may be equally informative.

PROCESSING DIFFERENT STIMULUS TYPES: LANGUAGE-BASED, PERCEPTUAL–MOTOR, AND NONLINGUISTIC–COGNITIVE MEASURES

We believe that to characterize LI and RD best from a cognitive–linguistic perspective, it is necessary to explore converging evidence from performance on a range of measures. These measures may tap skills that lie at different points along a hypothetical information-processing continuum of sorts, or at least represent observably different types of task stimuli that are encountered in information processing. From this perspective, children are exposed to a range of stimuli in learning language that affect their performance in experimental tasks. For our purposes here, we have framed the range of stimuli as comprising three general task areas: language-based processing tasks, perceptual–motor processing tasks, and higher-level nonlinguistic–cognitive processing tasks.

Language-Based Processing Tasks

These kinds of tasks have a linguistic component but typically reduce experience-dependence by using language stimuli (sounds, words, or grammatical structures) that are highly familiar or novel to all participants. Nonword repetition, rapid automatic naming, and listening or reading span tasks are common instances of language-based or linguistic processing measures. As one example, nonword repetition has been found to identify LI in culturally diverse populations, specifically African American and European American children (Campbell, Dollaghan, Needleman, & Janosky, 1997; Rodekohr & Haynes, 2001). Nonword repetition performance also has been found to be associated with RD in monolingual European American groups with reading difficulties (e.g., Roodenrys & Stokes, 2001), although nonword repetition performance may not be associated with reading performance in the general population (Bishop, 2001). However, bilingual performance may well depend on proficiency in the language in which the processing task is administered (Ardila et al., 2000; Service, Simola, Metsänheimo, & Maury, 2002).

Given that language tasks inherently are experience-dependent, and because experience interacts with cognitive function beginning early in development, it may be that we cannot create a truly experience-independent language or other behavioral task. However, we may well be able to create language-based processing tasks that level the playing field for group or individual comparisons across diverse language learners by taking into account children's current state of accumulated language and other cognitive experiences and knowledge.

Perceptual–Motor and Higher-Level Nonlinguistic–Cognitive Processing Tasks

These types of tasks reduce the effect of individual language experiences by taking advantage of the nonlinguistic profile that accompanies at least some LI and RD subgroups. An increasing body of literature shows that it is not just language tasks on which children with LI are outperformed by age peers. Relative slowness and/or lower accuracy by LI groups on a range of nonlinguistic tasks, including perceptual–motor tasks (e.g., auditory and visual detection), as well as more complex cognitive tasks (e.g., mental rotation and visual search) have been documented (Johnston & Ellis Weismer, 1983; Miller, Kail, Leonard, & Tomblin, 2001). Children with RD also have been found to show difficulties in nonlinguistic tasks, such as spatial construction, temporal order judgments, and auditory and visual perception (e.g., Eden, Wood, & Stein, 2003). These deficits suggest that the poor language performance in LI and RD actually is part of a broader cognitive performance profile, and that vulnerability to stress in cognitive processes contributes to the spoken and written language performance deficits (Hayiou-Thomas, Bishop, & Plunkett, 2004). We leave open the issue of whether these broader deficits are causally related or reliably correlated with language and reading performance.

It is important to remember that not all nonlinguistic tasks are free of the influence of individual differences in experience and acquired knowledge simply because they are not language-based. Research on cognitive function in aging makes it clear that nonlinguistic tasks that carry a minimal cognitive load should reflect underlying cognitive constraints more directly. However, complex cognitive tasks can be expected also to reflect the effects of individual participant experience and task variables, such as acquired knowledge, strategies, exposure, and so on (Birren & Fisher, 1995). For example, elementary choice response time (RT) tasks (e.g., pressing one of two response buttons when one of two lights appears), Odd Man Out, and inspection time paradigms that emphasize motor response time with a minimal decision-making component appear to be useful in capturing underlying cognitive constraints for adults and children (Bates & Stough, 1998; Kranzler, Whang, & Jensen, 1994). However, very elementary tasks with a heavy perceptual–motor component but functionally zero cognitive decision component (e.g., simple RT tasks), as well as complex nonlinguistic tasks (e.g., mental rotation, visual pattern assembly), may represent differences in pure motor RT or mental strategies in addition to underlying cognitive skills (Cerella & Hale, 1994). Thus, as for language-processing tasks, not all nonlinguistic processing tasks are useful in differentiating biological and experiential factors among diverse groups.

OVERVIEW OF RESEARCH FINDINGS

In our recent research we have tried to build on the current literature to identify cognitive–linguistic processing measures with the potential to identify children with LI and RD, and to better inform theories of language breakdown. Here we review results from eight experimental cognitive–linguistic tasks to illustrate the three general types of processing measures, that is, language-based or linguistic processing, perceptual–motor processing, and higher-level nonlinguistic processing. Partly because we are interested in teasing apart a biological disposition for LI or RD from the effect of experiential factors, we have contrasted the performance of English-only monolingual children with LI with two other groups: typical English-only monolingual age peers and typical sequential Spanish–English bilingual age peers. All children's language performance inherently is influenced by language exposure and experience; however, there are different factors at play for different groups. Although environmental factors, such as maternal responsiveness, may be moderating variables for children with persistent LI (La Paro, Justice, Skibbe, & Planta, 2004), there is strong evidence of a genetic etiology for LI (Bishop, North, & Donlan, 1995; SLI Consortium, 2002); that is, biological influences are particularly relevant factors in language performance for this group. On the other hand, although control of the dual-language system is influenced by factors such as maturation and underlying cognitive development, as well as relative levels of skills in each language, amount of exposure to a second language is a key factor in typical bilingual children's performance in the second language (Kan & Kohnert, 2005; Kohnert & Bates, 2002); that is, experiential factors are particularly relevant in language performance for this group. The notion of varied biological and experiential influences on language performance is illustrated in Figure 5.1. The figure shows that typical monolingual English-speaking children and bilingual Spanish–English children might be expected to outperform monolingual English-speaking children with LI in language performance because of the presumed greater biological constraints in LI. At the same time, typical monolingual English-speaking children with and without LI might be expected to outperform typical bilingual children because of greater exposure to English. By comparing the monolingual LI group with typical monolingual peers (i.e., whose language experience is equivalent), we can make tentative inferences about the role of biological constraints in LI performance. The comparison with typical bilingual peers (i.e., who have no biological constraints on language learning) allows us to ensure that our interpretation about LI performance is not confounded by relative language experience.

Participants

The tasks were administered to 100 children ages 8–13 years: 50 typically developing monolingual English-only speakers (EO group), 22 typical bilingual Spanish–English speakers (BI group), and 28 monolingual English-only speakers with LI (LI group). The average age in the LI group (*M* = 10 years, 6 months; *SD* = 1 year, seven months) and the EO group (*M* = 10 years, 7 months; *SD* = 1 year, 10 months) was comparable; the BI group was about 9 months younger (*M* = 9 years, 9 months; *SD* = 1 year, 5 months). The children were recruited by advertisements in several large urban public schools and the surrounding communities. To be eligible for participation, children in the LI group met conventional criteria for specific language impairment (Leonard, 1998) and showed an observable deficit (greater than -1 *SD*) on standardized expressive and/or receptive language tests in the presence of normal nonverbal intelligence. There was a strong overlap between spoken language and reading performance in the LI group. Seventeen of the 28 children with LI also showed below-average reading performance, with standardized reading test scores greater than -1 *SD* in word identification and/or reading comprehension. All but 2 of the 28 chil-

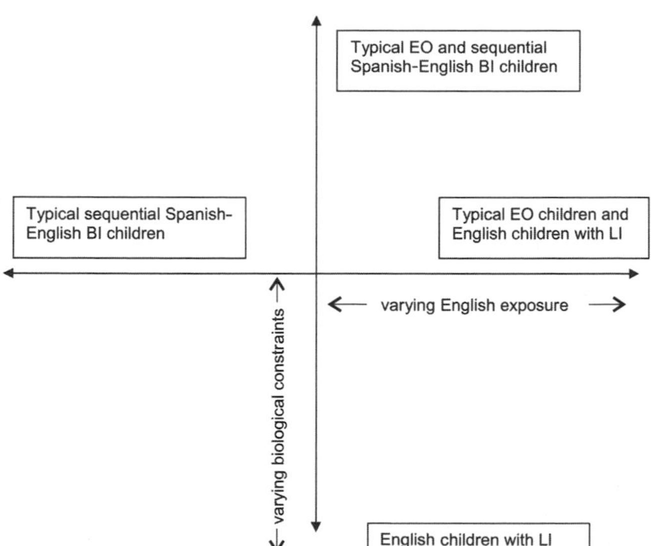

FIGURE 5.1. An illustration of biological and experiential influences on language performance. In all figures, EO, English-only group with no language impairment; BI, bilingual group with no language impairment; LI, English-only group with language impairment.

dren had a history of special educational services for reading and/or language.

Children in the EO and BI groups were typical language learners. Children in the EO group had English language and nonverbal IQ scores no greater than 1 *SD* below the mean. Children in the BI group all had learned Spanish as a first or primary language and attended English-only educational programs. The children had 4–8 years of English experience, and all were able to participate fully in the experimental tasks administered in English. Results from previous studies with bilingual children supported this approach (Kohnert & Bates, 2002; Kohnert, Bates, & Hernandez, 1999). Only bilingual children who had standard scores no greater than 1 *SD* below the mean on both English and Spanish standardized language tests, as well as normal nonverbal IQ scores and typical school achievement, as judged by parent/teacher report, were included as BI group participants. Each group's mean performance on key nonverbal IQ, spoken language, and reading standardized tests is given in Table 5.1. Complete participant details are given by Windsor and Kohnert (2004). Because the participants varied across a 6-year age span, all analyses for the following tasks were adjusted for age, with an expected developmental trend of older children outperforming younger children.

Cognitive–Linguistic Processing Tasks

An overview of the eight experimental tasks is given in Table 5.2. Two tasks emphasized linguistic processing: a word recognition task using phonological

TABLE 5.1. Participant Characteristics

Group	TONI	CELF-E	CELF-S	WRMT-WI	WRMT-PC
EO	110 (12)	114 (13)	—	113 (14)	110 (10)
LI	102 (12)	80 (9)	—	85 (16)	83 (12)
BI	114 (13)	102 (14)	116 (12)	—	—

Note. EO, English-only group with no language impairment; BI, bilingual group with no language impairment; LI, English-only group with language impairment; TONI, Test of Nonverbal Intelligence–3 (Brown, Sherbenou, & Johnsen, 1997); CELF-E and CELF-S, total scores from English (E) and Spanish (S) versions of the Clinical Evaluation of Language Fundamentals–3 (Semel, Wiig, & Secord, 1995, 1997); WRMT—WI and PC, Word Identification and Passage Comprehension subtests of the Woodcock Reading Mastery Tests—Revised (Woodcock, 1987). The WMRT subtests were administered to only the EO and LI groups; the CELF-S was administered to only the BI group. Standard deviations are given in parentheses.

TABLE 5.2. Overview of Tasks

Processing measure	Task	Stimuli and response
Linguistic	Phonological cognate	Two pictures are presented side by side on a computer screen. Children hear a Spanish word that shares some sounds with its English translation and identify the matching picture by pressing one of two response buttons.
	Rapid automatic naming	A series of colors, shapes, and colored shapes are presented for children to name.
Perceptual–motor	Simple auditory detection	Pure tones are presented through headphones. Children indicate a tone is present by pressing a response button.
	Simple visual detection	Blue shapes are shown on a computer screen. Children indicate that a shape is present by pressing a response button.
	Choice auditory detection	Low and high pure tones are presented through headphones. Children indicate which tone is present by pressing one of two response buttons.
	Choice visual detection	Blue and red shapes are shown on a computer screen. Children indicate which color shape is present by pressing one of two response buttons.
Nonlinguistic	Auditory serial memory	Pure tones are presented in paired sequences of 2, 3, 4, and 5 tones. Children make a same–different judgment about each pair by pressing one of two response buttons.
	Tallal Repetition Task	Two brief high and low pure tones are presented. Children replicate the tone sequence by pressing response buttons.

cognates (Kohnert et al., 2004) and a rapid automatic naming task. Four tasks emphasized elementary perceptual–motor processing; these included simple and choice versions of auditory and visual detection tasks (Kohnert & Windsor, 2004). Two tasks emphasized more complex cognitive processing of nonlinguistic stimuli: an auditory serial memory task (Yim, Kohnert, & Windsor, 2005) and the Tallal Repetition Task (Kohnert & Windsor, 2002). We describe each task in detail below, highlighting the central results.

Phonological Cognate Task

Spoken word recognition has long been of interest in LI (Edwards & Lahey, 1996; Windsor & Hwang, 1999). Although there are various explanations for the typical finding of poorer word recognition of children with LI compared to age peers, one underlying theme has been that these children show less detailed or salient phonological representations. This reasoning coincides with research indicating that children with RD (or learning disabilities) also perform more poorly than typical age peers on a wide range of tasks that emphasize phonology (Shankweiler et al., 1995). Investigation of the role of phonology in word recognition also fits well with MacDonald and Christiansen's (2002) proposal of precision of phonological representation as a central biological or cognitive constraint on language performance.

Finally, our previous research with a conventional word recognition task suggested that even when implemented to emphasize information-processing demands, the task was not successful in minimizing the effects of individual differences in language experience and did not reliably separate children with and without LI or RD in monolingual or linguistically diverse populations. Specifically, Windsor and Kohnert (2004) found that neither speed nor accuracy of performance in an online lexical decision task using common stimuli separated English monolingual children with LI from typical English monolingual and proficient Spanish–English bilingual age peers. Given this result, Kohnert et al. (2004) designed the word recognition task of interest here, which emphasized the phonological processing component of word recognition and further deemphasized the role of experience with the test language.

The phonological cognate task relied on "cross-linguistic cognates," which are word pairs from two different languages that share both meaning and form (either phonological or graphemic). For example, *bebe–baby* and *teléfono–telephone* are Spanish–English translation equivalents that show high phonological overlap. Word pairs such as *lago–lake* and *cuna–crib* are also translation equivalents, but here the phonological overlap between Spanish and English in each case is restricted to the initial phoneme. In the cognate task, children were presented with two pictures on a computer screen; one picture was of a common English word that was a member of a cognate pair, and the other picture was an equivalently common noncognate word. Children simultaneously heard the Spanish label for the cognate picture. They then identified the matching picture, with reaction time (RT) being the dependent variable of key interest. There were 80 picture pairs, 20 in each of four conditions of decreasing phonological overlap between the Spanish and English cognates.

In this task, the BI group served as a control group for the LI and EO groups. Whereas the BI group could complete the task through native lexical knowledge, children in the EO and LI groups needed to rely on phonological overlap across cognates rather than direct lexical knowledge to complete the task successfully. Task accuracy was very high for the BI group

(M = 98%) and, as expected, lower for the EO (M = 89.5%) and LI groups (M = 82.5%). For the EO and LI groups, it was expected that words such as *teléfono* and *bebe* would be identified quickly because of the high phonological overlap across the cognates, and that words such as *lago* and *cuna* would be identified more slowly because of the low phonological overlap.

Figure 5.2 shows that this prediction held, with the EO and LI groups showing a slower RT for accurate responses as phonological overlap between English and Spanish words decreased. The EO group was substantially faster in word identification than the LI group across all task conditions. As expected, the BI group had a very fast mean RT across all conditions. The task also was sensitive to the severity of language impairment in the LI group. A subgroup analysis showed that children with milder LI had a faster RT than children with more severe LI; there was a moderately high negative correlation (r = –.52) between language test score and RT (Kohnert et al., 2004).

Rapid Automatic Naming Task

Another well-established, language-based processing task in research on reading is rapid automatic naming (RAN). Although little research has been carried out with children labeled as LI, RAN has been found to be a reliable predictor of reading achievement for at least some subgroups of monolingual and bilingual children (Manis, Lindsey, & Bailey, 2004; Wolf & Bowers, 1999). Previous studies show that RAN performance predicts unique variance in poor readers' reading rate and overall reading achievement that is separate from the variance predicted by phonological processing, memory span, and general language ability. However, there is continued debate about whether RAN reflects a general cognitive-processing speed factor that is independent of language and/or motor processing (Catts, Gillespie, Leonard, Kail, & Miller, 2002; Fletcher et al., 1999). From our perspective, RAN is a linguistic processing task to the extent that performance relies on naming language stimuli, such as digits, colors, or common objects. Within MacDonald and Christiansen's (2002) framework, RAN may rely on both biological constraints of precision of phonological representations and processing speed.

In our research we have used standardized English and Spanish RAN tasks from the Clinical Evaluation of Language Fundamentals–3 (CELF-3; Semel, Wiig, & Secord, 1995, 1997), which rely on naming 36 colors, 36 shapes, or 36 colored shapes. In these tasks, children are asked to name the shape and color pictures as quickly as possible after practice with familiar items. Key dependent variables are accuracy and time taken to name the 36 colored shapes. Forty-five children in the EO group and 25 children in the

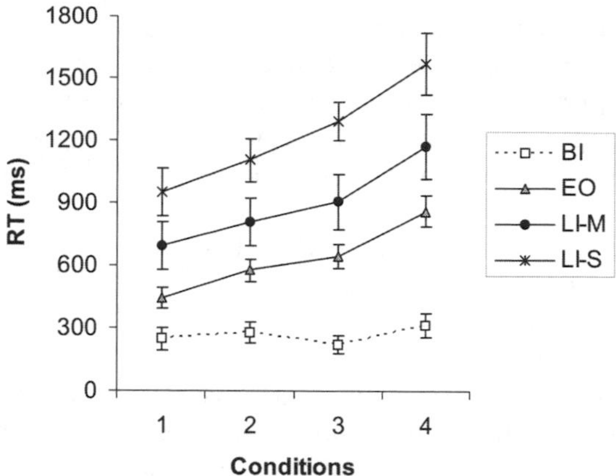

FIGURE 5.2. Mean RT (adjusted for age and perceptual–motor speed) across groups for the phonological cognate task. In all figures, the bars indicate 1 *SE* (standard error of measurement). LI-M and LI-S, mild and severe LI subgroups. Conditions 1–4 reflect decreasing phonological overlap of cognate pairs. This task was administered to five additional children in the BI group (*N* = 27) for a total of 103 participants. From Kohnert, Windsor, and Miller (2004). Copyright 2004. Reprinted with the permission of Cambridge University Press.

LI group were administered the English RAN task; 20 children in the BI group were administered both the English and Spanish task versions.

The results indicated that naming accuracy in English may be sufficient to distinguish between children with and without LI, regardless of native language experience (at least for these proficient bilingual children). Specifically, 84% (38/45) of children in the EO group and 80% (16/20) in the BI group versus 52% (13/25) of the LI group performed at age expectations on this task. Accuracy on the Spanish RAN task increased the percentage of BI children performing at age expectations to 89%. Given that the EO and BI groups comprise typical language learners, the overall accuracy is somewhat lower than expected; nonetheless, the LI group clearly is distinct from the other two groups. Importantly, there also was a significant positive correlation (r = .37) between Spanish and English RAN accuracy for the BI group. This finding suggests that RAN may tap into a common cognitive skills set that underlies performance across languages and reinforces the potential utility of this task for diverse language learners.

Auditory and Visual Detection Tasks

Subtle perceptual–motor difficulties have long been implicated in LI and are hypothesized to reflect a maturational delay in the development of skilled motor movements (Bishop, 1990). Notably, children with LI and RD often perform equivalently on perceptual–motor tasks to children with developmental coordination disorder (DCD), a classification identifying children who are delayed in reaching motor milestones, and are clumsy and uncoordinated (Hill & Bishop, 1998; Kaplan, Dewey, Crawford, & Wilson, 2001). A diagnosis of DCD appears to predict both current and later reading performance (Dewey, Kaplan, Crawford, & Wilson, 2002). Although here we do not assume that slowed or slightly atypical perceptual–motor skills cause language or reading difficulties, this type of overlap suggests that perceptual–motor tasks may well be informative in characterizing the profile of LI and RD. As noted earlier, RT on some perceptual–motor tasks may be a sensitive index of information-processing speed (Bates & Stough, 1998). Thus, investigation of perceptual–motor speed fits well with McDonald and Christiansen's (2002) second central cognitive constraints, that is, processing speed.

Much of the LI literature on perceptual–motor skills has focused on children's RT in auditory and visual detection tasks (responding as quickly as possible to the presence of a briefly presented pure tone or shape). Studies consistently have shown subtle slowing in RT at the group level for children with LI compared to age peers (e.g., Windsor & Hwang, 1999), although the differences often do not achieve statistical significance (for an overview, see Kohnert & Windsor, 2004). Although the RD literature contains a variety of visual tasks, such as visual tracking and discrimination (see Vellutino, Fletcher, Snowling, & Scanlon, 2004), little recent research has examined the perceptual–motor component of visual detection tasks in RD.

We have looked for detection tasks that robustly show performance differences not only between typical monolingual children with and without LI but also between monolingual children with LI and typical bilingual children. Kohnert and Windsor (2004) examined two auditory and two visual detection tasks. The four tasks are summarized here as a group. In both the auditory and visual modality, there was a simple RT task with 100 experimental trials (responding to the presence of a pure tone or colored shape) and a parallel choice RT task (responding differentially to a high/low tone and red/blue shape). To ensure that we emphasized motor processing versus other higher-level cognitive skills, children made their responses in four conditions of increasing motor difficulty. The response conditions included using the preferred or nonpreferred index finger to push a response button (conditions 1 and 2, respectively) and the preferred or nonpreferred foot to push a response pedal (conditions 3 and 4).

Although there was qualitative similarity among the three groups as a function of the motor difficulty of the four response conditions, the four detection tasks were not equal in discriminating among the LI, EO, and BI groups. As shown in Figure 3a, the LI group was substantially slower in all response conditions in the choice visual detection task than the EO and BI groups, with the latter two groups showing overlapping performance. Although individual analyses were not conducted, the standard error of measurement (*SE*) shown in Figure 3a suggests high within-group homogeneity of performance. For comparison, Figure 3b shows results from the parallel simple auditory detection task, in which there is no significant group effect. The difference across task results is striking and well in line with the distinction noted earlier that choice RT tasks are more sensitive than simple RT tasks to underlying processing speed, because they introduce a minimal decision-making component. Although the simple visual and choice auditory detection tasks did statistically separate the LI and EO groups, they did not separate the LI and BI groups, perhaps due to the smaller number of participants in this comparison. However, the trend in both of these tasks was for the BI group to have a faster RT than the LI group. To the extent that processing speed is an important aspect of typical and LI performance, the choice visual detection task seems well suited to differentiate among diverse language learners who may bring different experiences to even elementary cognitive tasks.

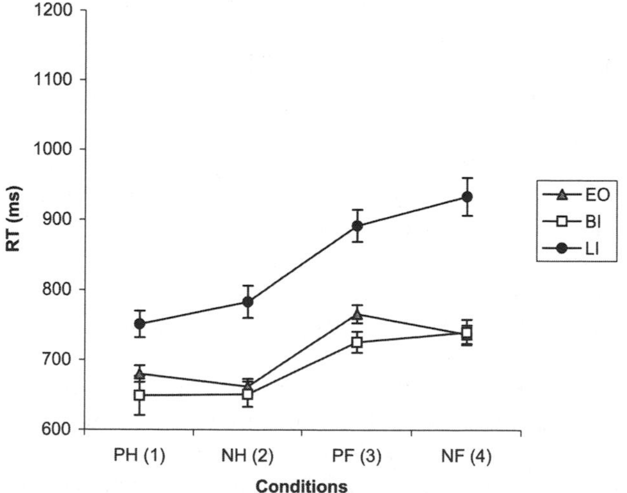

FIGURE 5.3a. Mean RT (adjusted for age) across groups for the choice visual detection task. Accuracy was above 95% for all groups in the choice visual and simple auditory detection tasks. PH (1), responding with preferred hand; NH (2), nonpreferred hand; PF (3), preferred foot; NF (4), nonpreferred foot. From Kohnert and Windsor (2004). Copyright 2004 by the American Speech–Language–Hearing Association. Reprinted by permission.

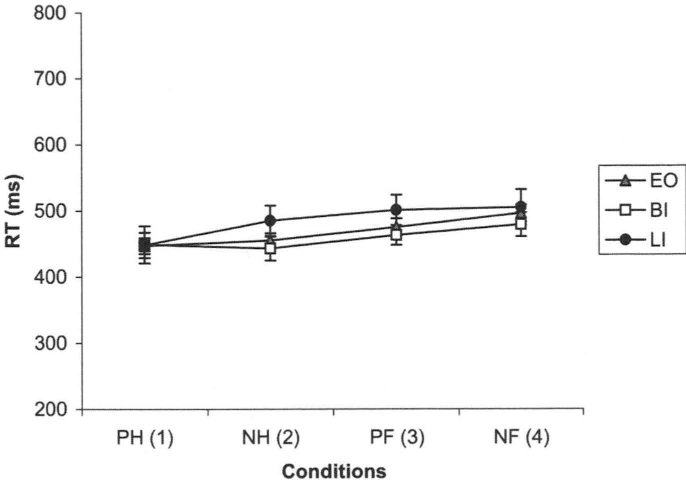

FIGURE 5.3b. Mean RT (adjusted for age) across groups for the simple auditory detection task. Copyright 2004 by the American Speech–Language–Hearing Association. Reprinted by permission.

Auditory Serial Memory Task

A great deal of attention has been paid to the concept of verbal working memory capacity deficits in LI and RD, from both a phonological working memory viewpoint and a broader functional working memory framework (for an overview, see Montgomery, 2002). As noted earlier, MacDonald and Christiansen (2002) have argued that verbal working memory is not a separate cognitive construct, but an aspect of language processing that is affected by an individual's underlying biology and language experience. Digit recall tasks, often considered a measure of phonological memory, provide one potential example to illustrate this perspective. Several investigations of digit recall tasks have shown that children with LI are outperformed by typical age peers on these recall tasks, suggesting that working memory capacity may be a relevant marker for LI (e.g., Conti-Ramsden, 2003). However, counting and recalling numbers may not be an automatic function in the second language for sequential bilinguals, and second-language learners may be outperformed by monolingual speakers, depending on the language in which the digits are to be recalled (Ardila et al., 2000). Less attention has been paid to nonlinguistic memory tasks, although children with LI have been found to be less accurate than age peers in making judgments about some nonlinguistic stimuli, such as brief serial presentations of scribble drawings (Fazio, 1998). Overall, it is possible that memory performance for nonlinguistic stimuli can deemphasize the role of experience across diverse language learners, yet remain a sensitive measure of LI.

The first of our two tasks that emphasized nonlinguistic cognitive processing rather than language or perceptual–motor processing was an auditory serial memory task. The task was administered to all 100 children (Yim et al., 2005). In this task children heard pairs of pure-tone patterns and judged whether the pairs were same or different. The patterns contained 2, 3, 4, and 5 tones in a series of 100 experimental trials (50 same and 50 different pairs). The dependent variables were accuracy and RT for the "same" pairs. Figure 5.4 shows that task accuracy statistically separated the LI group from the two typical groups in this task, with the BI and EO groups showing overlapping performance and equivalently stronger performance than the LI group. Task difficulty affected all groups in a qualitatively similar way, with a systematic decline in accuracy as the series of tones increased in length from two to five tones. A similar pattern of group differences was found for RT as a dependent measure; again, task difficulty affected all groups equivalently, with the hardest condition (memory for five-tone patterns) being particularly difficult for all three groups.

Tallal Repetition Task

In addition to the serial memory component of the auditory task we described, there are arguably other components involved, such as the discrimination of like-sounding stimuli and the same–different comparison of temporal patterns. We were interested in a second type of auditory task that more systematically separated the presumed underlying task components through a series of subtests. We chose the Tallal Repetition Task (Tallal, 1980), because it has a long history in the study of LI and RD. The traditional assumption is that task performance relies on the perception of rapidly presented acoustic information, which in turn underlies phonological representation/awareness, and spoken language and decoding skills. However, there has been continuing debate about whether the task assesses temporal, acoustic, and/or phonetic fundamentals (e.g., Studdert-Kennedy, 2002). In line with Bishop, Carlyon, Deeks, and Bishop (1999), who examined the task performance of children with LI and age peers, we do not necessarily assume that the Tallal Repetition Task assesses temporal processing per se, any more than it might assess nonverbal intelligence, attention, encoding, memory, and so forth. However, we were interested in the task as another measure with potential to deemphasize differences in language-learning experiences among children, so as to highlight the potential biological differences in information processing.

The Tallal Repetition Task includes a series of association, sequencing,

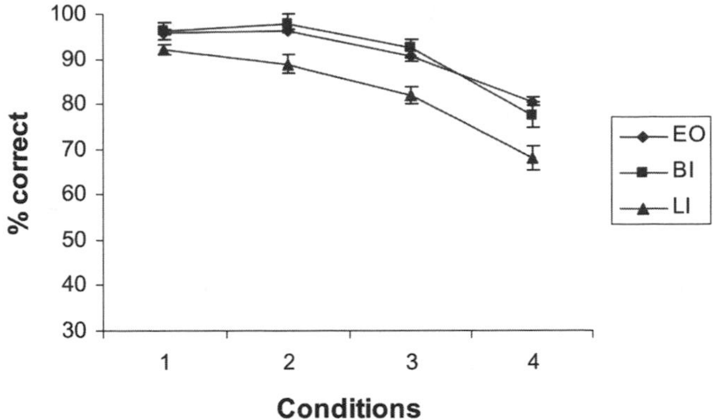

FIGURE 5.4. Mean accuracy (adjusted for age) across groups for the auditory serial memory task. Conditions 1–4 represent 2-, 3-, 4-, and 5-tone patterns. The dependent variable is percentage of correct identification of "same" paired patterns. An analysis of covariance followed by post hoc comparisons showed that the BI and EO groups had equivalent accuracy, $F(2\ 99) = .28$, $p = .60$; the LI group had lower accuracy than both the BI group ($p < .01$) and the EO group ($p < .01$).

discrimination, and serial memory subtests in which children hear two-tone (high and/or low) sequences and replicate these using response buttons. The task procedure is adaptive: The number of trials presented is a function of the child's performance. We administered the task in a conventional way following Tallal (1980): Children reached criterion performance in association and sequencing subtests before participating in the subtest of interest, in which they reproduced a sequence of two 75 ms tones with a 150 ms interstimulus interval. Children "passed" the task if they reached the level of 75% correct reproduction of the two-tone sequence. Kohnert and Windsor (2002) examined the Tallal Repetition Task performance of a subset of 30 randomly selected children in the larger cohort of 100 children, 10 children each in the LI, EO, and BI groups.

Table 5.3 shows the characteristics of the children who passed and failed the task using the conventional 75% criterion. Seven of the 10 children in each of the EO and BI groups, and only 3 children in the LI group, passed the task. Although these are group results from a small sample, the results suggest that this task may have some potential for distinguishing typical children from children with LI or RD. As shown in Table 5.3, English language skill did not appear substantially to influence whether children passed or failed the task in any group. Moreover, unlike the findings of Bishop et al. (1999), nonverbal intelligence did not appear to influence task performance. However, chronological age did contribute to performance. As noted earlier, there appears to be a developmental component to

TABLE 5.3. Performance across Groups for the Tallal Repetition Task

	Pass				Fail			
Group	No. of children	Mean age (yr, mo)	Nonverbal IQ score	Language score	No. of children	Mean age (yr, mo)	Nonverbal IQ score	Language score
EO	7	10,2	107	107	3	9,2	107	107
BI	7	10,2	110	99	3	8,6	112	107
LI	3	10,5	103	83	7	9,5	108	78

Note. EO, English-only group with no language impairment; BI, bilingual group with no language impairment; LI, English-only group with language impairment. $N = 10$ in each group. Scores are standardized test scores from the Test of Nonverbal Intelligence–3 and from the English version of the Clinical Evaluation of Language Fundamentals–3.

the task. Children in each group who failed the task tended to be younger than children who passed.

Theoretical and Educational Implications

The overall findings indicate some methodological utility for selected cognitive–linguistic processing measures in identifying children with LI and RD. Both language-based processing tasks (which deemphasized language experience), a nonlinguistic perceptual–motor task (choice visual detection), and both nonlinguistic auditory tasks separated the LI group in a predictable way from the two groups of typical language learners. It is also important to note that group performance across tasks was affected by chronological age, most clearly exemplified here by performance on the Tallal Repetition Task. This suggests that some cognitive–linguistic processing tasks may be more or less informative assessment tools at specific points in development. Although these key results from our group comparisons are an important first step, it is critical to move toward individual participant profiles across measures and to assess the sensitivity and specificity of these and other measures to move toward any type of diagnostic interpretations. Another point to remember in interpreting the results is that children in the BI group were proficient speakers of both Spanish and English. We have not yet investigated how useful these tasks would be with younger or less sophisticated bilinguals, or with children in the initial stages of learning a second language.

Notably, the monolingual EO and LI groups, as well as the two LI severity subgroups, performed in a qualitatively similar manner across the different conditions of task difficulty in the phonological cognate task; that is, all groups seemed to be affected to the same extent by increasing task demands. In the other processing tasks that emphasized perceptual–motor or higher-level processing for nonlinguistic stimuli, all three groups also performed similarly in response to increased task difficulty. This qualitative equivalence in response to task difficulty suggests that all groups are drawing on the same underlying cognitive processing mechanisms to complete tasks. As a practical correlate, this finding that general order of difficulty in these tasks was robust across groups indicates that the tasks may have high content validity across diverse language learners.

Applying MacDonald and Christiansen's (2002) framework to assessment and intervention, our perspective overall is that traditional measures of children's language performance are insufficient to distinguish among children with poor spoken language and/or literacy skills that are due to biological or experiential causes. Because they deemphasize the role of experience, assessments that focus on linguistic and nonlinguistic processing may be a very useful complement to these traditional measures. Importantly, instructional services are provided for children with poor language and reading performance, regardless of assumptions about the underlying cause. However, with an increasingly culturally and linguistically diverse population, there is abundant reason to separate more carefully the role of experience in distinguishing language disorders (Kan & Kohnert, 2005). Also, it may be that instruction emphasizing efficient processing of elementary linguistic and nonlinguistic material may be a useful complement to more traditional spoken language and reading instruction (see Windsor and Kohnert [in press] for specific assessment and intervention procedures that draw from this type of cognitive–linguistic perspective).

We may also gain some important theoretical insights in our research by specifying an explicit and testable framework for LI and RD. The framework referenced here is an initial attempt to disentangle biological and environmental contributions to language and literacy performance. By virtue of demonstrating that these tasks are not only sensitive (at the group level) to the presence of LI but also do not penalize bilingual children with different language experiences, we can begin to identify key cognitive–linguistic and experiential constructs that may provide increased insight about language and literacy performance. MacDonald and Christiansen's (2002) framework is appealing as a starting point, because it is a very parsimonious approach; that is, language and literacy breakdowns for both monolingual and bilingual language learners can be framed as related constructs within a model of typical variation rather than a priori introducing and reifying categorically separate LI and RD populations. Similarly, the approach to some extent makes moot the wide range of separate causal mechanisms that have been raised for LI and RD. For example, this approach does not introduce a broad range of specific heuristics, such as working memory deficits, or semantic or syntactic representational deficits, as necessary to explain LI or RD. Rather, the framework is compelling, in that it directs us to common biological and experiential constructs and terminology to explain the nature of human language.

ACKNOWLEDGMENTS

Funding for this chapter was provided by two grants from the National Institute of Deafness and Other Communication Disorders (Nos. DC04437 and DC05542) and by a grant from the National Institute of Child Health and Human Development (No. HD053222). Portions of the data reported here were presented at the 2003 Symposium on Research in Child Language Disorders and at the 2002 and 2005 American Speech–Language–Hearing Association Conventions. We gratefully acknowledge the contributions of the following individuals who assisted with task creation: Mark DeRuiter, Caren Dorman, Kerry Danahy, Ruth Miller, and Sara Turman.

REFERENCES

Ardila, A., Rosselli, M., Ostrosky-Solís, F., Marcos, J., Granda, G., & Soto, M. (2000). Syntactic comprehension, verbal memory, and calculation abilities in Spanish–English bilinguals. *Applied Neuropsychology, 7*, 3–16.

Bates, T., & Stough, C. (1998). Improved reaction time method, information processing speed, and intelligence. *Intelligence, 26*, 53–62.

Birren, J. E., & Fisher, L. M. (1995). Aging and speed of behavior: Possible consequences for psychological functioning. *Annual Review of Psychology, 46*, 329–353.

Bishop, D. (1990). Handedness, clumsiness and developmental language disorders. *Neuropsychologia, 28*, 681–690.

Bishop, D. (2001). Genetic influences on language impairment and literacy problems in children: Same or different? *Journal of Child Psychology and Psychiatry and Allied Disciplines, 42*, 189–198.

Bishop, D., Carlyon, R., Deeks, J., & Bishop, S. (1999). Auditory temporal processing impairment: Neither necessary nor sufficient for causing language impairment in children. *Journal of Speech, Language, and Hearing Research, 42*, 1295–1310.

Bishop, D., North, T., & Donlan, C. (1995). Genetic basis of specific language impairment: Evidence from a twin study. *Developmental Medicine and Child Neurology, 37*, 56–71.

Bishop, D., & Snowling, M. (2004). Developmental dyslexia and specific language impairment: Same or different. *Psychological Bulletin, 130*, 858–886.

Brown, L., Sherbenou, R., & Johnsen, S. (1997). *Test of Nonverbal Intelligence–3* (3rd ed.). Austin, TX: Pro-Ed.

Campbell, T., Dollaghan, C., Needleman, H., & Janosky, J. (1997). Reducing bias in language assessment: Processing dependent measures. *Journal of Speech, Language, and Hearing Research, 40*, 519–525.

Caplan, D., & Waters, G. (2002). Working memory and connectionist models of parsing: A reply to MacDonald and Christiansen (2002). *Psychological Review, 109*, 66–74.

Catts, H., Fey, M., Tomblin, J. B., & Zhang, X. (2002). A longitudinal investigation of reading outcomes in children with language impairments. *Journal of Speech, Language, and Hearing Research, 45*, 1142–1157.

Catts, H., Gillispie, M., Leonard, L., Kail, R., & Miller, C. (2002). The role of speed of processing, rapid naming, and phonological awareness in reading achievement. *Journal of Learning Disabilities, 35*, 510–525.

Cerella, J., & Hale, S. (1994). The rise and fall in information-processing rates over the life span. *Acta Psychologica, 86*, 109–197.

Conti-Ramsden, G. (2003). Processing and linguistic markers in young children with specific language impairment (SLI). *Journal of Speech, Language, and Hearing Research, 46*, 1029–1037.

Dewey, D., Kaplan, B., Crawford, S., & Wilson, B. (2002). Developmental coordination disorder: Associated problems in attention, learning, and psychosocial adjustment. *Human Movement Science, 21*, 905–918.

Dromi, E., Leonard, L., & Shteiman, M. (1993). The grammatical morphology of Hebrew-speaking children with specific language impairment: Some competing hypotheses. *Journal of Speech and Hearing Research, 36*, 760–771.

Eden, G., Wood, F., & Stein, J. (2003). Clock drawing in developmental dyslexia. *Journal of Learning Disabilities, 36*, 216–228.

Edwards, J., & Lahey, M. (1996). Auditory lexical decisions of children with specific language impairment. *Journal of Speech and Hearing Research, 39*, 1263–1273.

Fazio, B. (1998). The effect of presentation rate on serial memory in young children with specific language impairment. *Journal of Speech, Language, and Hearing Research, 41*, 1375–1383.

Fletcher, J., Foorman, B., Shaywitz, A., & Shaywitz, B. (1999). Conceptual and methodological issues in dyslexia research: A lesson for developmental disorders. In H. Tager-Flusberg (Ed.), *Neurodevelopmental disorders* (pp. 271–305). Cambridge, MA: MIT Press.

Håkansson, G., & Nettelbladt, U. (1996). Similarities between SLI and L2 children: Evidence from the acquisition of Swedish word order. In C. E. Johnson & J. H. V. Gilbert (Eds.), *Children's language* (Vol. 9, pp. 135–151). Mahwah, NJ: Erlbaum.

Hayiou-Thomas, M., Bishop, D., & Plunkett, K. (2004). Simulating SLI: General cognitive processing stressors can produce a specific linguistic profile. *Journal of Speech, Language, and Hearing Research, 47*, 1347–1362.

Hill, E., & Bishop, D. (1998). A reaching test reveals weak hand preference in specific language impairment and developmental coordination disorder. *Laterality, 3*, 295–310.

Johnston, J., & Ellis Weismer, S. (1983). Mental rotation abilities in language-disordered children. *Journal of Speech and Hearing Research, 26*, 397–403.

Just, M., & Varma, S. (2002). A hybrid architecture for working memory: Reply to MacDonald and Christiansen (2002). *Psychological Review, 109*, 55–65.

Kan, P. F., & Kohnert, K. (2005). Preschoolers learning Hmong and English: Lexical–semantic skills in L1 and L2. *Journal of Speech, Language, and Hearing Research, 48*, 1–12.

Kaplan, B., Dewey, D., Crawford, S., & Wilson, B. (2001). The term *comorbidity* is of questionable value in reference to developmental disorders. *Journal of Learning Disabilities, 34*, 555–565.

Kohnert, K., & Bates, E. (2002). Balancing bilinguals II: Lexical comprehension and cognitive processing in children learning Spanish and English. *Journal of Speech, Language, and Hearing Research, 45*, 347–359.

Kohnert, K., Bates, E., & Hernandez, A. (1999). Balancing bilinguals: Lexical–semantic production and cognitive processing in children learning Spanish and English. *Journal of Speech, Language, and Hearing Research, 42*, 1400–1413.

Kohnert, K., & Windsor, J. (2002, November). *Common ground? Language impairment and second language learners.* Paper presented at the American Speech–Language–Hearing Annual Convention, Atlanta, GA.

Kohnert, K., & Windsor, J. (2004). The search for common ground: Part II. Nonlinguistic performance by linguistically diverse learners. *Journal of Speech, Language, and Hearing Research, 47*, 891–903.

Kohnert, K., Windsor, J., & Miller, R. (2004). Crossing borders: Recognition of Spanish words by English-speaking children with and without language impairment. *Applied Psycholinguistics, 25*, 543–564.

Kohnert, K., Windsor, J., & Yim, D. (2006). Do language-based processing tasks separate children with language impairment from typical bilinguals? *Learning Disabilities Research and Practice, 21*, 19–29.

Kranzler, J., Whang, P., & Jensen, A. (1994). Task complexity and the speed and efficiency of elemental information processing: Another look at the nature of intellectual giftedness. *Contemporary Educational Psychology, 19*, 447–459.

La Paro, K., Justice, L., Skibbe, L., & Planta, R. (2004). Relations among maternal, child, and demographic factors and the persistence of preschool language impairment. *American Journal of Speech–Language Pathology, 13*, 291–303.

Leonard, L. (1998). *Children with specific language impairment.* Cambridge, MA: MIT Press.

MacDonald, M., & Christiansen, M. (2002). Reassessing working memory: Comment on Just and Carpenter (1992) and Waters and Caplan (1996). *Psychological Review, 109*, 35–54.

Manis, F., Lindsey, K., & Bailey, C. (2004). Development of reading in grades K–2 in Spanish-speaking English-language learners. *Learning Disabilities Research and Practice, 19*, 214–224.

Miller, C., Kail, R., Leonard, L., & Tomblin, J. B. (2001). Speed of processing in children with specific language impairment. *Journal of Speech, Language, and Hearing Research, 44*, 416–433.

Montgomery, J. (2002). Understanding the language difficulties of children with specific language impairments: Does verbal working memory matter? *American Journal of Speech–Language Pathology, 11*, 77–91.

Paradis, J., Crago, M., Genesee, F., & Rice, M. (2003). French–English bilingual children with SLI: How do they compare with their monolingual peers? *Journal of Speech, Language, and Hearing Research, 46*, 113–127.

Peña, E., Bedore, L., & Zlatic-Giunta, R. (2002). Category–generation performance of bilingual children: The influence of condition, category, and language. *Journal of Speech, Language, and Hearing Research, 45*, 938–947.

Rodekohr, R., & Haynes, W. (2001). Differentiating dialect from disorder: A comparison of two processing tasks and a standardized language test. *Journal of Communication Disorders, 34*, 255–272.

Roodenrys, C., & Stokes, J. (2001). Serial recall and nonword repetition in reading disabled children. *Reading and Writing, 14*, 379–394.

Semel, E., Wiig, E., & Secord, W. (1995). *Clinical Evaluation of Language Fundamentals* (3rd ed.). San Antonio, TX: Psychological Corporation.

Semel, E., Wiig, E., & Secord, W. (1997). *Clinical Evaluation of Language Fundamentals* (3rd ed.). San Antonio, TX: Psychological Corporation. [in Spanish]

Service, E., Simola, M., Metsänheimo, O., & Maury, S. (2002). Bilingual working memory span is affected by language skill. *European Journal of Cognitive Psychology, 14*, 383–408.

Shankweiler, D., Crain, S., Katz, L., Fowler, A., Liberman, A., Brady, S., et al. (1995). Cognitive profiles of reading-disabled children: Comparison of language skills in phonology, morphology, and syntax. *Psychological Science, 6*, 149–156.

SLI Consortium. (2002). A genome-wide scan identifies two novel loci involve in specific language impairment (SLI). *American Journal of Human Genetics, 70*, 384–398.

Snowling, M., Bishop, D., & Stothard, S. (2000). Is preschool language impairment a risk factor for dyslexia in adolescence? *Journal of Child Psychology and Psychiatry, 41*, 587–600.

Studdert-Kennedy, M. (2002). Deficits in phoneme awareness do not arise from failures in rapid auditory processing. *Reading and Writing, 15*, 5–14.

Swanson, H., Saez, L., Gerber, M., & Leafstedt, L. (2004). Literacy and cognitive functioning in bilingual and nonbilingual children at or not at risk for reading disabilities. *Journal of Educational Psychology, 96*, 3–18.

Tallal, P. (1980). Auditory temporal perception, phonics, and reading disabilities in children. *Brain and Language, 9*, 182–198.

Tomasello, M. (2003). *Constructing a language: A usage-based theory of language acquisition*. Cambridge, MA: Harvard University Press.

Tomblin, B. J., Records, N., Buckwalter, P., Zhang, X., Smith, E., & O'Brien, M. (1997). Prevalence of specific language impairment in kindergarten children. *Journal of Speech, Language, and Hearing Research, 40*, 1245–1260.

Vellutino, F., Fletcher, J., Snowling, M., & Scanlon, D. (2004). Specific reading disability: What have we learned in the past four decades? *Journal of Child Psychology and Psychiatry, 45*, 2–40.

Vellutino, F., Scanlon, D., & Sipay, E. (1997). Toward distinguishing between cognitive and experiential deficits as the primary sources of difficulty in learning to read: The importance of early intervention in diagnosing specific reading disability. In B. Blachman (Ed.), *Foundations of reading acquisition and dyslexia: Implication for early intervention* (pp. 347–379). Mahwah, NJ: Erlbaum.

Windsor, J., & Hwang, M. (1999). Children's auditory lexical decisions: A limited processing account of language impairment *Journal of Speech, Language, and Hearing Research, 42*, 990–1002.

Windsor, J., & Kohnert, K. (2004). The search for common ground: Part I. Lexical performance by linguistically diverse learners. *Journal of Speech, Language, and Hearing Research, 47*, 877–890.

Windsor, J., & Kohnert, K. (in press). Processing speed, attention, and perception: Implications for child language disorders. In R. G. Shwartz (Ed.), *The handbook of child language disorders*. Philadelphia, PA: Psychology Press.

Wolf, M., & Bowers, P. (1999). The double-deficit hypothesis for developmental dyslexias. *Journal of Educational Psychology, 91*, 415–438.

Woodcock, R. (1987). *Woodcock Reading Mastery Tests—Revised.* Circle Pines, MN: American Guidance Service.

Yim, D., Kohnert, K., & Windsor, J. (2005, November). *Sensitivity and specificity to LI for a non-linguistic processing task*. Paper presented at the American Speech–Language–Hearing Annual Convention, San Diego, CA.

6

Functional Neuroimaging Indices of Normal and Atypical Spoken Language

DEBORAH A. WEBER
WILLIAM DAVIS GAILLARD

This chapter considers normal and atypical language processes in children as shown by functional neuroimaging methods. The focus is primarily on atypical processing and organization of language in the brain as identified by functional magnetic resonance imaging (fMRI), with emphasis on epilepsy and, to an extent, stroke populations because these are the most extensively studied domains. fMRI language studies of normal and clinical populations provide insight into factors affecting language organization and reorganization, in addition to increased understanding of atypical language processes.

Although the majority of research to date has focused on adult populations, an increasing number of language studies are being performed in typically and atypically developing children. These studies demonstrate similar language networks in adults and children (Ahmad, Balsamo, Sachs, Xu, & Gaillard, 2003; Bookheimer, Zeffiro, Blaxton, Gaillard, & Theodore, 2000; Brown et al., 2005; Gaillard et al., 2002; Gaillard, Balsamo, Ibrahim, Sachs, & Xu, 2003; Gaillard, Pugliese, et al., 2001; Gaillard, Sachs, Whitnah, et al., 2003; Schlaggar et al., 2002). The focus of the chapter is on fMRI imaging techniques and typical and atypical language development.

fMRI PRINCIPLES

fMRI is increasingly being used to identify areas of the brain implicated in language processing. The noninvasiveness of fMRI studies of language allows investigation into the normal and pathological organization of the neural networks that process language functions. Basic fMRI principles relevant to pediatric studies and patients' studies are presented below. An in-depth review is beyond the scope of this chapter but is available elsewhere (Moonen & Bandettini, 2000).

Mechanism of fMRI

The blood-oxygenation-level-dependent (BOLD) technique is the primary method utilized by fMRI. BOLD fMRI allows for indirect measurement of altered neuronal activity based on detecting signal changes that result from an increase in the ratio of oxygenated to deoxygenated blood associated with increases in blood volume, composition, and flow. Measurements are related to differences in signals between an experimental, or target stimuli, and control, or baseline, conditions that typically alternate in a block design. The entire brain may be imaged, thus providing information regarding localization, in addition to identifying distributed brain networks. Most importantly, fMRI provides a safe means to study both normal and disease states, adding to the information currently available regarding the organization of neuronal systems.

Although the physiology of "activation" is reasonably well understood, that of deactivation is not. "Deactivation" is identified as a decrease in signal during the experimental in relation to the control condition. This may reflect not only decreased blood flow or blood volume but may also represent a "vascular steal," or increased consumption of oxygen without compensation of increased blood flow, among others. As a consequence studies that report deactivations must be interpreted with care.

There are two commonly employed fMRI paradigm designs: the block design and the event-related design. Block designs, which are most commonly used, maximize signal differences between conditions. In a block design, items for each condition are presented over a 20-to 40-second period; typically three to five blocks are obtained for each condition, including control. However, block designs lose the ability to distinguish within the block between individual responses, including the ability to distinguish between correct and incorrect responses. Event-related designs allow for more sophisticated item presentation and analysis. An event-related design presents task items on an individual basis; typically, 25–30 individual trial events are required per condition. The hemodynamic response function, in which peak signal occurs 5 seconds after item presentation and response, is then examined based on behavioral response to each event. In this manner, signal change can be examined on an individual-response basis. For example, memory paradigms may be analyzed between remembered items, in contrast to those not encoded; in a noun–verb generation paradigm, items matched for response time across ages may be examined (Schlaggar et al., 2002). Drawbacks for event-related designs are that the signal-to-noise ratio is less than for block designs, they generally require longer scan runs, and, for language paradigms, are mostly composed of single-word responses (e.g., noun–verb generation or decision rather than reading a sentence or story). Whether using a block or event-related design when working with young children, patient populations, or cognitively impaired individuals, one must ensure that the subject cooperates and can perform the task.

Several approaches differentiate child- and patient-based language studies. Individuals must be able to perform the required task; thus, tasks may need to be adjusted for ability and age. Choosing an appropriate control group is also important and requires a high contrast between experimental and control conditions (Balsamo & Gaillard, 2002; Gaillard, 2004). Random effects analysis is commonly used, because it allows the group finding to be extrapolated to broader populations by treating each individual dataset as an independent event, then examining the probability of activation in a particular region among the group. The older, fixed-effect analysis, employed to reduce the signal-to-noise ratio that derived from older [^{15}O] water position emission tomography (PET) techniques, summed signal in control and experimental conditions prior to statistical comparison between conditions and was more susceptible to outlier effects. Therefore, the results of a random effects analysis are applicable to the population, whereas those of fixed effects analysis are not, though, in practice, results are comparable. Although group studies are typically employed to identify common areas of activation (Gaillard, Grandin, & Xu, 2001), they assume a homogenous population and uniform network for various cognitive functions. However, normal developmental variants and pathological variants found in patient populations may be lost in this analysis strategy (Berl, Vaidya, & Gaillard, 2006). The power of fMRI resides in individual subject analysis, which allows for the study of developmental conditions and disease states.

Paradigm Development

fMRI paradigms can also target several distinct aspects of language processing. Though commonly used, caveats for patient and nonpatient populations include consideration of developmental differences, selection of a task almost everyone can do, and changing the difficulty of the task to match performance and highlight developmental differences. Tasks, such as word generation and naming, are commonly used to bring out developmental differences (see Berl et al. [2006] for more information regarding developmental difference). More recent studies report on sample sizes between 60 and 240 children, thus attaining power to identify factors with modest effects on language organization (Shaywitz et al., 2007; Holland et al., 2001). The literature regarding neural mechanisms of spoken language is small and dominated by PET studies. To date, the majority of fMRI language studies have relied heavily on covert (silent) paradigms, such as passive listening, lexical decision, silent reading, and category decision, due to motion artifacts produced by vocalization. Overall, fMRI provides an effective means to study language processes in normal and disease populations, and provides better understanding of language and other cognitive functions.

LANGUAGE ORGANIZATION IN THE BRAIN

Language processing in humans typically resides along perisylvian areas in the left hemisphere (Gaillard, Moore, Weber, Ritzl, & Berl, 2005). The asymmetry in the planum temporale in both infants and macaques provides evidence for left-hemisphere language dominance and suggests that the networks that process language are evolutionarily selected (Wada, Clarke, & Hamm, 1975).

Further evidence supports this view: Infants as young as 3 months old activate left posterior superior temporal gyrus and left angular gyrus when listening to stories presented in a woman's voice (Dehaene-Lambertz, Dehaene, & Hertz-Pannier, 2002). This activation is similar to left-sided language areas in older children and adults activated by speech perception (Ahmad et al., 2003; Balsamo, 2003; Balsamo et al., 2002; Balsamo, Xu, Sachs, & Gaillard, 2003; Booth et al., 1999, 2000; Dehaene-Lambertz et al., 2002; Moore, Berl, Ritzl, et al., 2003; Gaillard, Pugliesi, et al., 2001; Weber et al., 2005). The requisite need for exposure to and interactions with language early in life, and the ability to sustain language following early left-hemisphere insult, suggests that consolidation and environmental exposure also play a role in formulating mature language-processing networks. This observation supports previous studies that suggest a critical period for language development (Bates & Roe, 2001; Hacaen, 1983; Krashen, 1973; Lenneberg, 1967; Muller & Courchesne, 2000; Muter, Taylor, & Vargha-Khadem, 1997; for a contrary perspective, see Bruer, Chapter 3, this volume).

NORMAL LANGUAGE NETWORKS AS SHOWN BY fMRI

Group maps obtained with fMRI in healthy populations provide information regarding expected typical activation, whereas individual subject analyses in patient populations examine the effect of various developmental conditions and disease on language networks (Gaillard, Grandin, et al., 2001). fMRI allows for the study of healthy volunteers and patients, as young as age 4 years, and provides a framework for understanding the development of networks involved in language processing.

fMRI language studies in normal pediatric populations indicate a left-hemispheric distributed network of language processing fundamentally similar in hemisphic dominance and location to that found in adults. Verbal fluency (phonological and semantic), story listening, reading, sentence comprehension, and semantic–phonological decision paradigms identify networks involved in different aspects of language processing (Balsamo & Gaillard, 2002). When combined, these tasks identify the posterior language comprehension regions found in the left superior temporal sulcus associated with language comprehension, and the anterior "expressive," or word-retrieval network areas found in the inferior frontal gyrus (IFG), also implicated in grammatical processing and speech planning (Gaillard et al., 2004; Geschwind & Galaburda, 1985).

Expressive Language

"Expressive" language processing (i.e., recall, planning speech, fluency, decision) is typically associated with IFG activation. Verbal fluency tasks (semantic and phonological) and verb generation from nouns are among the most common tasks used to identify frontal language areas in fMRI studies (Bookheimer et al., 2000; Brown et al., 2005; Gaillard et al., 2002; Moore et al., 2005; Saling et al., 2006; Holland et al., 2001; Keene, Logan, & McAndrews, 2000; Liegeois et al., 2002; Logan, Smith, & McAndrews, 1999; Poldrack et al., 1999; Schlaggar et al., 2002; Wood et al., 2004). Phonological processing tasks activate areas in the more posterior and inferior aspect of the left IFG (Bookheimer et al., 2000). Areas anterior and inferior to the left IFG are activated by grammatical and semantic decisions (e.g., does a presented word [*duck*] match a given category [animal], or does a presented sentence sound syntactically correct; Poldrack et al., 1999). The left IFG is activated by tasks that require some single-word lexical processing (i.e., decision or word generation), whereas the left mid-frontal gyrus (MFG) is activated in tasks that call upon working memory and application of grammatical rules (Brown et al., 2005; Gaillard et al., 2000; Gaillard, Balsamo, et al., 2003; Holland et al., 2001; Liegeois et al., 2002; Muller, Kleinhans, & Courchesne, 2003; Schlaggar et al., 2002; Shaywitz et al., 2002; Wood et al., 2004).

Comprehension

Semantic comprehension tasks are consistently associated with activation in the left middle temporal gyrus (MTG), and the left temporal–parietal area (Bookheimer, 2002; McDermott, Petersen, Watson, & Ojemann, 2003). On an individual basis, the reading of sentences strongly identifies language comprehension cortex in the temporal region. In children ages 5–12 years, the reading of sentences and stories shows strong activation in the MTG, fusiform, and varying degrees of the MFG (Gaillard, Pugliese, et al., 2001; Gaillard, Balsamo, et al., 2003). Adults and children also show very similar patterns of lateralization and activation in temporal regions in the processing of listening comprehension tasks (Ahmad et al., 2003; Balsamo et al., 2002; Booth et al., 1999, 2000; Ulualp, Biswal, Yetkin, & Kidder, 1998). The basal temporal area (left fusiform and lingual gyrus) are commonly activated in tasks that involve identification, word detection, object naming, and, for reading, letter identification (Balsamo et al., 2003; Gaillard, 2004; Gaillard, Balsamo, et al., 2003; Gaillard, Pugliese, et al., 2001; Shaywitz et al., 2002). See Table 6.1 for examples of fMRI tasks and activation areas.

DEVELOPMENTAL EFFECTS IN LANGUAGE NETWORKS

Expressive and receptive language investigations (Gaillard, Balsamo, et al., 2003; Byars et al., 2002) emphasizing auditory comprehension (Ahmad et al., 2003) show left-hemisphere language activation and indicate that the networks that process language are well established by age 4–5 years. By this age, the patterns of activation, including location and laterality, are essentially the same in children as in adults (Gaillard et al., 2005). There are, however, some important observed developmental differences that we describe in the following sections: (1) laterality of language, especially in frontal regions (Gaillard et al., 2000; Gaillard, Balsamo, et al., 2003, Holland et al., 2001); (2) magnitude of activation, which is linked with age (Holland et al., 2001; Schapiro et al., 2004); (3) areas that grow up and grow down with age (i.e., magnitude); and (4) regional weighting of activation and language processing (Booth et al., 2001; Brown et al., 2005; Schlaggar et al., 2002).

Younger Children

Although verbal fluency, listening comprehension, and reading activation patterns in children are similar to those of adults and strongly left-lateralized, studies suggest that younger left-dominant children may exhibit greater bilateral activation due to recruitment in right homologous regions than that seen in older children and adults, especially in tasks that target IFG and MFG.

There is evidence to suggest that activation related to verbal fluency

TABLE 6.1. Examples of fMRI Tasks and Activation Areas

Language skill	Type of task	Example	Brodmann's area(s) activated
"Expressive" language	Object identification	"Is the object [picture of a dog] an animal?"	44, 45; 20
	Fluency tasks	Covert word generation	44, 45; less 46/9; variable 22
	Semantic fluency	Generate words to categories: animal, food, names Generate noun to verb (ball—throw, pitch, bat)	
	Phonemic fluency	Generate words to the letters *F, A, S* Generate word that rhymes with *cat* (*hat*, *fat*, *bat*)	
"Receptive" language			
Phonological processing	Speech discrimination tasks	"Same/ different" judgments Same: on the first phoneme of words (e.g., *shout–shower*) Different: on the phonetic voicing of the initial consonant (e.g., *dip–tip*)	44, 45
	Phonological decision task	Does presented word contain a certain sound?	44, 45
Decision tasks	Letter-string word identification	Decide if a letter string is a real word or not (*ocean* vs. *oaecn*)	44, 45, 20, 37
	Single-word semantic decision task	"Is presented word [*dog*] an animal?"	44, 45; 46/9; 20
	Sentence semantic decision task	Decide whether descriptions of named objects are correct "A large gray animal is an elephant."	44, 45, 47; 46/9; 22, 39; 37, 20
	Grammatical decision	Decide whether sentence is grammatically correct."A gray elephant leaves eat on the plain."	44, 45, 47; 46/9; 22, 39; 37, 20
Comprehension	Sentence comprehension (reading/visual)	"I like ice cream. Everyday my family goes to the ice cream store."	44, 45; 46/9; 22, 21, 39; 37, 20
	Passage comprehension (listening/auditory)	"Summer Day Story: On a sunny day in June three boys were . . ."	22, 21, 29; variable 44, 45; 46/9

Note. Areas activated include BA 44, 45, and 47 (inferior frontal gyrus); BA 46/9 (medial frontal gyrus); BA 21, 22 (superior/midtemporal gyrus and superior temporal sulcus); BA 39 (supramarginal gyrus); BA 37 (inferior temporal gyrus–occipital junction); and BA 20 (fusiform gyrus).

tasks becomes more unilateral in IFG over time (5- to 7-year olds vs. older children) in magnitude (mean t-score), extent, and laterality (voxel counts) (Moore et al., 2005; Gaillard et al., 2000; Holland et al., 2001). Schapiro and colleagues (2004) extended earlier findings (Holland et al., 2001) and looked at 332 healthy children; they found regionally specific increases in the BOLD effect—in left MFG, left Broca's areas (IFG), anterior cingulate, left Wernicke's area, and the left inferior parietal cortex—during a verb generation task that occurred in conjunction with an increase in age of the children.

Magnitude of Activation

Schlagger and Brown (Brown et al., 2005; Schlaggar et al., 2002) investigated developmental changes during three overt lexical generation and association tasks in an event-related task design: Volunteers generated a single word in response to a word that was visually presented (e.g., noun/verb). Most brain regions showed similar activation between children (7 years and older) and young adults, independent of age or performance. However, the investigators identified brain subregions that showed differences in the magnitude of activation when the task performance was equivalent between children and adults, supporting an age effect, and identified other areas that were performance- but not age-dependent. The left frontal and left parietal cortex, postulated to be associated with later anatomical maturation, exhibited age-related progressive increases in signal magnitude, whereas age-related regressive decreases were observed in areas implicated in regions achieving earlier anatomic maturation, such as the extrastriate cortex. The findings of Schlagger and Brown show continuing developmental specialization and maturational changes in cerebral functional organization for lexical processing. It is a challenge to image awake children in a systematic fashion. Therefore, it is important to recognize that studies in children, and especially in younger children (less than age 7 years), are susceptible to selection bias for cognitive capability and, as a consequence, may not be representative of typically developing children (Balsamo et al., 2003; Gaillard, Balsamo, et al., 2003; Moore et al., 2005).

Overall, evidence supports the theory that areas of language processing may be less consolidated and more bilateral in younger children. The differences observed in fluency tasks between children and young adults, including the degree of laterality in the frontal cortex, and age and performance, occur primarily in association cortex. The more diffuse activation signal sometimes observed in younger children may be a reflection of developmental immaturity of synaptic connections and myelinization in these later-maturing regions (Gaillard, Grandin, et al., 2001). These findings may also provide an explanation for the tendency of language networks in younger children to recover from a brain injury to the dominant hemisphere (Ahmad et al., 2003; Brown et al., 2005; Gaillard et al., 2005; Gaillard, Pugliese, et al., 2001; Gaillard, Sachs, Whitnah, et al., 2003; Holland et al., 2001; Schlaggar et al., 2002).

FMRI, HANDEDNESS, AND LANGUAGE DOMINANCE

fMRI may be used to identify language lateralization in healthy and patient populations. This is typically based on a region of interest (ROI) asymmetry index [AI = (L – R)/(L + R)]. Although language typically is a left-hemispheric process (L; right-hemispheric [R]), laterality and degree of laterality of language are affected by several factors, including task complexity, age, and handedness.

Left-hemispheric language dominance was found in 94% of 100 right-handed healthy adults in a semantic decision task that elicited the bulk of activation in frontal areas (Springer et al., 1999). These studies also found language comprehension activation along the left superior temporal sulcus. In a study of 50 right-handed and 50 left-handed adult volunteers (Pujol, Deus, Losilla, & Capdevila, 1999), left-sided language lateralization was found in 96% of normal right-handed adult volunteers (4% showed a bilateral activation pattern) in an fMRI verbal fluency study targeting frontal language regions. Left-sided language lateralization was found in 76% of normal left-handed volunteers (14% showed bilateral activation and 10% exhibited right-hemisphere language dominance). A follow-up study involving 50 left-handers found 78% of subjects left-dominant for language, 8% right-dominant, and 14% bilateral (Szaflarski et al., 2002). In typically left-dominant individuals, 10–30% activation is reported to occur in the right hemisphere (Ahmad et al., 2003; Gaillard et al., 2000; Moore et al., 2005; Gaillard, Sachs, Whitnah, et al., 2003; Holland et al., 2001; Springer et al., 1999). Few studies have specifically examined language comprehension laterality in temporal areas. However, Weber et al. (2005) found 86–95% dominance in left temporal comprehension cortex in right-handed individuals. Activation, however, is threshold-dependent, and some degree of activation in homologous regions in the nondominant hemisphere is observed in all tasks (Ahmad et al., 2003; Gaillard et al., 2000, 2002; Gaillard, Pugliese, et al., 2001; Gaillard, Sachs, Whitnah, et al., 2003). Increasing task difficulty also results in greater bilateral activation (Gaillard, Pugliese, et al., 2001; Just, Carpenter, Keller, Eddy, & Thulborn, 1996). Although the dominant hemisphere is widely assumed to be responsible for all essential language functions, varying degrees of lateralization of language are possible. Thus, it is unclear whether increased activation of homologous regions represents nonlinguistic aspects of language processing or a recruitment of additional processing for semantics (Gaillard et al., 2002).

fMRI AND SPOKEN LANGUAGE

Paradigms designed to study overt speech commonly comprise tasks such as oral reading, overt picture naming, repetition of heard speech, and speech generation (Huang, Thomas, & Cao, 2001). However, the fundamental assumption that internal speech and external speech are similar or valid replacements for each other appears to be unsupported (Gracco, Tremblay, & Pike, 2005).

For example, Bookheimer, Zeffiro, Blaxton, Gaillard, and Theodore (1995) compared cortical activation during silent compared to overt reading and picture-naming tasks in young adults, and raised the question regarding whether the internal voice actually shares a neural substrate with speaking. They found evidence for a shift from semantic to phonological processing strategies when tasks required overt rather than silent reading. Results from the PET study revealed difference among the tasks. An fMRI study by Huang and colleagues (2001) comparing overt and silent speech also identified differences in silent speech compared to overt speech. Results indicated that silent (covert speech) task paradigms were preferable to overt speech paradigms due to motion artifacts produced by vocalization. However, Huang et al. acknowledged that this was a problem in expanding our understanding of the extent to which neural substrates differ between overt and covert speech.

Similar results were also supported by other studies (e.g., Barch et al., 1999; Price et al., 1994). Palmer and colleagues (2001) looked at overt and covert word-generation tasks with 10 normal adult volunteers and found similar regions of activation during overt and covert task performance. However, the magnitude of activation during the overt task was greater than that during the covert condition. Overt speech studies in children are possible when careful attention is paid to differences in signal change associated with movement in contrast to the delayed BOLD response, as performed in the elegant studies of Brown, Schlagger, and colleagues (Brown et al., 2005; Schlaggar et al., 2002) discussed earlier.

ATYPICAL LANGUAGE DEVELOPMENT

The immature brain has an impressive capacity for reorganization and plasticity; however, differences between children and adults in neurological outcomes suggest some limitation to the plasticity and functional capacity of the brain. Recovery following brain injury is dependent upon developmental status, neural structures under investigation, and the cognitive processes being considered (Booth et al., 2000). Behavioral studies by Booth et al. show that language functions are preferentially preserved in comparison to spatial functions (e.g., the "crowding hypothesis," which states that in cases of early insult or injury, early language will be spared or served by the typically nondominant (right) hemisphere; thus, right-hemispheric functions may be compromised by the sparing and reorganization of language to the right hemisphere). Injury to the left-hemispheric language-processing areas caused by stroke, trauma, or tumor in adults results in profound and persistent aphasia (Geschwind & Galaburda, 1985). In contrast, children experiencing similar insults may develop normal language function. These findings suggest that language functions reorganize to the contralateral hemisphere, which supports the view that at least some brain areas in each hemisphere hold equipotentiality for language function.

The window of plasticity observed in the brain depends in part on when language laterality is established and consolidated. The period of neural plasticity for language is believed to extend through age 5 or 6 years (Balsamo et al., 2002; Gaillard et al., 2005; Janszky, Jokeit, et al., 2003; Muller & Courchesne, 2000). Interhemispheric transfer of language function appears more likely to occur with early injury, whereas intrahemispheric reorganization is more likely to occur in later childhood (Ojemann, Ojemann, Lettichy, & Berger, 1989; Devinsky, Perrine, Llinas, Luciano, & Dogali, 1993). There appears to be a more limited capacity for language reorganization that extends into late childhood and early adolescence.

fMRI language studies in epilepsy, and to a lesser extent, in stroke populations, provide much of what we know regarding the functional neuroanatomy of atypical language representation. Various studies show increased atypical language dominance, including the local and remote effects of epilepsy on language functions, and reveal the patterns of atypical language. From 17 to 33% of adults with childhood-onset localization-related epilepsy exhibit atypical language representation identified by fMRI (Adcock, Wise, Oxbury, Oxbury, & Matthews, 2003; Gaillard, 2004; Springer et al., 1999; Thivard et al., 2005; Woermann et al., 2003). Many of these reports do not indicate the nature of early brain injury or MRI findings; thus, it is difficult to distinguish between the effect of epilepsy or its remote cause on language networks.

Patterns of Atypical Language Activation

Several patterns of activation can be identified that represent atypical language dominance using the paradigms previously described that identify frontal "expressive" cortex and temporal "receptive" cortex. Activation for anomalous language processing nearly always occurs in homologous regions in the right hemisphere (Weber et al., 2005; Gaillard, 2004) Rarely is activation seen outside the distributed language network (Berl et al., 2004; Gaillard, 2004). In epilepsy populations, approximately one-fifth of patients with atypical language are truly right-side dominant, with activation in homologues of Broca's and Wernicke's areas. The more commonly observed patterns are varying degrees of bilateral language that include (1) bifrontal activation, with unilateral temporal activation (bitemporal activation, with unilateral frontal activation is a less common variant); (2) bilateral activation of both temporal and frontal regions; (3) crossed dominance between the temporal and frontal regions (Baciu et al., 2003; Gaillard et al., 2004; Ries et al., 2004; Thivard et al., 2005); and, less commonly, (4) a pattern that is task-dependent (one task is right-, another is left-dominant, with the degree of activation reflecting the paradigm employed; Berl et al., 2004; Gaillard, 2004).

Bilateral activation is a continuum. It is unclear whether the observed bilateral activation is sufficient or necessary to sustain language functions, and it is likely to differ across populations (Gaillard, 2004; Gaillard et al., 2002). Most importantly, these observations highlight the different lateralizing roles of temporal and frontal areas in language processing.

Several studies (e.g., Moore et al., 2005; Springer et al., 1999; Woermann et al., 2003) support the view that age at the time of brain injury or insult, including seizure onset, is a key factor regulating interhemispheric language reorganization. Lesion type and location are also important factors for guiding the expression of atypical language networks. Individuals with congenital stroke/perinatal ischemia (left middle cerebral artery) confirm reorganization of language to homologous regions in the right hemisphere (Booth et al., 1999, 2000; Moore et al., 2005; Staudt et al., 2001, 2002). Perinatal ischemia restricted to frontal periventricular regions results in transfer of frontal processing networks to right homologous regions in proportion to the extent of white matter injury; left-sided language comprehension networks are preserved (Staudt et al., 2001, 2002).

For epilepsy populations, both epileptiform activity and the underlying remote cause contribute to language reorganization. All the patients we have studied in our series with early middle cerebral artery stroke have typical language representation. One-third of patients with neocortical epilepsy, one-fifth of patients with mesial temporal sclerosis, and only one-sixth of patients with tumors or focal cortical dysplasia exhibit atypical language (Labate, Briellmann, Waites, Harvey, & Jackson, 2004). Epilepsy patients with atypical language fall within the normal range of language abilities (though lower than controls in fMRI studies); the stroke population and epilepsy patients have lower language measures, as is expected, but this does not impact the language maps (Gaillard et al., 2005). Furthermore, we find little evidence for intrahemispheric reorganization for language in patients with a left-seizure focus or lesion but who remain left language dominant (Rosenberger et al., 2006).

The impact of dysplasia on language functions is mixed. A "dysplastic" cortex can sustain language processing, but when the dysplasia is extensive and encompasses the whole IFG or superior temporal gyrus, then language functions are more likely to shift to adjacent brain areas or to right homologues (Janszky, Ebner, et al., 2003; Keene, Olds, & Logan, 2004; Smith et al., 2004). Liegeois and colleagues (2004) found that four of five children with developmental lesions in the temporal lobe removed from Wernicke's area had atypical activation, whereas only one in five children with Broca's area lesions had right-dominant language. Their observations support a role for epilepsy, in addition to the pathological lesion, as a contributing factor in the establishment of atypical language networks.

Berl et al. (2005) found evidence for compensatory mechanisms in their study using a reading responsive naming task (What is a long yellow fruit?), which indicated both widespread and focal effects on regional and hemispheric distribution of language processing. fMRI studies suggested activation within a broad network, with localization and laterality determined by site of foci. Billingsley, McAndrews, Crawley, and Mikulis (2001) also provided evidence for compensatory mechanisms in a study comparing semantic and phonemic tasks in adults with childhood-onset right temporal lobe epilepsy (RTLE) and left temporal lobe epilepsy (LTLE). They reported greater left dorsolateral prefrontal activation and increased signal change in right middle temporal areas in patients (adults and children) with LTLE than in controls during a semantic decision task, but not during a phonological task. Poorer performance occurred during measures of linguistic skills in patients with TLE compared with healthy controls (Billingsley et al., 2001). Changes in the patterns of activation in language networks implicate shifts in cognitive strategies and compensation necessary to preserve language functions.

These findings support the notion that the cerebral plasticity and capacity of the nondominant right hemisphere for language functions depends upon the complexity of functions requiring compensation, age of onset of structural–functional damage, and the extent of the dominant hemisphere lesion (Muller & Courchesne, 2000; Gaillard et al., 2005). These observations suggest that only evolutionarily defined brain areas have the capacity to sustain language, but they also raise the question of whether right-hemisphere activation represents the persistence of an immature pattern or true transfer of language functions to the right hemisphere.

Autism and Dyslexia

Research also suggests that brain activation in children with dyslexia differs from that of typically developing children during auditory language tasks.

A popular experimental view suggests that dyslexia represents a disorder in the phonological processing system (Shaywitz, Lyon, & Shaywitz, 2006). In a study by Corina et al. (2001), children with dyslexia had more activity than control subjects in the left precentral gyrus and the right inferior temporal gyrus on a phonological judgment task. However, during a lexical judgment task, children with dyslexia had more activity in the left orbitofrontal cortex but less activity in the bilateral MFG than controls. Georgiewa et al. (1999) found significant activation pattern differences in the left inferior temporal region and in Broca's area in children with normal and dyslexic reading during phonological transformation and non-word-reading tasks. Shaywitz et al. (2002) found that children with dyslexia exhibited an alteration in activation patterns elicited by a reading single non-word-rhyming task involving posterior regions of the brain. Age-related changes in children with dyslexia identify increasing left inferior gyrus activation with age. In contrast, nonimpaired readers demonstrate increased activation in temporal–occipital cortex (Shaywitz et al., 2007). Eden et al. (2004) looked at phonologically targeted training in adults with dyslexia and found improved performance, with associated signal increases in left-hemisphere regions activated in normal readers, and additional recruitment in the right perisylvian cortex.

There are no language studies in children with autism, but there are studies in older patients with Asperger's within the autistic spectrum disorders, where language regression is not present, though mild impairments in language profiles are found. In a functional imaging study by Harris et al. (2006), adults with autism spectrum disorder showed reduced Broca's area activation. However, activation was increased in Wernicke's area (left temporal). Additionally, the autism group had differences in activation between abstract and concrete words. Just, Cherkassky, and Keller (2004) found similar group differences in connectivity in Wernicke's and Broca's areas. Specifically, the autism group had more reliable activation in Wernicke's area and reliably less activation in Broca's area compared to the control group.

A fundamental challenge in these developmental disorders is to study language when it is impaired; the studies are limited to single-word or pseudoword paradigms. Studies show that the classical areas for processing language are used, but they may show less robust activation. In addition, activation patterns do not show expected maturation with age (with some regions becoming more strongly activated [e.g., left] and others less utilized [e.g., right side]; Turkeltaub, Gareau, Flowers, Zeffilo, & Eden, 2003; Turkelbaub, Eden, Jones, & Zeffilo, 2002; Shaywitz et al., 2007). Some studies also show additional recruitment of areas outside classical language areas, suggesting recruitment of less mature or "efficient" strategies (e.g., for dyslexia, greater activation in the left IFG rather than BA 37) or areas implicated in attention and cognitive control. These findings are fundamentally different than those for epilepsy or stroke populations, in which language function is relatively well preserved and exhibits compensation within a broadly distributed network and its homologues.

CONCLUSIONS

fMRI studies of language provide a noninvasive means to study normal and atypical organization of the neural networks that process language. Studies of children with brain dysfunction provide insight into the plasticity of language networks. In particular, these studies provide information regarding the location, timing, and extent of reorganized language processing (Gaillard et al., 2005). Research confirms that the fundamental aspects of both comprehension and expression of language are well established by age 4 or 5 years, though abilities continue to be refined over the ensuing 5–10 years.

Furthermore, activation patterns are similar in relation to location and degree of left-hemisphere laterality in children this age and in adults. Studies of disease mechanisms (e.g.,, from stroke and epilepsy) suggest that reorganization of language functions to homologous regions in the typically nondominant right hemisphere usually occurs before the age of 6 years. Destructive disease processes (e.g., inflammation and stroke) are more likely to drive language reorganization, whereas developmental processes (e.g., tumors and dysplasia) are less likely to result in interhemispheric reorganization. Additionally, reorganization may be regional, may involve widespread hemispheric language networks, or may reflect an immature and less efficient strategy within a larger distributed language network. It is rare for activation to occur in regions outside traditional language-processing areas. Reorganization or compensation of language in response to focal brain injury can occur, with diminishing capacity, into late childhood and early adolescence, and is restricted to the distributed network for language processing in the left hemisphere and its homologues in the right hemisphere.

ACKNOWLEDGMENTS

This work was supported by Grant No. RO1 NS44280 from the National Institute of Neurological Disorders and Stroke; Mental Retardation and Developmental Disabilities Center Grant No. P30HD40677 from the National Institute of Child Health and Human Development; General Clinical Research Center Grant No. MO1RR020359; and the Clinical Epilepsy Section, National Institute of Neurological Disorders and Stroke, National Institutes of Health.

REFERENCES

Adcock, J. E., Wise, R. G., Oxbury, J. M., Oxbury, S. M., & Matthews, P. M. (2003). Quantitative fMRI assessment of the differences in lateralization of language-related brain activation in patients with temporal lobe epilepsy. *NeuroImage, 18*(2), 423–438.

Ahmad, Z., Balsamo, L. M., Sachs, B. C., Xu, B., & Gaillard, W. D. (2003). Auditory comprehension of language in young children: Neural networks identified with fMRI. *Neurology, 60*(10), 1598–1605.

Anderson, D. P., Harvey, A. S., Saling, M. M., Anderson, V., Kean, M., Abbott, D. F., Wellard, R. M., Jackson, G. D. (2006). fMRI lateralization of expressive language in children with cerebral lesions. *Epilepsia, 47*, 998–1008.

Baciu, M. V., Watson, J. M., McDermott, K. B., Wetzel, R. D., Attarian, H., Moran, C. J., et al. (2003). Functional MRI reveals an interhemispheric dissociation of frontal and temporal language regions in a patient with focal epilepsy. *Epilepsy and Behavior, 4*(6), 776–780.

Balsamo, L. (2003). *Neural representation and function of language in children with new onset partial epilepsy.* Unpublished doctoral dissertation, American University, Washington, DC.

Balsamo, L. M., & Gaillard, W. D. (2002). The utility of functional magnetic resonance imaging in epilepsy and language. *Current Neurology and Neuroscience Reports, 2*(2), 142–149.

Balsamo, L. M., Xu, B., Grandin, C. B., Petrella, J. R., Braniecki, S. H., Elliott, T. K., et al. (2002). A functional magnetic resonance imaging study of left hemisphere language dominance in children. *Archives of Neurology, 59*(7), 1168–1174.

Balsamo, L. M., Xu, B., Sachs, B., & Gaillard, W. D. (2003). Language networks underlying auditory based category decision in children identified with fMRI. *Annals of Neurology, 54*(Suppl. 7), S105.

Balsamo, L. M., Xu, B., Gaillard, W. D. (2006). Language lateralization and the role of the fusiform gyrus in semantic processing in young children. *NeuroImage, 31*, 1306–1314.

Barch, D. M., Sabb, F. W., Carter, C. S., Braver, T. S., Noll, D. C., & Cohen, J. D. (1999). Overt verbal responsing during fMRI scanning: Empirical investigations of problems and potential solutions. *NeuroImage, 10*, 642–657.

Bates, E., & Roe, K. (2001). Language development in children with unilateral brain injury. In C. A. Nelson & M. Luciano (Eds.), *Handbook of developmental cognitive neuroscience.* Cambridge, MA: MIT Press.

Berl, M. M., Balsamo, L. M., Xu, B., Moore, E. N., Weinstein, S.L., Conry, J. A., et al. (2005). Seizure focus affects regional language networks assessed by fMRI. *Neurology, 65*(10), 1604–1611.

Berl, M. M., Moore, E. N., Xu, B., Pearl, P. L., Conry, J. A., Weinstein, S. L., et al. (2004). Atypical language dominance and patterns of reorganization in epilepsy as assessed by a panel of fMRI tasks. *Epilepsia, 45*(Suppl. 7), 306.

Berl, M. M., Vaidya, C., Gaillard, W. D. (2006). Functional imaging of development and adaptive changes in neurocognition. *NeuroImage, 30*, 679–691.

Billingsley, R. L., McAndrews, M. P., Crawley, A. P., & Mikulis, D. J. (2001). Functional MRI of phonological and semantic processing in temporal lobe epilepsy. *Brain, 124*(6), 1218–1227.

Bookheimer, S. (2002). Functional MRI of language: New approaches to understanding the cortical organization of semantic processing. *Annual Review of Neuroscience, 25*, 151–188.

Bookheimer, S., Zeffiro, T. A., Blaxton, T., Gaillard, W., & Theodore, W. (1995). Regional cerebral blood flow during object naming and work reading. *Human Brain Mapping, 3*, 93–106.

Bookheimer, S. Y., Zeffiro, T. A., Blaxton, T. A., Gaillard, P. W., & Theodore, W. H. (2000). Activation of language cortex with automatic speech tasks. *Neurology, 55*(8), 1151–1157.

Booth, J. R., Burman, D. D., Van Santen, F. W., Harasaki, Y., Gitelman, D. R., Parrish, T. B., et al. (2001). The development of specialized brain systems in reading and oral language. *Neuropsychology, 7*(3), 119–141.

Booth, J. R., MacWhinney, B., Thulborn, K. R., Sacco, K., Voyvodic, J., & Feldman, H. M. (1999). Functional organization of activation patterns in children: whole brain fMRI imaging during three different cognitive tasks. *Progress in Neuropsychopharmacology and Biological Psychiatry, 23*(4), 669–682.

Booth, J. R., MacWhinney, B., Thulborn, K. R., Sacco, K., Voyvodic, J. T., & Feldman, H. M. (2000). Developmental and lesion effects in brain activation during sentence comprehension and mental rotation. *Developmental Neuropsychology, 18*(2), 139–169.

Brown, T. T., Lugar, H. M., Coalson, R. S., Miezin, F. M., Petersen, S., & Schlaggar, B. L. (2005). Developmental changes in human cerebral functional organization for word generation. *Cerebral Cortex, 15*(3), 275–290.

Byars, A. W., Holland, S. K., Strawsburg, R. H., Bommer, W., Dunn, R. S., Schmithorst, V. J., et al. (2002). Practical aspects of conducting large-scale functional magnetic resonance imaging studies in children. *Journal of Child Neurology, 17*(12), 885–890.

Corina, D. P., Richards, T. L., Serafini, S., Richards, A. L., Steury, K., Abbott, R. D., et al. (2001). fMRI auditory language difference between dyslexic and able reading children. *Neuroreport, 12*(6), 1195–1201.

Dehaene-Lambertz, G., Dehaene, S., & Hertz-Pannier, L. (2002). Functional neuroimaging of speech perception in infants. *Science, 298*, 2013–2015.

Devinsky, O., Perrine, K., Llinas, R., Luciano, D. J., & Dogali, M. (1993). Anterior temporal language areas in patients with early onset of temporal lobe epilepsy. *Annals of Neurology, 34*(5), 727–732.

Eden, G. F., Jones, K. M., Cappell, K., Gareau, L., Wood, F. B., Zeffiro, T. A., et al. (2004). Neural changes following remediation in adult developmental dyslexia. *Neuron, 44*, 411–422.

Gaillard, W. D. (2004). Functional MR imaging of language, memory, and sensorimotor cortex. *Neuroimaging Clinics of North America, 14*(3), 471–485.

Gaillard, W. D., Balsamo, L. M., Ibrahim, Z., Sachs, B. C., & Xu, B. (2003). fMRI identifies regional specialization of neural networks for reading in young children. *Neurology, 60*(1), 94–100.

Gaillard, W. D., Balsamo, L., Xu, B., Grandin, C. B., Braniecki, S. H., Papero, P. H., et al. (2002). Language dominance in partial epilepsy patients identified with an fMRI reading task. *Neurology, 59*(2), 256–265.

Gaillard, W. D., Balsamo, L., Xu, B., McKinney, C., Papero, P. H., Weinstein, S., et al. (2004). fMRI language task panel improves determination of language dominance. *Neurology, 63*(8), 1403–1408.

Gaillard, W. D., Grandin, C. B., & Xu, B. (2001). Developmental aspects of pediatric fMRI: Considerations for image acquisition, analysis, and interpretation. *NeuroImage, 13*(2), 239–249.

Gaillard, W. D., Hertz-Pannier, L., Mott, S. H., Barnett, A. S., LeBihan, D., & Theodore, W. H. (2000). Functional anatomy of cognitive development: fMRI of verbal fluency in children and adults. *Neurology, 54*(1), 180–185.

Gaillard, W. D., Moore, E. N., Weber, D. A., Ritzl, E. K., & Berl, M. M. (2005). fMRI of normal and pathological language development. In A. Arzimanogou (Ed.), *Cognitive dysfunction in children with temporal lobe epilepsy.* Surrey, England: John Libbey Eurotext.

Gaillard, W. D., Pugliese, M., Grandin, C. B., Braniecki, S. H., Kondapaneni, P., Hunter, K., et al. (2001). Cortical localization of reading in normal children: An fMRI language study. *Neurology, 57*(1), 47–54.

Gaillard, W. D., Sachs, B. C., Whitnah, J. R., Ahmad, Z., Balsamo, L. M., Petrella, J. R., et al. (2003). Developmental aspects of language processing: fMRI of verbal fluency in children and adults. *Human Brain Mapping, 18*(3), 176–185.

Georgiewa, P., Rzanny, R., Hopf, J. M., Knab, R., Glauche, V., Kaiser, W. A., et al. (1999). fMRI during word processing in dyslexic and normal reading children. *Neuroreport, 10*(16), 3459–3465.

Geschwind, N., & Galaburda, A. M. (1985). Cerebral lateralization: Biological mechanisms, associations, and pathology: A hypothesis and a program for research. *Archives of Neurology, 42*, 428–459.

Gracco, V. L., Tremblay, P., & Pike, B. (2005). Imaging speech production using fMRI. *NeuroImage, 26*, 294–301.

Hacaen, H. (1983). Acquired asphasia in children: Revisited. *Neuropsychologia, 21*, 581–587.

Harris, G. J., Chabris, C. F., Clark, J., Urban, T., Aharon, I., Steele, S., et al. (2006). Brain activation during semantic processing in autism spectrum disorders via functional magnetic resonance imaging. *Brain Cognition, 61*(1), 54–68.

Holland, S. K., Plante, E., Weber Byars, A., Strawsburg, R. H., Schmithorst, V. J., & Ball, W. S. (2001). Normal fMRI brain activation patterns in children performing a verb generation task. *NeuroImage, 14*, 837–843.

Huang, J., Thomas, H. C., & Cao, Y. (2001). Comparing cortical activations for silent and overt speech using event-related fMRI. *Human Brain Mapping, 15*, 39–53.

Janszky, J., Ebner, A., Kruse, B., Mertens, M., Jokeit, H., Seitz, R. J., et al. (2003). Functional organization of the brain with malformations of cortical development. *Annals of Neurology, 53*(6), 759–767.

Janszky, J., Jokeit, H., Heinemann, D., Schulz, R., Woermann, F. G., & Ebner, A. (2003). Epileptic activity influences the speech organization in medial temporal lobe epilepsy. *Brain, 126*(9), 2043–2051.

Just, M. A., Carpenter, P. A., Keller, T. A., Eddy, W. F., & Thulborn, K. R. (1996). Brain activity modulated by sentence comprehension. *Science, 274*, 114–116.

Just, M. A., Cherkassky, V. L., & Keller, T. A. (2004). Cortical activation and synchronization during sentence comprehension in high-functioning autism: Evidence of underconnectivity. *Brain, 127*(8), 1811–1821.

Keene, D. L., Logan, W. J., & McAndrews, M. P. (2000). A comparison of three functional MRI language paradigms in children. *Epilepsia, 41*, 193.

Keene, D. L., Olds, J., & Logan, W. J. (2004). Functional MRI study of verbal fluency in a patient with subcortical laminar heterotopia. *Canadian Journal of Neurological Sciences, 31*(2), 261–264.

Krashen, S. D. (1973). Lateralization, language learning, and the critical period: Some new evidence. *Language Learning, 23*(1), 63–74.

Labate, A., Briellmann, R., Waites, A. B., Harvey, A. S., & Jackson, G. (2004). Temporal lobe developmental tumors: An fMRI study for language lateralization. *Epilepsia, 41*, 1456–1462.

Lenneberg, E. H. (1967). *Biological foundations of language.* New York: Wiley.

Liegeois, F., Connelly, A., Cross, J. H., Boyd, S. G., Gadian, D. G., Vargha-Khadem, F., et al. (2004). Language reorganization in children with early-onset lesions of the left hemisphere: An fMRI study. *Brain, 127*(Pt 6), 1229–1236.

Liegeois, F., Connelly, A., Salmond, C. H., Gadian, D. G., Vargha-Khadem, F., & Baldeweg, T. (2002). A direct test for lateralization of language activation using fMRI: Comparison with invasive assessments in children with epilepsy. *NeuroImage, 17*(4), 1861–1867.

Logan, W. J., Smith, M. I., & McAndrews, M. P. (1999). Lateralization of language in chidren with functional MRI compared to intracarotid amobarbital procedures. *Epilepsia, 40*, 44.

McDermott, K. B., Petersen, S. E., Watson, J. M., & Ojemann, J. G. (2003). A procedure for identifying regions preferentially activated by attention to semantic and phonological relations using functional magnetic resonance imaging. *Neuropsychologia, 41*(3), 293–303.

Moonen, C. T. W., & Bandettini, P. A. (2000). *Functional MRI.* Heidelberg: Springer.

Moore, E. N., Berl, M. M., Ritzl, E. K., Cho, Y. W., Weber, D. A., Pearl, P. L., et al. (2005). Association between epilepsy and atypical language dominance assessed by a panel of fMRI tasks. *Epilepsia, 46*(Suppl. 8), 53–54.

Muller, R. A., & Courchesne, E. (2000). The duplicity of plasticity: A conceptual approach to the study of early lesion and developmental disorders. In M. Ernst & J. Rumsey (Eds.), *The foundation and future of functional neuroimaging in child psychiatry.* New York: Cambridge University Press.

Muller, R. A., Kleinhans, N., & Courchesne, E. (2003). Linguistic theory and neuroimaging evidence: An fMRI study of Broca's area in lexical semantics. *Neuropsychologia, 41*, 1199–1207.

Muter, V., Taylor, S., & Vargha-Khadem, F. (1997). A longitudinal study of early intellectual development in hemiplegic children. *Neuropsychologia, 35*(3), 289–298.

Ojemann, G., Ojemann, J., Lettichy, E., & Berger, M. (1989). Cortical languge localization in left, dominant hemisphere. *Journal of Neurosurgery, 71*, 316–326.

Palmer, E. D., Rosen, H. J., Ojemann, J. G., Buckner, R. L., Kelley, W. M., & Peteren, S. E. (2001). An event-related fMRI study of overt and covert word stem completion. *NeuroImage, 14*, 182–193.

Poldrack, R. A., Wagner, A. D., Prull, M. W., Desmond, J. E., Glover, G. H., &

Gabrieli, J. D. (1999). Functional specialization for semantic and phonological processing in the left inferior prefrontal cortex. *NeuroImage, 10*, 15–35.

Price, C. J., Wise, R. J. S., Watson, J. D. G., Patterson, K., Howard, D., & Frankowiak, R. S. J. (1994). Brain activity during reading: The effects of exposure duration and task. *Brain, 117*, 1255–1269.

Pujol, J., Deus, J., Losilla, J., & Capdevila, A. (1999). Cerebral lateralization of language in normal left-handed people studied by functional MRI. *Neurology, 52*(5), 1038–1043.

Ries, M., Boop, F. A., Griebel, M. L., Zou, P., Phillips, N. S., Johnson, S. C., et al. (2004). Functional MRI and Wada determination of language lateralization: A case of crossed dominance. *Epilepsia, 45*(1), 85–89.

Rosenberger, L. A., Berl, M. M., Ritzl, E. K., Moore, E. N., Fieldstone, S., Weber, D., et al. (2006). Atypical frontal language activation occurs in the right homologue of Broca's area. *Epilepsia, 47*(Suppl. 3), 1.179.

Schapiro, M. B., Schmithorst, V. J., Wilke, M., Weber Byars, A., Strawsburg, R. H., & Holland, S. (2004). Bold fMRI signal increases with age in selected brain regions in children. *Brain Imaging, 15*(17), 2575–2578.

Schlaggar, B. L., Brown, T. T., Lugar, H. M., Visscher, K. M., Miezin, F. M., & Petersen, S. E. (2002). Functional neuroanatomical differences between adults and school-age children in the processing of single words. *Science, 296*(5572), 1476–1479.

Shaywitz, B. A., Lyon, G. R., & Shaywitz, S. E. (2006). The role of functional magnetic resonance imaging in understanding reading and dyslexia. *Developmental Neuropsychology, 30*, 613–632.

Shaywitz, B. A., Shaywitz, S. E., Pugh, K. R., Mencl, W. E., Fulbright, R. K., Skudlarski, P., et al. (2002). Disruption of posterior brain systems for reading in children with developmental dyslexia. *Biological Psychiatry, 52*(2), 101–110.

Shaywitz, B. A., Skudlarski, P., Holahan, J. M., Marchione, K. E., Constable, R. T., Fulbright, R. K., et al. (2007). Age related changes in reading systems of dyslexic children. *Annals of Neurology, 61*, 363–370.

Smith, M. L., Bernal, B., Duchowny, M., Dunoyer, C., Jayakar, P., & Altman, N. R. (2004). Severity of focal cortical dysplasia and functional organization of the brain. *Epilepsia, 45*, 357.

Springer, J. A., Binder, J. R., Hammeke, T. A., Swanson, S. J., Frost, J. A., Bellgowan, P. S., et al. (1999). Language dominance in neurologically normal and epilepsy subjects: A functional MRI study. *Brain, 122*(11), 2033–2046.

Staudt, M., Grodd, W., Niemann, G., Wildgruber, D., Erb, M., & Krageloh-Mann, I. (2001). Early left periventricular brain lesions induce right hemispheric organization of speech. *Neurology, 57*, 122–125.

Staudt, M., Lidzba, K., Wolfgang, G., Wildgruber, D., Michael, E., & Krageloh-Mann, I. (2002). Right-hemispheric organization of language following early left-sided brain lesions: Functional MRI topography. *NeuroImage, 16*, 954–967.

Szaflarski, J. P., Binder, J. R., Possing, E. T., McKiernan, K. A., Ward, B. D., & Hammeke, T. A. (2002). Language lateralization in left-handed and ambidextrous people: fMRI data. *Neurology, 59*(2), 238–244.

Thivard, L., Hombrouck, J., Montcel, T., Delmaire, C., Cohen, L., Samson, S., et al.

(2005). Productive and perceptive language reorganization in temporal lobe epilepsy. *NeuroImage, 24*, 841–851.

Turkeltaub, P. E., Eden, G. F., Jones, K. M., Zeffiro, T. A. (2002). Meta-analysis of the functional neuroanatomy of single-word reading: Method and validation. *NeuroImage, 16*, 765–780.

Turkeltaub, P. E., Gareau, L., Flowers, D. L., Zeffiro, T. A., & Eden, G. F. (2003). Development of neural mechanisms for reading. *Nature Neuroscience, 6*, 767–773.

Ulualp, S. O., Biswal, B. B., Yetkin, F. Z., & Kidder, T. M. (1998). Functional magnetic resonance imaging of auditory cortex in children. *Laryngoscope, 108*, 1782–1786.

Wada, J. A., Clarke, R., & Hamm, A. (1975). Cerebral hemispheric asymmetry in humans: Cortical speech zones in 100 adults and 100 infant brains. *Archives of Neurology, 32*, 239–246.

Weber, D. A., Berl, M. M., Moore, E. N., Gioia, G. A., Ritzl, E. K., Ratner, N. B., et al. (2005). TLE and cognition in children: Will fMRI be of some help in better understanding the mechanisms involved? In A. Arzimanogou (Ed.), *Cognitive dysfunction in children with temporal lobe epilepsy*. Surrey, England: John Libbey Eurotext.

Woermann, F. G., Jokeit, H., Luerding, R., Freitag, H., Schulz, R., Guertler, S., et al. (2003). Language lateralization by Wada test and fMRI in 100 patients with epilepsy. *Neurology, 61*(5), 699–701.

Wood, A. G., Harvey, A. S., Wellard, R. M., Abbott, D. F., Anderson, V., Kean, M., et al. (2004). Language cortex activation in normal children. *Neurology, 63*(6), 1035–1044.

7

Magnetoencephalographic Indices of Brain Mechanisms for Language Comprehension

PANAGIOTIS G. SIMOS
SHIRIN SARKARI
ANDREW C. PAPANICOLAOU

The ability of humans to convey ideas, desires, and information through spoken and written language is a remarkable attribute that has facilitated progression of the human race to an intelligent, self-aware species. Humans are able to produce complicated utterances and attribute specific meanings to them—an ability resulting from cerebral complexity unparalleled in nature. The ability to comprehend spoken language involves a number of component processes, each designed to analyze distinct key features naturally embedded in the language stream. Comprehension necessarily involves identification of words as distinct entities, a process that in turn involves gaining access to general knowledge associated with each word and, sometimes, also to memories of the specific instances surrounding earlier encounters with the word and its referents. Comprehension also requires identification of morphosyntactic segments that provide additional information regarding what the word refers to and help the listener to establish mental links among words. It is customary to refer to the cognitive operations through which words are identified as meaningful entities and the associated memories that enter consciousness (or, in some cases, influence behavior without awareness) as "semantic." It is also assumed that lexical, semantic, and grammatic analyses are normally performed on neural representations that serve as a code for key acoustic and phonemic features of spoken language. Although some models of how these operations engage to make the "comprehension" function possible assume a rather serial progression from acoustic to phonemic–phonological, to semantic and grammatical–syntactic operations, there is little direct empirical evidence that component operations engage in a strictly serial manner. Moreover, there is an ongoing debate regarding the degree to which the essential steps in the analysis of speech sounds are served by operations that are speech-specific (i.e., dedicated exclusively to the processing of speech), or whether these operations are also normally involved in the analysis of nonspeech (e.g., environmental) sounds. Historically, the former view has been linked to the notion that speech processing involves not only analyzing specific sound cues by the auditory system but also relating these cues to the articulatory programs used by the listener to produce the spoken utterances in question ("motor" theory of speech perception; Liberman & Mattingley, 1985). Although an in-depth discussion of these issues is beyond the scope of this chapter, it suffices to say that the available empirical evidence from experimental studies with healthy volunteers and patients with focal brain damage is at least partly supportive of the view that neural signals related to motor–articulatory programs may be involved in speech perception, and, hence, in language comprehension.

In the context of psychological research, these phenomena can only be deduced by observing—and measuring—the overt responses of research participants. These *experimental* tasks comprise stimulus manipulations and/or specific instructions on how to process and respond to these stimuli. The purpose of the tasks is to re-create—in the laboratory—repeatable conditions that trigger the psychological function under investigation. If the phenomena that define the particular function are subjective, participants may be given specific instructions to indicate their occurrence by some prespecified "discriminant response," which can stand as objective proof that the phenomena have in fact occurred. If the stimuli and the task instructions do occasion the function, the task is said to be "ecologically valid" and capable of activating the brain mechanism of the function.

To support comprehension, the brain utilizes specific mechanisms. A "brain mechanism" is defined as sets of neurophysiological events that take place in particular brain areas in a particular order, resulting in the generation of phenomena indicating that comprehension has been accomplished. Relevant phenomena include the subjective experience of "knowing" what a word one just heard means, and experimental evidence indicating that access to stored memories associated with that word has taken place. The earliest method used to identify the components of the brain mechanism for comprehension relied on the study of the profile of related abilities in patients who had recently suffered a, preferably acute, focal brain lesion. This line of research attempts to establish reliable associations between particular deficits (indicated by worse than expected performance on one or more related language tasks) and damage to specific brain areas. In lesion analysis, it is implicitly assumed that the impact of a particular lesion on the ability to perform a specific task is proportional to the degree to which the operations normally required for the execution of that task (in the intact brain) depend on that area. Despite a number of potential flaws associated with this line of reasoning, this assumption underlies the conclusions of the vast majority of published lesion studies.

Alternative means of studying mechanisms in the intact brain entail recording the by-products of neurophysiological activity during the performance of experimental tasks that require the function under investigation. A number of functional brain imaging techniques are widely available to researchers. Some of these techniques are completely noninvasive (e.g., functional magnetic resonance imaging [fMRI], electroencephalography [EEG], and magnetoencephalography [MEG]), whereas others involve minimal risk for the individuals tested as subjects (i.e., positron emission tomography [PET], single-photon emission computed tomography [SPECT]). Each imaging method measures only one aspect of neural activity, namely, neuronal signaling, blood flow, or metabolism, and attempts to identify systematic variations in this activity that may serve as indices of brain function.

THE AUDITORY SYSTEM AND LANGUAGE

The quest for reliable signatures of neurophysiological processes that support language functions is guided by accumulated knowledge of the basic physiology of the auditory system over decades of animal experimental studies. Thus, it is known that the auditory system at the cortical level comprises several histologically distinct neocortical areas, organized in a parallel and hierarchical fashion (Galaburda & Sanides, 1980; Gueguin, Bouquin-Jeannes, Faucon, Chauvel, & Liégeois-Chauvel, 2006; Kaas & Hacket, 2000). A single region in each hemisphere (the primary auditory cortex located on the floor of the Sylvian fissure) serves as the primary recipient of neural signals that convey auditory information from the last subcortical relay station of the auditory system, the medial geniculate nucleus of the thalamus.

Electrophysiological studies of the primary auditory cortex in primate and nonprimate species that display auditory capabilities very similar to those of human listeners reveal an intriguing variety of neurons with respect to the pattern of electrical responses they produce in response to simple auditory stimuli. It is apparent that cortical neurons have the capacity to convey information regarding the frequency composition of a continuous sound and also of rapid changes in sound energy, such as the onset or offset of a short speech sound, and fluctuations in the intensity of a spoken utterance (Eggermont, 1995; Phillips, 1993; Steinschneider et al., 2005; Sussman, 1989). These neuronal properties are sufficient to serve as a "neural code" signaling the presence of a particular sound to the auditory cortex. Whereas some cells in the auditory cortex prefer simple stimuli of a particular frequency, many others display preference for complex sounds, especially natural sounds that have an intrinsic biological significance for the organism. For instance, natural vocalizations produce stronger responses from certain neurons than do equally complex but artificial sounds, such as a vocalization played backwards (Wang, Merzenich, Beitel, & Schreiner, 1995). Yet primate neurons that respond selectively (exclusively) to a particular vocalization, and not to others that may be very similar acoustically, have not been found. Rather, many cells show preference for complex spectral patterns and respond less vigorously to isolated frequency components of complex sounds. Newer recording and analytic techniques suggest that the complex spectral–temporal structure of a natural sound can be conveyed by the *joint activity* of an entire population of neurons.

Recent histological studies focused on the human auditory cortex have provided insights into patterns of connections (e.g., Kaur, Rose, Lazar, Liang, & Metherate, 2005; Imig & Morel, 1984). These studies reveal two major projections from the primary auditory cortex: one laterally, toward the secondary association cortex; and another toward the temporal plane that lies immediately posterior to Heschl's gyri inside the Sylvian fissure. Projections appear to be organized in a hierarchical manner, from primary to secondary to tertiary association cortices, which are located more laterally on the upper ridge of the superior temporal gyrus. It is cortex in the latter areas that appears to be indispensable for comprehension, as we see in more detail in subsequent sections.

LANGUAGE ORGANIZATION IN THE BRAIN

One of the most well-established facts in neuropsychology is that the left cerebral hemisphere contains structures that are indispensable components of the brain mechanism that supports comprehension and production of language. This is true for the majority of right-handed individuals. According to these estimates, the left hemisphere has a *dominant* role in the execution of language functions in 95–98% of right-handed individuals without a history of neurological disease. The concept of "hemispheric dominance" implies that the left hemisphere is normally indispensable for perception, comprehension, and production of intelligible, meaningful speech.

Initially, observations of linguistic deficits following focal brain damage, with the location verified postmortem, introduced the notion that language functions were "localized" in certain areas of the left hemisphere, namely, inferior frontal and superior temporal areas surrounding the Sylvian fissure. The prominent role of these perisylvian areas in the execution of language functions was later verified by electrical stimulation mapping (Lesser, Gordon, & Uematsu, 1994; Ojemann, Ojemann, Lettich, & Berger, 1989). In this chapter we concentrate on regions located in the temporal lobe that are histologically characterized as part of the association auditory cortex, because they receive all of their neural input from the auditory cortex (rather than the auditory thalamus).

The portion of the auditory association cortex located on the posterior portion of the left superior temporal gyrus (STGp) has been the focus of extensive clinical research following several reports that permanent damage or transient inactivation of this region causes severe deficits in the recognition of spoken words (Boatman, Lesser, & Gordon, 1995; Simos et al., 1999). There is ongoing debate on whether this region contains neurophysiological processes that are primarily responsible for high-level phonetic and phonological analysis (i.e., sub-word-level analysis of spoken utterances), and whether this region also serves as an access to stored lexical representations (word-level analysis of spoken language). It also remains unclear whether this region is also critically involved in lower perceptual-level analysis of speech stimuli, which presumably involves extraction of relevant phonetic cues, or whether its role extends to the analysis of nonspeech sounds having comparable acoustic complexity. The notion of a specialized perceptual mechanism for speech sounds has been advocated for many years (Liberman, 1996; Studdert-Kennedy & Shankweiler, 1970), and STGp is a plausible cortical substrate for such a mechanism. Alternatively, STGp may be critical for the analysis of certain complex acoustic stimuli, regardless of whether such stimuli are perceived as speech sounds or not. In other words, it is possible to create nonspeech stimuli that contain acoustic cues similar to those used by listeners to discriminate speech sounds. Along these lines, a specialization of the left STGp has been suggested for analyzing rapid temporal cues, regardless of whether they are embedded in a speech context (Liégeois-Chauvel, de Graaf, Laguitton, & Chauvel, 1999; Nicholls, 1996; Robin, Tranel, & Damasio, 1990).

Recently, accumulating evidence from lesion and functional brain imaging studies suggests that the temporal lobe regions lying immediately inferior to Wernicke's area are important for language comprehension. This area hosts neurophysiological processes involved in accessing stored representations for the form of familiar words, defined as the "orthographic" (or "graphemic") identity of a particular printed word, which is in part independent from its visual form (i.e., regardless of whether it is presented in uppercase or lowercase, in script, or printed). This process is usually referred to as lexical–semantic access, a terminology that is adopted here by virtue of the inherent difficulty in distinguishing between word form (associated with "lexical" representations) and word meaning. This region extends on the posterior portion of the middle temporal gyrus and partially encompasses Brodmann's areas 21 and 37. Involvement of the region in lexical–semantic analysis is suggested by several independent sources of evidence, including noninvasive functional imaging investigations (Hart, Kraut, Kremen, Soher, & Gordon, 2000; Mummery, Patterson, Hodges, & Price, 1998; Kuperberg et al., 2000) and lesion studies (Damasio & Damasio, 1989).

Having set the background for functional imaging studies of language comprehension, we concentrate on attempts (not always conclusive) to study these issues in the intact human brain using MEG. Studies we review explore the outline of the brain mechanism that supports language comprehension, which in turn forms the basis for the ability to process and analyze speech sounds and to comprehend words both in isolation and in context. Applications of MEG techniques to the search for signatures of aberrant brain function in language disorders will be reviewed.

OVERVIEW OF MEG

MEG is a noninvasive imaging method that allows investigation of cortical dynamics in a millisecond timescale. MEG offers significant advantages over functional brain imaging techniques that rely on hemodynamic measures, such as PET and fMRI.

MEG involves the measurement of neuromagnetic signals emanating from the brain (for detailed discussion, see Papanicolaou, 1998). Most of the magnetic activity measurable outside the head originates from the intracellular current flow associated with postsynaptic electrical events in the long apical dendrites of cortical pyramidal cells. Pyramidal neurons comprise nearly 70% of neocortical neurons, and their long dendritic processes are oriented perpendicularly to the cortical surface. The ionic current flowing along the length of the dendrite forms a current dipole: a source–sink pair of electric current poles separated by a small distance.

An advantage of MEG over EEG (and event-related potentials) is that the neuromagnetic signals are less affected by the exact shape and conductivity of the skull and tissues. Magnetic signals associated with bioelectrical activity are very weak, and special techniques have to be employed to discriminate them from extraneous magnetic fields (noise). The instrument used to measure the signals is called a neuromagnetometer, equipped with an array of magnetic field sensors (superconducting quantum interference device [SQUID]), each coupled to a special, low-noise amplifier. State-of-the-art systems are equipped with over 150 magnetic field sensors arranged to cover the entire head. The neuromagnetometer is placed over the person's head, and recording commonly takes place inside a magnetically shielded room designed to reduce extraneous magnetic fields (see Figure 7.1).

During the MEG recording session, the phenomenon that represents the function under investigation is repeated several times, while the magnetic field around the head is being sampled at regular intervals (typically every 2–4 msec for cognitive and language studies). An external stimulus is presented at each instance to elicit either the phenomenon (in the case of language comprehension) or to act as a time cue for speech (in the case of expressive language functions). Each segment of recorded activity, beginning 50–200 msec before and extending several hundred milliseconds after each repetition of the stimulus, is stored separately as an MEG epoch or event-related field (ERF). One such epoch is stored for each magnetic sensor.

The data are filtered and averaged to enhance quality and to remove

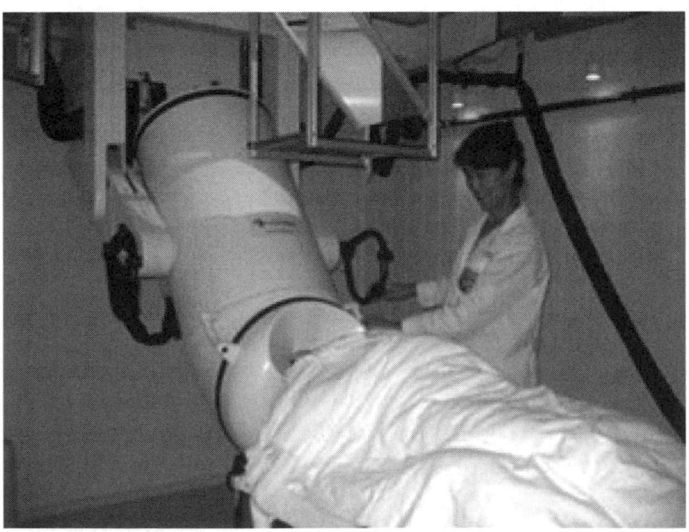

FIGURE 7.1. Neuromagnetometer (Magnes 3600, 4D-Neuroimaging, San Diego, California, equipped with 248 magnetic sensors) at the University of Texas Health Science Center.

components of the recorded magnetic field caused by extraneous sources (mechanical and biological artifacts). Typically, the average of the magnetic field across several repetitions of the experimental event is computed. The averaged magnetic response emerges as a waveform, or time series of magnetic field measurements at each recording site around the surface of the person's head. At each point in time the surface distribution of magnetic field can be reconstructed, resulting in a contour map. On the basis of the surface flux distribution, the position and strength of the brain source that produced it can be estimated by applying a mathematical algorithm, which considers the intracranial activity sources as equivalent-current dipoles (Papanicolaou, 1998).

CORTICAL ACTIVITY MAPS OBTAINED WITH MEG

Once estimates of the coordinates of the underlying electrical sources in the MEG coordinate system are made, they are registered on a set of anatomical images of the brain (MRI) to identify the anatomical location of each source. The procedures involved in reconstructing cortical activity maps based on MEG data are collectively referred to as magnetic source imaging (MSI). MSI provides several complementary indices of the characteristics of underlying neurophysiological activity. When combined, these indices provide information regarding *where* in the brain elevated levels of neurophysiological activity takes place, *when* this activity first occurs in relation to stimulus onset, *how* it evolves over time (duration and offset), and *what* its strength of activity was over time. Whereas alternative brain imaging methods (fMRI and PET) provide information regarding the strength and spatial extent of local increases in blood flow and metabolism resulting from task-specific increases in neurophysiological activity, MSI measures brain activity in real time, on a millisecond scale.

While the temporal resolution of MEG is, by definition, adequate for mapping regional activation in real time, it was necessary to establish empirically the degree of spatial (anatomical) resolution of the technique. The latter is primarily constrained by the signal-to-noise ratio of the recordings, the suitability of the activity–source model used to convert the raw data into functional images and, finally, the accuracy of the coregistration of these images onto the participant's MRI of the brain. Under ideal conditions the localization accuracy for dipolar current sources is in the order of 4–5 mm (Kwon, Lee, Kim, Park, & Kuriki, 2002). Under realistic conditions, the estimated spatial accuracy of MEG is only slightly worse; therefore, it is adequate for neurolinguistic investigations, as attested by the following facts.

First, intraparticipant reproducibility for the anatomical locations of the sources of both the early (50–200 msec) and late portions of the brain magnetic responses (200–800 msec) originating in primary and association auditory cortices, respectively, is in the millimeter range (Roberts, Disbrow, Robers, & Rowley, 2000; Simos, Sarkari, et al., 2005). This figure is well within the spatial resolution limits of invasive brain mapping procedures, which are considered as the "gold standard" in the field of neurolinguistics (i.e., less than 8 mm in all cases; Lesser et al., 1994; Ojemann & Whitaker, 1978). Second, test–retest differences in the location of language-related magnetic activity sources fall in the same range (Simos, Sarkari, et al., 2005). Third, MEG data agree with prior knowledge regarding the intrinsic organization of primary somatosensory–sensory cortex (somatotopy; Roberts, Ferrari, & Poeppel, 1998) and primary auditory cortex (tonotopy; Pantev et al., 1995).

The averaged ERF comprises an early portion (50–200 msec poststimulus onset) that correspond to activation of the sensory cortex, specific to the modality of stimulus (e.g., visual or auditory), and a late portion (200 to ~800 msec poststimulus onset) reflecting activation of the association cortex or higher functions. The stimuli and experimental design used in these studies, to a great extent, have been adopted from similar studies using event-related potentials as indices of brain activity (e.g., Kraus et al., 1996; Leppänen et al., 2002; Molfese, Molfese, Fonaryova-Key, & Kelly, 2003). Next, we briefly review basic research findings on what activity from the early and late portions of the ERF can reveal regarding the cortical mechanisms responsible for language comprehension.

THE EARLY PORTION OF THE ERF

Studies of Normal Language Processing

Most studies have focused on the most prominent early magnetic response, which peaks approximately 100 msec after stimulus onset (M100), and the amplitude of which is known to be affected by simple acoustic parameters in both speech and nonspeech sounds (e.g., stimulus intensity). In addition, the location of the neuronal population that gives rise to the magnetic field at the peak of the M100 response may vary as a function of both acoustic (e.g., frequency; Pantev et al., 1988) and phonetic features (e.g., place of articulation—the distinction between /b/, /d/, and /g/; Obleser, Elbert, Lahiri, & Eulitz, 2003).

Considerable recent research has been conducted on the timing of the M100 peak (i.e., latency after the onset of an auditory stimulus). M100 peak latency varies systematically with stimulus frequency (Roberts & Poeppel, 1996) and intensity (Stufflebeam, Poeppel, Rowley, & Roberts, 1998), with lower tone frequencies and lower tone intensities associated with longer latencies. An interesting observation is that the dynamic range of M100 latency modulation by stimulus frequency (i.e., the difference in peak latency between the M100 elicited by a 200 Hz tone and the latency of the M100 response to a 100 Hz tone, which is typically in the order of 10–15 msec) does not change significantly throughout childhood, although M100 peak latencies become progressively shorter with age (Roberts et al., 1998). At least one study has capitalized on this phenomenon to explore cortical auditory function in autism (Gage, Siegel, Callen, & Roberts, 2003; see discussion below).

Importantly, systematic variations in M100 amplitude and/or latency have been shown to parallel perceptual categorization boundaries for both speech and nonspeech stimuli. Latency-related effects have been demonstrated for phonetic identity (e.g., vowels /a/ and /u/) regardless of substantial acoustic variation among tokens of each vowel type (Makela, Alku, May, Makinen, & Tiitinen, 2005; Obleser, Eulitz, & Lahiri, 2004; Peoppel et al., 1997; Shestakova, Brattico, Soloviev, Klucharev, & Huotilainen, 2004). For instance, Obleser et al. (2004) presented participants with 42 stimuli exemplifying acoustic variations (seven different tokens) for each of six natural, German vowels. Despite these acoustic variations, adult, native German speakers could easily categorize each token into one of the seven vowel categories, a universal phenomenon in speech perception known as "categorical perception." Both the source locations of the magnetic field measured at the peak of the M100 response and its peak latency varied across tokens in a manner that paralleled categorical phonetic perception (identification of vowels based on phoneme identity). Thus, acoustically different tokens of /a/ elicited M100 responses with similar latencies and source locations, which were clearly different from the cluster of source locations elicited by each of the (acoustically different) tokens of /u/, which were also associated with longer peak latencies.

A similar finding has been reported for consonants varying on the acoustic parameter (known as voice onset time, or VOT) that speakers of most languages use to differentiate between voiced (e.g., /b/, /d/, /g/) and voiceless consonants (/p/, /t/, /k/, respectively) (Simos, Breier, Zouridakis, & Papanicolaou, 1998a, 1998b; Simos, Diehl, et al., 1998). It is possible to create synthetic consonant–vowel sounds that vary in VOT along a continuum, so that the acoustic difference between two phonetically similar sounds (e.g., sounds perceived by most listeners as /ga/) is equal to the acoustic difference between a sound that is perceived as /ga/ and one that is perceived as /ka/. In that study, changes in the peak amplitude of the M100 response paralleled participants' perceptual categorization performance (see Figure 7.2). Responses to phonetically similar but acoustically different tokens of /ga/ were similar to each other but clearly different from responses to tokens perceived as /ka/.

Numerous studies using a variety of tasks and stimuli generally indicate that neurophysiological activity in the early portion of the ERF is symmetrical across hemispheres in both amplitude and duration (Makela et al., 2005; Papanicolaou et al., 2004; Poeppel et al., 1996; Valaki et al., 2004). It has been shown, however, that the peak amplitude of the M100 response to speech sounds (vowels) is consistently greater than that in response to nonspeech sounds (tones) only in the left hemisphere (Gootjes, Raij, Salmelin, & Hari, 1999). This hemispheric difference was, on average, stronger and more systematic across right-handers (observed in approximately 80% of individuals) and significantly reduced in left-handers (Kirveskari, Salmelin, & Hari, 2006).

Teismann et al. (2004) reported another potentially interesting property of the auditory cortex in the left hemisphere on a small group of right-handed individuals. They found evidence that the expected attenuation of the M100 amplitude to repeated presentation of the same speech sound (a natural vowel token) was much more pronounced in the right than in the left hemisphere. This trend was not evident for trains of a nonspeech sound (a pure tone at the fundamental frequency of the vowel), suggesting enhanced capacity of the left hemisphere in processing rapidly changing complex sounds.

Studies of Disordered Language Processing

Several studies have searched for aberrant M100 profiles (in terms of amplitude, peak latency, duration, and location of underlying cortical sources) in language-related disorders, such as dyslexia and autism. The impetus behind these investigations rests on the view that these disorders are associated with abnormal organization of the auditory cortex, which may underlie evidence of reduced ability in processing the subtle acoustic variations that are normally crucial for making phoneme distinctions (Breier, Gray, Fletcher, Foorman, & Klaas, 2002; Breier, Fletcher, Foorman, Klaas, & Gray, 2003; Mody, Studdert-Kennedy, & Brady, 1997). First we summarize findings on specific reading disability (dyslexia).

Adults and Children with Dyslexia

In the earliest study, Helenius, Salmelin, Richardson, and Lyytinen (2002) reported increased M100 peak amplitudes for a group of adults with a history of dyslexia compared to a group of age-matched non-reading-impaired controls. This difference was found only for a synthetic vowel sound (/a/). There was also a latency difference between groups (the M100 peaked later in the group with dyslexia), which depended on the presence of a consonant sound (/ta/). Using a different stimulus (a synthetic /ba/ sound), Heim,

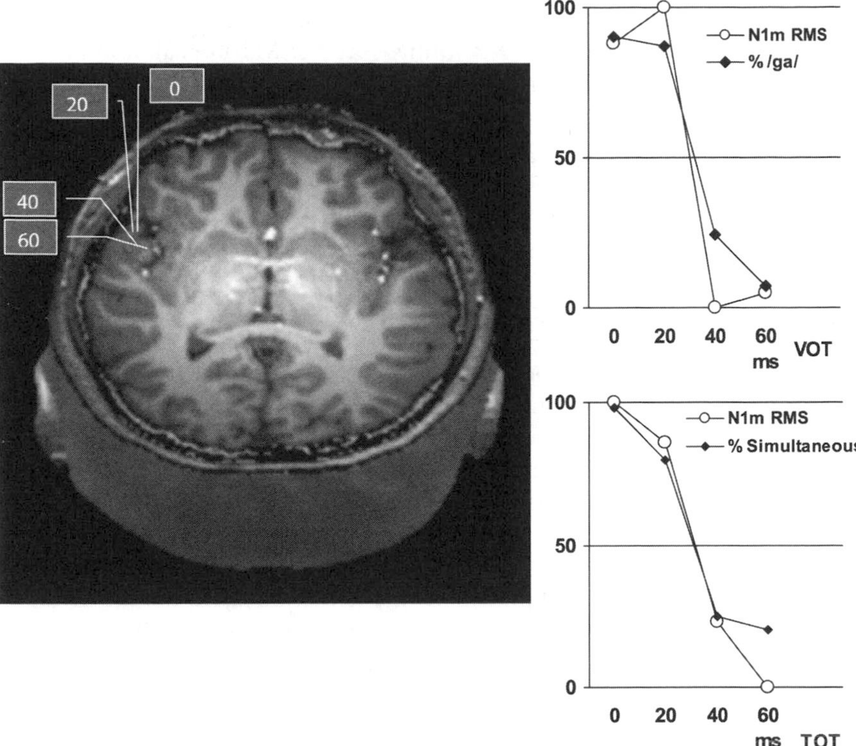

FIGURE 7.2. Change in N1m peak amplitude (left hemisphere) as a function of temporal cues embedded in speech (voice onset time [VOT]; upper left) and nonspeech, two-tone sounds (tone onset time [TOT]; lower left). The values on the *y* axis represent (1) percent of tokens perceived as /ga/ (upper graph) and percent of nonspeech sounds perceived as consisting of a single tone or two tones with simultaneous onsets (lower graph) and (2) difference of N1m peak amplitude from the maximum value elicited by any of the four stimuli used in each experiment expressed as percentage of the dynamic range of N1m peak amplitude. The locations of equivalent current dipoles representing the sources of the magnetic field at the peak of the N1m response elicited by each of the four speech stimuli (with VOT values of 0, 20, 40, or 60 msec) are shown on an axial view of the brain through the superior temporal gyrus.

Eulitz, and Elbert (2003) failed to find amplitude or latency differences between a group of children (ages 8–15 years) with dyslexia and a group of age-matched non-reading-impaired children. Instead, the authors reported that the expected asymmetry in the location of the cortical source of the M100 response (more anterior in the right compared to the left hemisphere) was observed in the control group, but not in the group of children with reading impairment.

In a more recent study, group differences between adults with dyslexia and age-matched controls were stimulus-specific: M100 peak amplitude in the left hemisphere was stronger for synthetic speech stimuli (/a/, /u/, /pa/, /ka/) than for nonspeech analogues (sounds composed of narrow bandwidth frequency transitions) for controls (Parviainen, Helenius, & Salmelin, 2005). This difference was not as pronounced for the group of adults with dyslexia, suggestive of weaker lateralization of speech–sound processing in readers with dyslexia.

Children and Adolescents with Autism

Two recent studies have focused on the characteristics of the M100 response elicited by tone stimuli in children and adolescents with autism. The first (Gage et al., 2003) examined changes in M100 peak latency as a function of tone frequency. Both groups showed the expected effect (increased latency with decreasing tone frequency). Nevertheless, the dynamic range of M100 modulation (the difference between the M100 latency at the lowest frequency and at the highest frequency tested) was significantly smaller in the right hemisphere and greater in the left hemisphere for the group of children with autism compared to the age-matched controls. To the extent that a reduced dynamic range of a response representing synchronous activity in thousands of neurons can be considered as evidence of deficient neurophysiological processes involved in the spectral analysis of sounds, these data are promising. Further research is required, however, to establish not only the reproducibility of this phenomenon but also its relationship with individual differences in verbal and/or nonverbal abilities in individuals with autism.

In the second study, Oram Cardy, Flagg, Roberts, Brian, and Roberts (2005) used a two-tone procedure to examine the degree of attenuation of the magnetic field amplitude elicited by the second stimulus in each pair. Given the length of the delay between the two tones (150 msec), only responses from the early portion of the ERF were examined, namely, the M100 and an earlier, less pronounced, response that peaks at around 50 msec poststimulus onset (M50). Results showed a trend for reduced probability for detecting either of the two early components of the ERF in response to the second tone among children and adolescents with autism compared to typically developing children. This trend reached statistical significance between the group of typically developing children and children with specific language impairment in the same study. Although the relationship of this phenomenon to auditory (including speech) perception has yet to be established, second-tone response attenuation may serve as an index of the capacity of the auditory cortex to respond adequately to a rapid stream of acoustic events, similar to those occurring in natural speech. The relevance of this capacity to the ability to identify sounds in natural speech remains to be established.

Mismatch Magnetic Field Approach

Studies reviewed thus far examined early magnetic responses to speech sounds, while participants were engaged in either passive listening or identification tasks. In the latter case, they were presented with a series of auditory stimuli (usually one every 2–3 seconds) and were asked to indicate manually the phonetic identity of each stimulus. An alternative experimental technique is to use higher presentation rates (at least one stimulus per second) and series of stimuli that contain a majority of identical tokens (the standard stimulus), some of which are followed by a different token (the deviant or oddball stimulus). The ERF elicited by the latter contains an amplified segment compared to that elicited by standard (frequent) stimuli. This segment, known as the mismatch magnetic field (MMF), occurs during and immediately after the resolution of the M100 response and originates from the auditory cortex (usually slightly anterior to the cortical patch that generates the peak of the M100 response). Given that the MMF does not require sustained, focused attention to the stimuli, it is believed to reflect neurophysiological activity in neuronal populations tuned to the particular attribute (phonetic and/or acoustic) that constitutes the difference between the standard and the deviant stimulus. Whereas an MMF response can typically be observed for deviants that are acoustically, as well as phonetically, different than the preceding standard stimuli, it is also found when the difference between standard and deviant stimuli is merely acoustic. There is evidence that the magnitude of the MMF parallels the perceptual discriminability of the standard and deviant stimuli (Näätänen et al., 1997; Pihko et al., 2005). Recent studies have used this experimental technique to search for potential markers in clinical conditions (mainly autism).

Potential Markers of Autism

Positive findings have been reported, but the precise nature of these results differed across studies. For instance, Tecchio et al. (2003) reported that the MMF elicited by a frequency change in tone stimuli was significantly reduced in *amplitude* in a group of young patients diagnosed with autism when compared with a group of age-matched controls.

In a more recent study with a small group of boys diagnosed with autism, it was found that the *latency* of the MMF response to a change in either vowel identity or tone frequency was significantly prolonged compared to that in a group of children with typical development (Oram

Cardy, Flagg, Roberts, & Roberts, 2005). A similar latency prolongation (but no amplitude difference) was also found in a small group of adults with autism, in response to a change in vowel identity (Kasai et al., 2005).

Although these findings have opened the way for more systematic investigations of basic auditory function in autism, due to the small sample sizes and the lack of evidence regarding the reproducibility of the effects on a case-by-case basis, caution is advised when interpreting results. In addition to differences across studies in the age of the participants, these factors may have contributed to the mix of positive and negative results reported.

THE LATE PORTION OF THE ERF

Various parameters of late activity have been shown to change systematically as a function of variations in stimulus characteristics and task demands. Processing of simple verbal stimuli, such as consonant–vowel syllables (/ba/), elicits magnetic activity that persists for 200–300 msec after the M100 response, originating predominantly within the primary and adjacent association auditory cortices. A moderate but consistent tendency for greater amplitude (Eulitz, Diesch, Pantev, Hampson, & Elbert, 1995) and overall duration of this activity in the left hemisphere is typically found (Papanicolaou et al., 2003; Szymanski et al., 2001).

Dyslexia

It appears that the hemispheric asymmetry for this late activity may be reduced, on average, in children with severe reading difficulties compared to age- and performance IQ–matched controls, due to increased duration of late activity in the right-hemispheric association auditory cortices in the former group (Breier, Simos, et al., 2003). It should be noted that these group differences are much less pronounced compared to those observed for reading tasks. Several MSI studies of dyslexia (see Shaywitz, Gruen, & Shaywitz, Chapter 9, this volume) have demonstrated consistent hypoactivation of the left STG, paired with increased activation in the corresponding right-hemispheric region during reading (Simos, Brier, Fletcher, Bergman, & Papanicolaou, 2000; Simos, Brier, Fletcher, Foorman, et al., 2000; Sarkari et al., 2005).

Autism

Late magnetic field responses elicited by simple speech sounds were recently explored for indices of aberrant function of the auditory association cortex in children with autism (Flagg, Oram Cardy, Roberts, & Roberts, 2005). Although hemispheric asymmetries in the duration of late activity (measured between approximately 350 and 650 msec after stimulus onset) were not evident across groups, the tendency for increasing leftward asymmetries with age, which was present in the group of normally developing children, was reversed in the group of children with autism. Larger-scale longitudinal studies are needed to address this issue.

More Complex Verbal Stimuli

A different pattern of activity is produced in the processing of more complex and meaningful, or potentially meaningful, spoken utterances (isolated real words and pseudowords). Initially, within the first 200 msec or so after stimulus onset, neurophysiological processes involved in the analysis of spoken words take place in and around the primary auditory cortex bilaterally, regardless of the particular task demands. The spatial layout of cortical activity within the next 500 msec depends largely upon the type of verbal stimulus used and the task that participants are asked to perform. When the task explicitly required analysis of spoken words into their constituent phonemes, activity was found primarily among neuronal populations in the left STG. Sustained neurophysiological activity was particularly prominent in the regions surrounding the primary auditory cortex, which are coextensive with Brodmann's area 22 (auditory association cortex; Castillo, Simos, Venkataraman, et al., 2001). This finding agrees with prior knowledge (acquired independently of functional imaging), regarding the location of Wernicke's area, which is specialized for high-level analysis of verbal input. Permanent damage or transient inactivation of this region severely impairs the ability to perceive spoken words as linguistic entities and to read meaningless letter strings (Boatman et al., 1995; Phillips & Farmer, 1990; Simos, Breier, Wheless, et al., 2000). Studies using hemodynamic indices of regional brain activity also support this notion (Binder et al., 2000; Demonet, Price, Wise, & Frackowiak, 1994; Shaywitz et al., 1998).

When the stimulus is adequate (real word) and/or the experimental task requires access to stored lexical–semantic representations, neurophysiological processes engaged the left posterior middle temporal gyrus (MTG) and mesial temporal cortex (Castillo, Simos, Davis, et al., 2001). Nonword stimuli that obey the phonotactic rules of the English language result in significantly reduced activation of these regions. Several independent sources of evidence, including noninvasive functional imaging investigations and lesion studies, suggest the involvement of the MTG in lexical–semantic analysis (Damasio & Damasio, 1989; Hart et al., 2000; Mummery et al., 1998; Kuperberg et al., 2000).

To ensure that the procedures used in the MEG studies described in the previous paragraph had sufficiently high fidelity and selectivity, several studies were undertaken to examine their degree of concurrent validity. In these clinical studies, there was near perfect agreement between MEG-derived maps of language-specific activity within the dominant hemisphere and the results of direct electrocortical stimulation regarding the precise location and extent of the receptive and expressive language cortex (Wernicke's and Broca's areas) (Castillo, Simos, Venkataraman, et al., 2001; Simos et al., 1999). These results are important in demonstrating that electrical inactivation of cortical regions that reliably show increased levels of activity associated with a particular linguistic function significantly impairs that function. In addition to providing the means for external validation, MEG-based mapping of language-specific cortex is generally promising as an adjunct to traditional invasive functional mapping methods, which can be used only in patients and suffer from time constraints and safety considerations (e.g., see, Simos, Brier, Wheless, et al., 2000).

It is noteworthy that hemispheric asymmetries in neurophysiological activity are evident for several complementary indices derived by MSI: (1) amplitude of the recorded magnetic field, (2) estimated amplitude of the underlying electrical current produced by the active population of neurons (Valaki et al., 2004), and (3) duration of neurophysiological activity sufficient to produce measurable magnetic fields (Maestú et al., 2002; Papanicolaou et al., 2004). MEG-derived hemispheric asymmetries are highly repeatable over time (Lee, Sawrie, Simos, Killen, & Knowlton, 2006; Simos, Fletcher, et al., 2005), and they are in excellent agreement with the results of a standard invasive procedure used clinically to determine hemispheric dominance (Wada test) in large, consecutive patient series (Maestú et al., 2002; Papanicolaou et al., 2004).

Functional Brain Reorganization

Several cases of functional reorganization of the brain as a result of focal lesions involving language-specific and somatosensory-specific cortex have been observed and documented with MEG and/or direct electrocortical stimulation mapping (Papanicolaou et al., 2001). In one of the few large patient series reported (Pataraia et al., 2004), patients with medically intractable epilepsy arising from the left temporal lobe showed significantly higher frequency of atypical lateralization of language (either right-hemisphere dominance or bilateral language representation) compared with patients sustaining focal lesions (43 vs. 13%, respectively). In fact, the majority of patients who experienced early seizure onset (before age 5) showed atypical lateralization of language. In contrast, the precise location of cortex involved in language comprehension within the dominant hemisphere was found to be atypical (outside of Wernicke's area) in 30% of patients with focal lesions, but only in 14% of the epilepsy patients (who also showed significant degeneration of the mesial temporal lobe). These findings indicate that there is an increased probability of a partial or total shift of the brain mechanism responsible for language comprehension to the nondominant hemisphere in patients with mesial temporal sclerosis (MTS).

In a subsequent study, reorganization of brain mechanisms for language comprehension as a result of resection of the anterior portion of the left temporal lobe was investigated (Pataraia et al., 2005). Each patient underwent preoperative Wada testing, pre- and postoperative neuropsychological testing, and MEG language mapping. Patients with atypical (bilateral) language lateralization (according to both the Wada procedure and preoperative MEG) were significantly more likely than patients with left-hemisphere dominance to show a shift in language representation toward greater right-hemispheric activity after surgery. Conversely, patients with left-hemispheric dominance preoperatively were more likely to show intrahemispheric changes involving a slight inferior shift of the putative location of Wernicke's area. Patients with bilateral representation tended to perform worse on neuropsychological test measures pre- and postoperatively (see also Breier et al., 2005). These preliminary findings show that MEG may not only contribute significantly to the precise localization of Wernicke's area for presurgical planning, but may also serve as an important tool for documenting postoperative intra- and interhemispheric language reorganization.

Monitoring Mismatched Meaning

The studies reviewed thus far in this section involve presentation of isolated meaningful (words) or meaningless spoken utterances (vowels, consonant–vowel syllables, or multisyllabic pseudowords). An alternative approach to investigating brain regions involved in phonological or lexical–semantic analysis involves presenting entire spoken sentences and asking participants to monitor each sentence for an inappropriate ending. The latter may consist of a semantically appropriate word that contains a phonologically unexpected/inappropriate initial phoneme or a semantically inappropriate word (Connolly, Phillips, & Forbes, 1995). In other studies, stimuli are presented in pairs that either match or do not match on a prespecified attribute (usually phonology or meaning; Kujala, Alho, Service, Ilmoniemi, & Connolly, 2004). Inappropriate or mismatching stimuli elicit stronger magnetic fields, between approximately 300 and 600 msec, after stimulus onset compared to appropriate or matching stimuli. The augmented portion of the ERF is referred to as the "N400m response." Although overall a left-hemisphere predominance in both the detectability and amplitude of this response is noted, the locations of underlying active neuronal populations show considerable variability both across participants in the same study and across studies. Overall, source locations cluster around the superior temporal sulcus, including the ventral bank of the STG and the dorsal bank of the MTG (Kwon et al., 2005; Halgren et al., 2002; Simos, Basile, & Papanicolaou, 1997). Exactly what type of process this response reflects (phonological or lexical–semantic) is still under debate. Some studies report two distinct magnetic components (an early one reflecting phonological processing, and a later one reflecting semantic processing; Inouchi, Kubota, Ferrari, & Roberts, 2005), whereas others relying on electrical recordings suggest a common underlying process (Connolly & Phillips, 1994; Haggort & Brown, 2000).

Production

Finally, performance on tasks that exemplify expressive language functions (overt or silent reading, picture-naming, and word generation or fluency tasks) is invariably associated with activation in posterior prefrontal areas of the dominant hemisphere (in the vicinity of Broca's area; Billingsley et al., 2004; Bowyer et al., 2004; Castillo, Simos, Davis, et al., 2001; Kober et al., 2001; Salmelin, Hari, Lounasmaa, & Sams, 1994). Typically, activity in Wernicke's area is observed within the first 200–500 msec after stimulus onset, followed by activity in Broca's area, which in turn precedes activity in motor cortices.

More recently, accumulating evidence, mainly from functional brain imaging studies, has introduced the notion that, in addition to Wernicke's area, inferior frontal regions (Broca's area) are also involved in phonological processing. It has been suggested that the neurophysiological processes that take place in this region are involved in the analysis of spoken utterances in terms of their articulatory features. In other words, the presumed contribution of Broca's area is in providing a description of speech stimuli with respect to the speaker's articulatory gestures involved in producing them, whereas Wernicke's area is primarily involved in the recognition of phonetic patterns that can be used to distinguish complex phonemic structure. The neuroimaging evidence in support of this notion presents some inconsistencies, highlighting the inherent ambiguity of functional brain imaging data as a means to identify the brain mechanisms that are necessary for a particular cognitive function. Evidence that a given area shows increased levels of neurophysiological activity associated with the performance of the function in question does not mean that this region is an indispensable component of the mechanism specialized for this function. Nevertheless, this view is strengthened by reports of phoneme discrimination and identification deficits in Broca's aphasia (Blumstein et al., 1998) and more directly by results from electrocortical stimulation studies suggesting a role of the left inferior frontal region in phonological processing (Boatman et al., 1995).

FUTURE DIRECTIONS AND APPLICATIONS

Whereas issues we mentioned in the previous section concern the external validity of functional imaging findings, it is equally important to consider fidelity and reliability issues when interpreting imaging data. Thus, we should emphasize that "functional images" are mere reflections of underlying neurophysiological activity and, depending on the technique, they are derived from the products of this activity in more or less indirect ways.

Although MEG provides the most direct measures of neuronal activity (signaling among neurons), it is not void of methodological problems that may affect the fidelity of results, or the accuracy with which the spatial and temporal aspects of this activity are indexed. The majority of studies reviewed in this chapter were based on very small samples for current standards in psychological research, but some researchers attempt to compensate for this potential problem by presenting data on a case-by-case basis, and few go a step further to include reproducibility estimates. Adoption of such simple procedures could render functional imaging as a powerful method for outlining the brain mechanisms involved in the processing of aural language.

With MEG, meaningful studies can be performed on children and adults that allow researchers to examine faint signs of the neurophysiological activity taking place inside the networks responsible for the processing of language. We are now beginning to understand the neurobiological mechanisms of functions involved in the appreciation of the phonemic, phonological, lexical–semantic, and morphosyntactic aspects of language. By studying speech processing at the level of the acoustic mechanisms that subserve it, we are beginning to understand the fundamental neurobiological underpinnings of language. Existing data provide preliminary clues that the outline of these mechanisms (i.e., the nature of component brain areas and neurophysiological processes) may be affected by cognitive task demands. Moreover, the neurophysiological phenotype associated with processing various language stimuli may parallel behavioral phenotypes, within both the "normal" and "subnormal" range of the distribution of language-related abilities.

REFERENCES

Billingsley, R. L., Simos, P. G., Castillo, E. M., Sarkari, S., Pataraia, E., et al. (2004). Spatio-temporal cortical dynamics of phonological and semantic fluency. *Journal of Clinical and Experimental Neuropsychology, 26*, 1031–1043.

Binder, J. R., Frost, J. A., Hammeke, T. A., Bellgowan, P. S. F., Springer, J. A., Kaufman, J. N., et al. (2000). Human temporal lobe activation by speech and nonspeech sounds. *Cerebral Cortex, 10*, 512–528.

Blumstein, S. E., Byma, G., Kurowski, K., Hourihan, J., Brown, T., & Hutchinson, A. (1998). On-line processing of filler-gap constructions in aphasia. *Brain and Language, 61*, 149–168.

Boatman, D., Lesser, R. P., & Gordon, B. (1995). Auditory speech processing in the left temporal lobe: an electrical interference study. *Brain and Language, 51*, 269–290.

Bowyer, S. M., Moran, J. M., Mason, K. M., Constantinou, J. E., Smith, B. J., Barkley, G. L., et al. (2004). MEG localization of language-specific cortex utilizing MR-FOCUSS. *Neurology, 62*, 2247–2255.

Breier, J. I., Castillo, E. M., Simos, P. G., Billingsley-Marshall, R. L., Pataraia, E., Sarkari, S., et al. (2005). Atypical language representation in patients with chronic seizure disorder and achievement deficits with magnetoencephalography. *Epilepsia, 46*, 540–548.

Breier, J. I., Fletcher, J. M., Foorman, B. R., Klaas, P., & Gray, L. C. (2003). Auditory temporal processing in children with specific reading disability with and without attention deficit/hyperactivity disorder. *Journal of Speech, Language, and Hearing Research, 46*, 31–42.

Breier, J. I., Gray, L. C., Fletcher, J. M., Foorman, B., & Klaas, P. (2002). Perception of speech and nonspeech stimuli by children with and without reading disability and attention deficit hyperactivity disorder. *Journal of Experimental Child Psychology, 82*, 226–250.

Breier, J. I., Simos, P. G., Fletcher, J. M., Castillo, E. M., Zhang, W., & Papanicolaou, A. C. (2003). Abnormal activation of temporoparietal language areas during phonetic analysis in children with dyslexia. *Neuropsychology, 17*, 610–621.

Castillo, E. M., Simos, P. G., Davis, R. N., Breier, J. I., Fitzgerald, M. E., & Papanicolaou, A. C. (2001). Levels of word processing and incidental memory: Dissociable mechanisms in the temporal lobe. *Neuroreport, 12*, 3561–3566.

Castillo, E. M., Simos, P. G., Venkataraman, V., Breier, J. I., Wheless, J. W., & Papanicolaou, A. C. (2001). Mapping of expressive language cortex using magnetic source imaging. *Neurocase, 7*, 419–422.

Connolly, J. F., & Phillips, N. A. (1994). Event-related components reflect phonological, semantic processing of the terminal words of spoken sentences. *Journal of Cognitive Neuroscience, 6*, 256–266.

Connolly, J. F., Phillips, N. A., & Forbes, K. A. (1995). The effects of phonological and semantic features of sentence-ending words on visual event-related brain potentials. *Electroencephalography and Clinical Neurophysiology, 94*, 276–287.

Damasio, H., & Damasio, A. (1989). *Lesion analysis in neuropsychology.* New York: Oxford University Press.

Demonet, J. F., Price, C., Wise, R., & Frackowiak, R. S. (1994). A PET study of cognitive strategies in normal subjects during language tasks: Influence of phonetic ambiguity and sequence processing on phoneme monitoring. *Brain, 117*, 671–682.

Eggermont, J. J. (1995). Representation of voice onset time continuum in primary auditory cortex of the cat. *Journal of the Acoustic Society of America, 98*, 911–920.

Eulitz, C., Diesch, E., Pantev, C., Hampson, S., & Elbert, T. (1995). Magnetic and electric brain activity evoked by the processing of tone and vowel stimuli. *Journal of Neuroscience, 15*, 2748–2755.

Flagg, E. J., Oram Cardy, J. E., Roberts, W., & Roberts, T. P. L. (2005). Language lateralization development in children with autism: Insights from the late field magnetoencephalogram. *Neuroscience Letters, 386*, 82–87.

Gage, N. M., Siegel, B., Callen, M., & Roberts, T. P. L. (2003). Cortical sound processing in children with autism disorder: An MEG investigation. *Neuroreport, 14*, 2047–2051.

Galaburda, A., & Sanides, F. (1980). Cytoarchitectonic organization of the human auditory cortex. *Journal of Comparative Neurology, 190*, 597–610.

Gootjes, L., Raij, T., Salmelin, R., & Hari, R. (1999). Left-hemisphere dominance for processing of vowels: A whole-scalp neuromagnetic study. *Neuroreport, 10*, 2987–2991.

Gueguin, M., Bouquin-Jeannes, R., Faucon, G., Chauvel, P., & Liegeois-Chauvel, C. (2007). Evidence of functional connectivity between auditory cortical areas revealed by amplitude modulation sound processing. *Cerebral Cortex, 17*, 304–313.

Haggort, P., & Brown, C. M. (2000). ERP effects of listening to speech: Semantic ERP effects. *Neuropsychologia, 38*, 1518–1530.

Halgren, E., Dhond, R. P., Christensen, N., Van Petten, C., Marinkovic, K., Lewine, J. D., et al. (2002). N400-like magnetoencephalography responses modulated by semantic context, word frequency, and lexical class in sentences. *NeuroImage, 17*, 1101–1116.

Hart, J., Kraut, M. A., Kremen, S., Soher, B., & Gordon, B. (2000). Neural substrates of orthographic lexical access as demonstrated by functional brain imaging. *Neuropsychiatry, Neuropsychology, and Behavioral Neurology, 13*, 1–7.

Heim, S., Eulitz, C., & Elbert, T. (2003). Altered hemispheric asymmetry of auditory P100m in dyslexia. *European Journal of Neuroscience, 17*, 1715–1722.

Helenius, J., Salmelin, R., Richardson, U., & Lyytinen, H. (2002). Abnormal auditory cortical activation in dyslexia 100 msec after speech onset. *Journal of Cognitive Neuroscience, 14*, 603–617.

Imig, T. J., & Morel, A. (1984). Topographic and cytoerchitectonic organization of thalamic neurons related to their targets of low-, middle-, and high-frequency representations in the cat auditory cortex. *Journal of Comparative Neurology, 227*, 511–539.

Inouchi, M., Kubota, M., Ferrari, P., & Roberts, T. P. L. (2005). The elicitation of the phonological and semantic neuromagnetic field components by nonwords in human auditory sentence comprehension. *Neuroscience Letters, 380*, 116–121.

Kaas, J. H., & Hacket, T. A. (2000). Subdivisions of auditory cortex and processing streams in primates. *Proceedings of the National Academy of Science USA), 97*, 11793–11799.

Kasai, K., Hashimoto, O., Kawakubo, Y., Yumoto, M., Kamio, S., Itoh, K., et al. (2005). Delayed automatic detection of change in speech sounds in adults with autism: A magnetoencephalographic study. *Clinical Neurophysiology, 116*, 1655–1664.

Kaur, S., Rose, H. J., Lazar, R., Liang, K., & Metherate, R. (2005). Spectral integration in primary auditory cortex: Laminar processing of afferent input, *in vivo* and *in vitro*. *Neuroscience, 134*, 1033–1045.

Kirveskari, E., Salmelin, R., & Hari, R. (2006). Neuromagnetic responses to vowels vs. tones reveal hemispheric lateralization. *Clinical Neurophysiology, 117*, 643–648.

Kober, H., Möller, M., Nimsky, C., Vieth, J., Fahlbusch, R., & Ganslandt, O. (2001). New approach to localize speech relevant brain areas and hemispheric dominance using spatially filtered magnetoencephalography. *Human Brain Mapping, 14*, 236–250.

Kraus, N., McGee, T. J., Carrell, T. D., Zecker, S. G., Nicol, T. G., & Koch, D. B. (1996). Auditory neurophysiologic responses and discrimination deficits in children with learning problems. *Science, 273*, 971–973.

Kujala, A., Alho, K., Service, E., Ilmoniemi, R. J., & Connolly, J. F. (2004). Activation in the anterior left auditory cortex associated with phonological analysis of speech input: Localization of the phonological mismatch negativity response with MEG. *Cognitive Brain Research, 21*, 106–113.

Kuperberg, G. R., McGuire, P. K., Bullmore, E. T., Brammer, M. J., Rabe-Hesketh, S., Wright, I. C., et al. (2000). Common and distinct neural substrates for pragmatic, semantic, and syntactic processing of spoken sentences: An fMRI study. *Journal of Cognitive Neuroscience, 12*, 321–341.

Kwon, H., Kuriki, S., Kim, J. M., Lee, Y. H., Kim, K., & Nam, K. (2005). MEG study on neural activities associated with syntactic and semantic violations in spoken Korean sentences. *Neuroscience Research, 51*, 349–357.

Kwon, H., Lee, Y. H., Kim, J. M., Park, Y. K., & Kuriki, S. (2002). Localization accuracy of single current dipoles from tangential components of auditory evoked fields. *Physics in Medicine and Biology 47*, 4145–4154.

Lee, D., Simos, P. G., Sawrie, S. M., Killen, J., & Knowlton, R. C. (2006). Reliability of language mapping with magnetic source imaging in epilepsy surgery candidates. *Epilepsy and Behavior, 8*, 742–749.

Leppänen, P. H. T., Richardson, U., Pihko, E., Eklund, K. M., Guttorm, T. K., Aro, M., et al. (2002). Brain responses to changes in speech durations differ between infants with and without familial risk for dyslexia. *Developmental Neuropsychology, 22*, 407–422.

Lesser, R., Gordon, B., & Uematsu, S. (1994). Electrical stimulation and language. *Journal of Clinical Neurophysiology, 11*, 191–204.

Liberman, A. M. (1996). *Speech: A special code*. Cambridge, MA: MIT Press.

Liberman, A. M., & Mattingley, I. G. (1985). The motor theory of speech revised. *Cognition, 21*, 1–36.

Liégeois-Chauvel, C., de Graaf, J. B., Laguitton, V., & Chauvel, P. (1999). Specialization of left auditory cortex for speech perception in man depends on temporal coding. *Cerebral Cortex, 9*, 484–496.

Maestú, F., Ortiz, T., Fernández, A., Amo, C., Martin, P., Fernández, S., et al. (2002). Spanish language mapping using MEG: A validation study. *NeuroImage, 17*, 1579–1586.

Makela, A. M., Alku, P., May, P. J., Makinen, V., & Tiitinen, H. (2005). Left-hemispheric brain activity reflects formant transitions in speech sounds. *Neuroreport, 16*, 549–553.

Mody, M., Studdert-Kennedy, M., & Brady, S. (1997). Speech perception deficits in poor readers: Auditory processing or phonological coding? *Journal of Experimental Child Psychology, 64*, 199–231.

Molfese, D. L., Molfese, V. J., Fonaryova-Key, A., & Kelly, S. D. (2003). Influence of environment on speech–sound discrimination: Findings from a longitudinal study. *Developmental Neuropsychology, 24*, 541–558.

Mummery, C. J., Patterson, K., Hodges, J., & Price, C. J. (1998). Organization of the semantic system: Divisible by what? *Journal of Cognitive Neuroscience, 10*, 766–777.

Näätänen, R., Lehtokoski, A., Lennes, M., Cheour, M., Huotilainen, M., Livonen, A., et al. (1997). Language-specific phoneme representations revealed by electric and magnetic responses. *Nature, 385*, 432–433.

Nicholls, M. E. R. (1996). Temporal processing asymmetries between the cerebral hemispheres: Evidence and implications. *Laterality, 1*, 97–137.

Obleser, J., Elbert, T., Lahiri, A., & Eulitz, C. (2003). Cortical representation of vowels reflects acoustic dissimilarity determined by formant frequencies, *Cognitive Brain Research, 15*, 207–213.

Obleser, J., Lahiri, A., & Eulitz, C. (2004). Magnetic brain response mirrors extraction of phonological features from spoken vowels. *Journal of Cognitive Neuroscience, 16*, 31–39.

Ojemann, G., Ojemann, J., Lettich, E., & Berger, M. (1989). Cortical language localization in left, dominant hemisphere: An electrical stimulation mapping investigation in 117 patients. *Journal of Neurosurgery, 71*, 316–326.

Ojemann, G. A., & Whitaker, H. A. (1978). Language localization and variability. *Brain and Language, 6*, 239–260.

Oram Cardy, J. E., Flagg, E. J., Roberts, W., Brian, J., & Roberts, T. P. L. (2005). Magnetoencephalography identifies rapid temporal processing deficit in autism and language impairment. *Neuroreport, 16*, 329–332.

Oram Cardy, J. E., Flagg, E. J., Roberts, W., & Roberts, T. P. L. (2005). Delayed mismatch field for speech and non-speech sounds in children with autism. *Neuroreport, 16*, 521–525.

Pantev, C., Bertrand, O., Eulitz, C., Verkindt, C., Hampson, S., Schuirer, G., et al. (1995). Specific tonotopic organizations of different areas of the human auditory cortex revealed by simultaneous magnetic and electric recordings. *Electroencephalography and Clinical Neurophysiology, 94*, 26–40.

Pantev, C., Hoke, M., Lehnertz, K., Lutkenhoner, B., Anogianakis, G., & Wittkowski, W. (1988). Tonotopic organization of the human auditory cortex revealed by transient auditory evoked magnetic fields. *Electroencephalography and Clinical Neurophysiology, 69*, 160–170.

Papanicolaou, A. C. (1998). *Fundamentals of functional brain imaging: A guide to the methods and their applications to psychology and behavioral neurosciences.* Lisse: Swets & Zeitlinger.

Papanicolaou, A. C., Castillo, E. M., Breier, J. I., Davis, R. N., Simos, P. G., & Diehl, R. L. (2003). Differential brain activation patterns during perception of voice and tone onset time series: A MEG study. *NeuroImage, 18*, 448–459.

Papanicolaou, A. C., Simos, P. G., Breier, J. I., Wheless, J. W., Mancias, P., Baumgartner, J. E., et al. (2001). Brain plasticity for sensory and linguistic functions: A functional imaging study using MEG with children and young adults. *Journal of Child Neurology, 16*, 241–252.

Papanicolaou, A. C., Simos, P. G., Castillo, E. M., Breier, J. I., Sarkari, S., Pataraia, E., et al. (2004). Magnetoencephalography: A non-invasive alternative to the Wada procedure. *Journal of Neurosurgery, 100*, 867–876.

Parviainen, T., Helenius, P., & Salmelin, R. (2005). Cortical differentiation of speech and nonspeech sounds at 100 ms: Implications for dyslexia. *Cerebral Cortex, 15*, 1054–1063.

Pataraia, E., Billingsley-Marshall, R. L., Castillo, E. M., Breier, J. I., Simos, P. G., Sarkari, S., et al. (2005). Organization of receptive language-specific cortex before and after left temporal lobectomy. *Neurology, 64*, 481–487.

Pataraia, E., Simos, P. G., Castillo, E. M., Billingsley-Marshall, R. L., McGregor, A. L., Breier, J. I., et al. (2004). Reorganization of language-specific cortex in patients with lesions or mesial temporal epilepsy. *Neurology, 63*, 1825–1832.

Phillips, D. P. (1993). Representation of acoustic events in primary auditory cortex. *Journal of Experimental Psychology: Human Perception and Performance, 19*, 203–216.

Phillips, D. P., & Farmer, M. E. (1990). Acquired word deafness, and temporal grain of sound representation in the primary auditory cortex. *Behavioural Brain Research, 40*, 85–94.

Pihko, E., Kujala, T., Mickos, A., Antell, H., Alku, P., Byring, R., et al. (2005). Magnetic fields evoked by speech sounds in preschool children. *Clinical Neurophysiology, 116*, 112–119.

Poeppel, D., Phillips, C., Yellin, E., Rowley, H. A., Roberts, T. P. L., & Marantz, A. (1997). Processing of vowels in supratemporal auditory cortex. *Neuroscience Letters, 221*, 145–148.

Poeppel, D., Yellin, E., Phillips, C., Roberts, T. P. L., Rowley, H. A., Wexler, K., et al. (1996). Task-induced asymmetry of the auditory evoked M100 neuromagnetic field elicited by speech sounds. *Cognitive Brain Research, 4*, 231–242.

Roberts, T. P. L., Disbrow, E. A., Roberts, H. C., & Rowley, H. A. (2000). Quantification and reproducibility of tracking cortical extent of activation by use of functional MR imaging and magnetoencephalography. *American Journal of Neuroradiology, 21*, 1377–1387.

Roberts, T. P. L., Ferrari, P., & Poeppel, D. (1998). Latency of evoked neuromagnetic M100 reflects perceptual and acoustic stimulus attributes. *Neuroreport, 9*, 3265–3269.

Roberts, T. P. L., & Poeppel, D. (1996). Latency of auditory evoked M100 as a function of tone frequency. *Neuroreport, 7*, 1138–1140.

Robin, D. A., Tranel, D., & Damasio, H. (1990). Auditory perception of temporal and spectral events in patients with focal left and right cerebral lesions. *Brain and Language, 39*, 539–555.

Salmelin, R., Hari, R., Lounasmaa, O. V., & Sams, M. (1994). Dynamics of brain activation during picture naming. *Nature, 368*, 463–465.

Shaywitz, S. E., Shaywitz, B. A., Pugh, K. R., Fulbright, R. K., Constable, R. T., Mencl, W. E., et al. (1998). Functional disruption in the organization of the brain for reading in dyslexia. *Neurobiology, 95*, 2636–2641.

Shestakova, A., Brattico, E., Soloviev, A., Klucharev, V., & Huotilainen, M. (2004).

Orderly cortical representation of vowel categories presented by multiple exemplars. *Brain Research, 21*, 342–350.

Simos, P. G., Basile, L. F. H., & Papanicolaou, A. C. (1997). Source localization of the N400 response in a sentence-reading paradigm using evoked magnetic fields and magnetic resonance imaging. *Brain Research, 762*, 29–39.

Simos, P. G., Breier, J. I., Fletcher, J. M., Bergman, E., & Papanicolaou, A. C. (2000). Cerebral mechanisms involved in word reading in dyslexic children: A magnetic source imaging approach. *Cerebral Cortex, 10*, 809–816.

Simos, P. G., Breier, J. I., Fletcher, J. M., Foorman, B. R., Bergman, E., Fishbeck, K., et al. (2000). Brain activation profiles in dyslexic children during nonword reading: A magnetic source imaging study. *Neuroscience Letters, 290*, 61–65.

Simos, P. G., Breier, J. I., Wheless, J. W., Maggio, W. W., Fletcher, J. M., Castillo, E. M., et al. (2000). Brain mechanisms for reading: The role of the superior temporal gyrus in word and pseudoword naming. *Neuroreport, 11*, 2443–2446.

Simos, P. G., Breier, J. I., Zouridakis, G., & Papanicolaou, A. C. (1998a). MEG correlates of categorical-like temporal cue perception in humans. *Neuroreport, 9*, 2475–2479.

Simos, P. G., Breier, J. I., Zouridakis, G., & Papanicolaou, A. C. (1998b). Magnetic fields elicited by a tone onset time continuum in humans. *Cognitive Brain Research, 6*, 285–294.

Simos, P. G., Diehl, R., Breier, J. I., Molis, M., Zouridakis, G., & Papanicolaou, A. C. (1998). MEG correlates of categorical perception of a voice onset continuum in humans. *Cognitive Brain Research, 7*, 215–219.

Simos, P. G., Fletcher, J. M., Sarkari, S., Billingsley-Marshall, R. L., Francis, D. J., Castillo, E. M., et al. (2005). Early development of neurophysiological processes involved in normal reading and reading disability. *Neuropsychology, 19*, 787–798.

Simos, P. G., Papanicolaou, A. C., Breier, J. I., Wheless, J. W., Constantinou, J. E., Gormley, W. B., et al. (1999). Localization of language-specific cortex by using magnetic source imaging and electrical stimulation mapping. *Journal of Neurosurgery, 91*, 787–796.

Simos, P. G., Sarkari, S., Castillo, E. M., Billingsley-Marshall, R. L., Pataraia, E., Clear, T., et al. (2005). Estimates of neurophysiological activity in Wernicke's area: Reproducibility of complementary measures using magnetoencephalography. *Clinical Neurophysiology, 116*, 2381–2391.

Steinschneider, M., Volkov, I. O., Fishman, Y. I., Oya, H., Arezzo, J. C., Howard, M. A., III. (2005). Intracortical responses in human and monkey primary auditory cortex support a temporal processing mechanism for encoding of the voice onset time phonetic parameter. *Cerebral Cortex, 15*, 170–186.

Studdert-Kennedy, M., & Shankweiler, D. (1970). Hemispheric specialization for speech perception. *Journal of the Acoustical Society of America, 48*, 579–594.

Stufflebeam, S. M., Poeppel, D., Rowley, H. A., & Roberts, T. P. L. (1998). Perithreshold encoding of stimulus frequency and intensity in the M100 latency. *Neuroreport, 9*, 91–94.

Sussman, H. M. (1989). Neural coding of relational invariance in speech: Human language analogs to the barn owl. *Psychological Review, 96*, 631–642.

Szymanski, M. D., Perry, D. W., Gage, N. M., Rowley, H. A., Walker, J., Berger, M. S., et al. (2001). Magnetic source imaging of late evoked field responses to vowels: Toward an assessment of hemispheric dominance for language. *Journal of Neurosurgery, 94*, 445–453.

Tecchio, F., Benassi, F., Zappasodi, F., Gialloreti, L. E., Palermo, M., Seri, S., et al. (2003). Auditory sensory processing in autism: A magnetoencephalographic study. *Biological Psychiatry, 54*, 647–654.

Teismann, I. K., Soros, P., Manemann, E., Ross, B., Pantev, C., & Knecht, S. C. A. (2004). Responsiveness to repeated speech stimuli persists in left but not right auditory cortex. *Neuroreport, 15*, 1267–1270.

Valaki, C. E., Maestu, F., Simos, P. G., Zhang, W., Fernandez, A., Amo, C. M., et al. (2004). Cortical organization for receptive language functions in Chinese, English, and Spanish: A cross-linguistic MEG study. *Neuropsychologia, 42*, 967–979.

Wang, X., Merzenich, M. M., Beitel, R., & Schreiner, C. E. (1995). Representation of a species-specific vocalization in the primary auditory cortex of the common marmoset: Temporal and spectral characteristics. *Journal of Neurophysiology, 74*, 2685–2706.

8

Dyslexia

A New Look at Neural Substrates

SALLY E. SHAYWITZ
JEFFREY R. GRUEN
BENNETT A. SHAYWITZ

Developmental dyslexia is characterized by an unexpected difficulty in reading in children and adults who otherwise possess the intelligence and motivation considered necessary for accurate and fluent reading. More formally:

> Dyslexia is a specific learning disability that is neurobiological in origin. It is characterized by difficulties with accurate and/or fluent word recognition and by poor spelling and decoding abilities. These difficulties typically result from a deficit in the phonological component of language that is often unexpected in relation to other cognitive abilities and the provision of effective classroom instruction. (Lyon, Shaywitz, & Shaywitz, 2003, p. 2)

Dyslexia (or specific reading disability) is the most common and most carefully studied of the learning disabilities, affecting 80% of all individuals identified as learning disabled. This chapter reviews recent advances in our knowledge of the epidemiology, etiology, cognitive influences, and neurobiology of reading and dyslexia in children and adults.

Historically dyslexia in adults was first noted in the latter half of the 19th century, and developmental dyslexia in children was first reported in 1896 (Morgan, 1896). Our understanding of the neural systems for reading had its roots as early as 1891, when Dejerine suggested that a portion of the posterior brain region (which includes the angular gyrus and supramarginal gyrus in the inferior parietal lobule, and the posterior aspect of the superior temporal gyrus) was critical for reading. Another posterior brain region, this more ventral in the occipital–temporal area was also described by (Dejerine, 1892) as critical in reading.

EPIDEMIOLOGY, ETIOLOGY, AND COGNITIVE INFLUENCES

Epidemiology

Recent epidemiological data indicate that, like hypertension and obesity, dyslexia fits a dimensional model. In other words, within the population, reading ability and reading disability occur along a continuum, with reading disability representing the lower tail of a normal distribution of reading ability (Gilger, Borecki, Smith, DeFries, & Pennington, 1996; S. E. Shaywitz, Escobar, Shaywitz, Fletcher, & Makuch, 1992).

Dyslexia is perhaps the most common neurobehavioral disorder affecting children, with prevalence rates ranging from 5 to 17.5% (Interagency Committee on Learning Disabilities, 1987; S. E. Shaywitz, 1998). Longitudinal studies, both prospective (Francis, Shaywitz, Stuebing, Shaywitz, & Fletcher, 1996; B. A. Shaywitz, Fletcher, et al., 1995) and retrospective (Bruck, 1992; Felton, Naylor, & Wood, 1990; Scarborough, 1990), indicate that dyslexia is a persistent, chronic condition; it does not represent a transient "developmental lag" (see Figure 8.1). Over time, poor readers and good readers tend to maintain their relative positions along the spectrum of reading ability (Francis et al., 1996; B. A. Shaywitz, Holford, et al., 1995). This newer conceptualization contrasts with an earlier, categorical view of dyslexia, that envisioned a bimodal distribution of reading in children with dyslexia, forming a so-called "hump" at the lower tail of the distribution (Rutter & Yule, 1975; Yule & Rutter, 1985).

Genetics

Dyslexia is both familial and heritable (Pennington & Gilger, 1996). Family history is one of the most important risk factors, with 23% to as much as 65% of children who have a parent with dyslexia reported to have the disorder (Scarborough, 1990). The rate among siblings of affected persons is approximately 40% and, among parents, rates range from 27 to 49% (Pennington & Gilger, 1996). Knowledge of these rates provides opportunities for early identification of affected siblings and, often, for delayed but helpful identification of affected adults. Yet despite the strong familial nature, both recessive and dominant transmission is frequently observed within a

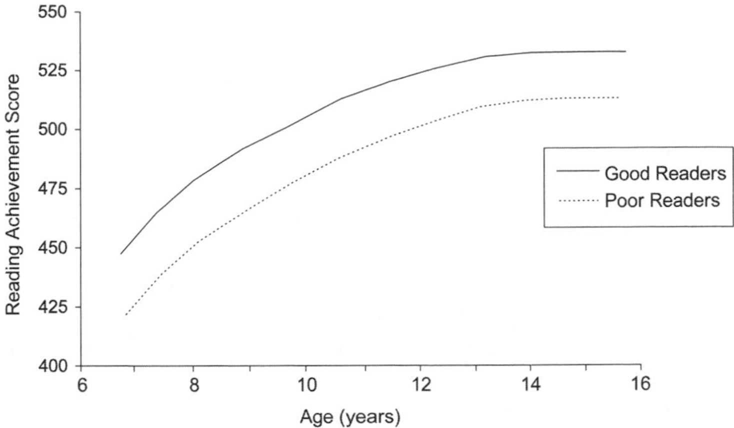

FIGURE 8.1. Trajectory of reading skills over time in nonimpaired readers and readers with dyslexia. Ordinate is Rasch scores (*W* scores) from the Woodcock–Johnson Reading Test (Woodcock & Johnson, 1989), and abscissa is age in years. Both readers with dyslexia and nonimpaired readers improve their reading scores as they get older, but the gap between them remains. Thus, dyslexia is a deficit and not a developmental lag. Figure derived from data in Francis et al. (1996). From S. E. Shaywitz (2003). Copyright 2003 by S. E. Shaywitz. Reprinted by permission.

single family. These data are consistent with a complex etiology. Studies of heritability show that between 44 and 77% of the variance is explained by genetic factors and the remaining variance by environmental factors (DeFries, Olson, Pennington, & Smith, 1991). These genetic factors are alleles of more than one gene that act in concert to produce the dyslexia phenotype (i.e., they are polygenic). Because of this polygenic nature, confusing transmission patterns are created that do not follow Mendelian rules governing recessive, dominant, or sex-linked single-gene disorders.

Segregation Analysis

In 1907, James Hinshelwood, a Scottish ophthalmologist, described four brothers with "word blindness" among 11 siblings in a single family. This condition, Dr. Hinshelwood wrote, "frequently assumes a family type." Today, "word blindness" is recognized as dyslexia, but it is noteworthy that Hinshelwood correctly recognized familial clustering 100 years ago, suggesting for the first time a genetic etiology.

The first large study of dyslexic families was conducted by Hallgren (1950). By documenting dyslexia in parents and children in each family (a method known as "segregation analysis"), Hallgren showed that when one parent was dyslexic, approximately one-half of the children were also affected. This pattern, consistent with an autosomal dominant pattern of inheritance, suggested that dyslexia was caused by a single major gene effect. Lewitter, DeFries, and Elston (1980) conducted the first segregation analysis based on actual tests of reading in probands (the family member presenting with symptoms), his or her parents, and siblings. They found that a multifactorial pattern—whereby multiple genes act together with environmental factors—was a better fit than a single major gene model (Lewitter et al., 1980).

Since the early 1980s, more sophisticated methods of segregation analysis have been developed that quantify "heritability," which is the fraction of the variance attributable to a total gene effect. Estimations of heritability are influenced by different models of inheritance, sample sizes, ascertainment, pedigrees, the reading tests administered, and the cut points that distinguish affected from unaffected individuals. For dyslexia, as mentioned earlier, the range of heritability is .44 to .77. This means that genes account for a significantly large percentage of the variance in normal reading ability. Relative to other multifactorial disorders, the heritability for dyslexia is similar to the heritability for schizophrenia (.82), schizoaffective disorders (.85), and Alzheimer's disease (.79), and reasonably close to that for autism (.90).

Genetic Linkage Analysis

The availability of large numbers of genetic markers beginning in the 1980s provided the means for achieving the next level of genetic resolution: estimating the number of dyslexia genes and their approximate locations on human chromosomes. The power of "genetic markers," short segments of DNA bases encoded in unique chromosomal locations, lies in their ability to tag and trace transmission of chromosomal segments from grandparents to parents to grandchildren within a single family. By correlating reading ability with inheritance of tagged chromosomal segments within families (a method known as "genetic linkage analysis"), the location of dyslexia genes (called "DYX" loci) could be confined to chromosomal regions of 1 to 10 million bases in size. Beginning in 1983, genetic linkage analyses of families from the United States, the United Kingdom, Germany, Canada, and Italy, have identified nine chromosomal regions, called DYX1 through DYX9, each spanning several million bases (Online Mendelian Inheritance in Man, 2000).

Identification of Dyslexia Genes

The means to achieve the next level of genetic resolution, identifying specific dyslexia genes within DYX loci, was provided by the Human Genome

Project, and the resulting sequencing and cataloguing of all human genes. Since 2004, four dyslexia genes have been identified, two by characterizing rare translocation breakpoints in individuals with dyslexia from Finland, and two by genetic association studies in common garden-variety dyslexia. A "translocation" involves the breakage and removal of a large segment of DNA from one chromosome, followed by the segment's attachment to a different chromosome.

Taipale et al. (2003) identified the first dyslexia gene in the DYX1 locus, subsequently named *DYX1C1*, which was present in a father and son, both of whom had dyslexia (Nopola-Hemmi et al., 2000; Taipale et al., 2003). In this case, a chromosome 15 translocation breakpoint (where part of chromosome 2 was exchanged with part of chromosome 15) disrupted the DNA coding sequence for *DYX1C1*. Although one independent study from Canada showed weak statistical association between sequence variations of *DYX1C1* in cases of dyslexia compared to controls (Wigg et al., 2004), the association could not be replicated in studies from the United Kingdom (Cope, Hill, et al., 2005; Scerri et al., 2004), Italy (Marino et al., 2005), or the United States (Meng, Hager, et al., 2005). In another family from Finland, Hannula-Jouppi et al. (2005) reported an individual with dyslexia and a translocation involving chromosomes 3 and 8 that disrupted a portion of the axon guidance receptor gene *ROBO1*. A sibling of the proband also had dyslexia but not the translocation.

Of the nine described DYX loci, the most often reproduced locus in genetic linkage analyses has been DYX2, located on chromosome 6. Using statistical association analysis, Francks et al. (2004) showed association between genetic markers in a gene called *KIAA0319* encoded in the DYX2 locus in cases from England. This finding was replicated in cases from Cardiff, Wales (Cope, Harold, et al., 2005) and Australia (Luciano et al., 2007). Using a high-density genetic marker panel, another research group studying the DYX2 locus identified a second dyslexia gene in that locus, called *DCDC2*, using statistical association. Meng, Smith, et al. (2005) investigated persons who were well-characterized for dyslexia from the United States. They reported associations with several reading-related phenotypes in the context of preserved IQ. This finding suggested a specific effect on reading performance (Meng, Smith, et al., 2005). In the human brain, *DCDC2* expression correlates with the location of reading centers in the temporal, prefrontal, and posterior cingulate regions.

Summary

The cumulative data from segregation and genetic linkage analyses provide compelling support for a largely genetic etiology for normal reading and susceptibility for dyslexia. To date four dyslexia genes have been identified;

two of them, *KIAA0319* and *DCDC2*, have been independently replicated. Three—*DYX1C1, KIAA0319*, and *DCDC2*—have significant effects on neuronal migration in the developing brain. However, it is too early to speculate about how these genes and/or their respective proteins work, or perhaps interact, to enable the neurophysiological infrastructure for language and reading. Also, it is premature to conjecture about the nature of the undiscovered genes and proteins encoded in other DYX loci. But the questions remain fascinating and are the driving force for current studies of the clinical effects of genetic variations, neuroembryology, neurophysiology, and genetic imaging. With the advent of genetic imaging, cellular processes may be visualized in space and time at the molecular–genetic level.

Cognitive Influences: Theories of Developmental Dyslexia

At least five theories of dyslexia have been proposed. These include (1) the phonological processing theory (Liberman, Shankweiler, & Liberman, 1989; Ramus et al., 2003); (2) the rapid auditory processing theory (Tallal, 1980, 2000; Tallal, Miller, & Fitch, 1993); (3) the visual theory (Livingstone, Rosen, Drislane, & Galaburda, 1991; Lovegrove, Bowling, Badcock, & Blackwood, 1980); (4) the cerebellar theory (Nicolson & Fawcett, 1990; Nicolson, Fawcett, & Dean, 2001); and (5) the magnocellular theory (Galaburda, Menard, & Rosen, 1994; Livingstone et al., 1991; Stein, 2003; Stein & Walsh, 1997). The reader is referred to Ramus et al. (2003) for a review and critique of the various theories.

Among investigators in the field there is now a strong consensus supporting the phonological processing theory. This theory recognizes that speech is natural and inherent, whereas reading is acquired and must be taught. To read, the beginning reader must recognize that letters and letter strings (the "orthography") represent the sounds of spoken language. To read, a child has to develop the insight that spoken words can be pulled apart into the elemental particles of speech ("phonemes"), and that the letters in a written word represent these sounds (S. E. Shaywitz, 2003). Such awareness is largely missing in children and adults with dyslexia (Bruck, 1992; J. M. Fletcher et al., 1994; Liberman & Shankweiler, 1991; Shankweiler, Liberman, Mark, Fowler, & Fischer, 1979; S. E. Shaywitz, 2003; Torgesen & Wagner, 1995; Wagner & Torgesen, 1987).

Results from large and well-studied populations with reading disability confirm that in young school-age children (J. M. Fletcher et al., 1994; Stanovich & Siegel, 1994), as well as adolescents (S. E. Shaywitz et al., 1999), a deficit in phonological processing represents the most robust and specific correlate of reading disability (Morris et al., 1998; Ramus et al.,

2003). Such findings form the basis for the most successful and evidence-based interventions designed to improve reading (National Reading Panel Report, 2000).

Implications of the Phonological Core Deficit Model of Dyslexia

Modern views envision reading as part of the language system; the language system itself is conceptualized as a hierarchy of component modules (Fodor, 1983), and at the lowest level of the hierarchy is the phonological module, dedicated to processing the elemental units of language, phonemes. In dyslexia, a deficit at the level of the phonological module impairs the ability to segment the spoken word into its underlying phonological elements, then link each letter(s) to its corresponding sound, and is referred to as a "phonological processing deficit." As a result, the reader experiences difficulty first in decoding the word, then in identifying it. The phonological processing deficit is domain-specific; that is, it is independent of other, nonphonological, abilities. In particular, the higher-order cognitive and linguistic functions involved in comprehension, such as general intelligence and reasoning, vocabulary (Share & Stanovich, 1995), and syntax (Shankweiler et al., 1995), are generally intact and serve to differentiate dyslexia from specific language impairment (Catts, Adlof, Hogan, & Weismer, 2005). This pattern—a deficit in phonological processing contrasted with intact, higher-order cognitive abilities—offers an explanation for the paradox of otherwise intelligent, often gifted people who experience great difficulty in reading (S. E. Shaywitz, 1996, 2003).

According to the model, a circumscribed deficit in a lower-order linguistic function (phonological processing) blocks access to higher-order processes and the ability to draw meaning from text. The problem is that the affected reader cannot use his or her higher-order linguistic skills to access the meaning until the printed word has first been decoded and identified. Suppose, for example, an individual knows the precise meaning of the spoken word *apparition*; however, she cannot use her knowledge of the meaning of the word until she can decode and identify the printed word on the page, and it will appear that she does not to know the word's meaning.

NEUROBIOLOGICAL STUDIES

To a large degree these advances in understanding the cognitive basis of dyslexia have informed and facilitated studies examining the neurobiological underpinnings of reading and dyslexia. Thus, a range of neurobiological investigations using postmortem brain specimens (Galaburda, Sherman,

Rosen, Aboitiz, & Geschwind, 1985), and, more recently, brain morphometry (Brown et al., 2001; Eliez et al., 2000; Filipek, 1996) and DTI (diffusion tensor magnetic resonance imaging [MRI]; Klingberg et al., 2000) suggests that there are differences in the temporal–parietal–occipital brain regions of readers with and without dyslexia. Although the focus of this chapter is on functional brain imaging, particularly, functional magnetic resonance imaging (fMRI), these other brain imaging studies are also discussed in more detail below.

Functional Brain Imaging: General Principles

Rather than being limited to examining the brain in an autopsy specimen, or measuring the size of brain regions with static morphometric indices based on computed tomography (CT) or MRI, functional imaging offers the possibility of examining brain function during performance of a cognitive task. We use the term "functional imaging" to refer to technologies that measure performance-related changes in metabolic activity and blood flow in specific brain regions, while an individual is engaged in a cognitive task.

The principles of fMRI depend on the principle of autoregulation of cerebral blood flow. When an individual is asked to perform a discrete cognitive task, that task places processing demands on particular neural systems in the brain. To meet those demands requires activation of neural systems in specific brain regions, and those changes in neural activity are reflected by changes in brain metabolic activity. These metabolic changes are in turn reflected by changes in cerebral blood flow and in the cerebral utilization of metabolic substrates, such as glucose. The term "functional imaging" has also been applied to magnetic source imaging, which uses magnetoencephalography (MEG), an electrophysiological method that has superior temporal resolution and may be used to delineate the time course of cognitive processes in the brain (Mody, 2004). Studies employing MEG are discussed following our discussion of studies using positron emission tomography (PET) and fMRI.

PET Studies

Some of the first functional imaging studies of dyslexia used PET (Gross-Glenn et al., 1991; Hagman et al., 1992). In practice, PET requires administration of a radioactive isotope to the individual, so that cerebral blood flow or cerebral utilization of glucose can be determined while the person is performing the task. Positron-emitting isotopes of nuclei of biological interest have very short biological half-lives and are synthesized in a cyclotron immediately prior to testing, a factor that mandates the time course of the experiment to conform to the short half-life of the radioisotope.

In one of the initial studies, (Rumsey et al., 1992) noted that adult readers with dyslexia failed to activate the left parietal and left middle temporal regions in response to an aurally presented rhyming task; no differences were found between readers with dyslexia and control adult readers on an aurally presented semantic judgment task (Rumsey et al., 1994). Paulesu and colleagues (1996) used a visually presented single-letter rhyming task to examine a hypothesis originally proposed by Geshwind (1965) that the neural underpinnings of dyslexia occur by a functional disconnection between written-language-related visual areas and spoken-language-related frontal brain regions. Paulesu et al. (1996) reported a disconnection between the anterior and posterior language regions, a theory supported by their finding of underactivation in the insula in a small group of university students with compensated dyslexia. Finally, Rumsey et al. (1997) noted that adults with dyslexia demonstrated reduced blood flow in temporal cortex and inferior parietal cortex, especially on the left, during tasks tapping phonological processing.

Functional Magnetic Resonance Imaging

Among the various methods that may be used to map an individual brain's response to specific cognitive stimuli, fMRI appears to hold the most promise. It is noninvasive and safe, and can be used repeatedly, properties that make it ideal for studying humans, especially children.

In principle, the signal used to construct MRI images changes by a small amount (typically on the order of 1–5%), in regions that are activated by a stimulus or task. The increase in signal results from the combined effects of increases in the tissue blood flow, volume, and oxygenation, though the precise contribution of each of these is still somewhat uncertain. MRI intensity increases when deoxygenated blood is replaced by oxygenated blood. A variety of methods can be used to record the changes that occur, but one preferred approach makes use of ultrafast imaging, such as echo planar imaging, in which complete images that cover the whole brain are acquired in times substantially shorter than a second. Echo planar imaging can provide images at a rate fast enough to capture the time course of changes in blood flow and blood oxygenation in the brain in response to neural activation, and to permit use with a wide variety of imaging paradigms. Details of fMRI are reviewed elsewhere (Anderson & Gore, 1997; Frackowiak et al., 2004; Jezzard, Matthews, & Smith, 2001).

Functional MRI has proven to be a powerful tool for understanding the brain organization for reading. Studies have examined a number of domains, each of which is detailed below.

Identification and Localization of Specific Systems and Their Differences in Good and Poor Readers

A number of research groups, including our own, have used fMRI to examine the functional organization of the brain for reading in readers with dyslexia (DYS) and nonimpaired (NI) controls. We (S. E. Shaywitz et al., 1998) studied 61 right-handed adult subjects, 29 DYS readers (14 men and 15 women, ages 16–54 years) and 32 NI readers (16 men and 16 women, ages 18–63 years), focusing on those brain regions that previous research had implicated in reading and language (Demonet, Price, Wise, & Frackowiak, 1994; Henderson, 1986; Petersen, Fox, Snyder, & Raichle, 1990). We found significant differences in brain activation patterns between DYS and NI readers, differences that emerged during tasks that made progressive demands on phonological analysis. Thus, during nonword rhyming in DYS readers, we found a disruption in a posterior region involving the superior temporal gyrus and angular gyrus, with a concomitant increase in activation in the inferior frontal gyrus anteriorly.

When studying adults with dyslexia there is always the concern that the findings may represent the consequences of a lifetime of poor reading, so it is important to study children to examine the neural systems for reading during the acquisition of literacy. We (B. A. Shaywitz et al., 2002) used fMRI to study 144 right-handed children, 70 readers with dyslexia (DYS; 21 girls and 49 boys, ages 7–18 years, mean age 13.3 years) and 74 nonimpaired (NI) readers (31 girls and 43 boys, ages 7–17 years, mean age 10.9 years) as they read pseudowords and real words. This study was designed to minimize some of the problems encountered in previous studies by examining a relatively large sample, particularly for a functional imaging study, that covered a broad age range and included both boys and girls. We found significant differences in brain activation patterns during phonological analysis in the NI compared to DYS children. Specifically, children who were normal readers demonstrated significantly greater activation than did children with dyslexia in predominantly left-hemisphere sites (including the inferior frontal, superior temporal, parietal–temporal and middle temporal–middle occipital gyri) and a few right-hemisphere sites (including an anterior site around the inferior frontal gyrus and two posterior sites, one in the parietal–temporal region, the other in the occipital–temporal region; Plate 8.1).

These data converge with reports from many investigators using functional brain imaging that have shown a failure of left-hemisphere posterior brain systems in individuals with dyslexia to function properly during reading (Brunswick, McCrory, Price, Frith, & Frith, 1999; Helenius, Tarkiainen, Cornelissen, Hansen, & Salmelin, 1999; Horwitz, Rumsey, & Donohue, 1998; Paulesu et al., 2001; Rumsey et al., 1992; Salmelin, Service, Kiesila, Uutela, & Salonen, 1996; Seki et al., 2001; B. A. Shaywitz et al., 2002; S. E. Shaywitz et al., 2003; Temple et al., 2000), as well as during nonreading visual processing tasks (Demb, Boynton, & Heeger, 1998; Eden et al., 1996). These findings indicate that dysfunction in left-hemisphere posterior reading circuits is already present in children with dyslexia and cannot be ascribed simply to a lifetime of poor reading.

Compensatory Systems in Readers with Dyslexia

The design of our study (B. A. Shaywitz et al., 2002) also allowed for the examination of compensatory systems that develop in readers with dyslexia. Two kinds of information were helpful in examining this issue. One involved the relationship between brain activation and age. During the most difficult and specific phonological task (nonword rhyming), *older* compared to younger readers with dyslexia engaged the left and right inferior frontal gyrus. In contrast, both older and younger readers without impairment primarily engaged the left inferior frontal gyrus.

Another clue to compensatory systems comes from the findings of the relationship between reading skills and brain activation, in which a significant positive correlation was noted between reading skills and activation in the left occipital–temporal word form area. We also found a *negative* correlation between brain activation and reading skills in the *right* occipital–temporal region; that is, the poorer the reader, the greater the activation in the right occipito-temporal region. Thus compensatory systems seem to involve areas around the inferior frontal gyrus in both hemispheres and, perhaps, the right-hemisphere homologue of the left occipital–temporal word form area as well.

Computational Roles of the Component Systems

These data from laboratories around the world indicate that a number of interrelated neural systems are used in reading, at least two in posterior brain regions, as well as distinct and related systems in anterior regions. The two posterior systems appear to parallel the two systems proposed by Logan (1988, 1997) as critical in the development of skilled automatic reading. One system involves word analysis, operates on individual units of words such as phonemes, requires attentional resources, and processes relatively slowly. It is reasonable to propose that this system involves the parietal–temporal posterior reading system. As noted previously, as early as 1891, (Dejerine) suggested that a portion of the posterior brain region (which includes the angular gyrus and supramarginal gyrus in the inferior parietal lobule, and the posterior aspect of the superior temporal gyrus) was critical for reading. Since that time, a large literature on acquired inability to read (acquired alexia) describes neuroanatomical lesions most prominently centered about the angular gyrus as a region considered pivotal in mapping the visual percept of the print onto the phonological structures of the language system (Damasio & Damasio, 1983; Friedman, Ween, & Albert, 1993; Geschwind, 1965). Thus, it is reasonable to suggest that this temporal–parietal reading system may be critical for analyzing the written word; that is, transforming the orthography into the underlying linguistic structures.

Perhaps of even more importance to reading is the second system proposed by Logan, a system that operates on the whole word (word form), an obligatory system that does not require attention and that processes very rapidly. This system, which also has historical roots described by Dejerine (1892), is located in another posterior brain region, the occipital–temporal area. Converging evidence from a number of lines of investigation indicates that the left occipital–temporal area is critical for the development of skilled reading and functions as an automatic, instant word-recognition system, the visual word form area (Cohen et al., 2000, 2002; McCandliss, Cohen, & Dehaene, 2003). Not only does brain activation in this region increase as reading skills increase (B. A. Shaywitz et al., 2002; Plate 8.2), but this region also responds preferentially to rapidly presented stimuli (Price, Moore, & Frackowiak, 1996), responding within 150 msec after presentation of a stimulus (Salmelin et al., 1996). This system is engaged even when the word has not been consciously perceived (Dehaene et al., 2001). Still another reading-related neural circuit involves an anterior system in the left inferior frontal gyrus (Broca's area), a region that has long been associated with articulation and also serves an important function in silent reading and naming (Fiez & Peterson, 1998; Frackowiak et al., 2004).

Plasticity of Neural Systems for Reading

Given the converging evidence of a disruption of posterior reading systems in dyslexia, an obvious question relates to the plasticity of these neural systems, that is, whether they are malleable and can be changed by an effective reading intervention. In a report (B. A. Shaywitz et al., 2004), we hypothesized that the provision of an evidence-based, phonologically mediated reading intervention would improve reading fluency and the development of the neural systems serving skilled reading. The experimental intervention was structured to help children gain phonological knowledge (develop an awareness of the internal structure of spoken words) and, at the same time, develop their understanding of how the orthography represents the phonology (Blachman, Ball, Black, & Tangel, 1994). Children in the community intervention received a variety of interventions within the school setting.

We recruited 78 right-handed children, ages 6.1–9.4 years, for three experimental groups: experimental intervention (EI, *N* = 37); community intervention (CI, *N* = 12) and community controls (i.e., nonimpaired readers; CC, *N* = 28). Children in the community intervention met criteria for reading disability and received a variety of interventions commonly provided within the school. Specific, systematic, explicit, phonologically-based interventions comparable to the experimental intervention were not used in any of reading programs that were provided to the community group. The experimental intervention provided second- and third-grade poor readers with 50 minutes of daily, explicit and systematic individual tutoring and focused on helping children understand the alphabetic principle (how letters and combinations of letters represent the small segments of speech known as "phonemes"), and provided many opportunities to practice applying the letter–sound linkages taught. Children were imaged on three occasions—preintervention, immediately postintervention, and 1 year after the intervention was complete.

Children who received the experimental intervention improved their reading accuracy, reading fluency, and reading comprehension. Compared to the CI group, both CC and EI groups demonstrate increased activation in left-hemisphere regions, including the inferior frontal gyrus and the posterior aspect of the middle temporal gyrus. One year after the experimental intervention had ended (Plate 8.3), compared to their preintervention images, EI group members were activating bilateral inferior frontal gyri, left superior temporal sulcus, the occipital–temporal region involving the posterior aspects of the middle and inferior temporal gyri, and the anterior aspect of the middle occipital gyrus, the inferior occipital gyrus, and the lingual gyrus.

These findings indicate that the nature of the remedial educational intervention is critical to successful outcomes in children with reading disabilities, and that the use of an evidence-based reading intervention facilitates the development of those fast-paced neural systems that underlie skilled reading. Our findings indicate that a phonologically based reading intervention leads to the development of neural systems both in anterior (inferior frontal gyrus) and posterior (middle temporal gyrus) brain regions. This is the first imaging study of a reading intervention in either children or adults that reports its effects on reading fluency, a critical but often neglected reading skill (National Reading Panel Report, 2000). It is also the largest imaging study of a reading intervention and the first report of the effects of a reading intervention on fMRI in children to examine not only children with reading disability who received an experimental reading intervention but also children with reading disabilities who did not receive such an intervention. Some of the previous studies have used fMRI to examine the effects of a commercial language intervention program (Fast ForWord) first in adults, and then in children with dyslexia (Temple et al.,

2000, 2003). In the first study, the authors examined three adults with dyslexia who received Fast ForWord training during a task that required subjects to respond to a high-pitched stimulus. Following 33 days of training for 100 minutes a day, two of the three subjects demonstrated greater activation in the left prefrontal cortex after training compared to before training. These two adults also showed improvement on both rapid auditory processing and auditory language comprehension after training; the one adult who did not show a change in fMRI after training failed to show behavioral changes (Temple et al., 2000). In a more recent study, immediate short-term improvement in reading accuracy and brain activation changes were observed in 20 children with dyslexia, changes that included the areas observed in our study, as well as in the right hemisphere and cingulate cortex (Temple et al., 2003). In yet another study, Richards et al. (2000) used proton magnetic resonance spectroscopy (MRS) to measure brain lactate concentrations at two time points, 1 year apart, in eight boys with dyslexia and seven control boys, before and after a 3-week phonologically based reading intervention. Before treatment, the group with dyslexia demonstrated increased lactate concentration (compared to controls) in left anterior brain areas, while listening to aurally presented words and nonwords. After treatment, brain lactate concentrations were no different in the two groups, and phonological decoding, measured by the Word Attack subtest of the Woodcock Reading Mastery Test—Revised (Woodcock, 1987) improved after treatment. More recently, this same group reported fMRI changes in areas similar to those reported in our studies following 28 hours of an intensive phonological and morphological reading intervention (Aylward et al., 2003).

Simos and colleagues (2002) used magnetoencephalography (MEG) in eight children with dyslexia and eight controls before and after an 8-week phonologically based reading intervention. Prior to intervention, the dyslexic readers demonstrated little or no activation of the posterior portion of the left superior temporal gyrus. After intervention, reading improved and activation increased in the left superior temporal gyrus.

Eden and her associates (2004) examined brain activation in adults with dyslexia. Two conditions involving aurally presented single words were used. In the word repetition condition, subjects repeated each word presented over the headphones. In the sound deletion condition, subjects were asked to repeat the word after deleting the initial sound (e.g., in response to the stimulus *cat*, the response would be *at*). Intervention lasted 8 weeks and used a phonologically based commercial program delivered by the staff from the Lindamood–Bell Learning Corporation. Intervention-related increases in brain activation were observed in the left parietal cortex and left fusiform gyrus, as well as right-hemispheric parietal–temporal regions.

Findings here with reading intervention suggest plasticity of the neural systems for reading in children, and parallel those observed after a variety of therapies in individuals with stroke (Carey et al., 2002) and after surgical removal of a hemisphere in a child with Rasmussen syndrome (Hertz-Pennier et al., 2002). Importantly, the effects of the experimental intervention, both on promoting skilled reading and on the activation of the occipital–temporal word form area shown to be critical for skilled reading (B. A. Shaywitz et al., 2002), are similar to the co-occurrence of visual–spatial proficiency and cortical specialization reported in adults. Thus, Gauthier and her associates (Gauthier, 2000; Gauthier et al., 2000) have demonstrated a progressive increase of activation of the right-hemisphere fusiform face area and right lateral occipital cortex, with increasing proficiency in identifying novel face-like stimuli they called "Greebles." The current findings suggest that, as in the recognition of Greebles, an intervention that improved proficiency in reading was the most important element in functional reorganization of the neural systems for reading. Such findings, which have important implications for understanding the effect of phonologically based reading programs on neural systems of young children, have been shown to be effective in the educational equivalent of clinical trials.

In summary, these data demonstrate that an intensive evidence-based reading intervention brings about significant and durable changes in brain organization, so that brain activation patterns resemble those of typical readers in the left occipital–temporal area and reading fluency improvement. These data have important implications for public policy on teaching children to read: The provision of an evidence-based reading intervention at an early age improves reading fluency and facilitates the development of those neural systems that underlie skilled reading.

Implications of fMRI Studies for Identifying Types of Reading Disability

Longitudinal Patterns

Using data from participants in a longitudinal, epidemiological study, we (S. E. Shaywitz et al., 2003) compared the neural systems for reading in nonimpaired readers to two groups of young adults who were poor readers as children. One group comprised relatively compensated poor readers (i.e., poor readers who improved their reading accuracy as young adults but were impaired in reading fluency), whereas another group comprised poor readers with persistent difficulties in reading accuracy from early childhood, as well as impaired fluency. In addition, we wanted to determine whether any factors that distinguished between the compensated and persistently poor readers might account for their different outcomes. To this end we took advantage of the availability of a cohort participating in the Connecticut Longitudinal Study, a representative sample of young adults who have been prospectively followed since 1983, when they were age 5 years. Members of this cohort had their reading performance assessed yearly throughout their primary and secondary schooling (Ferrer et al., 2007; B. A. Shaywitz, Fletcher, Holahan, & Shaywitz, 1992; S. E. Shaywitz et al., 1999; S. E. Shaywitz, Shaywitz, Fletcher, & Escobar, 1990).

Three groups of young adults, ages 18.5–22.5 years, were classified as follows:

1. Persistently poor readers (PPR; *N* = 24), if they met criteria for poor reading in second or fourth grade and again in grade 9 or 10.
2. Accuracy (but not fluency) improved (compensated) readers (AIR; *N* = 19), if criteria were satisfied for poor reading in second or fourth grade but not in grade 9 or 10.
3. Nonimpaired readers (NI; *N* = 27) were selected on the basis of (a) not meeting the criteria for poor reading in any of the grades 2–10; (b) having a reading standard score 94 (above the 40th percentile) to prevent overlap with the PPR and AIR groups; and (c) having average Full Scale IQ lower than 130 to avoid a supernormal control group.

Findings during pseudoword rhyming in both groups of poor readers (AIR, PPR) were similar to those observed in previous studies, that is, a relative underactivation in posterior neural systems located in the superior temporal and the occipital–temporal regions. But when reading real words, findings were quite surprising. Brain activation patterns in the AIR and PPR readers diverged. As they had for the pseudoword rhyming task, compared to NI, AIR demonstrated relative underactivation in left posterior regions (Plate 8.4, column 2). In contrast, during real-word reading, PPR subjects activated posterior systems (Plate 8.4, column 3); thus, there was comparable activation in NI and PPR groups in the posterior reading systems, a finding that was both new and unexpected. Despite the significantly better reading performance in the NI compared to the PPR group on every reading task administered, left posterior reading systems were activated during the reading of real words in both NI and PPR groups.

We hypothesized that the PPR readers were reading real words very differently from NI readers, reading the very simple real words primarily by memory. Support for this belief came from their performance on an out-of-MR magnet word pronunciation task. PPR readers were accurate while reading high-frequency words, but far less accurate when reading low-frequency and unfamiliar words. Further support for this hypothesis comes

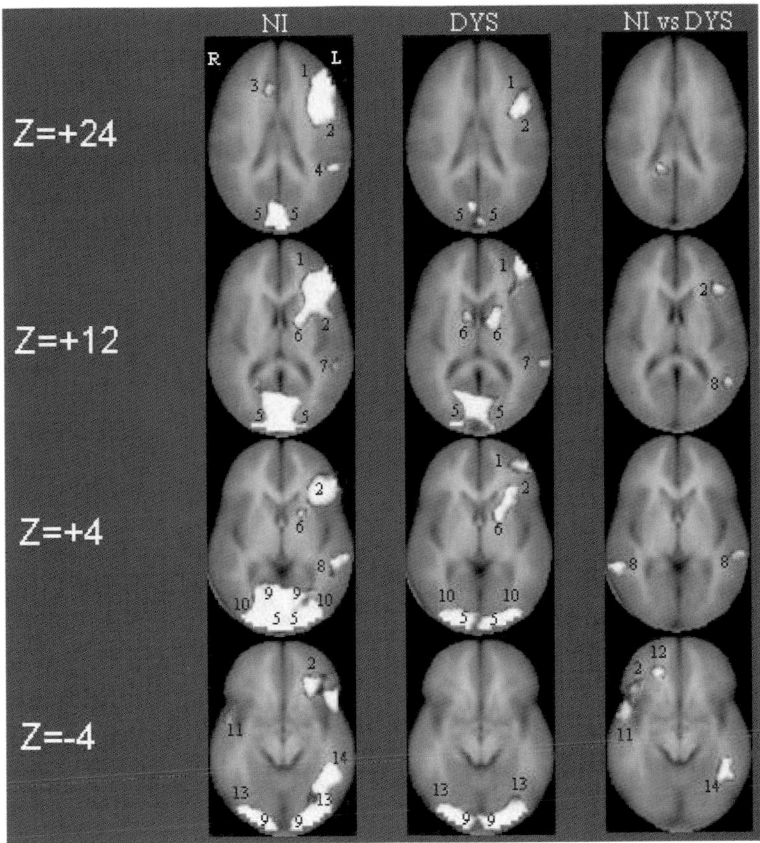

PLATE 8.1. Composite maps (columns 1 and 2) demonstrating brain activation in nonimpaired (NI) readers and readers with dyslexia (DYS) readers as they determined whether two pseudowords rhymed (NWR, nonword rhyme), and composite contrast maps (column 3) comparing directly the brain activation of the two groups. In columns 1 and 2, red–yellow indicates areas that had significantly greater activation (p = .05) in the NWR task compared to the line task, and in column 3, red–yellow indicates brain regions that were more active in NI compared to DYS during the NWR task. The four rows of images from top to bottom show axial slices at z = +23, +14, +5, and –5 in Talairach space (Talairach & Tournoux, 1988), where smaller z coordinate values correspond to lower slices. Following standard MRI convention, the right side of the axial slice corresponds to the left hemisphere. The legend for brain activation is (1) middle frontal gyrus, (2) inferior frontal gyrus, (3) anterior cingulate gyrus, (4) supramarginal gyrus, (5) cuneus, (6) basal ganglia, (7) superior temporal gyrus, (8) superior temporal sulcus and posterior aspect of the superior and middle temporal gyri, (9) lingual gyrus, (10) middle occipital gyrus, (11) anterior aspect of superior temporal gyrus, (12) medial orbital gyrus, (13) inferior occipital gyrus, and (14) posterior aspect of middle temporal gyrus and anterior aspect of middle occipital gyrus. Reprinted from B. A. Shaywitz et al. (2002). Copyright (2002) with permission from Elsevier.

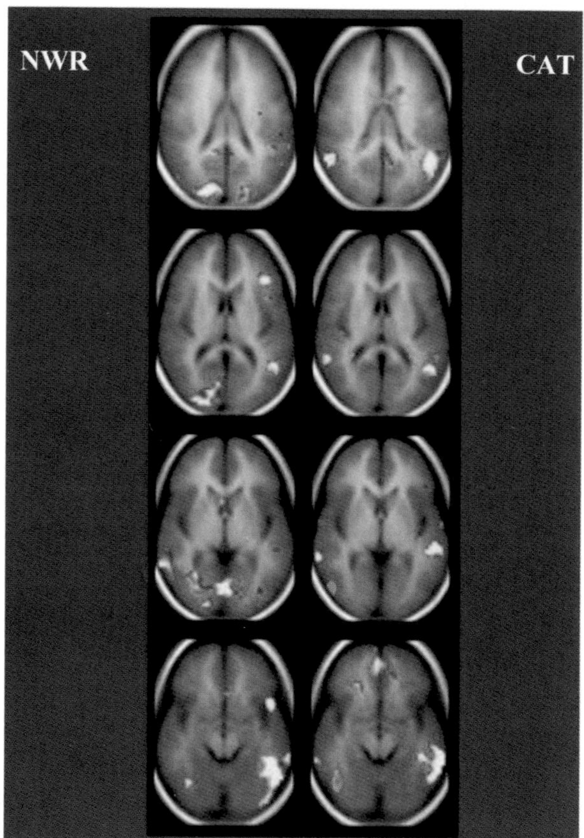

PLATE 8.2. Correlation map between reading skills as measured by the Word Attack Subtest of the Woodcock–Johnson Reading Test (R. W. Woodcock & Johnson, 1989) performed during two out-of-magnet activation tasks, judging whether two pseudowords rhymed (NWR) and whether two real words were in the same category (CAT). At each voxel, a Pearson correlation coefficient (r) was calculated, with age included as a covariate; a normal distribution test was used (Hays, 1988). Areas in yellow–red show a positive correlation of in-magnet tasks with the out-of-magnet reading test (threshold, $p < .01$). The four rows of images from top to bottom correspond to $z = +23$, $+14$, $+5$ and -5 coordinates (see Plate 8.1) in the Talairach and Tournoux (1988) brain atlas. Following standard MRI convention, the right side of the axial slice corresponds to the left hemisphere. Strong correlation was found in the inferior aspect of the temporal–occipital region (fourth row), in the more superior aspect of the temporal–occipital regions (second and third rows), and in the parietal regions (top row). Reprinted from B. A. Shaywitz et al. (2002). Copyright (2002) with permission from Elsevier.

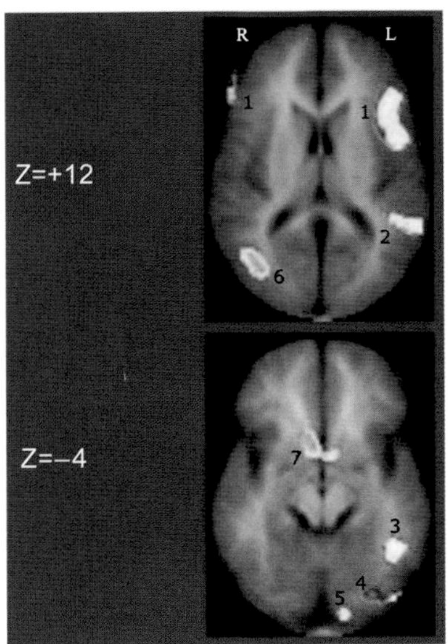

PLATE 8.3. Composite maps indicating the difference in activation between Year 3 and Year 1 in the experimental intervention (EI) study group (n = 25). Red–yellow indicates brain regions that were more active (p = .05) in the third year; blue–purple indicates brain regions that were more active (p = .05) in the first year. The slice locations are z = 12 and –4 in Talairach space (Talairach & Tournoux, 1988). Brain regions (Talairach x, y, z coordinates in parentheses) more active in the third year compared to the first were (1) bilateral inferior frontal gyri (±41, 23, 12), (2) the left superior temporal sulcus (51, –42, 12), (3) the occipital–temporal region involving the posterior aspects of the middle and inferior temporal gyri and the anterior aspect of the middle occipital gyrus (42, –49, –4), (4) the inferior occipital gyrus (34, –71, –4), and (5) the lingual gyrus (13, –88, –4). The brain regions more active in the first year compared to the third year were (6) the right middle temporal gyrus (35, –69, 12) and (7) the caudate nucleus (–7, 10, –4). Following standard MRI convention, the right side of the axial slice corresponds to the left hemisphere. Reprinted from B. A. Shaywitz et al. (2004). Copyright (2004) with permission from Elsevier.

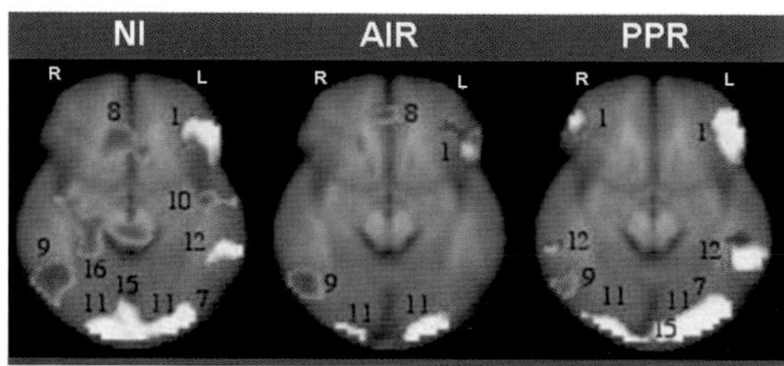

PLATE 8.4. Composite maps demonstrating brain activation in readers who are nonimpaired (NI), accuracy improved (AIR), and persistently poor (PPR) during the CAT (real-word categorization) reading task. Red–yellow indicates areas that had significantly greater activation ($p = .05$) in the rhyme task compared to the line task. Blue–purple indicates areas that had significantly greater activation ($p = .05$) in the line task compared to the rhyme task. The slice locations correspond to a z level of –4 in the Talairach and Tournoux atlas (Talairach & Tournoux, 1988). Following standard MRI convention, the right side of the axial slice corresponds to the left hemisphere. The legend for regional brain activation is as follows: (1) inferior frontal gyrus, (2) precentral gyrus, (3) insula, (4) superior temporal gyrus and superior temporal sulcus, (5) middle temporal gyrus and superior temporal sulcus, (6) cuneus, (7) middle occipital gyrus, (8) anterior cingulate sulcus and adjacent aspects of the cingulate gyrus and superior frontal gyrus, (9) posterior middle temporal gyrus and anterior middle occipital gyrus, (10) anterior aspect of the superior temporal gyrus, (11) inferior occipital gyrus, (12) middle temporal gyrus, (13) superior frontal gyrus, (14) posterior cingulate gyrus, (15) lingual gyrus, (16) medial occipital–temporal gyrus (parahippocampal region), and (17) basal ganglia. Adapted from S. E. Shaywitz et al. (2003). Copyright (2003) with permission from Elsevier.

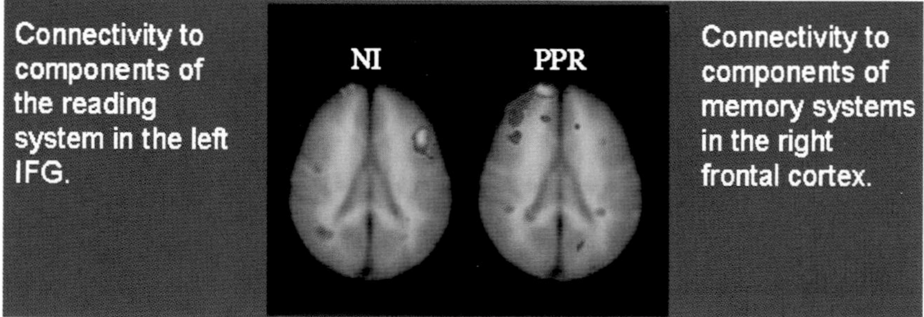

PLATE 8.5. Group connectivity profiles between the "seed voxel" in the left occipital–temporal region (Talairach x, y, z coordinates –55, –36, –5) and other brain regions during the CAT (real-word categorization) reading task. Red–yellow indicates significant positive correlations ($p < .02$); blue–purple indicates negative correlation. The images correspond to $z = +24$ in Talairach space (Talairach & Tournoux, 1988). Following standard MRI convention, the right side of the axial slice corresponds to the left hemisphere. In the nonimpaired readers (on the left), a strong positive correlation is observed between the left occipital–temporal region and the left inferior frontal gyrus (IFG; Broca's area), a traditional language region. In contrast, for persistently poor readers, the occipital–temporal region is correlated with regions in the right superior, middle, and IFGs, brain regions believed to play a role in attention and memory. Reprinted from S. E. Shaywitz et al. (2003). Copyright (2003) with permission from Elsevier.

from an analysis of the functional connections between different brain regions. This strategy involves selecting and interrogating a specific group of activated voxels termed "seed voxels," in this case, voxels in the left occipital–temporal region, then determining other brain regions most functionally related (connected) to the seed voxels (McIntosh, Bookstein, Haxby, & Grady, 1996; McIntosh, Nyberg, Bookstein, & Tulving, 1997).

Results indicated that NI readers demonstrated connectivity between the left occipital–temporal seed region and the left inferior frontal gyrus, a traditional language region (Plate 8.5, column 1). In contrast, PPR subjects (Plate 8.5, column 2) demonstrated functional connectivity between the seed region and right prefrontal areas often associated with working memory and memory retrieval (P. Fletcher, Frith, & Rugg, 1997; MacLeod, Buckner, Miezin, Petersen, & Raichle, 1998). This finding suggests that in the persistently poor readers, the occipital–temporal area functions as a component of a memory network, and that this group resorts less to linguistic (i.e., phonological) mediation in the rhyme task. A more recent fMRI study (B. A. Shaywitz et al., 2007) also demonstrates the importance of memory systems in readers with dyslexia. This study found that brain regions developing with age in readers with dyslexia differ from those in NI readers, primarily in being localized to a more left posterior and medial, rather than a more left anterior and lateral occipital–temporal region. This difference in activation patterns between readers with dyslexia and NI readers has parallels to reported brain activation differences observed during reading of two Japanese writing systems: *Kana* and *Kanji*. *Kana* script employs symbols that are linked to the sound (comparable to English and other alphabetic scripts); *Kanji* script uses ideographs in which each character must be memorized. In the imaging study of these writing systems, activation, similar to that seen in NI readers, occurred during the reading of *Kana*. In contrast, activation, comparable to that observed in readers with dyslexia, was noted during reading of *Kanji* script, suggesting that the portion of the word form region developing in readers with dyslexia functions as part of a memory-based system.

Possibilities Underlying Compensation versus Persistence

Because it is a longitudinal study, data from the Connecticut Longitudinal Study as early as kindergarten and first grade were available and indicated that the two groups of disabled readers (PPR and AIR) began school with comparable reading skills, but with PPR, compared to AIR, having poorer cognitive, primarily verbal, ability and attending more disadvantaged schools. These findings suggest that PPR readers may be doubly disadvantaged in being exposed to a less rich language environment at home, then less effective reading instruction at school. In contrast, protective factors in the AIR group, for example, the presence of compensatory factors, such as stronger verbal ability and exposure to a richer language environment at home, allowed AIR readers to minimize, in part, the consequences of their phonological processing deficit, so that as adults the AIR readers were indistinguishable from NI readers on a measure of reading comprehension.

These findings are consonant with a large body of evidence indicating that the impact of dyslexia can be modified by the availability of compensatory resources, for example, semantic knowledge (Snowling, 2000), use of context (Frith & Snowling, 1983; Nation & Snowling, 1998), and verbal ability (Torgesen et al., 2001) to compensate for phonological processing deficits. In adults, verbal abilities, as measured by Verbal IQ, directly predict reading accuracy, with phonological factors influencing reading indirectly through their effects on Verbal IQ (Berninger, Abbott, & Thomson, 2001). The current study extends such findings by demonstrating that *childhood* cognitive ability may be an important influence on the development of reading skills in later childhood and into adult life. Beginning reading is most related to phonological processing skills, and within a few years, other language skills, for example, semantic knowledge, gain in importance. The current findings suggest that greater cognitive abilities may provide some degree of compensation for a reading difficulty. Intuitively this makes sense, because a larger vocabulary and better reasoning skills are helpful when a struggling reader is trying to decipher unknown words. If the word is in a child's spoken-language vocabulary, the beginning reader may recognize the word even if he or she can only partially sound it out. Strong reasoning abilities also help this reader to use the context around an unknown word to figure out its meaning. The imaging findings noted earlier that demonstrated a greater number of ancillary systems in AIR compared to PPR, for example, activation in right frontal and right occipital–temporal regions, as well as greater activation in left frontal areas, may represent the neural correlates of this compensation.

Magnetoencephalography

Magnetoencephalography (MEG), also referred to as magnetic source imaging (MSI), has been used to study reading and dyslexia. In principle, MEG depends on measuring changes in extracranial magnetic fields generated by postsynaptic currents in cortical pyramidal cells in response to stimulus presentation. Compared to fMRI, which has good spatial resolution but is somewhat insensitive to the time course of events, MEG is most useful in examining the time course of cognitive processes, that is, the sequence of activation in millisecond resolution.

In a series of experiments in adults and typically reading children, Papanicolaou and his associates (2003) described a sequence of brain activation profiles in aurally and visually presented word recognition tasks (see a recent review of these studies by Papanicolaou et al., 2003.) Only a brief summary of the findings is included here. This pattern comprises the following:

- An initial engagement (within the first 100–150 msec) of primary sensory cortices (the floor of the Sylvian fissure for aurally presented real words, and the occipital cortex for real written words).
- This is followed by activation (150–250 msec) of the posterior portion of the left superior temporal gyrus for aurally presented words, and the left fusiform and lingual gyri for written words.
- These activations are followed by activations in the left superior and middle temporal areas, inferior parietal regions (including the angular and supramarginal gyri), as well as the inferior frontal cortex, including Broca's area.
- When the visual stimuli are "pseudowords" rather than real words, the left superior temporal, left inferior parietal, and left inferior frontal regions are activated primarily, and the middle temporal and hippocampus do not activate.

The principal difference observed in children with dyslexia is activation initially of *right* temporal and *right* temporoparietal systems, before moving to left hemisphere systems, rather than the typical *left*-hemisphere activation. These hemispheric differences are observed as well in even younger children at risk for reading problems. Provision of an effective intervention program resulted in significant activity increases in the left superior temporal and left inferior parietal regions (Papanicolaou et al., 2003).

Structural Sources of Evidence

Postmortem Studies of Dyslexia

As noted earlier, postmortem studies of adults with acquired alexia suggested two posterior brain regions influential in the reading process. Using traditional neuropathological methods, Galaburda and his associates (1985) were able to examine the neurobiological underpinnings of dyslexia more than two decades ago. Subjects were adults with a childhood history suggestive of reading difficulties, who had died suddenly, usually in automobile or motorcycle accidents. Galaburda et al. described a pattern that comprised symmetry of the planum temporale, rather than the asymmetric pattern of larger left planum observed in adults assumed not to be reading impaired. In addition, affected individuals exhibited gray matter heterotopias, most commonly observed along the left Sylvian fissure. However, these findings have not been replicated with technological advances.

Structural MRI Studies of Dyslexia

Building on the postmortem findings, a number of structural MRI studies have attempted to demonstrate the asymmetrical planum in individuals with dyslexia. Earlier MR imaging studies of dyslexia have assessed asymmetries in such measures as gross regional volumes (Jernigan, Hesselink, Sowell, & Tallal, 1991) and the lengths of various posterior temporal regions, such as the planum temporale (Leonard et al., 1993). We have examined this issue and discussed this early literature previously, and the reader is referred to that paper for more details (Schultz et al., 1994). Other studies have demonstrated a reduction in temporal lobe volume, particularly on the left side, in right-handed adult males with dyslexia (Eliez et al., 2000), and localized to temporal lobe gray matter (Brown et al., 2001). A more recent study examining children indicates, in dyslexia, smaller right anterior lobes of the cerebellum and pars triangularis, and smaller total brain volume (Eckert et al., 2003). These studies have not supported the adult postmortem findings.

Advances in computer technology now allow a much more detailed examination of brain cortical changes. For example, Sowell and her associates (2002) have used such technology to map cortical change across the lifespan, and to map the sulcal pattern asymmetry *in vivo*. Such studies are currently underway in children with and without dyslexia in our laboratory, in collaboration with Dr. Sowell.

Reading and Dyslexia in Languages Other Than English

Phonological processing deficits characterize dyslexia in non-English languages that use an alphabetic script. For example, Paulesu et al. (2001) noted a comparable disruption to native English speakers in posterior reading systems in college students with dyslexia in Italy and in France. Recent studies have also begun to examine dyslexia in nonalphabetic languages, such as Chinese. In nonimpaired Chinese readers, Siok, Jin, Fletcher, and Tan (2003) suggested that the left middle frontal gyrus was critical for skilled Chinese reading. This region appeared critical in processing syllables, whereas the left inferior frontal gyrus mediated the processing of phonemes. This pattern of findings offers compelling evidence for the existence of cortical areas relevant to the representation of syllables and phonemes. In a later report, Siok, Perfetti, Jin, and Tan (2004) found that Chinese children with dyslexia demonstrated reduction in activation of the left middle frontal gyrus. Brain imaging during a word recognition task indicated that Chinese children with dyslexia showed reduced activation in both left and right middle frontal gyri, left and right inferior frontal gyri, and the left fusiform gyrus. The readers with dyslexia demonstrated increased activation in the right occipital cortex. Thus, in a similar pattern with English readers with dyslexia, Chinese children with dyslexia exhibited reduced activation in left frontal and left occipital–temporal regions. However, in contrast to American children with dyslexia, no differences were observed in parietal–temporal regions.

CONCLUSIONS AND FUTURE DIRECTIONS

Within the last two decades, overwhelming convergent evidence from many laboratories indicates the cognitive basis for dyslexia: Dyslexia represents a disorder within the language system and, more specifically, within a particular subcomponent of that system, phonological processing. Recent advances in imaging technology and the development of tasks that sharply isolate the subcomponent processes of reading now allow the localization of phonological processing in brain, and, as a result, for the first time provide the potential to elucidate a biological signature for reading and reading disability. Converging evidence from a number of laboratories using functional brain imaging indicates a disruption of left-hemisphere posterior neural systems in dyslexia in both child and adult readers while performing reading tasks. There is also the additional suggestion for an associated, increased reliance on ancillary systems, for example, in the frontal lobes and right-hemisphere posterior circuits.

The discovery of neural systems that serve reading has significant implications. At the most fundamental level, it is now possible to investigate specific hypotheses regarding the neural substrate of dyslexia, and to verify, reject, or modify suggested cognitive models. From a more clinical perspective, findings from laboratories around the world, in every language tested, indicate a neural signature for dyslexia (a disruption of posterior reading systems, primarily systems serving skilled, automatic [fluent] reading) and implications for the acceptance of dyslexia as a valid disorder, a necessary condition for its identification and treatment. Simply put, they provide for the first time, convincing, irrefutable evidence that what has been considered a hidden disability is "real."

This demonstration of a neurobiological signature for dyslexia has implications not only for reading instruction but also for the provision of accommodations, a critical component of management for older children attending postsecondary and graduate programs. Such neurobiological findings should make testing agencies, certification boards, and others more willing to allow children and adolescents with dyslexia to receive accommodations on high-stakes tests. The utilization of advances in neuroscience to inform educational policy and practices provides an exciting example of translational science being used for the public good (S. E. Shaywitz, Mody, Shaywitz, 2006).

ACKNOWLEDGMENTS

The work described in this review was supported by grants from the National Institute of Child Health and Human Development (Nos. P50 HD25802, RO1 HD046171, and R01 HD057655) to Sally E. Shaywitz and Bennett A. Shaywitz. Portions of this chapter have appeared whole or in part in earlier publications (B. A. Shaywitz & Shaywitz, 2006; S. E. Shaywitz, 1998, 2003; S. E. Shaywitz & Shaywitz, 2005).

REFERENCES

Anderson, A., & Gore, J. (1997). The physical basis of neuroimaging techniques. *Child and Adolescent Psychiatric Clinics of North America, 6*, 213–264.

Aylward, E., Richards, T., Berninger, V., Nagy, W., Field, K., Grimme, A., et al. (2003). Instructional treatment associated with changes in brain activation in children with dyslexia. *Neurology, 61*, 212–219.

Berninger, V., Abbott, R., & Thomson, J. (2001). Language phenotype for reading and writing disability: A family approach. *Scientific Studies of Reading, 5*(1), 59–106.

Blachman, B. A., Ball, E. W., Black, R. S., & Tangel, D. M. (1994). Kindergarten teachers develop phoneme awareness in low-income, inner-city classrooms. *Reading and Writing: An Interdisciplinary Journal, 6*, 1–18.

Brown, W. E., Eliez, S., Menon, V., Rumsey, J. M., White, C. D., & Reiss, A. L. (2001). Preliminary evidence of widespread morphological variations of the brain in dyslexia. *Neurology, 56*(6), 781–783.

Bruck, M. (1992). Persistence of dyslexics' phonological awareness deficits. *Developmental Psychology, 28*(5), 874–886.

Brunswick, N., McCrory, E., Price, C. J., Frith, C. D., & Frith, U. (1999). Explicit and implicit processing of words and pseudowords by adult developmental dyslexics: A search for Wernicke's Wortschatz. *Brain, 122*, 1901–1917.

Carey, J., Kimberley, T., Lewis, S., Auerbach, E., Dorsey, L., Rundquist, P., et al. (2002). Analysis of fMRI and finger tracking training in subjects with chronic stroke. *Brain, 125*, 773–788.

Catts, H., Adlof, S., Hogan, T., & Weismer, S. (2005). Are specific language impairment and dyslexia distinct disorders? *Journal of Speech, Language, and Hearing Research, 48*, 1378–1396.

Cohen, L., Dehaene, S., Naccache, L., Lehericy, S., Dehaene-Lambertz, G., Henaff, M., et al. (2000). The visual word form area: Spatial and temporal characterization of an initial stage of reading in normal subjects and posterior split-brain patients. *Brain, 123*, 291–307.

Cohen, L., Lehéricy, S., Chochon, F., Lemer, C., Rivaud, S., & Dehaene, S. (2002).

Language-specific tuning of visual cortex?: Functional properties of the visual word form area. *Brain, 125*, 1054–1069.

Cope, N. A., Harold, D., Hill, G., Moskvina, V., Stevenson, J., Holmans, P., et al. (2005). Strong evidence that *KIAA0319* on chromosome 6p is a susceptibility gene for developmental dyslexia. *American Journal of Human Genetics, 76*(4), 581–591.

Cope, N. A., Hill, G., van den Bree, M., Harold, D., Moskvina, V., Green, E. K., et al. (2005). No support for association between dyslexia susceptibility 1 candidate 1 and developmental dyslexia. *Molecular Psychiatry, 10*(3), 237–238.

Damasio, A. R., & Damasio, H. (1983). The anatomic basis of pure alexia. *Neurology, 33*, 1573–1583.

DeFries, J. C., Olson, R. K., Pennington, B. F., & Smith, S. D. (1991). Colorado Reading Project: An update. In D. D. Duane & D. B. Gray (Eds.), *The reading brain: The biological basis of dyslexia* (pp. 53–87). Parkton, MD: York Press.

Dehaene, S., Naccache, L., Cohen, L., Le Bihan, D., Mangin, J., Poline, J., et al. (2001). Cerebral mechanisms of word masking and unconscious repetition priming. *Nature Neuroscience, 4*, 752–758.

Dejerine, J. (1891). Sur un cas de cécité verbale avec agraphie, suivi d'autopsie. *Comptes Rendus Société du Biologie, 43*, 197–201.

Dejerine, J. (1892). Contribution a l'etude anatomo-pathologique et clinique des differentes varietes de cecite verbale. *Memoires de la Société de Biologie, 4*, 61–90.

Demb, J., Boynton, G., & Heeger, D. (1998). Functional magnetic resonance imaging of early visual pathways in dyslexia. *Journal of Neuroscience, 18*, 6939–6951.

Demonet, J., Price, C., Wise, R., & Frackowiak, R. (1994). A PET study of cognitive strategies in normal subjects during language tasks: Influence of phonetic ambiguity and sequence processing on phoneme monitoring. *Brain, 117*, 671–682.

Eckert, M. A., Leonard, C. M., Richards, T. L., Aylward, E. H., Thomson, J., & Berninger, V. W. (2003). Anatomical correlates of dyslexia: Frontal and cerebellar findings. *Brain, 126*(2), 482–494.

Eden, G., Jones, K., Cappell, K., Gareau, L., Wood, F., Zeffiro, T., et al. (2004). Neural changes following remediation in adult developmental dyslexia. *Neuron, 44*(3), 411–422.

Eden, G. F., VanMeter, J. W., Rumsey, J. M., Maisog, J. M., Woods, R. P., & Zeffiro, T. A. (1996). Abnormal processing of visual motion in dyslexia revealed by functional brain imaging. *Nature, 382*, 66–69.

Eliez, S., Rumsey, J. M., Giedd, J. N., Schmitt, J. E., Patwardhan, A. J., & Reiss, A. L. (2000). Morphological alteration of temporal lobe gray matter in dyslexia: An MRI study. *Journal of Child Psychology and Psychiatry and Allied Disciplines, 41*(5), 637–644.

Felton, R. H., Naylor, C. E., & Wood, F. B. (1990). Neuropsychological profile of adult dyslexics. *Brain and Language, 39*, 485–497.

Ferrer, E., McArdle, J., Shaywitz, B., Holahan, J., Marchione, K., & Shaywitz, S. (2007). Longitudinal models of developmental dynamics between reading and cognition from childhood to adolescence. *Developmental Psychology, 43*(6), 1460–1473.

Fiez, J. A., & Peterson, S. E. (1998). Neuroimaging studies of word reading. *Proceedings of the National Academy of Sciences USA, 95*(3), 914–921.

Filipek, P. (1996). Structural variations in measures in the developmental disorders. In R. Thatcher, G. Lyon, J. Rumsey, & N. Krasnegor (Eds.), *Developmental neuroimaging: Mapping the development of brain and behavior* (pp. 169–186). San Diego: Academic Press.

Fletcher, J. M., Shaywitz, S. E., Shankweiler, D. P., Katz, L., Liberman, I. Y., Stuebing, K. K., et al. (1994). Cognitive profiles of reading disability: Comparisons of discrepancy and low achievement definitions. *Journal of Educational Psychology, 86*(1), 6–23.

Fletcher, P., Frith, C., & Rugg, M. (1997). The functional anatomy of episodic memory. *Trends in Neuroscience, 20*, 213–218.

Fodor, J. A. (1983). *The modularity of mind.* Cambridge, MA: MIT Press.

Frackowiak, R., Friston, K., Frith, C., Dolan, R., Price, C., Zeki, S., et al. (2004). *Human brain function* (2nd ed.). San Diego: Academic Press.

Francis, D. J., Shaywitz, S. E., Stuebing, K. K., Shaywitz, B. A., & Fletcher, J. M. (1996). Developmental lag versus deficit models of reading disability: A longitudinal, individual growth curves analysis. *Journal of Educational Psychology, 88*(1), 3–17.

Francks, C., Paracchini, S., Smith, S. D., Richardson, A. J., Scerri, T. S., Cardon, L. R., et al. (2004). A 77-kilobase region of chromosome 6p22.2 is associated with dyslexia in families from the United Kingdom and from the United States. *American Journal of Human Genetics, 75*(6), 1046–1058.

Friedman, R. F., Ween, J. E., & Albert, M. L. (1993). Alexia. In K. M. Heilman & E. Valenstein (Eds.), *Clinical neuropsychology* (3rd ed., pp. 37–62). New York: Oxford University Press.

Frith, U., & Snowling, M. (1983). Reading for meaning and reading for sound in autistic and dyslexic children. *British Journal of Developmental Psychology, 1*, 329–342.

Galaburda, A. M., & Kemper, T. L. (1979). Cytoarchitectonic abnormalities in developmental dyslexia: a case study. *Annals of Neurology, 6*(2), 94–100.

Galaburda, A. M., Menard, M., & Rosen, G. D. (1994). Evidence for aberrant auditory anatomy in developmental dyslexia. *Proceedings of the National Academy of Sciences USA, 91*, 8010–8013.

Galaburda, A. M., Sherman, G. F., Rosen, G. D., Aboitiz, F., & Geschwind, N. (1985). Developmental dyslexia: Four consecutive patients with cortical anomalies. *Annals of Neurology, 18*(2), 222–233.

Gauthier, I. (2000). What constrains the organization of the ventral temporal cortex. *Trends in Cognitive Sciences, 4*, 1–2.

Gauthier, I., Tarr, M., Moylan, J., Skudlarski, P., Gore, J. C., & Anderson, A. (2000). The fusiform "face area" is part of a network that processes faces at the individual level. *Journal of Cognitive Neuroscience, 123*, 495–504.

Geschwind, N. (1965). Disconnection syndromes in animals and man. *Brain, 88*, 237–294.

Gilger, J. W., Borecki, I. B., Smith, S. D., DeFries, J. C., & Pennington, B. F. (1996). The etiology of extreme scores for complex phenotypes: An illustration using reading performance. In C. H. Chase, G. D. Rosen & G. F. Sherman (Eds.), *De-*

velopmental dyslexia. Neural, cognitive, and genetic mechanisms (pp. 63–85). Baltimore: York Press.

Gross-Glenn, K., Duara, R., Barker, W. W., Loewenstein, D., Chang, J.-Y., Yoshii, F., et al. (1991). Positron emission tomographic studies during serial word-reading by normal and dyslexic adults. *Journal of Clinical and Experimental Neuropsychology, 13*(4), 531–544.

Hagman, J. O., Wood, F., Buchsbaum, M. S., Tallal, P., Flowers, L., & Katz, W. (1992). Cerebral brain metabolism in adult dyslexic subjects assessed with positron emission tomography during performance of an auditory task. *Archives of Neurology, 49*, 734–739.

Hallgren, B. (1950). Specific dyslexia ("congenital word-blindness"): A clinical and genetic study. *Acta Psychiatrica Neurologica Scandinovica, Supplementum, 65*, 179–189.

Hannula-Jouppi, K., Kaminen-Ahola, N., Taipale, M., Eklund, R., Nopola-Hemmi, J., Kaariainen, H., et al. (2005). The axon guidance receptor gene *ROBO1* is a candidate gene for developmental dyslexia. *PLoS Genetics, 1*(4), e50.

Hays, W. L. (1988). *Statistics*. Orlando, FL: Holt, Rinehart & Winston.

Helenius, P., Tarkiainen, A., Cornelissen, P., Hansen, P. C., & Salmelin, R. (1999). Dissociation of normal feature analysis and deficient processing of letter-strings in dyslexic adults. *Cerebral Cortex, 4*, 476–483.

Henderson, V. W. (1986). Anatomy of posterior pathways in reading: A reassessment. *Brain and Language, 29*, 119–133.

Hertz-Pennier, L., Chiron, C., Jambaque, I., Renaux-Kieffer, V., Van de Moortele, P., Delalande, O., et al. (2002). Late plasticity for language in a child's non-dominant hemisphere: A pre- and post- surgery fMRI study. *Brain, 125*, 361–372.

Hinshelwood, J. (1907). Four cases of congenital word-blindness occurring in the same family. *British Medical Journal, 2*, 1229–1232.

Horwitz, B., Rumsey, J. M., & Donohue, B. C. (1998). Functional connectivity of the angular gyrus in normal reading and dyslexia. *Proceedings of the National Academy of Sciences, USA, 95*, 8939–8944.

Humphreys, P., Kaufmann, W. E., & Galaburda, A. M. (1990). Developmental dyslexia in women: neuropathological findings in three patients. *Annals of Neurology, 28*(6), 727–738.

Interagency Committee on Learning Disabilities. (1987). Learning disabilities: A report to the U.S. Congress. Washington, DC: U.S. Government Printing Office.

Jernigan, T. L., Hesselink, J. R., Sowell, E., & Tallal, P. A. (1991). Cerebral structure on magnetic resonance imaging in language- and learning-impaired children. *Archives of Neurology, 48*, 539–545.

Jezzard, P., Matthews, P., & Smith, S. (2001). *Functional MRI: An introduction to methods*. Oxford, UK: Oxford University Press.

Klingberg, T., Hedehus, M., Temple, E., Salz, T., Gabrieli, J., Moseley, M., et al. (2000). Microstructure of temporo-parietal white matter as a basis for reading ability: Evidence from diffusion tensor magnetic resonance imaging. *Neuron, 25*, 493–500.

Leonard, C. M., Voeller, K. S., Lombardino, L. J., Morris, M. K., Hynd, G. W., Alexander, A. W., et al. (1993). Anomalous cerebral morphology in dyslexia revealed with MR imaging. *Archives of Neurology, 50*, 461–469.

Lewitter, F., DeFries, J., & Elston, R. (1980). Genetic models of reading disability. *Behavioral Genetics, 10*, 9–30.

Liberman, I. Y., & Shankweiler, D. (1991). Phonology and beginning to read: A tutorial. In L. Rieben & C. A. Perfetti (Eds.), *Learning to read: Basic research and its implications* (pp. 3–17). Hillsdale, NJ: Erlbaum.

Liberman, I. Y., Shankweiler, D., & Liberman, A. M. (1989). The alphabetic principle and learning to read. In D. Shankweiler & I. Y. Liberman (Eds.), *Phonology and reading disability: Solving the reading puzzle.* (Vol. 6, pp. 1–33). Ann Arbor: University of Michigan Press.

Livingstone, M. S., Rosen, G. D., Drislane, F. W., & Galaburda, A. M. (1991). Physiological and anatomical evidence for a magnocellular defect in developmental dyslexia. *Proceedings of the National Academy of Sciences USA, 88*(18), 7943–7947.

Logan, G. (1988). Toward an instance theory of automatization. *Psychological Review, 95*, 492–527.

Logan, G. (1997). Automaticity and reading: Perspectives from the instance theory of automatization. *Reading and Writing Quarterly, 13*, 123–146.

Lovegrove, W. J., Bowling, A., Badcock, D., & Blackwood, M. (1980). Specific reading disability: Differences in contrast sensitivity as a function of spatial frequency. *Science, 210*, 439–440.

Luciano, M., Lind, P. A., Duffy, D. L., Castles, A., Wright, M. J., Montgomery, G. W., et al. (2007). A haplotype spanning *KIAA0319* and *TTRAP* is associated with normal variation in reading and spelling ability. *Biological Psychiatry, 62*(7), 811–817.

Lyon, G. R., Shaywitz, S. E., & Shaywitz, B. A. (2003). A definition of dyslexia. *Annals of Dyslexia., 53*, 1–14.

MacLeod, A., Buckner, R., Miezin, F., Petersen, S., & Raichle, M. (1998). Right anterior prefrontal cortex activation during semantic monitoring and working memory. *NeuroImage, 7*, 41–48.

Marino, C., Giorda, R., Luisa Lorusso, M., Vanzin, L., Salandi, N., Nobile, M., et al. (2005). A family-based association study does not support *DYX1C1* on 15q21.3 as a candidate gene in developmental dyslexia. *European Journal of Human Genetics, 13*(4), 491–499.

McCandliss, B., Cohen, L., & Dehaene, S. (2003). The visual word form area: Expertise in reading in the fusiform gyrus. *Trends in Cognitive Sciences, 7*(7), 293–299.

McIntosh, A., Bookstein, F., Haxby, J., & Grady, C. (1996). Spatial pattern analysis of functional brain images using partial least squares. *NeuroImage, 3*, 143–157.

McIntosh, A., Nyberg, L., Bookstein, F., & Tulving, E. (1997). Differential functional connectivity of prefrontal and medial temporal cortices during episodic memory retrieval. *Human Brain Mapping, 5*, 323–327.

Meng, H., Hager, K., Held, M., Page, G. P., Olson, R. K., Pennington, B. F., et al. (2005). TDT-association analysis of *EKN1* and dyslexia in a Colorado twin cohort. *Human Genetics, 118*, 87–90.

Meng, H., Smith, S. D., Hager, K., Held, M., Liu, J., Olson, R. K., et al. (2005). *DCDC2* is associated with reading disability and modulates neuronal development in the brain. *Proceedings of the National Academy of Sciences, USA, 102*(47), 17053–17058.

Mody, M. (2004). Neurobiological correlates of language and literacy impairments. In C. Stone, E. Silliman, B. Ehren, & K. Apel (Eds.), *Handbook of language and literacy: Development and disorders*. New York: Guilford Press.

Morgan, W. P. (1896). A case of congenital word blindness. *British Medical Journal*, 1378.

Morris, R. D., Stuebing, K. K., Fletcher, J. M., Shaywitz, S. E., Lyon, G. R., Shankweiler, D. P., et al. (1998). Subtypes of reading disability: Variability around a phonological core. *Journal of Educational Psychology, 90*, 347–373.

National Reading Panel Report. (2000). *Teaching children to read: An evidence based assessment of the scientific research literature on reading and its implications for reading instruction* (NIH Publication No. 00-4754): Washington, DC: U.S. Department of Health and Human Services, Public Health Service, National Institutes of Health, National Institute of Child Health and Human Development.

Nation, K., & Snowling, M. (1998). Individual differences in contextual facilitation: Evidence from dyslexia and poor reading comprehension. *Child Development, 69*, 996–1011.

Nicolson, R. I., & Fawcett, A. J. (1990). Automaticity: A new framework for dyslexia research? *Cognition, 35*(2), 159–182.

Nicolson, R. I., Fawcett, A. J., & Dean, P. (2001). Developmental dyslexia: The cerebellar deficit hypothesis [see comment]. *Trends in Neurosciences, 24*(9), 508–511.

Nopola-Hemmi, J., Taipale, M., Haltia, T., Lehesjoki, A. E., Voutilainen, A., & Kere, J. (2000). Two translocations of chromosome 15q associated with dyslexia. *Journal of Medical Genetics, 37*(10), 771–775.

Online Mendelian Inheritance in Man. (2000). OMIM™. McKusick–Nathans Institute for Genetic Medicine, Johns Hopkins University (Baltimore, MD) and National Center for Biotechnology Information, National Library of Medicine (Bethesda, MD). Retrieved December 20, 2005, from *www.ncbi.nlm.nih.gov/omim/*.

Papanicolaou, A. C., Simos, P. G., Breier, J. I., Fletcher, J. M., Foorman, B. R., Francis, D., et al. (2003). Brain mechanisms for reading in children with and without dyslexia: A review of studies of normal development and plasticity. *Developmental Neuropsychology, 24*(2–3), 593–612.

Paulesu, E., Demonet, J.-F., Fazio, F., McCrory, E., Chanoine, V., Brunswick, N., et al. (2001). Dyslexia: Cultural diversity and biological unity. *Science, 291*, 2165–2167.

Paulesu, E., Frith, U., Snowling, M., Gallagher, A., Morton, J., Frackowiak, R. S. J., et al. (1996). Is developmental dyslexia a disconnection syndrome?: Evidence from PET scanning. *Brain, 119*, 143–157.

Pennington, B. F., & Gilger, J. W. (1996). How is dyslexia transmitted? In C. H. Chase, G. D. Rosen, & G. F. Sherman (Eds.), *Developmental dyslexia: Neural, cognitive, and genetic mechanisms* (pp. 41–61). Baltimore: York Press.

Petersen, S. E., Fox, P. T., Snyder, A. Z., & Raichle, M. E. (1990). Activation of extrastriate and frontal cortical areas by visual words and word-like stimuli. *Science, 249*, 1041–1044.

Price, C., Moore, C., & Frackowiak, R. S. J. (1996). The effect of varying stimulus rate and duration on brain activity during reading. *NeuroImage, 3*(1), 40–52.

Ramus, F., Rosen, S., Dakin, S., Day, B., Castellote, J., White, S., et al. (2003). Theories of developmental dyslexia: Insights from a multiple case study of dyslexic adults. *Brain, 126*, 841–865.

Richards, T., Corina, D., Serafini, S., Steury, K., Echelard, D., Dager, S., et al. (2000). Effects of a phonologically driven treatment for dyslexia on lactate levels measured by proton MRI spectroscopic imaging. *American Journal of Neuroradiology, 21*, 916–922.

Rumsey, J. M., Andreason, P., Zametkin, A. J., Aquino, T., King, C., Hamburber, S. D., et al. (1992). Failure to activate the left temporoparietal cortex in dyslexia. *Archives of Neurology, 49*, 527–534.

Rumsey, J. M., Nace, K., Donohue, B., Wise, D., Maisog, J. M., & Andreason, P. (1997). A positron emission tomographic study of impaired word recognition and phonological processing in dyslexic men. *Archives of Neurology, 54*, 562–573.

Rumsey, J. M., Zametkin, A. J., Andreason, P., Hanahan, A. P., Hamburger, S. D., Aquino, T., et al. (1994). Normal activation of frontotemporal language cortex in dyslexia, as measured with oxygen 15 positron emission tomography. *Archives of Neurology, 51*, 27–38.

Rutter, M., & Yule, W. (1975). The concept of specific reading retardation. *Journal of Child Psychology and Psychiatry and Allied Disciplines, 16*, 181–197.

Salmelin, R., Service, E., Kiesila, P., Uutela, K., & Salonen, O. (1996). Impaired visual word processing in dyslexia revealed with magnetoencephalography. *Annals of Neurology, 40*, 157–162.

Scarborough, H. S. (1990). Very early language deficits in dyslexic children. *Child Development, 61*, 1728–1743.

Scerri, T. S., Fisher, S. E., Francks, C., MacPhie, I. L., Paracchini, S., Richardson, A. J., et al. (2004). Putative functional alleles of *DYX1C1* are not associated with dyslexia susceptibility in a large sample of sibling pairs from the UK. *Journal of Medical Genetics, 41*(11), 853–857.

Schultz, R. T., Cho, N.K., Staib, L.H., Kier, L.E., Fletcher, J.M., Shaywitz, S.E., et al. (1994). Brain morphology in normal and dyslexic children: The influence of sex and age. *Annals of Neurology, 35*, 732–742.

Seki, A., Koeda, T., Sugihara, S., Kamba, M., Hirata, Y., Ogawa, T., et al. (2001). A functional magnetic resonance imaging study during reading in Japanese dyslexic children. *Brain and Development, 23*, 312–316.

Shankweiler, D., Crain, S., Katz, L., Fowler, A. E., Liberman, A. M., Brady, S. A., et al. (1995). Cognitive profiles of reading-disabled children: Comparison of language skills in phonology, morphology, and syntax. *Psychological Science, 6*(3), 149–156.

Shankweiler, D., Liberman, I. Y., Mark, L. S., Fowler, C. A., & Fischer, F. W. (1979). The speech code and learning to read. *Journal of Experimental Psychology: Learning, Memory, and Cognition, 5*(6), 531–545.

Share, D. L., & Stanovich, K. E. (1995). Cognitive processes in early reading development: Accommodating individual differences into a model of acquisition. *Issues in Education: Contributions from Educational Psychology, 1*(1), 1–57.

Shaywitz, B. A., Fletcher, J. M., Holahan, J. M., & Shaywitz, S. E. (1992). Discrepancy compared to low achievement definitions of reading disability: Results from the Connecticut Longitudinal Study. *Journal of Learning Disabilities, 25*(10), 639–648.

Shaywitz, B. A., Fletcher, J. M., Holahan, J. M., Shneider, A. E., Marchione, K. E., Stuebing, K. K., et al. (1995). Interrelationships between reading disability and attention-deficit/hyperactivity disorder. *Child Neuropsychology, 1*(3), 170–186.

Shaywitz, B. A., Holford, T. R., Holahan, J. M., Fletcher, J. M., Stuebing, K. K., Francis, D. J., et al. (1995). A Matthew effect for IQ but not for reading: Results from a longitudinal study. *Reading Research Quarterly, 30*(4), 894–906.

Shaywitz, B. A., & Shaywitz, S. E. (2006). Dyslexia. In K. Swaiman, S. Ashwal, & D. Ferriero (Eds.), *Pediatric neurology: Principles and practice* (4th ed., pp. 855–870). St. Louis: Mosby.

Shaywitz, B. A., Shaywitz, S. E., Blachman, B., Pugh, K., Fulbright, R., Skudlarski, P., et al. (2004). Development of left occipito-temporal systems for skilled reading in children after a phonologically-based intervention. *Biological Psychiatry, 55*, 926–933.

Shaywitz, B. A., Shaywitz, S. E., Pugh, K., Mencl, W., Fulbright, R., Skudlarski, P., et al. (2002). Disruption of posterior brain systems for reading in children with developmental dyslexia. *Biological Psychiatry, 52*(2), 101–110.

Shaywitz, B. A., Skudlarski, P., Holahan, J., Marchione, K., Constable, R., Fulbright, R., et al. (2007). Age-related changes in reading systems of dyslexic children. *Annals of Neurology, 61*, 363–370.

Shaywitz, S. E. (1996). Dyslexia. *Scientific American, 275*(5), 98–104.

Shaywitz, S. E. (1998). Current concepts: Dyslexia. *New England Journal of Medicine, 338*(5), 307–312.

Shaywitz, S. E. (2003). *Overcoming dyslexia: A new and complete science-based program for reading problems at any level.* New York: Knopf.

Shaywitz, S. E., Escobar, M. D., Shaywitz, B. A., Fletcher, J. M., & Makuch, R. (1992). Evidence that dyslexia may represent the lower tail of a normal distribution of reading ability. *New England Journal of Medicine, 326*(3), 145–150.

Shaywitz, S. E., Fletcher, J., Holahan, J., Shneider, A., Marchione, K., Stuebing, K., et al. (1999). Persistence of dyslexia: The Connecticut Longitudinal Study at adolescence. *Pediatrics, 104*(6), 1351–1359.

Shaywitz, S. E., Mody, M., & Shaywitz, B. A. (2006). Neural mechanisms in dyslexia. *Current Directions in Psychological Science, 15*(6), 278–282.

Shaywitz, S. E., & Shaywitz, B. (2005). Dyslexia (specific reading disability). *Biological Psychiatry, 57*, 1301–1309.

Shaywitz, S. E., Shaywitz, B., Fletcher, J., & Escobar, M. (1990). Prevalence of reading disability in boys and girls: Results of the Connecticut Longitudinal Study. *Journal of the American Medical Association, 264*(8), 998–1002.

Shaywitz, S. E., Shaywitz, B., Fulbright, R., Skudlarski, P., Mencl, W., Constable, R., et al. (2003). Neural systems for compensation and persistence: Young adult outcome of childhood reading disability. *Biological Psychiatry, 54*(1), 25–33.

Shaywitz, S. E., Shaywitz, B., Pugh, K., Fulbright, R., Constable, R., Mencl, W., et al.

(1998). Functional disruption in the organization of the brain for reading in dyslexia. *Proceedings of the National Academy of Sciences, USA, 95*, 2636–2641.

Simos, P. G., Fletcher, J. M., Bergman, E., Breier, J. I., Foorman, B. R., Castillo, E. M., et al. (2002). Dyslexia-specific brain activation profile becomes normal following successful remedial training [See comment]. *Neurology, 58*(8), 1203–1213.

Siok, W. T., Jin, Z., Fletcher, P., & Tan, L. H. (2003). Distinct brain regions associated with syllable and phoneme. *Human Brain Mapping, 18*(3), 201–207.

Siok, W. T., Perfetti, C. A., Jin, Z., & Tan, L. H. (2004). Biological abnormality of impaired reading is constrained by culture. *Nature, 431*(7004), 71–76.

Snowling, M. (2000). *Dyslexia* (2nd ed.). Oxford, UK: Blackwell.

Sowell, E. R., Thompson, P. M., Rex, D., Kornsand, D., Tessner, K. D., Jernigan, T. L., et al. (2002). Mapping sulcal pattern asymmetry and local cortical surface gray matter distribution *in vivo*: Maturation in perisylvian cortices. *Cerebral Cortex, 12*(1), 17–26.

Stanovich, K. E., & Siegel, L. S. (1994). Phenotypic performance profile of children with reading disabilities: A regression-based test of the phonological-core variable-difference model. *Journal of Educational Psychology, 86*(1), 24–53.

Stein, J. (2003). Visual motion sensitivity and reading. *Neuropsychologia, 41*(13), 1785–1793.

Stein, J., & Walsh, V. (1997). To see but not to read: The magnocellular theory of dyslexia. *Trends in Neurosciences, 20*(4), 147–152.

Taipale, M., Kaminen, N., Nopola-Hemmi, J., Haltia, T., Myllyluoma, B., Lyytinen, H., et al. (2003). A candidate gene for developmental dyslexia encodes a nuclear tetratricopeptide repeat domain protein dynamically regulated in brain. *Proceedings of the National Academy of Sciences USA, 100*(20), 11553–11558.

Talairach, J., & Tournoux, P. (1988). *Coplanar stereotaxic atlas of the human brain: Three-dimensional proportional system: An approach to cerebral imaging*. New York: Thieme.

Tallal, P. (1980). Auditory temporal perception, phonics, and reading disabilities in children. *Brain and Language, 9*(2), 182–198.

Tallal, P. (2000). The science of literacy: From the laboratory to the classroom. *Proceedings of the National Academy of Sciences USA, 97*, 2402–2404.

Tallal, P., Miller, S., & Fitch, R. (1993). Neurobiological basis of speech: A case for the preeminence of temporal processing. *Annals of the New York Academy of Sciences, 682*, 27–47.

Temple, E., Deutsch, G., Poldrack, R., Miller, S., Tallal, P., Merzenich, M., et al. (2003). Neural deficits in children with dyslexia ameliorated by behavioral remediation: Evidence from fMRI. *Proceedings of the National Academy of Sciences USA, 100*(5), 2860–2865.

Temple, E., Poldrack, R., Protopapas, A., Nagarajan, S., Salz, T., Tallal, P., et al. (2000). Disruption of the neural response to rapid acoustic stimuli in dyslexia: Evidence from functional MRI. *Proceedings of the National Academy of Sciences USA, 97*, 13907–13912.

Torgesen, J., Alexander, A., Wagner, R., Rashotte, C., Voeller, K., & Conway, T. (2001). Intensive remedial instruction for children with severe reading disabilities: Immediate and long-term outcomes from two instructional approaches. *Journal of Learning Disabilities, 34*(1), 33–58.

Torgesen, J. K., & Wagner, R. K. (1995, May 11). *Alternative diagnostic approaches for specific developmental reading disabilities*. Paper presented at the National Research Council's Board on Testing and Assessment workshop on IQ Testing and Educational Decision Making, Washington, DC.

Wagner, R., & Torgesen, J. (1987). The nature of phonological processes and its causal role in the acquisition of reading skills. *Psychological Bulletin, 101*, 192–212.

Wigg, K. G., Couto, J. M., Feng, Y., Anderson, B., Cate-Carter, T. D., Macciardi, F., et al. (2004). Support for *EKN1* as the susceptibility locus for dyslexia on 15q21. *Molecular Psychiatry, 9*, 1111–1121.

Woodcock, R. W. (1987). *Woodcock Reading Mastery Test—Revised*. Circle Pines, MN: American Guidance Service.

Woodcock, R. W., & Johnson, M. B. (1989). *Woodcock–Johnson Psycho-Educational Battery—Revised (WJ-R)*. Allen, TX: Developmental Learning Materials.

Yule, W., & Rutter, M. (1985). *Reading and other learning difficulties* (2nd ed.). Oxford, UK: Blackwell.

9

Reading Development in Children at Risk for Dyslexia

BRIAN BYRNE
DONALD P. SHANKWEILER
DONALD W. HINE

In this chapter we review research from our group on the characteristics of young children in families with a history of reading difficulties, and on early intervention to help these children. We preface the research with short surveys of familial risk for developmental reading disability, of behavior–genetic studies of early literacy growth, and of other groups' work on children at familial risk. We summarize research demonstrating that:

1. Preschool children at risk show deficits in insights and abilities characteristic of older children with established reading problems and are consequently not as well resourced as children not at risk for learning to read; these compromised resources include aspects of linguistic processing (the "phonological core"), as well as emergent literacy knowledge.
2. The performance pattern in these preschool children cannot be the result of differential response to literacy instruction.
3. The phonological core deficit does not extend to the quality of phonological representations, but manifests as the less efficient retrieval or activation of the phonological code.
4. Children at risk are less responsive to preschool instruction in pho-

nemic awareness than children not at risk, but they can be brought up to grade-appropriate average levels of reading with intensive preschool intervention.

5. Early intervention does not equate to full prevention.

FAMILIAL RISK FOR DEVELOPMENTAL READING DISABILITY

The populationwide prevalence of reading disability is usually estimated to be from around 3 to 10%, depending on the restrictiveness of the adopted definition. But it has been known for a century that the within-family incidence of reading disability—and, therefore the risk associated with being a member of an affected family—is well above the prevalence rate. In 1905, Thomas noted that children with reading disabilities often had affected relatives. Subsequent early case studies reported similar findings (Fisher, 1905; Hinshelwood, 1911; Marshall & Ferguson, 1939; Orton, 1937; Stephenson, 1907). In later studies, a reasonable amount of agreement has been achieved concerning the percentage of parents and siblings of probands that are affected, with values ranging from 27 to 49%, and an average of 42% in the cited studies (Finucci, Guthrie, Childs, Abbey, & Childs, 1976; Gilger, Pennington, & DeFries, 1991; Hallgren, 1950; Vogler, DeFries, & Decker, 1985).

Researchers have also attempted to estimate the degree of risk imposed on a child with one or both parents (and/or older siblings) with a reading disability (Badian, 1988; Gilger et al., 1991; Pennington & Lefly, 2001; Scarborough, 1989, 1990; Snowling, Gallagher, & Frith, 2003; Vogler et al., 1985). Scarborough (1998) summarized eight of these studies and reported estimates of reading disability ranging from 23 to 62%, with an average of approximately 38.5%.

EVIDENCE FROM BEHAVIOR–GENETIC STUDIES

The mechanism of familial transmission of reading disability is of scientific and practical interest. Family members share genes *and* the home environment, so either or both could drive the familial aggregation we have summarized. In fact, it is now known from twin and adoption studies that genetic influences on reading ability, including both marked disability and normal-range and high-end ability, are substantial, with estimates of the proportion of variance attributable to genes ranging from .5 to .8, depending on which aspect of reading is measured, and in what population (for overviews, see Pennington & Olson, 2005; Olson & Byrne, 2005).

Recently, a twin study employing preschool-age children in four countries demonstrated that aspects of phonological processing and learning known to be linked to reading growth in school-age children are influenced by genes prior to the onset of formal reading instruction (Byrne et al., 2002; Samuelsson et al., 2005). However, the same study indicated that other processes, also known to be important for reading, such as vocabulary and early letter and printed word knowledge, appear to be largely determined by the home and preschool environment. Later observations of these same children have shown that the genetic influences detected at the preschool level continue to affect literacy levels in kindergarten and grade 1, whereas the influence of the home/preschool environment appears to attenuate as children proceed through school. It also appears that genetic influences, in addition to those detected in preschool, come into play for reading and related processes, such as phonological awareness and verbal fluency, as children develop (Byrne et al., 2005, 2007; Byrne, Samuelsson, et al., 2007).

MOTIVATING INTERVENTION STUDIES FROM BEHAVIOR–GENETIC RESEARCH

Practitioners may view the figures in the previous section with dismay. If reading ability is so highly heritable, what are the prospects of successful intervention?

The prospects are good, at least in principle. To see this, it is important to bear in mind that in reviewing behavior–genetic research, we have been considering *differences* among children, not absolute levels of reading skill. Imagine, optimistically, the discovery of a new method of instruction that raises the reading ability of every child, such that no child is hampered in school progress by low literacy capabilities. Differences in skills would no doubt still exist, as they do now among, say, graduating college students (or Nobel Prize winners, for that matter), though they would largely be of scientific rather than practical interest. Importantly, those differences could be as highly heritable as the present ones are. Keep in mind, too, that going to school raises the reading levels of all children, year by year, even though the differences among children are substantially genetically driven; that is, instruction is effective. So it is perfectly plausible that more intensive instruction with appropriate content is even more effective—indeed, we should be surprised if it were not. Empirical studies confirm this. For instance, instruction in the phonemic structure of the speech delivered before the start of formal schooling has been shown to foster reading skills for up to 6 years (Byrne, Fielding-Barnsley, & Ashley, 2000; for a summary of such research, see Bus & van IJzendoorn, 1999).

The lesson is that the search for better ways to teach literacy should go on, and practitioners should not be discouraged by the conclusions reached on the basis of family and behavior–genetic studies of the sort we have summarized. Rather, they should note them, note as well that some children start school with a genetic burden, and reach the justifiable conclusion that well-devised and well-delivered preschool and school support, over and above the normal curriculum, are exactly what is called for in these cases. With that in mind, we turn to the main topic of this chapter, the children at family risk for reading disability and what can be done about their situation.

CHARACTERISTICS OF CHILDREN AT RISK FOR DEVELOPMENTAL READING DISABILITY

It is frequently pointed out that by the time a child is diagnosed as having a reading disability, identifying the factors that led to the disability is clouded by the reciprocal relationship that can develop between reading itself and the hypothesized underlying deficits. For example, Morais, Cary, Alegria, and Bertelson (1979) showed that phonemic awareness can be enhanced by learning to read, so failures of phonemic awareness could, in principle, be the outcome, not the cause, of reading disability (see also Cunningham & Stanovich, 1997; Ehri, 1993).

One way to gain a clearer picture of the nature of the deficit in developmental reading disability, unconfounded by the effects of reading failure, is to study prereading children who are at increased risk for reading failure. Several research groups have reported prospective studies of children at familial risk for reading disability (Byrne, Fielding-Barnsley, Ashley, & Larsen, 1997; Elbro, Borstrom, & Petersen, 1998; Gallagher, Frith, & Snowling, 2000; Lefly & Pennington, 1996; Locke et al., 1997; Lyytinen, 1997; Lyytinen, Poikkeus, Laasko, Eklund, & Lyytinen, 2001; Lyytinen et al., 2004; Scarborough, 1991; Snowling et al., 2003). We now summarize the findings.

Processes Close to Reading: Print Knowledge and Phonological Awareness

First, we clarify our use of terms and how we have chosen to assess them. "Phonological awareness," a broad-brush term that defines a person's metalinguistic sensitivity to the sound structure of language, with the sound units unspecified, can include words, syllables, onsets and rimes, phonemes, allophones, and phonetic features. "Phonemic awareness" is more restrictive, defining sensitivity to the phonemes that comprise a language. Within these structures, a range of assessment measures reflect in part the explicitness of sensitivity. In most of our work with preliterate children, for example, we have chosen to assess recognition of the same phoneme occurrences in different spoken words, "phoneme identity," as we call it. We test children's ability to judge that words such as *sun* and *sail* begin with the same sound, and that words such as *bus* and *horse* end with the same sound. This ability is usually lacking in at-risk preschoolers, and it can be regarded as an "emerging" awareness, one that falls short of the ability to perform more deliberate tasks, such as the explicit segmentation of a word into its phonemic constituents. Gombert (1992) provides perhaps the most comprehensive analysis for forms of phonological awareness and their emergence.

Children at familial risk for reading disability have been found to have fewer resources than other children in terms of the prerequisite knowledge they bring to reading. This includes reading-related phonological skills and familiarity with letter names and layout of books (Byrne et al., 1997; Gallagher et al., 2000; Scarborough, 1991). For instance, in the study reported by Byrne et al. (1997), only 8% of the 4-year-olds in the at-risk group performed above chance on the test of phoneme identity, compared with 29% in the normal group.

Other Phonological Processes

Phonological Processing Abilities

Preschoolers from families with a history of reading problems have also been found to have poorer phonological processing abilities than controls. Differences in short-term phonological memory (Locke et al., 1997) and verbal repetition (Snowling et al., 2003) have been observed. Although differences in short-term phonological memory have not always been found to discriminate between children from families with and without reading disabilities (Lefly & Pennington, 1996), they have been found to discriminate between children who go on to have reading problems and those who do not (Elbro et al., 1998; Gallagher et al., 2000). Differences in naming speed and accuracy have also been found between at-risk and not at-risk preschoolers (Lefly & Pennington, 1996; Locke et al., 1997). Rhyme recognition has consistently been found to discriminate between these groups of children (Byrne et al., 1997; Lefly & Pennington, 1996; Locke et al., 1997; Scarborough, 1991; Snowling et al., 2003).

Speech Perception and Speech Production Abilities

As early as 6 months of age, speech processing differences have been demonstrated between at-risk and non-at-risk infants in a Finnish study that used both behavioral and ERP (event-related potential) techniques (see Lyytinen et al. [2004] for a substantial summary, including evidence that some of these very early measures predict later reading skills; see also Van der Leij, Lyytinen, & Zwarts, 2001). Locke et al. (1997) and Elbro et al. (1998) found that at-risk prekindergarten children perform significantly more poorly than controls on speech discrimination tasks. However, not all studies have detected group differences in speech perception (e.g., Lefly & Pennington, 1996; Scarborough, 1990).

The evidence on speech production is also somewhat equivocal. Whereas some studies failed to find any differences between children from families with and without reading disabilities, other studies did find differences. Scarborough (1991) found that at 30 months of age, children from families with reading disabilities were less accurate than controls in their pronunciation of consonants, and that their expressive phonological abilities at this age were strongly predictive of outcome reading status in the sample. Although Elbro et al. (1998) found no differences between children from families with reading disabilities and controls in terms of vowel pronunciation accuracy (the number of vowels in complex words, such as *crocodile*, that were given maximally distinct pronunciations by the child) at the prekindergarten level, differences in this distinctness metric of early phonological representations was found to be a strong predictor of both phoneme awareness and reading outcome at the grade 2 level. "Distinctness" means the degree of separation between a phonological representation and its neighbors, and Elbro et al. suggested that it may in turn be a function of the number of distinct phonetic features specified in the representation. The success of this measure as a predictor of later reading attests to the value of grounding commonly used concepts in linguistic theory.

Higher-Level Language Processes

Vocabulary

Preschoolers from families with a history of reading problems have also been found to display deficits in semantic and syntactic processes relative to controls. The most consistently reported deficits are in vocabulary, and these differences are among the largest detected between at-risk and control children (Byrne et al., 1997; Elbro et al., 1998; Gallagher et al., 2000; Locke et al., 1997; Lyytinen et al., 2004; Scarborough,1990; Snowling et al., 2003).

Syntactic Comprehension

The picture with syntactic processing is less consistent. Locke et al. (1997) found that, relative to the control group, their at-risk group obtained significantly lower scores on a test measuring comprehension of verbal commands administered at 42 months of age, a finding at odds with that of

Lyytinen et al. (2001), who found no differences between the groups on comprehension of instructions at the same age. Lyytinen at al. found a difference in favor of the non-at-risk group in maximum sentence length at 24 months, though Locke et al. (1997) found that the at-risk group did not score significantly more poorly on measures of syntactic complexity at 30 months of age.

Syntactic Production

In contrast to these findings, clear group differences in sentence production have emerged when the analyses are restricted to at-risk children who turned out to have a reading disability. For instance, in the at-risk sample studied by Scarborough (1990), the group identified as having a reading disability at the grade 2 level scored more poorly on measures of syntactic complexity at 30 months of age than the group assessed as having normal reading skills. Similarly, in the at-risk sample studied by Gallagher et al. (2000), the group identified as having delayed literacy at age 6 produced significantly shorter sentences at 45 months of age than the group identified as developing literacy skills at the normal rate. Finally, Lyytinen at al. (2004) found a marginally significant group difference on control of Finnish inflectional morphology at 42 months.

Summary

From this review of the literature, it is apparent that children who are at familial risk for developmental reading disability:

1. Are not as well resourced as other children for learning to read.
2. Appear to be lacking in the development of phoneme awareness, which is known to be subject to genetic influence.
3. Have less knowledge of letters and less background knowledge of the purposes and mechanics of written language, processes that appear particularly responsive to the home and preschool environment but also show some genetic influence.
4. Also display a range of linguistic processing deficits similar to those displayed by children who have already failed at learning to read. Although the most consistently reported linguistic deficits are in the phonological domain and vocabulary, deficits in syntactic processing, particularly production measures, have been observed.

We use the term "deficit" to describe differences between children at risk and those not at risk throughout this chapter. But we need to acknowledge here that whether the differences are in reality delays (quantitative differences) or genuine deficits (qualitative differences) is an open question that will not necessarily resolve with time. Another open question is whether the inconsistencies apparent across studies are a sign that the risk for dyslexia is associated with broader language problems for only some children, whereas for others it is specific to literacy development. These are issues that take us further afield than we can go in this chapter, except to note that both questions are the subject of ongoing research, with some kind of consensus emerging that children with language difficulties restricted to short-term articulation problems are less likely than those with longer-term difficulties of this kind to develop reading problems or associated receptive language problems (Bishop & Adams, 1990; Nathan, Stackhouse, Goulandris, & Snowling, 2004; see also Catts & Kamhi [2005], for a volume devoted to these issues).

EARLY INTERVENTION FOR AT-RISK CHILDREN

Having surveyed the characteristics of children at familial risk for reading difficulties, we now review findings on early intervention. We summarize a published longitudinal study from Denmark and one from Australia, and present further data from the Australian project, which follows the children through 2 more years of schooling.

The Danish Longitudinal Study

To the best of our knowledge, the only early intervention study other than ours that has specifically targeted children at familial risk is that of Elbro and colleagues (Borstrom & Elbro, 1997; Elbro and Petersen, 2004). In this Danish study, the focus was on teaching 6-year-old children about individual phonemes in words (rather than the larger phonological unit of rhyme), supported by letter instruction. Regular kindergarten teachers who had participated in lengthy training administered the teaching program on a whole-class basis for about half an hour each day for 17 weeks, with one or more at-risk children in each class. Comparison children, both at risk and not at risk, were taught in classes that included some attention to phonological awareness, but at a considerably less extensive and intensive level than the experimental training.

In grades 2 and 3, the instructed at-risk children outperformed the at-risk controls on each measure of reading administered, including measures of silent and oral reading, real and nonword reading, and fluency (speed and accuracy). By grade 7, the trained children were still ahead of the controls on three of eight measures, including real word and nonword reading fluency and pseudohomophone detection (selecting which nonword sounds like a real word, e.g., *brane* vs. *brone*). The lack of advantage on five of the tests—real and nonword reading accuracy, orthographic coding (selecting which is the real word, *flight* or *flite*), and reading comprehension accuracy and efficiency—contrasts the situation in the earlier grades, when the trained group outperformed the risk controls on all measures.

The experimental training was not a panacea. At grade 7, many more at-risk than non-at-risk children, including those receiving the experimental training, were below the 5th and 20th percentile cutoffs determined by the non-at-risk group. Averaged over the reading measures, approximately 16% of the trained at-risk children were below the 5% cutoff, and 42% were below the 20% cutoff. The trained at-risk children generally fared better than the untrained ones (25 and 47%, respectively, compared with the 16 and 42% just reported), but this was only significant in two out of 16 cases (where "case" indicates the 5th or 20th percentile on a test, with eight tests in all). Thus, the additional kindergarten focus on phonemic awareness and letters assisted the at-risk children in achieving higher than otherwise expected levels of reading, especially in early school grades, but by grade 7, at least some of the advantage over untrained at-risk children had dissipated. It is not clear from the data whether the untrained children had caught up (perhaps through special support within the Danish school system), or whether the trained children had slipped back (perhaps through the continuing expression of the underlying, presumably partly genetic deficiencies that led to the diagnosis of being *at risk* in the first place).

The Australian Longitudinal Study

We have conducted two training studies of at-risk preschool children ranging in age from 41 to 70 months. The first report (Byrne et al., 1997) can be considered pilot work, because it lacked a dedicated control group. Its findings have been replicated in the larger, more recent study reported in Hindson et al. (2005), so although the methods of the larger project were pioneered in the pilot study, we do not consider the latter study further here.

In presenting this study, we describe the children and selection of them, the results of preintervention assessments, the intervention and its outcomes within the preschool and kindergarten phases (all described in more detail in Hindson et al., 2005), and finally longer-term outcomes in the next two school years (not previously presented).

The Children and Selection of Them

The study included 101 at-risk children, 48 females and 53 males (mean age = 54.6 months), and 68 non-at-risk controls, 41 females and 27 males (mean age = 55.5 months). These children were all assessed for relevant linguistic and cognitive characteristics prior to the intervention, but not all children were able to complete the intervention, generally because they moved from the area during the 3-month course of the study or declined to continue. Of the non-at-risk children, 65 participated in the full intervention. Of the at-risk children, 69 participated, and a further 17 (7 females and 10 males, mean age = 54.2 months) children were allocated to an at-risk waiting-list control group; they were pre- and posttested over the same 3-month period but were not given the intervention until after the posttest.

We recruited the children primarily through notices placed in preschools throughout the Sydney metropolitan area. We solicited involvement from parents who could recall having difficulties learning to read, and also from parents who could not recall such an experience. We insisted on English as the first language in the families because of the parent testing we planned; although we administered a substantial battery of language tests to the children, we did not rule out a child's participation on the basis of any suspected oral language impairment. As it turned out, the at-risk group did not score significantly lower than the non-at-risk controls in the two tests we used, the Goldman–Fristoe Test of Articulation (Goldman & Fristoe, 1986) and Bishop's test of speech discrimination (Bishop, 1985).

We identified a child as being at risk if one or both parents reported a history of marked reading difficulties, and this we confirmed with objective testing of word and nonword reading, reading rate, and reading comprehension based on a criterion of 1 standard deviation or more below the level that could be expected on the basis of the parent's age and years of schooling (for full details, see Hindson et al., 2005). Parental occupational status was assessed on a 9-point scale (from 1 = managers, 2 = professionals, to 9 = laborers and other low-skilled jobs). In at-risk families, the mean level corresponded to intermediate clerical and service workers, and in non-at-risk families, to advanced clerical and service workers. Covarying group comparisons on occupational status did not affect the significance of results (Hindson et al., 2005).

The Preintervention Assessment

We assessed a broad range of abilities and compared the at-risk and non-at-risk samples. In addition to the main battery, we administered a more extensive set of tests, requiring six to seven sessions of up to 30 minutes, to convenience subsamples of the at-risk (N = 49) and non-at-risk (N = 41) children. We present the results as a whole in Table 9.1, which identifies the tests and shows group comparisons. In the summary below, we add descriptions and explanations of tests that were tailor-made for the project or are otherwise likely to be unfamiliar to some readers.

TABLE 9.1. Performance of At-Risk and Non-at-Risk Children.

	Means (and *SD*s)			
Test	At-Risk	Non-at-Risk	*t*	Cohen's *d*[a]
Phoneme identity recognition (max. = 20, chance = 10)	10.26 (2.92)	11.78 (3.09)	3.20**	0.49
Letter recognition (chance = 6.5)	10.04 (5.64)	13.76 (6.00)	4.04**	0.62
Rhyme recognition (max. = 10, chance = 3.3)	5.11 (2.66)	6.99 (2.63)	4.50**	0.71
Concepts about print (max. = 24)	5.55 (3.05)	7.57 (3.20)	4.11**	0.63
PPVT (R)	93.99 (14.25)	104.78 (12.77)	4.73**	0.84
Confrontation naming (max. = 100)	73.77 (11.31)	81.88 (8.26)	5.03**	0.98
WPPSI Block Design	11.82 (2.72)	13.74 (2.65)	4.35**	0.72
Raven's Progressive Matrices	11.67 (3.59)	12.96 (3.15)	2.37	0.41
Phoneme blending[b] (max. = 10)	5.00 (2.63)	7.31 (2.28)	4.32**	1.01
Word Span total[b] (max. = 18)	7.57 (1.51)	8.49 (1.52)	2.86**	0.61
WPPSI Sentence Memory[b] (scaled score)	11.07 (4.78)	13.98 (4.53)	2.89**	0.64
Nonword repetition[a] (max. = 40)	32.42 (5.23)	35.29 (3.99)	2.72**	0.72
Word repetition[b] (max. = 40)	38.41 (1.68)	39.00 (1.45)	1.72	0.40
Speech Discrimination[b] (max. = 24)	16.79 (5.31)	18.33 (5.14)	1.21	0.30
Goldman–Fristoe Test[b] (incorrect articulations, max. = 44)	4.66 (3.47)	3.78 (4.81)	0.95	0.18
Word identification point[b] (mean proportion of gates required for correct identification)	0.71 (0.10)	0.69 (0.09)	0.83	0.22
Articulation rate[b] (total time for all items in msec)	25,702 (4,282)	22,285 (3,392)	3.92**	1.01
Temporal terms[b] (mean errors per condition, max. = 6)	1.99 (1.06)	1.43 (1.13)	2.38*	0.50
Visual matching[b]	7.50 (3.50)	7.80 (3.34)	0.39	0.09
Phoneme blending[b] (max. = 10)	5.00 (2.63)	7.31 (2.28)	4.32**	1.01
Temporal terms[b] (mean errors per condition, max. = 6)	1.99 (1.06)	1.43 (1.13)	2.38*	0.50
Visual matching[b]	7.50 (3.50)	7.80 (3.34)	0.39	0.09

Note. PPVT (R), Peabody Picture Vocabulary Test (Revised); WPPSI, Wechsler Preschool and Primary Scale of Intelligence. Adapted from Hindson et al. (2005). Copyright 2005 by the American Psychological Association. Adapted by permission.

[a]We elected to use the non-at-risk group's standard deviations in calculating the effect size measure.

[b]Test administered to subsample of children.

$^{*}p < .05$; $^{**}p < .01$.

The at-risk group's mean scores were lower than those of controls on the majority of measures. Vocabulary, the expressive phonological ability of articulation rate, and aspects of phonological awareness discriminated between the two groups most clearly, with the at-risk group close to or at 1 standard deviation below the non-at-risk group's mean. Articulation rate was assessed for familiar one- and three-syllable words, following Gathercole and Baddeley (1990) and Gathercole and Adams (1993). Phoneme blending and rhyme recognition were the phonological awareness tests that generated the largest group differences. We also found substantial differences in favor of non-at-risk children on measures of verbal short-term memory, nonword repetition, word span, and sentence memory, and on our primary nonverbal measure, Block Design from the Wechsler Preschool and Primary Scale of Intelligence (WPPSI). Scores on familiarity with print (Concepts about Print [CAP]; Clay, 1975) and letter names were also superior in the non-at-risk group.

The groups did not differ on auditory word identification point ("gating"), a test in which increasingly long fragments of words are presented, until the child can recognize the word (the first 100, 160, 220 msec, etc.). Metsala (1993, 1997) and Metsala and Walley (1998) have argued that the test taps a child's level of phonological representation, with recognition at shorter exposure durations indicating a phonemic rather than, say, a syllabic basis of representation.

Although we found a group difference in the measure of syntactic control that we used, interpretation of temporal terms (e.g., *before* and *after*) in spoken act-out sentences, such as *before you pick up the truck, touch the horse* (Macaruso, Bar-Shalom, Crain, & Shankweiler, 1989), overall error rates, including those of the at-risk group, were low, indicating interpretive control over these structures. Furthermore, the group difference did not survive statistical control using our nonverbal IQ measure, Block Design (all other reported differences did).

Summary and Conclusions

1. The overall picture emerging from these language-based tests is consistent with the phonological core deficit model that so frequently is proposed to capture differences between older children with and without reading deficits (e.g., Snowling, 2000). Efficient retrieval or activation of the phonological code is said to be a central feature of the deficit, one that also underlies the slow development of phonological awareness, also confirmed by our results.
2. Short-term and working memory deficiencies were also evident in the at-risk group. Phonological problems are said to create a bottle-

neck that leads to these memory deficits and, in turn, to slower development of vocabulary, one of our biggest effects (Shankweiler & Crain, 1986; Shankweiler, Crain, Brady, & Macaruso, 1992).

3. The deficit appears to be in place prior to formal literacy instruction; therefore, it is not a product of differing responses to that instruction.
4. The failure to identify an at-risk group deficit on the gating task suggests that the phonological core deficit does not extend to the quality of the representations themselves (see also Griffiths & Snowling, 2001).
5. The at-risk group did not show the kinds of articulation and speech discrimination difficulties typical of a language-delayed group.
6. Likewise, there was no clear evidence that the at-risk group was delayed, or deficient, in control of syntax, although, of course, our assessment was limited to just one structure, temporal terms.
7. Risk children are less familiar with letters and other print conventions.

Intervention

The intervention program was based on two main elements, dialogic book reading and phoneme identity instruction (phoneme identity was defined earlier). "Dialogic reading," developed and tested by Whitehurst and colleagues (Arnold, Lonigan, Whitehurst, & Epstein, 1994; Whitehurst et al., 1988; Whitehurst, Arnold, et al., 1994; Whitehurst, Epstein, et al., 1994), seeks active engagement of the child through questioning procedures linked to the material being read. Children were also encouraged to follow the text as it was read. The goal was to advance the child's familiarity with the technology of print and books, and to stimulate vocabulary (Sénéchal & LeFevre, 2002; Sénéchal, LeFevre, Thomas, & Daley, 1998).

As for phoneme identity, we developed and used a teaching kit, entitled *Sound Foundations*, previously shown to enhance children's literacy prospects when administered at preschool (Byrne & Fielding-Barnsley, 1991b; Byrne et al., 2000) The kit focuses on a subset of consonants and vowels, a design feature justified by a demonstration that phoneme identity detection ability readily generalizes from taught to untaught phonemic sites (Byrne & Fielding-Barnsley, 1991a). The kit contains large pictorial scenes in which about 60% of the objects and actions have names that begin (or end) with the critical phoneme. We also taught the letters representing the phonemes we used. The order of instructional elements was phoneme identity training, letter training, and book reading. Children were taught individually by one of two trained instructors.

Teaching phoneme identity focused on a single phoneme in a single position each day (initial /s/ one day, initial /m/ the next, final /s/ another day, etc.). We selected from the Sound Foundations kit a subset of five consonants, /s, m, p, l, t/, in both initial and final positions, and two vowels, /æ and e/ (as in *axe* and *egg*), in initial position only. The vowels were taught in a single session; thus, there were 11 lessons. Details are in Byrne et al. (1997) and Hindson et al. (2005).

The minimum number of sessions, 11, may seem rather meager to practitioners searching for effective ways to ameliorate reading disabilities. We believe, however, it is important to note that each session approached an hour in length; that the number of sessions was variable depending on the progress of the child (see next section); and that in an epidemiological sample, a reduced version of this program delivered in preschool had beneficial effects lasting for 6 years (Byrne et al., 2000). The crucial factor underlying this last encouraging result, and those to be presented later, may be that this is the first taste of formal instruction relating to literacy for all the children, and that, as such, it may be quite formative.

Index of Responsiveness to Instruction

As well as reassessing the children on letter knowledge, phoneme identity, vocabulary, and concepts of print postintervention, we developed a criterion for the rate of progression though the program. After each session, we tested children on mastery of the phoneme taught in that session by asking them to sort 12 picture cards into two piles, one with names starting (or ending) with the target phoneme, the other with names starting or ending with a different phoneme. If they did not reach the relatively stringent criterion of 10/12, the lesson was repeated, including all the elements described earlier. Thus, we created an index of responsiveness to instruction, namely, the number of lessons required to complete the program, ranging from 11 to 17 (the limit we imposed on the total number of sessions). The value for each child reflected the number of lessons that needed repetition, as determined by the postlesson criterion test (e.g., 11 = 0 lessons repeated, 17 = 6 lessons repeated). In principle, this index is independent of the actual level of achievement reached, as determined by a postintervention test of phoneme identity.

Outcomes in Preschool

The intervention succeeded in raising the trained children's levels of (1) phonological awareness (both phoneme identity and rhyme recognition), (2) CAP, and (3) receptive vocabulary (Peabody Picture Vocabulary Test [PPVT]). The primary evidence for this is pre- to postintervention (Time) difference for the trained groups combined with a Group × Time interaction for the two at-risk groups, trained and waiting-list, in which the waiting-list group advanced less. Letter name knowledge also increased significantly, but the waiting-list control group improved as much as the instructed groups, so activities occurring with the passage of time (about 3 months for most children for pretest to postintervention test) were sufficient to advance this skill. Because letter names, other than the seven for the taught phonemes, were not the subject of instruction, this result is understandable. Likewise, expressive vocabulary (Hundred Pictures Naming Test [HPNT]) grew equally in all three groups. We do not have an explanation for the difference between receptive and expressive vocabulary in effects of the intervention.

The improvement for the at-risk group was slightly less than the non-at-risk group, as revealed by covarying the change scores on preintervention scores. Without that covariation, change scores were not significantly different: The altered pattern with covariance is probably due to the fact that the non-at-risk group had higher preintervention scores and, hence, less chance to improve, masking a sample difference.

The risk group needed more lessons to complete the program than the non-at-risk group (13.64 vs. 12.48, significant beyond .01, with a Cohen's d of 0.67, a medium-to-large effect). Thus, although the at-risk children benefited from the instruction, they were immediately less responsive than non-at-risk controls, both in terms of postintervention levels and, more clearly, rate of response, as indicated by number of lessons required.

Prediction of Response to Instruction

We were able to account for 52% of the variance in outcome phonemic awareness using a combination of predictors, including preintervention phoneme identity, rhyme recognition, letter knowledge, vocabulary, and verbal short-term memory (a composite of Word Span, Nonword Repetition, and Sentence Memory). Only the two phonological awareness tests, phoneme identity and rhyme recognition, made independent contributions to the prediction. Their zero-order correlations with the dependent variable, postintervention phoneme identity, were .53 for phoneme identity and .38 for rhyme recognition. Risk status did not in itself contribute additionally to variance explained, indicating that status had its effect through the variables we assessed at pretest. The fact that Vocabulary and Block Design, our best proxies for IQ, also did not contribute indicates that factors underlying this measure of response to intervention are cognitively specific rather than general. It seems that children who already have a degree of phonological awareness, including at the rhyme level, benefit most from additional early instruction. The specific contribution of rhyming ability is encouraging, because many risk children who lacked any detectable phonemic awareness were nevertheless able to judge rhyme successfully in our pretests. Sensitivity to large-scale units, rhymes, apparently paves the way for sensitivity to small-scale units, phonemes, in suitably prepared children (Goswami & Bryant, 1990). Because rhymes appear easier to teach than phonemes, early rhyme instruction in difficult cases can be recommended.

The rate at which children advanced through the program, a variable we have dubbed "Progress" (Hindson et al., 2005), was determined by the phoneme identity criterion tests, but its predictors patterned differently than those for the actual level of phoneme identity achieved postintervention. Using the same suite of predictors, we found that vocabulary and verbal short-term memory were the only ones that made independent contributions to variance explained in Progress, which totaled 54%. The zero-order correlations were .64 and .55, respectively. Because vocabulary predicts this outcome measure, it may be more subject than postintervention phoneme identity level to general rather than specific cognitive factors, using the assumption that vocabulary is a proxy for verbal intelligence. That issue aside, the fact that Progress and outcome phoneme identity do not engage their predictor variables in the same way indicates that they capture different aspects of response to instruction, indicating in turn that responsiveness is not a unitary construct. We return to this distinction again when we consider determinants of later outcome measures, those in school.

The third response measure we investigated was Concepts about Print (CAP) measured postintervention. Here we found that our noverbal IQ measure, Block Design, preintervention phoneme identity, and preintervention CAP all made independent contributions to explaining the outcome variance, with the largest influence coming from the last of these, as might be expected. The zero-order correlations for Block Design, preintervention phoneme identity, and preintervention CAP were .35, .59, and .65, respectively.

Kindergarten Outcomes

The kindergarten data are reported in detail in Hindson et al. (2005). There we showed that the non-at-risk group outperformed the risk group by a considerable margin in Word Identification (the Woodcock Reading Mastery Test—Revised (WRMT-R; Woodcock, 1987) subtest, Nonword Reading (using a specially created list of 20 one-syllable items from two to five letters in length), and Spelling (a list of 10 words and 4 nonwords, scored to value phonemic as well as orthographic accuracy).

Despite the superiority of the non-at-risk group, there were reasons to believe that the at-risk children were performing about as well as a non-at-risk group that had not been subjected to special, early intervention. The mean Woodcock standard score for the at-risk group was 109.7 (*SD* =

17.4) and 117.9 (*SD* = 15.1) for the non-at-risk group. Although the norms are based on a U.S. sample whose applicability to Australia is uncertain, the value is above the U.S. mean and very close to the 108.6 obtained by the control (uninstructed) group in our earlier evaluation of the Sound Foundations kit (Byrne & Fielding-Barnsley, 1993). Likewise, the Spelling scores, also used in that earlier study, were similar at 54.3 (15.4) for the intervention group in the risk study, and 53.4 (13.6) for the control group in the evaluation study. Elbro and Petersen (2004) also reported that their experimental risk group achieved levels typical of untrained normal samples directly following the training and also in grade 2 (though with a nonsignificant tendency to lag behind on some tests in grade 2). Grade 1 in Denmark is equivalent to Australian kindergarten, in that it is the first year of formal literacy instruction in Danish schools.

Grade 1 Outcomes

In grade 1, 94 children were available for testing, 53 at-risk children and 41 non-at-risk children. The attrition was primarily due to families leaving the area or otherwise not being contactable. The attrition appears not to have been selective in terms of children's preschool performance levels. For example, the children available for assessment in Grade 1 had preschool scores of 11.42, 12.98, and 96.72 on phoneme identify, letter knowledge, and PPVT compared with 11.28, 12.13, and 96.19 for children who were not available for follow-up. We re-administered three of the kindergarten tests, Woodcock Word Identification, Spelling and Nonword Reading. In addition, we gave the Word Attack subtest from the Woodcock. All tests were given individually, toward the end of the school year. Details of performance by group are presented in Table 9.2.

There are two obvious features of the grade 1 results in the Woodcock subtests, the superior performance of the non-at-risk group, and the grade-level performance of the at-risk group. Both group differences are significant beyond .05, as are those for Spelling and Nonword Reading, with effect sizes in the medium range and the percentage of nonoverlap between the two samples in a range around 30 to 40 (Cohen, 1998). As with the kindergarten data, uncertainty about the appropriateness of the U.S. Woodcock norms for these Australian children tempers the confidence we may place in these data as far as grade level is concerned. However, what we can say is that the at-risk group is performing at a level that meets a reasonable absolute standard, that of average U.S. children in grade 1.

The continued higher performance of the non-at-risk group is consistent with evidence from our earlier work that preschool instruction in phoneme identity can advance the reading skills of unselected children (Byrne & Fielding-Barnsley, 1991a, 1993, 1995; Byrne et al., 2000), indicating

TABLE 9.2. Means (and Standard Deviations) of At-Risk and Non-at-Risk Groups in Grades 1 and 2 Literacy Tests

Grade	Test	Group		*d*
		At-risk (N = 53)	Non-at-risk (N = 41)	
1	WWI	109.7 (13.7)	117.5 (15.1)	0.52
	WWA	104.2 (13.6)	111.0 (13.7)	0.50
	Spelling[a]	68.9 (13.2)	75.0 (9.1)	0.67
	Nonword reading[b]	47.4 (12.8)	52.4 (10.4)	0.48
		Risk (N = 49)	Non-at-risk (N = 39)	
2	WWI	106.5 (18.0)	116.1 (16.9)	0.57
	WWA	103.4 (15.5)	111.6 (12.7)	0.65
	WPC	101.5 (16.3)	110.8 (10.2)	0.92
	Regular words[c]	20.3 (8.6)	24.0 (6.2)	0.60
	Irregular words[c]	13.8 (7.5)	17.7 (4.9)	0.80
	Nonwords[c]	15.1 (9.5)	19.5 (8.6)	0.51

Note. WWI, Woodcock Word Identification; WWA, Woodcock Word Attack; WPC, Woodcock Passage Comprehension.
[a]Max. = 84; [b]max. = 64; [c]max. = 30.

that its benefits are nonspecific, that is, not limited to children at risk. The relative intensity of the one-on-one instruction, including interactive book reading, as well as phonemic awareness, may explain the substantial boost to performance in these. At a practical level, this kind of early instruction is unlikely to become standard practice because of its expense, but in cases of likely risk, the results may well be worth the cost in the long run.

Grade 2 Outcomes

We were able to test 48 at-risk children and 39 non-at-risk children, and administered the test battery in the final 2 months of the school year. The grade 2 tests included the two Woodcock subtests used in grade 1, Word Identification and Word Attack, and we added Passage Comprehension from the same test. In addition, we administered three lists devised by Castles (1994; see also Coltheart & Leahy, 1996): (1) regularly spelled words, such as *flannel*; (2) irregularly spelled words, such as *blood*; and (3) pseudowords, such as *tapple*. Each list contained 30 items, which were mixed into a single test of 90 items. Children were told that some of the words were not real. The test is untimed, and the scores are the numbers correct for each item type. Table 9.2 contains the descriptive statistics. The pattern of grade 1 is repeated here, namely, a group difference along with grade-appropriate scores in the Woodcock subtests from the at-risk group (the cautions about interpretation of these are still relevant). All group differences were significant beyond .05, with effect sizes that appeared somewhat larger than for grade 1. It may be that although the at-risk children still appeared to be at grade level, they may not quite have been keeping up with the control children.

Following Elbro and Petersen (2004), we identified the numbers of at-risk children falling below the 5 and 20% cutoff values established by the non-at-risk sample. We did this for our oldest group, grade 2. For the Woodcock Word Identification subtest, the percentages were 10.4, and 54.2, respectively; for Word Attack, they were 10.6 and 46.8, respectively; and for Passage Comprehension, they were 23.9 and 54.3, respectively, with means of 15.0 and 51.8%, respectively, for the at-risk and non-at-risk groups. Recall that the analogous means from Elbro and Petersen (2004) were 16 and 42%, so there is reasonable agreement across the samples that substantially more at-risk children are performing below the level of similarly instructed non-at-risk children. The relatively higher numbers of at-risk children below the 5% cutoff for Passage Comprehension (23.9 vs. 10.4% for Word Identification, for example) might indicate that more pervasive language problems exist in the at-risk group. We know from the longitudinal twin study that at grade 1, most of the phenotypic and almost all of the genetic variance is shared in common between word-level processes and reading comprehension (Byrne et al., 2007). But at higher grades, this picture changes, with language factors, as captured by measures of listening comprehension playing an increasing role, although still genetically mediated (Keenan, Betjemann, Wadsworth, DeFries, & Olson, 2006).

Overall, the at-risk children did not perform as well as the instructed non-at-risk children, but they probably achieved grade-level performance over the 3-year follow-up on average. This is encouraging. But we also noted that more of the at-risk children were reading at levels that classified them as reading disabled, so, as Elbro and Petersen (2004) also found, early intervention is not full prevention. It would be helpful, of course, to know more about the failing children from both groups, so now we consider what predicts response to intervention in these samples.

Predicting Responsiveness

In our earlier evaluation study (Byrne et al., 2000), we were able to follow the children from preschool to grade 5, giving us ample opportunity to determine which of the early variables predicted later reading growth. The clear finding was that the single best predictor was the number of preschool lessons it took before a child showed that he or she grasped the idea of phoneme identity, the primary subject of the instruction. This variable, akin to Progress in the current risk study, outdid the outcome level of phoneme identity as predictor of most reading and spelling measures from kindergarten to grade 5. Thus, for the kindergarten phase of this risk project, reported in Hindson et al. (2005), we ran the same kind of analysis, using Progress and postintervention phoneme identity as the predictors. For Spelling and Nonword Reading, only Progress accounted for unique variance when both measures were entered simultaneously, for a total of 25% of the variance. For Word Identification, only the postintervention phoneme identity score contributed uniquely to variance explained, accounting for a total of 29% of the variance. It may be that Spelling and Nonword Reading place heavier demands on phonological coding, and that Progress was largely determined by the rate at which children mastered phoneme identity in the program.

We ran similar analyses for grades 1 and 2, which we report for the first time here. We extended the analyses in two ways, refining the dependent variable and adding preintervention phoneme identity to the predictor list. Because our total sample contracted in size with each passing year (N = 97 in grade 1 and N = 89 in grade 2), we created a single and therefore more stable dependent variable from our follow-up reading and spelling measures. To do so, we checked on the overlap among the dependent variables at each grade by running a principal components analysis. In each case we identified a single factor accounting for a substantial percentage of variance, 79.8 at grade 1 and 62.4 at grade 2. In neither case did the eigenvalue for the second factor approach 1. Thus, we considered it justifiable to treat the separate measures as contributing to a single literacy factor. We formed a composite dependent variable for each grade by summing and averaging within-grade standardized scores for the tests, four at grade 1 and six at grade 2.

The other change to the analyses was the addition of preintervention phoneme identity to the predictors. The correlation between the pre- and postintervention phoneme identity tests was just .53, suggesting that they may make partially independent contributions to predicting other variables. Thus, we subjected the hypothesis that Progress would account for the lion's share of variance in each of the two dependent variables to a more searching test, by including an additional and plausible independent variable. The results of the analyses are presented in Tables 9.3 and 9.4.

In grade 1, where 34% of variance was explained by the preschool predictors we used, postintervention phoneme identity and Progress each made an independent contribution in the model. In grade 2, 22% of variance of the composite literacy scores was explained by the predictors. Once again, both postintervention phoneme identity and Progress made significant unique contributions to the model. Thus, as in the Hindson et al. (2005) kindergarten analysis, responsiveness of the children to early intervention (where responsiveness is measured by the rate at which they

TABLE 9.3. Summary of Regression Analyses for Variables Predicting Grade 1 Composite Literacy Scores

Predictors	R^2	*B*	*SE B*	ß
Model	.34**			
Preintervention phoneme identity		–.01	.32	–.05
Postintervention phoneme identity		.14*	.07	.28
Progress		–.16*	.05	–.39

Note. *$p < .05$; **$p < .01$.

showed gains from the instruction rather than the final outcome level) was an important predictor of literacy levels 2 and 3 years after the preschool intervention. At neither grade did these preschool variables account for more than a modest amount of variance, but perhaps this is not surprising given the time that has elapsed and the school instruction that has occurred in the meantime.

SUMMARY OF INTERVENTION

1. Intensive, one-on-one tuition in phoneme identity supported by interactive reading raises at-risk children's preschool levels of phonological awareness, vocabulary, and knowledge of print conventions.
2. At-risk children are less responsive to this instruction than at non-at-risk children, particularly in the number of sessions required.
3. Preexisting levels of phonological awareness, including rhyme, predict postintervention levels of phoneme awareness, but different variables predict the rate of response—vocabulary and short-term memory.
4. In kindergarten, grade 1, and grade 2, the instructed at-risk children achieved grade-average levels on word reading and reading comprehension, but lagged behind their non-at-risk counterparts.

TABLE 9.4. Summary of Regression Analyses for Variables Predicting Grade 2 Composite Literacy Scores

Predictors	R^2	*B*	*SE B*	ß
Model	.22**			
Preintervention phoneme identity		–.02	.04	–.07
Postintervention phoneme identity		.15*	.08	.28
Progress		–.12*	.06	–.29

Note. *$p < .05$; **$p < .01$.

5. Substantial numbers of at-risk children remained poor readers, as defined by cutoff values within the non-at-risk comparison group.
6. The rate of response to instruction and the actual outcome levels were independent predictors of school progress in reading.

OVERALL SUMMARY AND IMPLICATIONS

Effects of Early Intervention and Its Educational Implications

Children who present with a familial risk factor for reading disability can be assisted by timely, targeted intervention. This does not guarantee freedom from reading problems, however, and it stands to reason that continued support is required. The kind of support needed can be implied from the major, novel findings of our research that at-risk children require more extensive instruction than non-at-risk children to reach comparable levels in the foundations of literacy, and that the rate at which they progress is a good indicator of future prospects. Thus, teaching needs to be more sustained, and opportunities for practice more abundant, for these compromised children if we are to avoid early difficulties and regression later to lower skills levels.

The Nature of the Learning Deficit

Our data promote the idea that reading disability is first and foremost a *learning* deficiency, one that affects early stages in which phonological awareness and letter knowledge are emerging, and later stages, in which more integrated orthographic and semantic processes come online to contribute to reading mastery under all plausible models of literacy growth (e.g., Coltheart, 2005; Ehri, 2002; Harm & Seidenberg, 1999; Liberman, Shankweiler, Camp, Blachman, & Werfelman, 1980; Plaut, 2005). Others have drawn attention to learning processes as central (e.g., Reitsma, 1983; Snowling et al., 2003; Vellutino, Scanlon, & Sipay, 1997). Learning, of course, can be disrupted by many factors, from impaired levels of basic neural plasticity (Garlick, 2002) to attentional control (Willcutt et al., 2002). Clearly, much more research is required if we are to describe the learning impairment that leads specifically to literacy difficulties, and we return to this issue in the final section. But for the moment, we wish to make the point that a focus on learning processes can and should complement the attention given so far to difficulties with phonological awareness as a cause of reading disability. Without detracting from the impressive amount of evidence in favor of the role of phonemic awareness, we believe that it is only part of the etiological story.

A major issue in considering the nature of a learning deficit is its scope.

Is there a deficiency that is limited to aspects of literacy, or does it extend to other domains of academic achievement, such as mathematics, or indeed to domains outside traditional school subjects? We do not know at present, but Plomin and Kovas (2005) argue a case for "generalist genes" of relatively wide scope, underlying learning disabilities within and across the domains of language, literacy, and mathematics. Space prohibits us from comparing their arguments that favor our position here. But we do note that among the basic processes that these genes may affect (and that therefore account for the generalist effects), researchers are considering ones that could govern learning, such as dendritic density and basic neural plasticity (Grant, 2003; Plomin & Kovas, 2005; see also Garlick, 2002).

Another issue relates to the precise routes via which fundamental learning processes affect literacy development. We consider some possibilities in the final section on genetics and literacy, but here we note that this is likely to be a complex question. To illustrate this, consider as a start our observation that vocabulary (along with working memory) was a good predictor of our preschool learning rate parameter, Progress, which in turn predicted subsequent literacy growth. Vocabulary levels are themselves in part the obvious products of learning processes, so the relationship with Progress might be based on a common underlying parameter. Alternatively, and in accordance with the phonological restructuring hypothesis (Metsala & Walley, 1998), larger vocabularies enhance acquisition of the insights that the program was teaching, shared phonemes across words, leading to quicker completion of the program. As it turns out, our data relevant to the lexical restructuring hypothesis from the gating experiments lend little support to that hypothesis, but this illustrates the kinds of questions that will have to be addressed in delineating the paths (and there will be many) from basic learning processes to literacy competence (and deficiencies).

This additional emphasis on learning has the practical implications to which we alluded earlier. Perhaps most important is that children who show signs of reading difficulties early are likely to need continued support, because learning is an ongoing process. Put another way, reading disability is unlikely to yield to a one-time targeted intervention, such as early phoneme awareness training linked to letter knowledge, however justified that is based on available evidence (and it is). The nature of that continued support should be the subject of an extensive research effort, but it plainly should afford compromised children with extensive exposure to written language as a way of building up their stock of print–speech links (Ehri, 2002).

We close with some cross-links to our behavior–genetic study of early reading development (Byrne et al., 2002, 2005; Byrne, Olson, Samuelsson, Wadsworth, et al., 2006; Samuelsson et al., 2005), motivated by the familial aggregation of reading problems that has been central to the current research. As a preface, we quote Snowling et al. (2003) as they speculate about the fundamental deficiency underlying dyslexia, based on their findings of slow vocabulary development and lower levels of nursery rhyme and letter knowledge in at-risk children.

> A speculative interpretation of these findings is that a cognitive marker of dyslexia that characterizes not only affected individuals but also unaffected relatives is one of verbal association learning. Such a deficit could account for the slow rate of learning of nursery rhymes and letters in both (their) high-risk groups, with the letter learning deficit having an effect downstream on decoding and encoding processes that engage grapheme–phoneme correspondences. (p. 371)

In our twin study we observed that although preschool letter and print knowledge was largely under the influence of home/preschool factors, it was subject to a modest genetic influence as well. Knowledge of how graphic forms map onto linguistic ones can be seen as a prototypical instance of verbal association learning. The extensive variability in home and preschool literacy practices that exists in the United States and Australia, from which the samples primarily came, probably contributes to the dominance of environmental processes in print familiarity at this early developmental stage. Because opportunities for gaining familiarity with elements of print and explicit awareness of phonological structures tend to be informal rather than structured for preschool children, the genetic source may be determining, in part, the ability to fix these associations from ambient information. This genetic source for print also affected preschool phonological awareness.

At the end of kindergarten, when the twins had completed a year of formal instruction in reading, word identification efficiency was substantially affected by genes (Byrne et al, 2005). *Importantly, multivariate analysis showed that the genes that (modestly) affected print familiarity in preschool contributed substantially to the total heritability of kindergarten reading*. It is as if their genetic effects "amplified" in the course of development. Although the interpretation of these links must remain tentative, it is possible that we are seeing a genetic basis for early reading growth (and for familial aggregation of reading problems) that drives, in part, the learning process in both formal and informal settings, with early evidence of the process at work centering on letter knowledge and familiarity with print structures. The dominant predictive role of the Progress variable in the risk study is consistent with this interpretation: Some children make more efficient use of learning opportunities than others, and this difference is determined in part by genes.

As a further example of learning opportunities, consider the acquisition of word-specific spelling patterns in English. Share (1999) has proposed that successful decoding of newly encountered words affords children the opportunity to commit to memory those words' spelling patterns, the so-called "self-teaching hypothesis." There is a considerable amount of evidence in favor of this hypothesis (e.g., Cunningham, Perry, Stanovich, & Share, 2002; Nation, Angell, & Castles, 2006; Share, 1999). In typical tests of the theory, children read novel words that could be spelled in at least two ways, such as *vade*, and are subsequently required to spell those words. In our ongoing twin study, we have been able to show that among second graders, (1) the ability to learn word-specific spelling patterns under these circumstances is moderately affected by genes, and (2) the same genes are the major influence on levels of concurrent spelling achievement (Byrne et al., 2008). New learning and existing achievement in the same domain show high genetic overlap. Thus, we could say that spelling achievement represents the "crystallized" product of the genes that determine the ability to fix new spellings in mind.

The learning opportunities we have been illustrating are but some of the many insights and associations required for a successful start, and successful continuation, on the path to reading and spelling competence: insights, such as the fact that words share phonemes; and associations such as the letters that stand in for these phonemes. Some of these opportunities are informal, some are formal, but all play a role in literacy growth.

In any case, integration of phenotypic research of the sort we have outlined in this chapter, and research within a behavior–genetic framework of the kind that we and others are conducting (e.g., Harlaar, Spinath, Dale, & Plomin, 2005; Petrill, Deater-Deckard, Schatschneider, & Davis, 2005), including rapid advances in identifying genes contributing to developmental reading disability (e.g., Cope et al., 2005; Hannula-Jouppi et al., 2005; Meng et al., 2005), can only advance our understanding of reading difficulties and enhance our prospects for devising intelligent interventions. Here we have presented a case for including learning processes among those to be given prominence in this program of research.

REFERENCES

Arnold, D. H., Lonigan, C. J., Whitehurst, G. J., & Epstein, J. N. (1994). Accelerating language development through picture book reading: Replication and extension of videotape training format. *Journal of Educational Psychology, 86*, 235–243.

Badian, N. A. (1988). The prediction of good and poor reading before kindergarten entry: A nine-year follow-up. *Journal of Learning Disabilities, 21*, 98–123.

Bishop, D. V. (1985). Spelling ability in congenital dysarthria: Evidence against articulatory coding in translating between phonemes and graphemes. *Cognitive Neuropsychology, 3*, 229–251.

Bishop, D. V., & Adams, C. (1990). A prospective study of the relationship between specific language impairment, phonological disorders, and reading retardation. *Journal of Child Psychology and Psychiatry and Allied Disciplines, 31*, 1027–1050.

Borstrom, I., & Elbro, C. (1997). Prevention of dyslexia in kindergarten: Effects of phoneme awareness training with children of dyslexic parents. In C. Hulme & M. Snowling (Eds.), *Dyslexia: Biology, cognition and intervention* (pp. 235–253). London: Whurr.

Bus, A. G., & van IJzendoorn, M. H. (1999). Phonological awareness and early reading: A meta-analysis of experimental training studies. *Journal of Educational Psychology, 91*, 403–414.

Byrne, B., Coventry, W. L., Olson, R. K., Hulslander, J., Wadsworth, S., DeFries, J. C., et al. (2008). A behavior-genetic analysis of orthographic learning, spelling, and decoding. *Journal of Research in Reading, 31*, 8–21.

Byrne, B., Delaland, C., Fielding-Barnsley, R., Quain, P., Samuelsson, S., Hoien, T., et al. (2002). Longitudinal twin study of early reading development in three countries: Preliminary results. *Annals of Dyslexia, 52*, 49–73.

Byrne, B., & Fielding-Barnsley, R. (1991a). Evaluation of a program to teach phonemic awareness to young children. *Journal of Educational Psychology, 83*, 451–455.

Byrne, B., & Fielding-Barnsley, R. (1991b). *Sound Foundations: An introduction to prereading skills*. Sydney: Peter Leyden Educational.

Byrne, B., & Fielding-Barnsley, R. (1993). Evaluation of a program to teach phonemic awareness to young children: A 1-year follow-up. *Journal of Educational Psychology, 85*, 104–111.

Byrne, B., & Fielding-Barnsley, R. (1995). Evaluation of a program to teach phonemic awareness to young children: A 2- and 3-year follow-up, and a new preschool trial. *Journal of Educational Psychology, 87*, 488–503.

Byrne, B., Fielding-Barnsley, R., & Ashley, L. (2000). Effects of preschool phoneme identity training after six years: Outcome level distinguished from rate of response. *Journal of Educational Psychology, 92*, 659–667.

Byrne, B., Fielding-Barnsley, R., Ashley, L., & Larsen, K. (1997). Assessing the child's and the environment's contribution to reading acquisition: What we know and what we don't know. In B. Blachman (Ed.), *Foundations of reading acquisition and dyslexia: Implications for early intervention* (pp. 265–286). Mahwah, NJ: Erlbaum.

Byrne, B., Olson, R. K., Samuelsson, S., Wadsworth, S., Corley, R., DeFries, J. C., et al. (2006). Genetic and environmental influences on early literacy skills: A review and update. *Journal of Research in Reading, 29*, 33–49.

Byrne, B., Samuelsson, S., Wadsworth, S., Hulslander, J., Corley, R., DeFries, J. C., et al. (2007). Longitudinal twin study of early literacy development: Preschool through grade 1. *Reading and Writing: An Interdisciplinary Journal, 20*, 77–102.

Byrne, B., Wadsworth, S., Corley, R., Samuelsson, S., Quain, P., DeFries, J. C., et al. (2005). Longitudinal twin study of early literacy development: Preschool and kindergarten phases. *Scientific Studies of Reading, 9*, 219–235.

Castles, A. (1994). *Varieties of developmental dyslexia*. Unpublished PhD thesis, Macquarie University, Sydney, Australia.

Catts, H., & Kamhi, A. (2005). *The connections between language and reading disabilities*. Mahwah, NJ: Erlbaum.

Clay, M. (1975). *The early detection of reading difficulties: A diagnostic survey.* Auckland: Heinemann.

Cohen, J. (1998). *Statistical power analysis for the behavioral sciences* (2nd ed.) Hillsdale, NJ: Erlbaum.

Coltheart, M. (2005). Modeling reading: The dual-route approach. In M. J. Snowling & C. Hulme (Eds.), *The science of reading: A handbook* (pp. 6–23). Oxford, UK: Blackwell.

Coltheart, M., & Leahy, J. (1996). Assessment of lexical and nonlexical reading abilities in children: Some normative data. *Australian Journal of Psychology, 48*, 136–140.

Cope, N. A., Harold, D., Hill, G., Moskvina, V., Holmans, P., Owen, M. J., et al. (2005). Strong evidence that *KIAA0319* on chromosome 6p is a susceptibility gene for developmental dyslexia. *American Journal of Human Genetics, 76*, 581–591.

Cunningham, A. E., Perry, K. E., Stanovich, K. E., & Share, D. L. (2002). Orthographic learning during reading: Examining the role of self-teaching. *Journal of Experimental Child Psychology, 82*, 185–199.

Cunningham, A. E., & Stanovich, K. E. (1997). Early reading acquisition and its relation to reading experience and ability ten years later. *Developmental Psychology, 33*, 934–945.

Ehri, L. C. (1993). How English orthography influences phonological knowledge as children learn to read and spell. In R. J. Scholes (Ed.), *Literacy and language analysis* (pp. 21–43). Hillsdale, NJ: Erlbaum.

Ehri, L. C. (2002). Phases of acquisition in learning to read words and implications for teaching. in R. Stainthorpe & P. Tomlinson (Eds.), *Learning and teaching reordering* (pp. 7–28). London: British Journal of Educational Psychology Monograph Series I.

Elbro, C., Borstrom, I., & Petersen, D. K. (1998). Predicting dyslexia from kindergarten: The importance of distinctness of phonological representations of lexical items. *Reading Research Quarterly, 33*, 36–60.

Elbro, C., & Petersen, D. K. (2004). Long-term effects of phoneme awareness and letter sound training: An intervention study with children at risk for dyslexia. *Journal of Educational Psychology, 96*, 660–670.

Finucci, J. M., Guthrie, J. T., Childs, A. L., Abbey, H., & Childs, B. (1976). The genetics of specific reading disability. *Annals of Human Genetics, 40*, 1–23.

Fisher, J. H. (1905). Case of congenital word blindness (inability to learn to read). *Ophthalmic Review, 24*, 315–318.

Gallagher, A., Frith, U., & Snowling, M. J. (2000). Precursors of literacy delay among children at genetic risk for dyslexia. *Journal of Child Psychology and Psychiatry, 41*, 203–213.

Garlick, D. (2002). Understanding the nature of the general factor in intelligence: The role of individual differences in neural plasticity as an explanatory mechanism. *Psychological Review, 109*, 116–136.

Gathercole, S. E., & Adams, A. (1993). Phonological working memory in very young children. *Developmental Psychology, 29*, 770–778.

Gathercole, S. E., & Baddeley, A. D. (1990). Phonological memory deficits in language disordered children: Is there a causal connection? *Journal of Memory and Language, 29*, 336–360.

Gilger, J. W., Pennington, B. F., & DeFries, J. C. (1991). Risk for reading disability as a function of parental history in three family studies. *Reading and Writing: An Interdisciplinary Journal, 3*, 205–219.

Goldman, R., & Fristoe, M. (1986). *Goldman–Fristoe Test of Articulation.* Circle Pines, MN: American Guidance Service.

Gombert, J.-E. (1992). *Metalinguistic development.* Hemel Hempstead: Harvester Wheatsheaf.

Goswami, U., & Bryant, P. E. (1990). *Phonological skills and learning to read.* Hove, UK: Erlbaum.

Grant, S. G. N. (2003). An integrative neuroscience program linking genes to cognition and disease. In R. Plomin, J. C. DeFries, I. W. Craig, & P. McGuffin (Eds.), *Behavioral genetics in the postgenomic era* (pp. 123–138). Washington, DC: American Psychological Association.

Griffiths, Y. M., & Snowling, M. J. (2001). Auditory word identification and phonological skills in dyslexic and average readers. *Applied Psycholinguistics, 22*, 419–439.

Hallgren, B. (1950). Specific dyslexia: A clinical and genetic study. *Acta Psychiatrica et Neurologica Scandinavica, 65*(Suppl.), 179–189.

Hannula-Jouppi, K., Kaminen-Ahola, N., Taipale, M., Eklund, R., Nopola-Hemmi, J., Kääriäinen, H., et al. (2005). The axon guidance receptor gene *ROBO1* is a candidate gene for developmental dyslexia. *PLS: Genetics, 1*(4)e50, 0467–0474.

Harlaar, N., Spinath, F. M., Dale, P. S., & Plomin, R. (2005). Genetic influences on word recognition abilities and disabilities: A study of 7-year-old twins. *Journal of Child Psychology and Psychiatry, 46*, 373–384.

Harm, M. W., & Seidenberg, M. S. (1999). Phonology, reading acquisition, and dyslexia: Insights from connectionist models. *Psychological Review, 106*, 491–528.

Hindson, B. A., Byrne, B., Fielding-Barnsley, R., Newman, C., Hine, D., & Shankweiler, D. (2005). Assessment and early instruction of preschool children at risk for reading disability. *Journal of Educational Psychology, 94*, 687–704.

Hinshelwood, J. (1911). Two cases of congenital hereditary word-blindness. *British Medical Journal, 60*, 608–609.

Keenan, J. M., Betjemann, R. S., Wadsworth, S. J., DeFreis, J. C., & Olson, R. K. (2006). Genetic and environmental influences on reading and listening comprehension. *Journal of Research in Reading, 29*, 75–91.

Lefly, D. L., & Pennington, B. F. (1996). Longitudinal study of children at high family risk for dyslexia: The first two years. In M. L. Rice (Ed.), *Towards a genetics of language* (pp. 49–76). Hillsdale, NJ: Erlbaum.

Liberman, I. Y., Shankweiler, D., Camp, L., Blachman, B., & Werfelman, M. (1980). Steps toward literacy: A linguistic approach. In P. Levinson & C. Sloan (Eds.), *Auditory processing and language* (pp 189–215). New York: Grune & Stratton.

Locke, J. L., Hodgson, J., Macaruso, P., Roberts, J., Lambrecht-Smith, S., & Guttentag, C. (1997). The development of developmental dyslexia. In C. Hulme & M. Snowling (Eds.), *Dyslexia: Biology, cognition and intervention* (pp. 72–96). London: Whurr.

Lyytinen, H. (1997). In search of the precursors of dyslexia: A prospective study of children at risk for reading problems. In C. Hulme & M. Snowling (Eds.), *Dyslexia: Biology, cognition and intervention* (pp. 97–107). London: Whurr.

Lyytinen, H., Aro, M., Eklund, K., Erskine, J., Guttorm, T., Laakso, M.-L., et al. (2004). The development of children at familial risk for dyslexia: Birth to early school age. *Annals of Dyslexia, 54*, 184–220.

Lyytinen, H., Poikkeus, A.-M., Laakso, M.-L., Eklund, K., & Lyytinen, P. (2001). Language development and symbolic play in children with and without familial risk for dyslexia. *Journal of Speech, Language and Hearing Research, 44*, 873–885.

Macaruso, P., Bar-Shalom, E., Crain, S., & Shankweiler, D. (1989). Comprehension of temporal terms by good and poor readers. *Language and Speech, 32*, 45–67.

Marshall, W., & Ferguson, J. (1939). Hereditary word-blindness as a defect of selective association. *Journal of Nervous and Mental Disease, 89*, 164–173.

Meng, H., Smith, S. D., Hager, K., Held, M., Liu, J., Olson, R. K., et al. (2005). *DCDC2* is associated with reading disability and modulates neuronal development in the brain. *Proceedings of the National Academy of Sciences USA, 102*, 17053–17058.

Metsala, J. L. (1993). *An examination of speech perception in reading disabled and normally achieving children using the gating paradigm*. Unpublished PhD thesis, University of Toronto, Toronto, Canada.

Metsala, J. L. (1997). Spoken word recognition in reading disabled children. *Journal of Educational Psychology, 89*, 159–169.

Metsala, J. L., & Walley, A. C. (1998). Spoken vocabulary growth and the segmental restructuring of lexical representations: Precursors to phonemic awareness and early reading ability. In J. L. Metsala & L. C. Ehri (Eds.), *Word recognition and beginning literacy* (pp. 89–120). Hillsdale, NJ: Erlbaum.

Morais, J., Carey, L., Alegria, J., & Bertelson, P. (1979). Does awareness of speech as a sequence of phonemes arise spontaneously? *Cognition, 7*, 323–334.

Nathan, L., Stackhouse, J., Goulandris, N., & Snowling, M. J. (2004). The development of early literacy skills among children with speech difficulties: A test of the "critical age" hypothesis. *Journal of Speech, Hearing, and Language Research, 47*, 377–391.

Nation, K., Angell, P., & Castles, A. (2006). Orthographic learning via self-teaching in children learning to read English: Effects of exposure, durability, and context. *Journal of Experimental Child Psychology, 96*, 71–84.

Olson, R. K., & Byrne, B. (2005). Genetic and environmental influences on reading and language ability and disability. In H. Catts (Ed.), *Connections between language and reading disorders* (pp. 173–200). Mahwah, NJ: Erlbaum.

Orton, S. J. (1937). *Reading, writing and speech problems in children*. London: Chapman & Hall.

Pennington, B. F., & Lefly, D. L. (2001). Early reading development in children at family risk for dyslexia. *Child Development, 72*, 816–833.

Pennington, B. F., & Olson, R. K. (2005). Genetics of dyslexia. In M. J. Snowling & C. Hulme (Eds.), *The science of reading: A handbook* (pp. 453–472). Oxford: Blackwell.

Petrill, S. A., Deater-Deckard, K., Schatschneider, C., & Davis, C. (2005). Measured environmental influences on early reading: Evidence from an adoption study. *Scientific Studies of Reading, 9*, 237–259.

Plaut, D. C. (2005). Connectionist approaches to reading. In M. J. Snowling & C. Hulme (Eds.), *The science of reading: A handbook* (pp. 24–38). Oxford, UK: Blackwell.

Plomin, R., & Kovas, Y. (2005). Generalist genes and learning disabilities. *Psychological Bulletin, 131*, 592–617.

Reitsma, P. (1983). Printed word learning in beginning readers. *Journal of Experimental Child Psychology, 75*, 321–339.

Samuelsson, S., Byrne, B., Quain, P., Corley, R., DeFries, J. C., Wadsworth, S., et al. (2005). Environmental and genetic influences on pre-reading skills in Australia, Scandinavia, and the United States. *Journal of Educational Psychology, 97*, 705–722.

Samuelsson, S., Olson, R. K., Wadsworth, S., Corley, R., DeFries, J. C., Willcutt, E., et al. (2007). Genetic and environmental influences on prereading skills and early reading and spelling development in the United States, Australia, and Scandinavia. *Reading and Writing: An Interdisciplinary Journal, 20*, 51–75.

Scarborough, H. S. (1989). Prediction of reading disability from familial and individual differences. *Journal of Educational Psychology, 81*, 101–108.

Scarborough, H. S. (1990). Very early language deficits in dyslexic children. *Child Development, 61*, 1728–1743.

Scarborough, H. S. (1991). Antecedents to reading disability: Preschool language development and literacy experiences of children from dyslexic families. *Reading and Writing: An Interdisciplinary Journal, 3*, 219–234.

Scarborough, H. S. (1998). Early detection of children at risk for reading disabilities: Phonological awareness and other promising predictors. In B. K. Shapiro, P. J. Accardo, & A. J. Capute (Eds.), *Specific reading disability: A view of the spectrum* (pp. 75–119). Timonium, MD: York Press.

Sénéchal, M., & LeFevre, J. (2002). Parental involvement in the development of children's reading skill: A five-year longitudional study. *Child Development, 73*, 445–460.

Sénéchal, M., LeFevre, J., Thomas, E. M., & Daley, K. E. (1998). Differential effects of home literacy experiences on the development of oral and written language. *Reading Research Quarterly, 33*, 96–116.

Shankweiler, D., & Crain, S. (1986). Language mechanisms and reading disorder: A modular approach. *Cognition, 24*, 139–168.

Shankweiler, D., Crain, S., Brady, S., & Macaruso, P. (1992). Identifying the causes of reading disability. In P. B. Gough, L. C. Ehri, & R. Treiman (Eds.), *Reading acquisition* (pp. 275–305). Hillsdale, NJ: Erlbaum.

Share, D. L. (1999). Phonological recoding and orthographic learning: A direct test of the self-teaching hypothesis. *Journal of Experimental Child Psychology, 72*, 95–129.

Snowling, M. J. (2000). *Dyslexia*. Oxford, UK: Blackwell.

Snowling, M. J., Gallagher, A., & Frith, U. (2003). Family risk of dyslexia is continuous: Individual differences in the precursors of reading skill. *Child Development, 74*, 358–373.

Stephenson, S. (1907). Six cases of congenital word-blindness affecting three generations of one family. *Opthalmoscope, 5*, 482–484.

Thomas, C. J. (1905). Congenital word-blindness and its treatment. *Ophthalmoscope, 3*, 380–385.

Van der Leij, A., Lyytinen, H., & Zwarts, F. (2001). The study of infant cognitive processes in dyslexia. In A. J. Fawcett (Ed.), *Dyslexia: Theory and good practice* (pp. 160–181). London: Whurr.

Vellutino, F. R., Scanlon, D. M., & Sipay, E. R. (1997). Towards distinguishing between cognitive and experiential deficits as primary sources of difficulty in learning to read: The importance of early intervention in diagnosing specific reading disability. In B. A. Blachman (Ed.), *Foundations of reading acquisition and dyslexia: Implications for early intervention* (pp. 347–379). Hillsdale, NJ: Erlbaum.

Vogler, G. P., DeFries, J. C., & Decker, S. M. (1985). Family history as an indicator of risk for reading disability. *Journal of Learning Disabilities, 18*, 419–421.

Whitehurst, G. J., Arnold, D. S., Epstein, J. N., Angell, A. L., Smith, M., & Fischel, J. E. (1994). A picture book reading intervention in daycare and home for children from low-income families. *Developmental Psychology, 30*, 679–689.

Whitehurst, G. J., Epstein, J. N., Angell, A. L., Payne, A. C., Crone, D. A., & Fischel, J. E. (1994). Outcomes of an emergent literacy intervention in Head Start. *Journal of Educational Psychology, 86*, 542–555.

Whitehurst, G. J., Falco, F., Lonigan, C. J., Fischel, J. E., Valdez-Manchaca, M. C., & Caulfield, M. (1988). Accelerating language development through picture-book reading. *Developmental Psychology, 24*, 552–558.

Willcutt, E. G., Pennington, B. F., Smith, S. D., Cardon, L. R., Gayán, J., Knopik, V. S., et al. (2002). Quantitative trait locus for reading disability on chromosome 6p is pleiotropic for attention deficit hyperactivity disorder. *American Journal of Medical Genetics: B. Neuropsychiatric Genetics, 114*, 260–268.

Woodcock, R. W. (1987). *Woodcock Reading Mastery Tests—Revised.* Circle Pines, MN: American Guidance Service.

Part III

The Role of Experience

INTRODUCTION

Learning to Read and Reading to Learn

The Interaction among Cognitive Capacity, Linguistic Abilities, and the Learning Environment

MARIA MODY
ELAINE R. SILLIMAN

The importance of evidence-based practices in communication disorders has had a positive influence in the field of developmental reading and language research. However, the emphasis on scientific definitions and empirical validation has led to an oversight of two useful, though seemingly less concrete, constructs that play a central role in our understanding of disorders: "interaction" and "experience." More specifically, reading and language outcomes reflect the interaction among neurobiology, behavior, and experience. This last section of the book highlights the role of experience in complex cognitive phenomena such as language and literacy.

In Chapter 10, van Kleeck and Littlewood address the very core of experience in reading and oral language development by taking on the issue of how best to prevent and/or ameliorate later literacy and language issues in at-risk children through a meta-analysis of the literature. In addition to cognitive deficits, hearing impairments, and attention disorders, the risk factors they cite in their review include limited English proficiency, nonstandard English dialects, and low socioeconomic status (SES). Inherent in these latter factors is the influence of experience, especially the nature of home experience, the social context in which children first learn about the rules of spoken language and print as they engage in verbal play and literary activities, with or without interaction with adults. The authors point to a large number of studies that demonstrate the positive effects of joint or dialogic book reading, for example, on oral language skills, preliteracy skills, and beginning reading achievement. Dialogic book sharing has been found to boost vocabulary learning in young children, including those from low SES households with oral language delays, though to a lesser extent. Clearly, book sharing provides opportunities for an enhanced language experience whose positive effects appear to have propagated through various levels of oral language development and reading performance.

Recently, an emerging area of research combines storybook sharing with a focus on print form (i.e., a decoding-oriented approach to reading). This combined approach of reading for meaning with reading for sound in informal literacy activities fits well with a dynamic "tricky" mix model (DTM) of learning. In Chapter 11, the model's proponents, Nelson and Arkenberg, present the DTM as an optimal mix of learning conditions for accelerating a child's learning. According to them, the DTM is based on the premise that learning is dependent on a complex, tricky-to-achieve, converging set of conditions that must cooperate at high levels for children to achieve elevated rates of learning. Additionally, the mix needs to be tailored to the constraints represented by the learner's biological makeup and experience-based differences. The DTM approach has shown promise in the areas of vocabulary and syntactic development.

In the final Chapter 12, Silliman and Mody pull together the various interacting components of experience, neurobiology, and individual response behaviors to explain differences in developmental trajectories. The authors examine three critical building blocks relating to speech perception, word learning, and construction of syntax in the development of the oral language register and their impact on language-reading relationships. It appears that individual differences interact with variations in experience (in frequency and quality) to yield a continuum of oral and language reading ability. We put forth a differentiated continuity perspective—that genes code individual predispositions for different outcomes—evident in the varying profiles of normal and atypical development.

10

Fostering Form and Meaning in Emerging Literacy Using Evidence-Based Practice

ANNE VAN KLEECK
ELIZABETH NORLANDER

The literacy skills with which children enter school matter very much. "Children who start school behind in these areas are likely to stay behind" (Whitehurst & Lonigan, 2001, p. 21; see also B. A. Shaywitz et al., 1995). Indeed, this achievement gap shows up even before children enter school. Individual differences in preliteracy skills appear to be in place by age 4, and children who are poor at them tend to remain poor at them (e.g., Whitehurst & Fischel, 2000; Whitehurst & Lonigan, 2001). Studies of somewhat older children once again echo this disturbing finding: Children who are poor readers in the early school years typically remain poor readers across the next several years (Baker, Decker, & DeFries, 1984; Juel, 1988; McKinney & Feagans, 1984; Scarborough & Parker, 2003; B. A. Shaywitz et al., 1995; Smith, 1997).

Not only is this achievement gap persistent across time, but it also represents a strikingly large number of children. Some research indicates that as many as one-third of all children have significant difficulty learning how to read (S. E. Shaywitz, Escobar, Shaywitz, Fletcher, & Makuch, 1992), whereas other research places the prevalence substantially lower at

5 to 17% (e.g., Shaywitz, 1998). Snow, Burns, and Griffin (1998) reviewed evidence showing that some preschoolers are more likely to be among this rather large group that has later difficulty learning to read. This included children with language delays, cognitive deficits, hearing impairments, attention deficit disorder, limited English proficiency, and nonstandard English dialects. Children who are low on the socioeconomic scale (SES), who live in poor neighborhoods and attend schools serving predominantly those from such backgrounds, are also at higher risk for later literacy difficulties.

What can we do to help these at-risk preschoolers, ideally, in an attempt to prevent, or at least to ameliorate, later literacy difficulties? Answering this question relies on answering at least three other questions.

- First, what is meant by a reading disability (or, more generally, by literacy difficulties)? There is a long history of subgrouping children with reading disabilities into different categories reflecting the different kinds of problems they experience. Do children in some groups need one kind of support and those in others need another kind of support?
- Another question we might reasonably ask is, "What should we teach?" Long a subject of controversy, it seems that there is finally at least the beginning of a consensus on this particular issue, as we discuss later. However, questions still remain when we consider *how* children best learn literacy skills. Should we focus on discrete skills and later integrate this knowledge into meaningful activities? Or should we focus on meaningful activities and embed information about discrete skills into these more authentic literacy contexts? Does the answer to this question interact with the answer to the previous question regarding different types of reading disabilities?
- Finally, how do these questions regarding reading disabilities and the teaching of reading relate to fostering foundations for literacy in young, preliterate children, the focus of this chapter?

The answers to all of these questions, as well as the source of controversy, where it exists, arise at the most basic level from the same universal property of language: Language conveys meaning via form. In oral English, the form comprises approximately 45 individually meaningless sounds that combine in systematic sequences to form words, which in turn combine in systematic ways to form sentences. In written English, the form comprises 26 individually meaningless letters or graphemes that (singly or in two-letter combinations) generally correspond to individual sounds within spoken words. The different types of reading difficulties, what is taught to prereaders and beginning readers, and how it is taught are all fundamentally related to the relative emphasis one places on either the form or the meaning of the written code, as well as how one emphasizes each. The different kinds of evidence we have, and the level of trust we believe we can place in it, more often than not relate to this distinction as well.

There are two sections in this chapter. The first considers how form and meaning underlie the nature of oral and written language, and how a relative emphasis on print form or on print meaning underlies models predicting later reading disability among preschoolers, categories of reading disability, approaches to the teaching of beginning reading, and the separate strands of preliteracy research. The second section then reviews research on meaning-focused and form-focused interventions that foster various dimensions of preliteracy and later literacy skill in young prereaders. We conclude the chapter by circling back to the questions just posed, and considering them in light of the information reviewed.

FORM AND MEANING IN ORAL AND WRITTEN LANGUAGE, PRELITERACY, READING DISABILITY, READING PEDAGOGY, AND READING RESEARCH

Form and Meaning in Oral Language

When young children learn their native language, the form and meaning of the messages they hear and attempt to produce are in large measure inextricably bound. They learn to speak their native tongue as they go about hearing and using the form of the language in the naturally occurring, meaningful contexts of living life in the community into which they were born. Even if they are on occasion told what specifically to say (e.g., "say, thank you"), they are not explicitly taught the smallest elements of the language—the individual sounds or phonemes that comprise words. Nor are they explicitly taught the rules for how phonemes can combine to form words, or how words combine to form sentences. Most likely, their caregivers could not explicate how the system works anyway, even though they unconsciously apply their knowledge of the system to every sentence they utter and comprehend. It is only years later that children might learn some things about the formal properties of language, such as how its grammatical and phonological systems operate. Unless they are learning an alphabetic written language, they never need to (and likely would not) become aware of the small finite set of individual phonemes, or sounds, that combine in systematic ways to comprise the words of their spoken language.

Form and Meaning in Written Language

This all changes if children are learning an alphabetic script, such as English, that requires them to become aware of the alphabetic principle: Individual letters correspond to individual sounds within spoken words (nuances and exceptions to this general principle are typically learned as later refinements). The small set of individual units of which they need to become aware—phonemes and letters—are meaningless by themselves. Although the individual phonemes comprising spoken words are also meaningless, children do not need to become aware of them to use language orally. When learning written language, however, children are required to become aware of individually meaningless sounds, and the individually meaningless letters that correspond with them. So, at this basic level, knowledge of print form consists of alphabetic knowledge (letter names, shapes, and sounds) and an awareness of the sound units within spoken words. Phonological awareness (PA) is the more general skill referring to the awareness of the various sound components of spoken language, including syllables, subsyllabic units called onsets and rimes, and individual sounds within syllables. Phonemic awareness is the more specific term reserved for the latter (awareness of the smallest sound units within words).

Not only are the individual sounds that comprise spoken English words meaningless, but they also cannot be isolated in the acoustic signal; that is, the sounds within spoken words are not individually and separately articulated, but are instead simultaneously coarticulated. The acoustic signal does not provide information regarding where one sound ends and the next begins. To figure out that there are individual sounds in spoken words as such is not a perceptual task, but a *conceptual* one: Knowledge of individual sounds must be cognitively imposed on the acoustic signal. Given that individual sounds are meaningless and cannot be directly detected individually in the acoustic signal, they are not discoverable by the child without at least some level of assistance, nor are the letters that correspond to them. For this reason, written English distinguishes itself from oral English in this critically important way: One must become consciously aware of the smallest, meaningless units of both spoken language form (phonemes) and written language form (graphemes or letters) to "break the code" or "decode" written language.

Gough and Tunmer's (1986) widely cited and researched simple view of reading "divides" reading (R) into the two broad areas of decoding (D), which relies on knowledge of print form, and comprehension (C), which relies on oral language comprehension ($R = D \times C$). In the beginning stages of learning to read independently, children, of necessity, are focused on learning to decode more and more fluently. Once decoding becomes more fluent, increasing amounts of mental energy during independent reading can be devoted to comprehension. For this reason, we often talk about these as two relatively separate stages of learning to read.

Form and Meaning in Preliteracy Development

The two dimensions of reading (decoding and comprehension) are also captured in the two broad types of preliteracy skills that have been posited in three independently developed models of emergent literacy (Scarborough, 2001; van Kleeck, 1998; Whitehurst & Lonigan, 1998). Each of these models divides the foundational skills for later literacy development into two broad categories, one containing skills related to meaning or comprehension, and the other containing skills related to the formal aspects of print (e.g., alphabet knowledge and PA skills that underlie later decoding and/ or "word attack" skills).

Form and Meaning in Reading Disability

The form and meaning dimensions of preliteracy development also underlie theoretical models of the different causal pathways to later disability. In the last decade, a single-path model predominated that viewed phonological processing difficulties in prereading children as the single causal pathway responsible for difficulties with decoding. From this perspective, difficulties with decoding caused by difficulties with phonological processing in turn caused difficulties with later comprehension (because individual words must be decoded before sentences and longer connected text can be understood).

More recently however, scholars have been moving from a single-path to a two-path model that relates preliterate skills to later reading disability. The single-path model is often referred to as the phonological hypothesis, or the "phonological core deficit hypothesis," which is grounded in children's awareness that words comprise component sounds or phonemes. Scarborough (2005) notes how "in response to much eloquent theorizing and compelling empirical evidence from research with beginning readers and students with reading disabilities, a consensus has coalesced around the view that phonological abilities are the most crucial language skills for successfully learning to read, and that phonological weaknesses underlie most reading disabilities" (p. 3). Scarborough suggests this theory became so popular that it served to overshadow research that did not support it. As a result, research refuting the idea that phonological processing was not at the root of *all* reading disorders became virtually ignored by researchers engaged in work that supported the hypothesis.

Scarborough (2005) goes on to discuss how this "beautiful hypothesis" (p. 3), while not inaccurate for some children, is simply too limited. Many children who have adequate phonological abilities and are able to decode print nonetheless develop reading disabilities focused on reading comprehension. This has led to numerous researchers recently positing two-path models that propose both a phonological and nonphonological (e.g., lexical, semantic, syntactic) causal path to later reading difficulties (McCardle, Scarborough, & Catts, 2001; Scarborough, 2005; Storch & Whitehurst, 2002; Share & Leikin, 2004). Children with phonological difficulties have difficulty in learning to decode print and recognize words;

that is, their difficulties relate to the code, or print form. Children with nonphonological difficulties are able to decode print, but later in the process of learning to read, have difficulties with text comprehension. Of course, children can have both phonological and nonphonological difficulties, hence experiencing difficulties both in decoding and in text comprehension.

The two-path models that attempt to look at preliteracy difficulties of children and predict two different pathways to later literacy difficulties have much in common with efforts to classify older children who have reading disabilities into different categories. While there have been a wide array of such categorization schemes over the years, at some level, all of them once again make a distinction between difficulties with print meaning and difficulties with print form. Catts, Hogan, and Fey (2003) used Gough and Tunmer's (1986) simple model of reading discussed earlier to classify 604 children as either good or poor on word recognition (decoding) and listening comprehension, resulting in three categories of children with reading disabilities. Of the children with reading disabilities, there were those with (1) poor decoding and good listening comprehension (35.5%), (2) good decoding and poor comprehension (15.4%), and (3) both poor decoding and poor listening comprehension (35.7%). An additional 13.4% of the poor readers had reading problems for reasons not specified by the model.

Form and Meaning in Reading Pedagogy

The relative emphasis on the form or meaning components of written language also relates to the two opposing schools of thought regarding beginning reading pedagogy, sometimes broadly referred to as "code-oriented" (or "skills-oriented") and "meaning-oriented approaches." Many advocates of the two currently best known examples of these approaches—phonics and whole language—continue to be locked in heated debate about both how, and how much, form or meaning should be emphasized in the teaching of beginning reading (although other scholars have begun to find common ground in supporting balanced approaches that combine a focus on form and meaning; see the volume edited by Flippo, 2001). An overly simplified version of the debate is that one group believes basic decoding skills—those related to print form—are critical, and should be taught in a systematic fashion to all children in the early elementary grades, if not sooner. This orientation encompasses the myriad kinds of phonics approaches that have in their essence existed for hundreds of years. On the other extreme are those who decry breaking reading down into meaningless little parts, and advocate teaching children in a holistic fashion via interesting, meaningful, and useful activities involving authentic connected text.

Authentic text, such as children's unabridged literature, is distinguished from decodable text, which is expressly designed to contain words that allow easy application of phonics principles. "Dan can fan Nan" is an extreme version of decodable text (example from Pearson, 2004, p. 240).

Initially, many whole-language advocates believed that specific decoding skills would be "caught" or inferred in the process of pursuing meaning during immersion in authentic reading activities (Pearson, 2004). Somewhat more moderate whole-language advocates believed that skills should be taught, but only when children indicated their need to know them as they worked to better access or express meaning in their holistic activities. More recently, some supporters of whole language have suggested the importance of more explicitly and systematically teaching children about sounds and letters, and their relationships, but only when these lessons are embedded in holistic, meaningful activities involving connected text (e.g., Coles, 2003). These whole-language advocates still tend to deplore programs for any children that separately teach sounds and letters and focus initially on single words rather than on connected text (whereas other more moderate whole-language advocates do not take this strong of a stance).

Current educational legislation in the United States (the No Child Left Behind Act of 2001) was founded on the hope that requiring evidence-based practice would allow educators and policymakers to turn to research for answers, and avoid the emotional brouhaha that often continues to surround discussion of how best to teach early reading. What does the scientific evidence say about meaning-oriented versus code-oriented approaches? It turns out that different lines and kinds of research have been more or less privileged in answering this question.

Form and Meaning in Research on Reading

Although exceptions certainly exist, research on meaning-oriented approaches to the teaching of beginning reading have embraced more qualitative research methodologies since the early 1980s. "Treatises pointing out the shortcomings of traditional forms of quantitative inquiry, especially experimental research, appeared frequently in educational journals," particularly in *Educational Researcher* (Pearson, 2004, p. 225). Much of the research inspired by the whole-language philosophy came from the qualitative tradition. Alternatively, research on skills-oriented approaches to the teaching of beginning reading was more likely to use experimental paradigms generating quantitative evidence.

Of the number of documents synthesizing research in reading pedagogy that have been published in the last few years, none has had the policy impact of the National Reading Panel (NRP) report (2000) used to establish guidelines for the No Child Left Behind Act of 2001. The NRP report considered only experimental and quasi-experimental studies meeting certain quantitative research standards. As such, the panel reviewed only those topics that had a large enough number of experimental studies from which to draw conclusions. Although the report called for a balanced approach to reading instruction, it did offer qualified endorsement of a phonics approach, noting that phonics helps children if it is taught early (it is not much help beyond grade 1), and in a systematic and explicit fashion. Phonics approaches help more with recognizing individual words than with text comprehension, and work best if embedded in a rich curriculum (Pearson, 2004, p. 239).

The NRP decisions regarding what constitutes high-quality research basically excluded the qualitative research base upon which whole language was grounded. It led, not surprisingly, to scathing critiques of the science included in that report, as the title of some recent publications attests. Some examples include books, such as *Unspeakable Acts, Unnatural Practices: Flaws and Fallacies in "Scientific" Reading Instruction*, (Smith, 2003), *Big Brother and the National Reading Curriculum: How Ideology Trumped Evidence* (Allington, 2002), and *Reading the Naked Truth: Literacy, Legislation, and Lies* (Coles, 2003), as well as journal articles such as "Beyond the Smoke and Mirrors: A Critique of the National Reading Panel Report on Phonics" (Garan, 2001).

This current scenario in the early reading instruction debate lays the foundation for understanding similar issues regarding how to provide preschoolers with foundations for later literacy development. In the late 1980s, Teale and Sulzby (1987) called for attention to the nascent field of inquiry called "emerging literacy," a term they had adopted from the seminal work of Marie Clay (1966). By the late 1980s, research from the emerging literacy perspective was beginning to provide substantial evidence (primarily, although not exclusively, from mainstream culture families) on the specific activities, and resultant skills and knowledge about literacy that young children can acquire in their home environments before they begin formal schooling. One general conclusion of this body of work suggests that, in their everyday informal interactions with print used by adults in their worlds, in the context of sharing books with adults, and in their own explorations with writing, children become aware first and foremost that print is meaningful and useful. These attitudes and beliefs lay important foundations for children's eventual transition to becoming conventional readers and writers. Becoming literate came to be seen as a social process heavily influenced by the search for meaning. The ways in which children engaged in literate acts in their play and other activities, long before they possessed conventional literacy skills, also highlighted that becoming a reader and writer were closely related skills.

The role of the home environment in later literacy development continued to be viewed as a context in which children learned about print naturally as they were engaged in meaningful literacy activities on their own or with the guidance of an adult. Sharing books with young prereaders, in particular, often took center stage in research agendas and in recommendations to parents. The major literacy policy document of the 1980s, *Becoming a Nation of Readers* (Anderson, Hiebert, Scott, & Wilkinson, 1985), was very instrumental in promoting the virtue of this family activity with preschoolers. A frequently quoted conclusion of this document was that "the single most important activity for building the knowledge required for eventual success in reading is reading aloud to children" (p. 23).

While research from the emerging literacy perspective continued to accrue, a second, quite different line of research with preschoolers that focused on print form was also gaining momentum. Researchers became interested in how PA skills developed in young children, as well as how they predicted children's ability to decode print later as they began to learn to read. Researchers from the emerging literacy perspective, being interested in meaning-focused, natural interactions with print, often chose not to consider these form-focused skills in their views of important emerging literacy abilities (e.g., McGee & Purcell-Gates, 1997; Yaden, Rowe, & MacGillivray, 2000).

MEANING- AND FORM-FOCUSED INTERVENTION RESEARCH

Given our discussion thus far, it should not be surprising that preliteracy intervention research can also be roughly divided into two broad areas: (1) storybook-sharing interventions that, as indicated by the weight of evidence, foster skills related to later reading comprehension (and predict later reading comprehension but usually do not predict decoding skills) and (2) the usually more formal and structured interventions to foster PA and letter knowledge skills (that predict early decoding, but usually do not predict later reading comprehension). An emerging third area of research combines storybook sharing with a focus on print form. Before reviewing this evidence, we offer a very brief introduction to evidence-based practice to provide a foundation for discussion of the different levels of evidence provided by various kinds of preliteracy intervention studies.

Evidence-Based Practice

Evidence-based practice (EBP) is defined as "the conscientious, explicit, and judicious use of current best evidence in making decisions about the care of individual patients . . . [by] integrating individual clinical expertise with the best available external clinical evidence from systematic research" (Sackett, Rosenberg, Gray, Haynes, & Richardson, 1996, p. 71). A major tenet of EBP is that, although a range of evidence may be used in making treatment decisions, not all evidence is equally credible. Levels of quality and credibility for treatment efficacy studies progress from the following (Robey, 2004, 2005):

1. The "gold standard" of a well-designed meta-analysis of numerous randomized controlled trials (Level Ia) to
2. A single, well-designed randomized controlled trial (Level Ib) to
3. A well-designed controlled study without randomization, or intervention studies without controls (quasi-experimental) (Level II) to
4. Observational, nonexperimental studies with controls (e.g., correlational and case studies) (Level III) to
5. Observational case studies without controls (Level IV) to
6. The expert committee report, consensus conference, and clinical experience of respected authorities (Level V).

A well-designed experimental study that is controlled will have participants who are randomly assigned to at least two groups, one receiving intervention (the experimental group) and one not receiving intervention or receiving a "dummy" intervention. Participants must be randomly assigned for the design to be considered experimental. If, for example, all of the students in one classroom are assigned to the experimental group and students from another classroom are assigned to the control group, the design is considered quasi-experimental, because there is now the additional confounding factor of each teacher's individual teaching style that cannot be factored out of any outcome differences that might be observed.

The NRP (2000), mentioned earlier, reviewed studies in its report that met the standards of Levels I and II, but in doing so, it chose to exclude areas of research for which that level of evidence was not yet available. Pearson (2004) recently called into question this overly narrow view of what constitutes valid science as applied by the NRP. He claimed that "research can never be truly rigorous, indeed truly scientific, until and unless it privileges all of the empirical and theoretical methodologies that characterize the scientific disciplines" (p. 234). He noted that randomized field trials, when used in medicine and pharmacology, are typically the last 10% of the research process. To get to the point where such trials are feasible, a wide range of methodologies is employed, "including much observation, description, examination of relationships, and just plain messing around (that is a technical term used by scientists to describe what they spend most of their time doing)" (p. 235). Pearson sums up by saying, "in short, we need all the tools we can muster to address the inherent complexity of research involving human beings who live and work in groups" (p. 237). In a similar fashion, Dollaghan (2004) discusses how far more attention is often paid to some parts of the definition of EBP ("evidence from systematic research") than to others ("clinical experience"). She suggests that "the first myth that needs to be dispelled is the idea that evidence from systematic research is the only acceptable basis for clinical decision-making" (p. 4).

In the next section, we examine an array of different studies on book-sharing interventions. The review is organized according to the impact of interventions on children's exposure to and participation in book sharing, and according to the different kinds of emerging literacy skills they foster. Within the discussion of each type of outcome, studies are further organized according to the level of evidence they provide using EBP guidelines we just discussed (see Table 10.1 for a summary of these levels of evidence). We also note where research is available on children with language delays, in addition to children who are typically developing.

Establishing Print Meaning Foundations Using Book-Sharing Interventions

Increasing Children's Exposure to Book Sharing in the Home

Interventions aimed at increasing the amount of book sharing that young, prereading children experience at home are based on other research that has shown clear relationships between the amount of book sharing to which children are exposed and a number of child outcomes in literacy skills or skills related to literacy achievement. The most comprehensive review looking at these outcomes as a function of the frequency of children's book-sharing experience was conducted by Bus, van IJzendoorn, and Pellgrini (1995).

Bus and her colleagues (1995) conducted a Level III meta-analysis of 41 correlational, longitudinal, and experimental studies that analyzed effects of joint book reading on language growth, preliteracy skills, and reading achievement. All studies included in the analysis focused on the effects of the frequency of book sharing with toddlers and preschoolers who were typically developing. The child outcome measures were divided into three categories: (1) standardized receptive and expressive language measures, (2) preliteracy print form skills developed before school (i.e., phoneme blending, letter naming, and name writing and reading), and (3) reading achievement during school. Average effect sizes for the frequency of book sharing on language skills (Cohen's $d = 0.67$), preliteracy skills ($d = 0.58$), and reading achievement ($d = 0.55$) were all medium to strong, and the frequency of book reading explained approximately 8% of the variance in all of the measures.

TABLE 10.1. Levels of Quality for Treatment Efficacy

Level of evidence	Description
Ia	"Gold standard" of a well-designed meta-analysis of numerous randomized controlled trials
Ib	A single, well-designed randomized controlled trial
II	A well-designed controlled study without randomization, or intervention studies without controls (quasi-experimental)
III	Observational, nonexperimental studies with controls (e.g., correlational and case studies)
IV	Observational case studies without controls
V	The expert committee report, consensus conference, and clinical experience of respected authorities

Note. Data from Robey (2004, 2005).

Based on the positive effects of book sharing in a large number of studies evaluating early predictors of later reading achievement, and the national focus on the importance of reading aloud to young, preliterate children, several large-scale interventions have been conducted. Their aim has been to increase the amount of parents' book sharing with their preliterate children. Most have not measured subsequent child outcomes, although we mention some exceptions in the section on vocabulary development. One of the most widely implemented interventions of this nature is a pediatric, clinically based program called Reach Out and Read (ROR), which focuses on families with children ages 6–72 months (for an overview of the program, see Needlman, Klass, & Zuckerman, 2002). During well-child visits, pediatricians participating in ROR give parents information about the importance of reading aloud to their young, preliterate children, and provide them with free picture books.

A number of Level II quasi-experimental studies comparing convenience samples of families from low, middle, and high SES backgrounds have shown a positive correlation between participation in ROR and the home literacy environment (High, Hopmann, LaGasse, & Linn, 1998; Needlman, Toker, Dreyer, Klass, & Mendelsohn, 2005; Silverstein, Iverson, & Lozano, 2002). In these studies, "improved reading environment" was defined as having parents whose favorite parental activity was reading aloud to the child 3 or more days a week, and ownership or 10 or more children's picture books. ROR has also been associated with (1) a reported increase of book sharing as a favorite activity and of sharing a book within the last 24 hours in a study of 79 English-speaking parents from low- and middle-class backgrounds, with a reported adjusted odds ratio (AOR) of 4.05, which means that families exposed to ROR are 4.05 times more likely to report book sharing as a favorite activity (Needlman, Fried, Morley, Taylor, & Zuckerman, 1991, Level II); (2) a significant increase in frequent (defined as reading aloud three or more times per week) book sharing in low-SES, Spanish-speaking households (odds ratio (OR) = 3.62; Sanders, Gershon, Huffman, & Mendoza, 2000, Level II); and (3) an increase in weekly bedtime reading in low-SES, multilingual households, reading to the child as a parent's favorite activity, and family ownership of more than 10 children's books (Silverstein et al., 2002). In a Level III, nonexperimental study, Weitzman, Roy, Walls, and Tomlin (2004) found that ROR contributed to 4.7% of variance in children's home literacy environment, as assessed by a standardized measure of home literacy in low-SES, English-speaking households.

The two components of the ROR intervention include providing free children's books to families and having the child's health care provider discuss the importance of sharing the books with the child's parents. The importance of both of these components was supported in a Level III correlational study of families of mixed-SES backgrounds (Kuo, Franke, Regalado, & Halfon, 2004). Analyzing data from the 2000 National Survey of Early Childhood Health, this study revealed that two of the significant predictors of daily reading to children, ages 4–35 months, were a greater number of children's books in the home (OR = 1.01) and discussion by the family's pediatric health care provider of the importance of parents' reading to young preliterate children (OR = 1.66). It should be noted that although the greater number of children's book in the home is a statistically significant predictor, the interpretation of the OR statistic indicates equal probability for children with a greater number of books and those with fewer books to be read to daily.

Although the ROR intervention has been shown to increase the quantity of book sharing, it does not indicate whether the manner of book sharing encourages the child's verbal participation. Other Level Ib and II studies have shown that when children actively and verbally participate in book sharing, they learn more from the experience (e.g., Hockenberger, Goldstein, & Haas, 1999, Level II; Huebner, 2000; Lonigan & Whitehurst, 1998, Level II; Sénéchal, 1997, Level Ib; Whitehurst et al., 1994, Level Ib; 1988, Level II; 1999, Level II). It appears, however, that many children may not receive much encouragement to participate verbally in book sharing. Survey data on over 11,000 families every year, collected by the federal government, indicate that an increasingly large percentage of preschoolers are read to at home (Federal Interagency Forum on Child and Family Statistics, 1999, 2003, 2005). However, in a Level Ib randomized controlled study designed to test the efficacy of an interactive reading style known as "dialogic reading" (see next section), most of the parents from low- and middle-SES backgrounds did not encourage much child participation during these interactions before intervention (Huebner, 2000). In a related vein, Hammett, van Kleeck, and Huberty (2003), in a Level III observational study, found that although some of the middle-class parents talked a great deal about the book they were sharing with their preschoolers, the majority engaged in much less discussion.

Increased Child Participation

In an effort to increase interaction during book sharing with preschoolers, Whitehurst and his colleagues created a program called "Dialogic Reading," in which adults are trained to ask children questions about the book, and to expand and praise children's verbal contributions to the discussion (Arnold & Whitehurst, 1994). This reflects an interaction style used more often by middle-class, European American families than by other groups. It also reflects a style often used in classroom discourse and, as such, prepares children to participate in the kinds of academic discussions they will later encounter (for a discussion, see van Kleeck, 2004). Multiple controlled studies without randomization (Level II evidence) have shown that this technique is successful in increasing children's participation during the book-sharing activity, as measured by their average length of utterance or total number of words. This increased child participation following adult training in Dialogic Reading techniques has been found in low-income households (Lonigan & Whitehurst, 1998), middle-income households (Whitehurst et al., 1988), and with children who are typically developing as well as those who have language delays (Dale, Crain-Thoreson, Notari-Syverson, & Cole, 1996; Huebner & Meltzoff, 2005).

In Dialogic Reading, the adult actively promotes the child's verbal participation. Another study showed that even when adults merely comment on the book content, the verbal participation of the children with whom they are sharing the book also increases. In a Level II intervention study with a multiple-baseline design, seven children of low-SES mothers were considered to be at risk due to their SES or diagnosed developmental delays. The mothers were trained to comment during storybook-sharing interactions. Six comments were suggested per book, with a sample comment such as the mother reading, "Clifford is a big red dog," then saying something like, "Aunt Diane has a big dog named Max." After training, there were significant increases in both the frequency of parental comments and in the number of children's conversational acts during book sharing (Hockenberger et al., 1999).

General Oral Language

In the Bus, van IJzendoorn, and Pellegrini (1995) meta-analysis discussed earlier, which analyzed the effects of the amount of joint book reading on language growth, preliteracy skills, and reading achievement, the effect size $d = 0.67$ for the frequency of book sharing with preschoolers on children's general oral language skills was considered medium to strong. A longitudinal correlational study (Level III data) of kindergartners with typical language skills from middle- and upper middle-class backgrounds also found that parent–child book sharing explained 9% of variance in the children's receptive language skills even when parent education, PA, and emergent literacy skills were controlled for in the equation (Sénéchal & LeFevre, 2002).

A more stringent test of the efficacy of book sharing in fostering oral language skills measured children's language ability outside of the book-sharing context. Huebner (2000, Level Ib) evaluated preschoolers from low- and middle-class backgrounds (most of whom had typically developing language). Results indicated that participation in a dialogic book-sharing intervention increased vocabulary skills and the ability to use language to express ideas when the children were assessed on three standardized tests outside the context of the book-sharing interaction.

Vocabulary

As children mature, their vocabularies grow both in breadth (the number of words that a child understands and uses) and in depth (the completeness of their understanding of words, e.g., multiple definitions and semantic relations with other words). When exposed to a new word, children often create a hypothesis of what the meaning of the word is, based on the context in which they encountered the word (called "fast mapping"); this is often a partial representation of the meaning of the word. If children are exposed to a word in more than one context—for example, if the definition of the word is given, synonyms are provided, and relations are detailed—they begin to increase their depth of knowledge regarding a word (an example of "slow mapping"). Many intervention studies have shown an increase in children's receptive and expressive vocabulary as a result of participating in book sharing, most often in the breadth, but occasionally in the depth of their knowledge.

Exposure to the ROR program we mentioned earlier was associated with an increase in the breadth of comprehension of vocabulary words in two Level III correlational studies of preschoolers with both typical and delayed language skills from low-SES backgrounds, as measured by a standardized assessment of receptive vocabulary (Mendelsohn et al., 2001; Sharif, Rieber, & Ozuah, 2002). The standardized vocabulary assessments that were used required only a shallow knowledge of the words that are assessed. Given the correlational designs of these studies and the inconsistency of their findings, a stricter experimental approach is warranted before concluding the effectiveness of the ROR program for improving preschoolers' vocabulary knowledge.

In the ROR studies, parents were simply given books by their child's health care provider and were encouraged to read them to their young children. Children's vocabulary skills were measured after varying amounts of time post-ROR exposure, and generally no baseline level of vocabulary was taken. Other studies that have trained adults to use dialogic book-sharing techniques have also shown an impact on the span of children's vocabulary. For example, in a Level Ib intervention study, preschoolers (most of whom had potential language delays) whose parents read to them using the Dialogic Reading techniques demonstrated significantly higher scores on a standardized test of their vocabulary recognition abilities than children who were read the same books in a noninteractive manner (Fielding-Barnsley & Purdie, 2003). A number of additional experiments studying middle- and upper-class preschoolers with typically developing and delayed language have found that dialogic book sharing results in greater vocabulary gains than does book sharing in which interaction is not encouraged (e.g., Arnold, Lonigan, Whitehurst, & Epstein, 1994, Level Ib; Ewers & Brownson, 1999, Level Ib; Rump, Walsh, & Blewitt, 2005, Level II; Whitehurst et al., 1988, Level II).

An interesting question arises from these studies that have measured vocabulary outcomes in book-sharing interventions. Lonigan (1994) commented on how Dialogic Reading interventions have "consistently larger and more enduring effects" (p. 307) on expressive rather than receptive vocabulary skills (i.e., Arnold et al., 1994; Valdez-Menchaca & Whitehurst, 1992; Whitehurst et al., 1991). Studies of the ROR program, however, reported receptive vocabulary gains but did not measure expressive vocabulary. It is important in future research to determine whether book sharing that is more or less interactive has differential effects on children's receptive versus expressive vocabulary skills.

The studies we just reviewed had adults engage in Dialogic Reading in which no special attention was given to specific vocabulary in the books, then measured the effects on general vocabulary growth. Other studies have focused on developing specific, targeted vocabulary in the books being shared. In one such study, incidental exposure to specific novel words during book sharing was effective in improving children's recognition of that specific vocabulary (Sénéchal & Cornell, 1993). Most studies have found, however, that discussion of specific vocabulary is more effective than incidental exposure to the vocabulary in improving children's ability to identify and label both targeted and general vocabulary.

The impact of incidental exposure was found in a study by Sénéchal and Cornell (1993). In this Level Ib, controlled experiment with randomization, preschoolers from middle- and upper-middle-class backgrounds were tested for their receptive knowledge of 10 vocabulary words that were not usually known to preschoolers (e.g., *corridor, elderly,* and *reposing*). To participate in the study, the children were required to be familiar with the synonyms of at least seven of the 10 targeted words. The children were then read a storybook presenting the target words in one of four different ways to determine the impact of these different styles on their subsequent knowledge of the target words. The reading styles varied in their amount of interaction—from verbatim reading to simply repeating the sentences containing the target work, to repeating the sentence with the target word with a synonym in place, to questioning the students about the target words. Sénéchal and Cornell found that reading a book just one time to preschoolers resulted in a significant increase in their ability to identify vocabulary specific to the book, with no significant differences noted among interaction styles.

The authors speculated that reading the story only once might have obscured any differences based on reading style that might accrue over more readings. In a later Level Ib study, Sénéchal (1997) divided middle-class preschoolers into three groups: single reading with no interaction, three readings with no interaction, and three readings with interaction encouraged through the use of questions. The preschoolers were assessed pre- and postintervention with researcher-constructed assessments of the target vocabulary. In the receptive vocabulary assessment, the children were asked to point to one of four pictures corresponding with an orally presented vocabulary word. In the expressive assessment, children were asked to label a picture. The results indicated that as the number of readings increased, preschoolers made significantly greater improvements in both receptive target vocabulary (d = 1.16) and expressive target vocabulary (d = 1.90) compared to the single-reading condition. In addition, children in the interactive book-sharing condition, in which the text was both read and discussed, made significantly greater improvements in both their receptive (d = 0.57) and expressive (d = 1.61) target vocabulary than did the children in conditions in which the text was read but not discussed. In another Level II study, Hargrave and Sénéchal (2000) found that children from low-SES households with expressive language delays made greater improvements in the breadth of both target vocabulary and general expressive vocabulary (d = 0.21) scores when involved in Dialogic Reading than children who were read to without discussion of the book.

Similar results were reported from a Level Ib single, randomized pre- to posttest comparison group experiment by Justice, Meier, and Walpole (2005) that involved low-SES kindergartners, the majority of whom had language delays. Children in the experimental group completed 20 small-group, storybook-sharing interactions that included targeted vocabulary, whereas those in the control group were not exposed to the targeted vocabulary. In addition, within the experimental group, half of the vocabulary words were defined (using a dictionary definition, i.e., "a *marsh* is a very wet place where there are wet lands covered with grasses") and explained (using the word in the context of a sentence, i.e., "We took a boat through the *marsh* and we saw lots of birds and animals"), and the other half were simply read as they occurred in the books but not discussed. The results indicated that reading books to kindergartners with language delays resulted in a significant increase in targeted expressive vocabulary, as measured by the quality of the child's definition of a word, but only if the meanings of the targeted vocabulary were explained (d = 1.22). Unlike the typically developing children in the Sénéchal and Cornell (1993) study we just discussed, simply exposing the children with language delays to vocabulary (without explaining it) did not result in significant gains in the target vocabulary (d = 0.53). However, some of this difference could also be explained by the fact that the outcome Sénéchal and Cornell studied was shallower than that of the Justice et al. (2005) study. Children in the former study merely had to use the targeted word to label a picture, whereas children in the latter study had to give a definition of the word.

A Level Ib study by Coyne, Simmons, Kame'enui, and Stoolmiller (2004) found advantages to discussion of targeted vocabulary on kindergartners' vocabulary growth. These researchers found that kindergartners at risk for later reading difficulties, based on preintervention assessment of letter-naming and PA skills, showed significant improvement in the depth of their knowledge of specific targeted vocabulary when they were exposed to discussion of the targeted vocabulary compared to exposure to a sounds and letters module of a commercial reading program (d = 0.85). In the experimental condition, the words were explicitly defined within the context of the story (e.g., "*rumpus* means wild play," p. 151), the definitions were used within the context of the story (e.g., "I'll say the sentence with the words that mean the same as *rumpus*. 'Let the wild play start,' " p. 151), and the words were incorporated into additional activities.

In summary, it appears that book sharing can facilitate vocabulary development in a number of different ways. Merely reading to children appears to be effective in providing incidental learning of new words, although interactive (dialogic) reading is even more effective. Although typically developing children can attain a basic knowledge of specific vocabulary just by hearing text containing those words read to them and using their fast-mapping skills, their vocabulary is better enhanced when target vocabulary is discussed, because this allows them to expand and refine their definition of the new words using slow-mapping skills. Fast mapping is important in the initial acquisition of words, because it allows children to hypothesize the meaning of a word to which they have only incidentally been exposed. However, when words are explicitly defined and explained, and children are asked to expand their understanding of a word by answering questions about it, a deeper understanding of the word is encouraged. Children with language delays appear to need this type of discussion to foster the ability to identify, label, and define specific vocabulary words, perhaps because they have impaired fast-mapping skills. Finally, sharing a book several times is more beneficial to children learning the meanings of new vocabulary words in that book than is sharing the book just once, particularly if the book sharing involves discussion of the text being read. The studies reviewed in this section are summarized in Table 10.2.

Reading Achievement

Book sharing with preschoolers has also been correlated with children's later reading achievement. In their meta-analysis of 41 correlational, longitudinal, and experimental studies, Bus et al. (1995) found what they considered a medium effect ($d = 0.55$) for the frequency of book reading during preschool on later reading achievement. While Bus and her colleagues examined longitudinal designs, another Level III correlational study looked retrospectively at 56 parents' reported book sharing when their second-grade children were preschoolers. Poor reading achievement in the second grade correlated with less frequent book-sharing interactions during the preschool years as reported by the parents ($p = .04$; Scarborough, Dobrich, & Hager, 1991).

It is important to note that the effect sizes in the Bus et al. (1995) meta-analysis of book sharing were larger for children's general oral language skills ($d = 0.67$) than for either preliteracy print form skills ($d = 0.58$) or early reading ($d = 0.55$). This is likely because, as we mentioned earlier, book sharing has a much greater impact on preliteracy and later literacy skills related to meaning than on skills related to print form, such as decoding ability (which is typically emphasized in tests of early reading ability). Most middle-class parents focus almost exclusively on the meaning of stories when they share books with their young preliterate children (e.g., Bus & van IJzendoorn, 1988; Ezell & Justice, 2000; Morrow, 1988; Phillips & McNaughton, 1990; Snow & Ninio, 1986; van Kleeck, 1998), as do their children (e.g., Yaden, Smolkin, & Conlon, 1989). Subsequently, in many studies, the amount of shared book reading at home (which is overwhelmingly with storybooks) does not predict children's letter knowledge or early word identification ability once they are in school (e.g., Evans, Shaw, & Bell, 2000; Sénéchal, LeFevre, Thomas, & Daley, 1998).

On the other hand, most middle-class parents report directly teaching their children literacy skills, such as letter names (Baker, Fernandez-Fein, Scher, & Williams, 1998; Evans et al., 2000; Haney & Hill, 2004; Sénéchal, LeFevre, Hudson, & Lawson, 1996; Sonnenschein, Baker, &

TABLE 10.2. Reviewed Print-Meaning Studies

Level of EBP	Study	Outcome examined	Sample size (N)	Ages studied	TDL/LD	SES	Length of intervention/observation
Ib	Huebner (2000)	Child participation, oral language	115	24–35 months	TDL	Low and middle	6 weeks
	Ewers & Brownson (1999)	Vocabulary	66	M = 6.0 years	Not reported	Middle	1 session
	Sénéchal & Cornell (1993)	Vocabulary	160	44–66 months	Not reported	Middle and upper-middle	1 session
	Sénéchal (1997)	Vocabulary	60	3 and 4 years	Not reported	Middle	2 sessions
	Justice, Meier, & Walpole (2005)	Vocabulary	57	60–78 months	TDL/LD	Low	10 weeks
	Coyne et al. (2004)	Vocabulary	32	Kindergarten	TDL/LD	Not reported	7 months
II	High, Hopmann, LaGasse, & Linn (1998)	Book exposure	151	12–38 months	Not reported	Low	Varied
	Needlman, Toker, Dreyer, Klass, & Mendelsohn (2005)	Book exposure	1,647	6–72 months	Not reported	Low and middle	Varied
	Silverstein, Iverson, & Lozano (2002)	Book exposure	55	6–72 months	Not reported	Low	Varied
	Needlman, Fried, Morley, Taylor, & Zuckerman (1991)	Book exposure	79	6–60 months	Not reported	Low and middle	Varied

	Sanders, Gershon, Huffman, & Mendoza (2000)	Book exposure	122	2–60 months	Not reported	Low	Varied
	Lonigan & Whitehurst (1998)	Child participation	91	33–60 months	LD	Low	6 weeks
	Whitehurst et al. (1988)	Child participation	29	21–35 months	TDL	Middle	1 month
	Dale, Crain-Thoreson, Notari-Syverson, & Cole (1996)	Child participation	33	36–72 months	LD	Not reported	6–8 weeks
	Huebner & Meltzoff (2005)	Child participation	95	2 to 3 years (M = 28.21 months)	TDL/LD	Low, middle, and high	8 weeks
	Hockenberger, Goldstein, & Haas (1999)	Child participation	7	53–65 months	LD	Low	4 weeks
	Fielding-Barnsley & Purdie (2003)	Vocabulary	49	Not reported	TDL/LD	Not reported	8 weeks
	Hargrave & Sénéchal (2000)	Vocabulary	36	31–61 months	LD	Low	4 weeks
III	Bus, van IJzendoorn, & Pellegrini (1995)	Book exposure, oral language, reading achievement	3,410	32–96 months	TDL	Low, middle, and high	Varied
	Weitzman, Roy, Walls, & Tomlin (2004)	Book exposure	100	18–30 months	Not reported	Low	Varied

(*continued*)

TABLE 10.2. *(continued)*

Level of EBP	Study	Outcome examined	Sample size (*N*)	Ages studied	TDL/LD	SES	Length of intervention/ observation
	Kuo, Franke, Regalado, & Halfon (2004)	Book exposure	2,068	4–35 months	Not reported	Low, middle, and high	Varied
	Hammett, van Kleeck, & Huberty (2003)	Child participation	96	40–49 months	TDL	Middle	1 session
	Mendelsohn et al. (2001)	Vocabulary	122	2 years to 5 years, 9 months	TDL/LD	Low	Varied
	Sharif, Rieber, & Ozuah (2002)	Vocabulary	200	M = 3.8 years	TDL/LD	Low	Varied
	Sénéchal & LeFevre (2002)	Vocabulary	93	4–6 years	TDL	Middle and upper-middle	K–third grade
	Scarborough, Dobrich, & Hager (1991)	Reading achievement	56	36 months–second grade	Poor and normally achieving readers	Middle	36 months–second grade
	Sénéchal & LeFevre (2001)	Reading achievement	111	Pre-K–third grade	Not reported	Middle	Pre-K–third grade

Note. EBP, evidence-based practice; TDL, typically developing language; LD, language delayed; SES, socioeconomic status.

Cerro, 1992). Doing so does influence their children's acquisition of print form skills, such as letter knowledge and early decoding (e.g., Evans et al., 2000; Haney & Hill, 2004; Lonigan, Dyer, & Anthony, 1996; Sénéchal et al., 1998).

We might expect that if middle-class parents both share books and directly teach print form skills, then we would find correlations between book sharing and early decoding, even though they might be spurious (because parents who read also taught the alphabet). Although the majority of middle-class families do teach alphabetic skills to their children, there is still substantial variation among even upper-middle-class professional families regarding whether they believe it is appropriate to do so (Rescorla, Hyson, Hirsh-Pasek, & Cone, 1990). This variation allowed Sénéchal and LeFevre (2001), in a Level III study, to sort out the impact of book sharing versus direct alphabet teaching practices on children's subsequent literacy outcomes. These researchers divided the middle-class families they studied into four groups, as determined by the amount of direct teaching of print form skills ("teach") and the amount of storybook sharing ("read"). This resulted in a "high-teach–high-read" group, a "high-teach–low-read" group, a "low-teach–high-read" group, and a "low-teach–low-read" group.

Children with high-teach–high-read parents performed well on all reading measures across time; that is, they did well in early decoding and alphabetic knowledge, and in reading comprehension in grade 3. Children with high-teach–low-read parents did well initially with alphabetic knowledge and early decoding but had a dramatic decline in their reading performance relative to peers on third-grade reading comprehension measures. Children with low-teach–high-read parents started off lower in decoding and alphabetic knowledge relative to the two high-teach groups, but their word reading and reading comprehension scores at the end of grade 3 almost caught up to those of the high-teach–high-read group. And finally, children with low-teach–low-read parents performed most poorly on all measures across time. This was true even though they had fairly good word reading skills at the end of grade 1, most likely due to instruction in school during that year. By grade 3, though, their reading comprehension was the lowest of any group.

The outcomes for the low-teach–high-read group prompt us to ask why these children would basically catch up by third grade. Even though they were initially behind in word decoding skills, it is possible that their first- and second-grade school reading instruction was adequate to teach them to decode, which is essential but not sufficient for good reading comprehension. By third grade, their parents' focus on book sharing with them as preschoolers put them at an advantage in reading comprehension. School instruction apparently did not compensate for this preschool experience of being read to because children who were not read to frequently at home did more poorly in reading comprehension in third grade.

These findings offer striking evidence of the long-term differential impact of the frequency of different preliteracy experiences. More direct teaching by parents leads to better decoding ability by their children in grade 1 but does not necessarily support later reading comprehension very well. More storybook sharing by parents leads to better reading comprehension by their children in grade 3 but does not support early decoding very well. This study provides evidence of the importance of parents' direct teaching of print form skills to give preschoolers a solid foundation for learning formally to decode in school and, therefore, to do well from the very beginning of their formal reading instruction. However, such teaching can also be accomplished in a preschool context, which leads us next to consider more structured, school-based interventions for teaching two critical print form skills to preliterate children—phonological awareness (PA) and letter knowledge.

In this section, we have discussed a wide variety of intervention studies that search to find answers to the question, "What should we teach children to give them a solid foundation in print meaning?" The interventions reviewed have targeted a variety of outcomes, from increasing children's exposure to books to experimentally manipulating the child's actual interaction with specific books. Given the diversity of outcomes researched, as well as the variety of levels of evidence presented, a sweeping, all-encompassing conclusion to this question is not appropriate. When attempting to determine what to teach in practice, whether in a classroom, therapy room, or the home, one must look not only at the outcomes of the studies but also at the quality of the studies themselves. The levels of evidence presented in this chapter provide the teacher, clinician, and parent with a framework to assess and interpret the evidence, and to decide what technique, or techniques, is appropriate for creating children's foundation for later reading comprehension, as well as early decoding skills.

Establishing Print Form Foundations for Later Reading Using Structured Programs

Numerous reviews and meta-analyses of the research on the impact of structured, systematic, directly taught PA interventions have appeared elsewhere (e.g., Bus & van IJzendoorn, 1999; Gillon, 2004; Troia, 1999). Consequently, we do not go into detail here on the extensive evidence supporting the effectiveness of such programs in fostering both children's PA skills and their subsequent early reading ability. Because a meta-analysis of a number of randomized, controlled experimental studies provides us with the highest level of empirical support for EBP (Level Ia evidence), we briefly summarize the results of a meta-analysis of 36 experimental studies by Bus and van IJzendoorn (1999), which included 3,000+ children with typical and delayed language. We also review one series of studies that reported on long-term outcomes in a longitudinal dataset of unusual duration by Byrne and colleagues (Byrne & Fielding-Barnsley, 1991, 1993; 1995; Byrne, Fielding-Barnsley, & Ashley, 2000; see Byrne, Shankweiler, & Hine, Chapter 9, this volume, for a complete review of this research).

In their meta-analysis of 36 studies, Bus and van IJzendoorn (1999) analyzed the effects that PA training had on the PA skills and reading skills of preschoolers, kindergartners, and primary school students. The PA training programs that were examined ranged from phonological blending training, to segmentation training, to PA above the level of the phoneme (i.e., rhyming). The overall effect size of PA training on short-term PA skills was very strong ($d = 1.04$), and for short-term reading skills (e.g., real-word identification and single-word decoding) was moderate ($d = 0.44$). Long-term (an average of 18.5 months), the effects on PA skills were moderate ($d = 0.48$) and on reading skills were nonsignificant ($d = 0.16$). Bus and van IJzendoorn concluded from their analysis that phonological awareness was a causal factor in children's learning to read, with experimentally manipulated PA accounting for 12% of the variance in short-term word identification skills. Although 12% might seem to be a modest amount of variation in reading skills, Bus and van IJzendoorn detailed how this variation results in important success rate differences between the experimental and control groups, especially when considered in light of the thousands of children that this could affect if PA training were put in place in schools throughout the world. They also found that PA training was more effective when paired with letter knowledge training than when implemented alone, and that such instruction with preschoolers ($d = 1.10$, strong) and kindergartners ($d = 1.26$, strong) was more effective than with children in primary school ($d = 0.50$, moderate).

One might question how training in PA skills is justified if the long-term effects on reading skills are not significant. It is important to consider the componential nature of reading and the evidence that word recognition (involving decoding) and text comprehension are distinct, somewhat independent skills influenced by different factors, as has been shown in recent studies using structural equation modeling (Storch & Whitehurst, 2002; Oakhill, Cain, & Bryant, 2003). Reading comprehension certainly involves word recognition, but it also involves oral language skills that go beyond word recognition (Nation, 2005; Snowling, 2005). As such, many children who may have quite good word recognition skills do quite poorly at reading comprehension. For this reason, fostering their word recognition skills via phonological awareness training will not have an impact on their later reading comprehension skills. For this reason, PA skills are more important to a vital component of early reading instruction—word recognition—than to later reading instruction, when text comprehension plays an increasingly important role. The following series of studies demonstrates the long-term impact of PA skills on the decoding component of reading ability.

In a Level Ib, randomized controlled intervention study, Byrne and Fielding-Barnsley (1991, 1993, 1995; Byrne et al., 2000), implemented a structured phonological awareness program within small groups in Australian preschool classes, then longitudinally followed the 128 children, the majority of whom had typical language development. The experimental group comprised 64 preschoolers exposed to explicit instruction of phonemic awareness principles using posters and worksheets. The control group was exposed to the same kind of materials, but with no phonological training. In the initial posttesting, the children in the experimental group showed significant improvement over the control group on phoneme identification, including both phonemes that were trained and those that were not directly trained (Byrne & Fielding-Barnsley, 1991).

When tested 1 year later at the end of kindergarten, the children in the experimental group still showed stronger phoneme identification skills than the control group, although the difference was no longer statistically significant (Byrne & Fielding-Barnsley, 1993). By the end of grade 5, the children in the experimental group performed significantly better on nonword decoding, reading irregularly spelled words (i.e., *yacht*), and decoding words in general than did children who had not received the preschool intervention (Byrne et al., 2000).

In this section, we have discussed print form interventions that lay the foundation for later decoding skills. These types of interventions have typically involved interventions using systematic, explicit teaching that was more decontextualized, in the sense that practice focused on word-level activities divorced from connected text (see Table 10.3 for a summary of the research reviewed in this section). In contrast, the intervention studies that incorporated book sharing have focused on fostering skills that primarily support later reading comprehension. Very few print form interventions have tried to use the more naturalistic and contextualized setting of book sharing to teach print form skills. In the next section, a recent series of studies that provide an exception to this trend is reviewed.

Embedding Print Form in Book-Sharing Activities

Print Awareness

Print awareness comprises a number of skills that can be categorized into four general areas: (1) print- and book-reading conventions, (2) concept of word, (3) alphabet knowledge, and (4) literacy terms (Justice & Ezell,

TABLE 10.3. Reviewed Print-Form Interventions Utilizing A Decontextualized Approach

Level of EBP	Study	Outcome examined	Sample size (N)	Ages studied	TDL/LD	SES	Length of intervention/ observation
Ia	Bus & van Ijzendoorn (1999)	Phonological awareness; reading skills	3,092	Pre-K–primary school	Varied	Varied	Varied
Ib	Byrne & Fielding-Barnsley (1991)	Phonological awareness; reading skills	128	M = 55 months	Primarily TDL	Not reported	12 weeks
	Byrne & Fielding-Barnsley (1993)	Phonological awareness; reading skills	119	M = 72.2 months	Primarily TDL	Not reported	1 year postintervention
	Byrne & Fielding-Barnsley (1995)	Phonological awareness; reading skills	118 and 115	M = 84.2 and M = 96.2 months	Primarily TDL	Not reported	2 and 3 years postintervention
	Byrne, Fielding-Barnsley, & Ashley (2000)	Phonological awareness; reading skills	103	M = 11 years	Primarily TDL	Not reported	6 years postintervention

2002). Justice and Ezell (2000, 2002; Ezell & Justice, 2000) conducted a number of Level Ib, controlled intervention studies with matched-pair randomization to determine the effects of a book-reading intervention with a focus on children's print awareness skills. Ezell and Justice (2000) initially determined that the video training of graduate students in speech and hearing sciences to use print-referencing verbal strategies (i.e., "That says *apple*," "Find the letter *B*," or "Do you see the word *Spot* on this page?") and nonverbal strategies (tracking and pointing to print) significantly increased the amount of verbal and nonverbal print referencing they subsequently used during book-sharing interactions with young children (Time × Group effect size of $\eta^2 = 0.454$ for verbal strategies, and $\eta^2 = 0.705$ for nonverbal strategies). In addition, when the adult used these print-referencing techniques, the children's use of utterances referring to print also increased significantly during book-sharing interactions (with significant main effects for Group, Time, and Time × Group interaction).

In another Level Ib, matched-pair randomized intervention study, Justice and Ezell (2000) trained parents instead of graduate students. Parent dyads in the experimental group were video-trained in print referencing, whereas members of the control group was asked to read to their children in their usual manner. All of the children were from middle-class backgrounds and were typically developing. After 4 weeks, compared to the control group, parents in the experimental group showed a significant increase from pretest to posttest both in their talk about print (comments, requests, and questions) and in pointing and tracking print while reading, indicating that the video training was effective in changing parent reading behavior. In addition, children in the experimental group showed a statistically significant increase in their gain scores from pre- to posttest on three of the early literacy subtests: words in print, word segmentation, and print concepts. No significant differences were noted in the gain scores on the alphabet knowledge or print recognition subtests. It should be noted that effect sizes were not reported in this study, so the results of this intervention should be interpreted cautiously.

The first two studies (Ezell & Justice, 2000; Justice and Ezell, 2000) used middle-class children as participants. A later Level Ib intervention study extended the findings to students from low-income households in Head Start programs, in addition to expanding to a small-group format in the classroom (Justice & Ezell, 2002). In this study, the first author (a licensed speech–language pathologist) read to small groups of children using a print focus, the experimental condition (utilizing comments and questions about print convention, i.e., "Show me where to start reading"; concept of word, e.g., "Count the number of words on this page"; and alphabet knowledge, i.e., "Where is the letter *F* on this page?"), or a picture focus, the control condition. Children who received reading intervention with a print focus showed significant improvements on three print awareness measures (print recognition, words in print, and alphabet knowledge), as well as in their overall print awareness compared to children who received intervention with a picture focus. There was a significant Time × Group interaction, with a moderate effect size ($\eta^2 = 0.548$).

Phonological Awareness

The vast majority of studies on PA intervention have involved systematic, structured training, as reviewed in the previous section. There has been far less research in which such training was incorporated into a more naturalistic context, such as storybook sharing.

For example, in an evidence-based Level V (refer to Table 10.1) discussion based on clinical experience, McFadden (1998) encouraged a more holistic approach to the phonemic awareness level of PA training. She acknowledged the success of explicit, structured instruction in phonemic awareness, but hypothesized that the incorporation of phonemic awareness into literacy activities, such as storybook sharing, would be appealing to many speech–language pathologists and also would be as effective as a structured program.

Skibbe and Justice (2005) began to test the effectiveness of such embedded PA training in interventions with children with language delays. They compared the effectiveness of mother–child storybook sharing on the children's development of print awareness and PA skills in a Level Ib intervention study. Mothers were trained to focus on either print awareness ($N = 11$), PA ($N = 11$), or on the pictures in the book (control group, $N = 7$). The research is still in progress and the data are tentative, with a not large enough dataset to calculate statistical significance or effect sizes, but the results so far suggest that children in the PA group possibly make greater gains in rhyming than do children in the print awareness or control groups, whereas the children in the print awareness group potentially make greater gains in alphabet knowledge, word awareness, and print awareness. Further research and data are necessary before conclusions can be drawn.

Other researchers have proposed that rhyming books are a more effective tool than narrative storybooks to increase children's PA skills. In a Level III observational study on parental reading habits, Stadler and McEvoy (2003) observed 72 parents from mixed-SES backgrounds, sharing both an alphabet-rhyming book and a storybook with their preschool child. Children with both typical and impaired language were included in the study. Parents, who were asked to read the books in their usual manner at home, were noted to spend more time teaching PA skills when reading the rhyming book than when reading the storybook. Furthermore, the parents of children with typically developing language skills were more likely than parents of children with language impairments to teach PA skills. It could be hypothesized that the parents of the children with language impairment perceived PA as a skill beyond their children's current abilities; therefore, they focused more attention on the content of the book (e.g., comments on the characters or setting) than on the form (sound–letter correspondence).

In a more stringent Level Ib experimental study that measured children's outcomes on specific skills rather than focusing on adult reading habits, Hayes (2001) found that preschoolers from middle-class backgrounds ($N = 20$) performed significantly better on rhyming–alliteration tasks after hearing a rhyming version of a story one time compared to the control group children ($N = 20$), who listened to a nonrhyming version of the same story. Given that parents may naturally incorporate the instruction of PA skills in rhyming book-sharing interactions, and that children showed an increased sensitivity to PA after only one exposure to a rhyming book, it is probable that the incorporation of rhyming books into a family's normal book-sharing routine could have more long-term effects on children's PA skills. In addition, the use of rhyming books to teach PA skills in a more naturalistic environment in the schools could also be beneficial. However, more research must be conducted to validate these conclusions.

Like the print meaning interventions discussed previously, the print form interventions studied a number of potential outcomes for preliteracy skills, such as print awareness and PA, as well as actual single-word reading achievement. Although there are extensive high-quality intervention studies with large numbers of subjects that address print form using structured, decontextualized programs, the print form intervention studies that use the more naturalistic environment of book sharing are just beginning to be published. As a result, there are fewer high-quality studies in this area, and there are often smaller sample sizes (see Table 10.4 for a summary of studies reviewed in this section). Again, this does not mean that these experiments are not useful, just that one must be more cautious in drawing conclusions regarding their efficacy.

CONCLUSIONS

Our review shows that the research on preliteracy intervention can be divided into two broad categories, one focusing on skills related to meaning, and the other focusing on skills related to print form. The meaning-focused approach uses book sharing to foster language skills that support children's later reading comprehension. The print form approaches may differ in whether aspects of print form (PA, print awareness, and/or alphabet knowledge) are initially taught in an embedded fashion, while children are engaged in meaningful

TABLE 10.4. Reviewed Print-Form Interventions Embedded in Book Sharing

Level of EBP	Study	Outcome examined	Sample size (N)	Ages studied	TDL/LD	SES	Length of intervention/ observation
Ib	Ezell & Justice (2000)	Print awareness	24	47–61 months	TDL	Not reported	1 session
	Justice & Ezell (2000)	Print awareness	28	3 years, 11 months–5 years, 2 months	TDL	Varied	4 weeks
	Justice & Ezell (2002)	Print awareness	30	41–62 months	TDL	Low	8 weeks
	Skibbe & Justice (2005)	Phonological awareness	29	M = 55 months	LD	Not reported	12 weeks
	Hayes (2001)	Phonological awareness	40	3–5 years	Not reported	Middle	1 session
III	Stadler & McEvoy (2003)	Phonological awareness	72	51–70 months	TDL/LD	Varied	1 session
V	McFadden (1998)	Phonological awareness	N/A	N/A	N/A	N/A	N/A

uses of connected text (i.e., using book sharing) or whether they are taught in a nonembedded fashion. In the nonembedded approach, the focus may be on the single-word level of meaning, or even on smaller and meaningless sound sequences (syllables). The latter approach is by far the most common type of intervention that concentrates on print form.

Which of these approaches should we consider using? This question hearkens back to the two key, interrelated questions we asked at the beginning of this chapter. In answering what area of reading is posing the problem, we are answering the related question regarding what we should teach. The intervention research to date rarely considers differences in children's initial strengths and weaknesses in skills. As we mentioned early in this chapter, current scholarship suggests two causal pathways that preschoolers may follow to later reading disabilities. In one, children have problems with phonological processing that primarily impede early decoding. Via the nonphonological pathway, children's weaknesses in oral language abilities place them at risk for difficulties with later reading comprehension. Some children have weaknesses in both areas. Perhaps it would make sense to focus on direct, systematic PA–letter knowledge interventions with children who appear to have only phonological processing problems. With children who primarily have weaknesses in oral language, but not in phonological processing, meaning-focused interventions would likely be most beneficial. Finally, for children who have difficulties in both areas, it might be most efficient to use techniques that not only focus on meaning, such as storybook sharing, but also embed print-form kinds of information into those activities (e.g., as Justice and her colleagues did with print referencing in the studies discussed; Ezell & Justice, 2000; Justice & Ezell, 2000; 2002). Of course, we need further intervention studies that take into account children's initial skills in each of these areas to provide evidence that different interventions might best benefit these different groups of children.

The intervention research reviewed here also does not take into account differences in families' values and practices related to children's early literacy that are often found among different cultural groups (for discussion of cultural differences in family practices relevant to the book-sharing context, see van Kleeck, 2004). As van Kleeck discussed, families may not value a talkative child; hence, they may not find it appropriate to encourage a child to participate verbally in book sharing. Or they may not believe preschoolers are old enough to benefit from having books read to them. Others may tend to center too much on print form, and may rarely engage their young child in discussions about print meaning. In applying intervention research findings, we need to consider these kinds of cultural variations to make sound decisions about how best to work with families in promoting family literacy practices.

Yet another factor to consider in choosing how best to foster young children's preliteracy skills relates to where they are developmentally in acquiring these sets of skills. In other work, van Kleeck (e.g., 1995, 1998, 2003) posited two stages of preliteracy development suggested primarily by the research on middle-class European American children. The goal of the first stage is to ensure that children are aware that print is meaningful and useful. In the first stage, meaning is an almost exclusive focus when storybooks are shared (e.g., Phillips & McNaughton, 1990; Snow & Ninio, 1986; van Kleeck, 1998; Yaden et al., 1989), and even alphabet books are treated primarily as picture books at this stage (Bus & van IJzendoorn, 1988; van Kleeck, 1998; Yaden, Smolkin, & MacGillivray, 1993). In the second stage, older preschoolers are introduced to various aspects of the print form. The focus of alphabet book reading shifts to print (Bus & van IJzendoorn, 1988; van Kleeck, 1998), while a continued and more complex exploration of meaning occurs in other contexts and with other genres.

Several scholars have described similar stages in early reading development, with a function–meaning foundation stage followed by a stage focused on teaching the formal aspects of print through techniques such as decoding. A third stage that incorporates skills from the two previous phases facilitates reading comprehension (Chall, 1983; Downing, 1979; McCormick & Mason, 1986). In a review of empirical studies comparing whole-language–language-experience approaches and basal reader approaches to beginning reading, Stahl and Miller (1989) provide support for emphasizing the meaning and functional aspect before the form aspect of print. This conclusion was upheld in an updated review by Stahl, McKenna, and Pagnucco (1994). Conclusions from both reports are similar. Whole-language–language-experience approaches might be most effective for teaching functional aspects of reading, whereas more direct approaches might be better for helping a student master the word recognition skills prerequisite to effective comprehension. Moreover, whole-language–language-experience approaches are more effective if used when children are in kindergarten, saving the more form-oriented approaches for first grade.

In applying these ideas related to stages of preliteracy and early reading development in choosing the most appropriate skills on which to focus and the most appropriate approach to teaching them, it is important to consider both children's experience with literacy in their homes, and where they are functioning in relation to these two stages of preliteracy development. Regardless of where we choose to start, any use of decontextualized approaches in fostering print form skills must be followed by gradually embedding skills in meaningful uses of print involving connected text.

REFERENCES

Allington, R. (2002). *Big brother and the national reading curriculum: How ideology trumped evidence*. Portsmouth, NH: Heinemann.

Anderson, R., Hiebert, E., Scott, J., & Wilkinson, I. A. G. (1985). *Becoming a nation of readers: The report of the Commission on Reading*. Washington, DC: National Institute of Education.

Arnold, D. S., Lonigan, C. J., Whitehurst, G., & Epstein, J. (1994). Accelerating language development through picture-book reading: Replication and extension to a videotape training format. *Journal of Educational Psychology, 86*, 235–243.

Arnold, D. S., & Whitehurst, G. J. (1994). Accelerating language development through picture book reading: A summary of dialogic reading and its effects. In D. K. Dickinson (Ed.), *Bridges to literacy: Children, families, and schools* (pp. 103–128). Cambridge, MA: Blackwell.

Baker, L., Decker, S. N., & DeFries, J. C. (1984). Cognitive abilities in reading-disabled children: A longitudinal study. *Journal of Child Psychology and Psychiatry, 23*, 111–117.

Baker, L., Fernandez-Fein, S., Scher, D., & Williams, H. (1998). Home experiences related to the development of word recognition. In J. L. Metsala & L. C. Ehri (Eds.), *Word recognition in beginning literacy* (pp. 263–287). Hillsdale, NJ: Earlbaum.

Bus, A. G., & van IJzendoorn, M. H. (1988). Mother–child interactions, attachment, and emergent literacy: A cross-sectional study. *Child Development, 59*, 1262–1272.

Bus, A. G., & van IJzendoorn, M. H. (1999). Phonological awareness and early reading: A meta-analysis of experimental training studies. *Journal of Educational Psychology, 91*, 403–414.

Bus, A. G., van IJzendoorn, M. H., & Pellegrini, A. (1995). Joint book reading makes for success in learning to read: A meta-analysis on intergenerational transmission of literacy. *Review of Educational Research, 65*, 1–21.

Byrne, B., & Fielding-Barnsley, R. (1991). Evaluation of a program to teach phonemic awareness to young children. *Journal of Educational Psychology, 83*, 451–455.

Byrne, B., & Fielding-Barnsley, R. (1993). Evaluation of a program to teach phonemic awareness to young children: A 1-year follow-up. *Journal of Educational Psychology, 85*(1), 104–111.

Byrne, B., & Fielding-Barnsley, R. (1995). Evaluation of a program to teach phonemic awareness to young children: A 2- and 3-year follow-up. *Journal of Educational Psychology, 87*(3), 488–503.

Byrne, B., Fielding-Barnsley, R., & Ashley, L. (2000). Effects of preschool phoneme identity training after six years: Outcome level distinguished from rate of response. *Journal of Educational Psychology, 92*(4), 659–667.

Catts, H. W., Hogan, T., & Fey, M. (2003). Subgrouping poor readers on the basis of individual differences in reading-related abilities. *Journal of Learning Disabilities, 36*(2), 151–164.

Chall, J. (1983). *Stages of reading development*. New York: McGraw-Hill.

Clay, M. (1966). *Emergent reading behavior*. Unpublished doctoral dissertation, University of Auckland, New Zealand.

Coles, G. (2003). *Reading the naked truth: Literacy, legislation, and lies.* Portsmouth, NH: Heinemann.

Coyne, M., Simmons, D., Kame'enui, E., & Stoolmiller, M. (2004). Teaching vocabulary during shared storybook readings: An examination of differential effects. *Exceptionality, 12*(3), 145–162.

Dale, P. S., Crain-Thoreson, C., Notari-Syverson, A., & Cole, K. (1996). Parent–child book reading as an intervention technique for young children with language delays. *Topics in Early Childhood Special Education, 16*(2), 213–235.

Dollaghan, C. (2004). Evidence-based practice: Myths and realities. *ASHA Leader, 9*(7), 4–5,12.

Downing, J. (1979). *Reading and Reasoning.* New York: Springer-Verlag.

Evans, M. A., Shaw, D., & Bell, M. (2000). Home literacy activities and their influence on early literacy skills. *Canadian Journal of Experimental Psychology, 54*, 65–75.

Ewers, C. A., & Brownson, S. M. (1999). Kindergartners' vocabulary acquisition as a function of active vs. passive storybook reading, prior vocabulary, and working memory. *Reading Psychology, 20*(1), 11–21.

Ezell, H. K., & Justice, L. M. (2000). Increasing the print focus of adult-child shared book reading through observational learning. *American Journal of Speech–Language Pathology, 9*, 36–47.

Federal Interagency Forum on Child and Family Statistics. (1999). *America's children: Key national indicators of well-being, 1999* (NCES 1999-019). Washington, DC: Superintendent of Documents.

Federal Interagency Forum on Child and Family Statistics. (2003). *America's children: Key national indicators of well-being, 2003.* Retrieved November 10, 2005, from *www.childstats.ed.gov/americaschildren/pdf/ac2003/ed.pdf.*

Federal Interagency Forum on Child and Family Statistics. (2005). *America's children: Key national indicators of well-being, 2005.* Retrieved November 28, 2005, from *www.childstats.gov/americaschildren/edu1.asp.*

Fielding-Barnsley, R., & Purdie, N. (2003). Early intervention in the home for children at risk of reading failure. *Support for Learning, 18*(2), 77–82.

Flippo, R. F. (2001). The "real" common ground: Pulling the threads together. In *Reading researchers search for common ground* (pp. 178–184). Newark, DE: International Reading Association.

Garan, E. M. (2001). Beyond the smoke and mirrors: A critique of the National Reading Panel report on phonics. *Phi Delta Kappan, 82*(7), 500–506.

Gillon, G. T. (2004). *Phonological awareness: From research to practice.* New York: Guilford Press.

Gough, P. B., & Tunmer, W. E. (1986). Decoding, reading, and reading disability. *Remedial and Special Education, 7*, 6–10.

Hammett, L. A., van Kleeck, A., & Huberty, C. (2003). Clusters of parent interaction behaviors during book sharing with preschool children. *Reading Research Quarterly, 38*, 442–468.

Haney, H., & Hill, J. (2004). Relationships between parent–teaching activities and emergent literacy in preschool children. *Early Child Development and Care, 17*(3), 215–228.

Hargrave, A. C., & Sénéchal, M. (2000). A book reading intervention with preschool children who have limited vocabularies: The benefits of regular reading and dialogic reading. *Early Childhood Research Quarterly, 15*(1), 75–90.

Hayes, D. S. (2001). Young children's phonological sensitivity after exposure to a rhyming or nonrhyming story. *Journal of Genetic Psychology, 162*, 253–259.

High, P., Hopmann, M., LaGasse, L., & Linn, H. (1998). Evaluation of a clinic-based program to promote book sharing and bedtime routines among low-income urban families with young children. *Archives of Pediatrics and Adolescent Medicine, 152*, 459–465.

Hockenberger, E. H., Goldstein, H., & Haas, L. S. (1999). Effects of commenting during joint book reading by mothers with low SES. *Topics in Early Childhood Special Education, 19*, 15–27.

Huebner, C. E. (2000). Promoting toddlers' language development through community-based intervention. *Journal of Applied Developmental Psychology, 21*(5), 513–535.

Huebner, C. E., & Meltzoff, A. (2005). Intervention to change parent–child reading style: A comparison of instructional methods. *Journal of Applied Developmental Psychology, 26*(3), 296–313.

Juel, C. (1988). Learning to read and write: A longitudinal study of 54 children from first through fourth grades. *Journal of Educational Psychology, 80*, 437–447.

Justice, L. M., & Ezell, H. K. (2000). Enhancing children's print and word awareness through home-based parent intervention. *American Journal of Speech–Language Pathology, 9*, 257–269.

Justice, L. M., & Ezell, H. K. (2002). Use of storybook reading to increase print awareness in at-risk children. *American Journal of Speech–Language Pathology, 11*, 17–29.

Justice, L. M., Meier, J. D., & Walpole, S. (2005). Learning new words from storybooks: An efficacy study with at-risk kindergartners. *Language, Speech, and Hearing Services in Schools, 36*(1), 17–32.

Kuo, A. A., Franke, T. M., Regalado, M., & Halfon, N. (2004). Parent report of reading to young children. *Pediatrics, 113*, 1944–1951.

Lonigan, C. J. (1994). Reading to preschoolers exposed: Is the emperor really naked? *Developmental Review, 14*, 303–323.

Lonigan, C. J., Dyer, S. M., & Anthony, J. L. (1996, April). *The influence of the home literacy environment on the development of literacy skills in children from diverse racial and economic backgrounds*. Paper presented at the Annual Conference of the American Educational Research Association, New York, NY.

Lonigan, C. J., & Whitehurst, G. (1998). Relative efficacy of parent and teacher involvement in shared reading intervention for preschool children from low-income backgrounds. *Early Childhood Research Quarterly, 13*, 263–290.

McCardle, P., Scarborough, H., & Catts, H. W. (2001). Predicting, explaining, and preventing reading difficulties. *Learning Disabilities Research and Practice, 16*, 230–239.

McCormick, C., & Mason, J. M. (1986). *Use of little books at home: A minimal intervention strategy that fosters early reading* (Technical Report No. 388). Champaign: University of Illinois at Urbana–Champaign, Center for the Study of Reading.

McFadden, T. U. (1998). Sounds and stories: Teaching phonemic awareness in interactions around text. *American Journal of Speech–Language Pathology, 7*(2), 5–13.

McGee, L. M., & Purcell-Gates, V. (1997). So what's going on in research on emergent literacy? *Reading Research Quarterly, 32*, 310–318.

McKinney, J. D., & Feagans, L. (1984). Academic and behavioral characteristics: Longitudinal studies of learning disabled children and average achievers. *Learning Disability Quarterly, 7*, 251–265.

Mendelsohn, A., Mogilner, L., Dreyer, B., Forman, J., Weinstein, S., Broderick, M., et al. (2001). The impact of a clinic-based literacy intervention on language development in inner-city preschool children. *Pediatrics, 107*(1), 130–134.

Morrow, L. M. (1988). Young children's responses to one-to-one story readings in school settings. *Reading Research Quarterly, 23*, 89–107.

Nation, K. (2005). Connections between language and reading in children with poor reading comprehension. In H. W. Catts & A. G. Kamhi (Eds.), *The connections between language and reading disabilities* (pp. 41–54). Mahwah, NJ: Erlbaum.

National Reading Panel. (2000). *Report of the National Reading Panel: Teaching children to read: Reports of the subgroups*. Washington, DC: National Institute of Child Health and Human Development.

Needlman, R., Fried, L., Morley, D., Taylor, S., & Zuckerman, B. (1991). Clinic-based intervention to promote literacy: A pilot study. *American Journal of Diseases of Children, 145*(8), 881–884.

Needlman, R., Klass, P., & Zuckerman, B. (2002). Reach out and get your patients to read. *Contemporary Pediatrics, 19*(1), 51.

Needlman, R., Toker, K., Dreyer, B., Klass, P., & Mendelsohn, A. (2005). Effectiveness of a primary care intervention to support reading aloud: A multicenter evaluation. *Ambulatory Pediatrics, 5*(4), 209–215.

Oakhill, J. V., Cain, K., & Bryant, P. E. (2003). The dissociation of word reading and text comprehension: Evidence from component skills. *Language and Cognitive Processes, 18*, 443–468.

Pearson, P. (2004). The reading wars. *Educational Policy, 18*(1), 216–252.

Phillips, G., & McNaughton, S. (1990). The practice of storybook reading to preschool children in mainstream New Zealand families. *Reading Research Quarterly, 25*, 196–212.

Rescorla, L., Hyson, M. C., Hirsh-Pasek, K., & Cone, J. (1990). Academic expectations in mothers of preschool children: A psychometric study of the Educational Attitude Scale. *Early Education and Development, 1*, 167–184.

Robey, R. R. (2004, April 13). Levels of evidence. *ASHA Leader*, p. 5.

Robey, R. R. (2005, May 24). An introduction to clinical trials. *ASHA Leader*, pp. 6–7, 22–23.

Rump, K. M., Walsh, B. A., & Blewitt, P. (2005, April). *Shared book reading: What helps children learn new words*. Paper presented at the Society for Research in Child Development, Atlanta, GA.

Sackett, D., Rosenberg, W., Gray, J., Haynes, R., & Richardson, W. (1996). Evidence based medicine: What it is and isn't. *British Medical Journal, 312*, 71–72.

Sanders, L., Gershon, T., Huffman, L., & Mendoza, F. (2000). Prescribing books for immigrant children: A pilot study to promote emergent literacy among the children of Hispanic immigrants. *Archives of Pediatrics and Adolescent Medicine, 154*(8), 771–777.

Scarborough, H. S. (2001). Connecting early language and literacy to later reading (dis)abilities: Evidence, theory, and practice. In S. B. Neuman & D. K. Dickinson (Eds.), *Handbook of early literacy research* (pp. 97–110). New York: Guilford Press.

Scarborough, H. S. (2005). Developmental relationships between language and reading: Reconciling a beautiful hypothesis with some ugly facts. In H. W. Catts & A. Kamhi (Eds.), *The connections between language and reading disabilities* (pp. 3–24). Mahwah, NJ: Erlbaum.

Scarborough, H. S., Dobrich, W., & Hager, M. (1991). Preschool literacy experience and later reading achievement. *Journal of Learning Disabilities, 24*, 508–511.

Scarborough, H. S., & Parker, J. L. (2003). Matthew effects in children with learning disabilities: Development of reading, IQ, and psychosocial problems from grade 2 to grade 8. *Annals of Dyslexia, 53*, 47–71.

Sénéchal, M. (1997). The differential effect of storybook reading on preschoolers' acquisition of expressive and receptive vocabulary. *Journal of Child Language, 24*, 123–138.

Sénéchal, M., & Cornell, E. H. (1993). Vocabulary acquisition through shared reading experiences. *Reading Research Quarterly, 28*, 360–374.

Sénéchal, M., & LeFevre, J. A. (2001). Storybook reading and parent teaching: Links to language and literacy development. *New Directions for Child and Adolescent Development, 92*, 39–52.

Sénéchal, M., & LeFevre, J. A. (2002). Parental involvement in the development of children's reading skill: A five-year longitudinal study. *Child Development, 73*, 445–460.

Sénéchal, M., LeFevre, J. A., Hudson, E., & Lawson, E. P. (1996). Knowledge of storybooks as a predictor of young children's vocabulary. *Journal of Educational Psychology, 88*, 520–536.

Sénéchal, M., LeFevre, J. A., Thomas, E., & Daley, K. (1998). Differential effects of home literacy experiences on the development of oral and written language. *Reading Research Quarterly, 33*(1), 96–116.

Share, D. L., & Leikin, M. (2004). Language impairment at school entry and later reading disability: Connections at lexical versus supralexical levels of reading. *Scientific Studies of Reading, 8*(1), 87–110.

Sharif, I., Rieber, S., & Ozuah, P. (2002). Exposure to Reach Out and Read and vocabulary outcomes in inner city preschoolers. *Journal of the National Medical Association, 94*(3), 171–177.

Shaywitz, B. A., Holford, T. R., Holahan, J. M., Fletcher, J. M., Stuebing, K. K., Francis, D. J., et al. (1995). A Matthew effect for IQ but not for reading: Results from a longitudinal study. *Reading Research Quarterly, 30*, 984–906.

Shaywitz, S. E. (1998). Current concepts: Dyslexia. *The New England Journal of Medicine, 338*(5), 307–312.

Shaywitz, S. E., Escobar, M. D., Shaywitz, B. A., Fletcher, J. M., & Makuch, R. W. (1992). Evidence that dyslexia may represent the lower tail of the normal distribution of reading ability. *New England Journal of Medicine, 326*, 145–150.

Silverstein, M., Iverson, L., & Lozano, P. (2002). An English-language clinic-based literacy program is effective for multilingual population. *Pediatrics, 109*(5), E76.

Skibbe, L., & Justice, L. M. (2005, June). *Explicit literacy instruction during book reading: Impact on preschoolers with SLI*. Paper presented at the Symposium on Research in Child Language Disorders, Madison, WI.

Smith, F. (2003). *Unspeakable acts, unnatural practices: Flaws and fallacies in "scientific" reading instruction*. Portsmouth, NH: Heinemann.

Smith, S. S. (1997). A longitudinal study: The literacy development of 57 children. In C. K. Kinzer, K. A. Hinchman & D. J. Leu (Eds.), *Inquiries in literacy theory and practices* (pp. 250–264). Chicago: National Reading Conference.

Snow, C. E., Burns, M. S., & Griffin, P. (Eds.). (1998). *Preventing reading difficulties in young children*. Washington, DC: National Academy Press.

Snow, C. E., & Ninio, A. (1986). The contracts of literacy: What children learn from learning to read books. In W. H. Teale & E. Sulzby (Eds.), *Emergent literacy: Writing and reading* (pp. 116–137). Norwood, NJ: Ablex.

Snowling, M. J. (2005). Literacy outcomes for children with oral language impairments: Developmental interactions between language skills and learning to read. In H. W. Catts & A. G. Kamhi (Eds.), *The connections between language and reading disabilities* (pp. 55–75). Mahwah, NJ: Erlbaum.

Sonnenschein, S., Baker, S. C., & Cerro, L. (1992). Mothers' views on teaching their preschoolers in everyday situations. *Early Education and Development, 3*(1), 5–26.

Stadler, M. A., & McEvoy, M. A. (2003). The effect of text genre on parent use of joint book reading strategies to promote phonological awareness. *Early Childhood Research Quarterly, 18*, 502–512.

Stahl, S. A., McKenna, M. C., & Pagnucco, J. R. (1994). The effects of whole language instruction: An update and a reappraisal. *Educational Psychologist, 29*, 175–185.

Stahl, S. A., & Miller, P. D. (1989). Whole language and language experience approaches for beginning reading: A quantitative research synthesis. *Review of Educational Research, 59*, 87–116.

Storch, S. A., & Whitehurst, G. J. (2002). Oral language and code-related precursors to reading: Evidence from a longitudinal structural model. *Developmental Psychology, 38*(6), 934–947.

Teale, W. H., & Sulzby, E. (1987). Literacy acquisition in early childhood: The roles of access and mediation in storybook reading. In D. A. Wagner (Ed.), *The future of literacy in a changing world* (pp. 111–129). New York: Pergamon Press.

Troia, G. A. (1999). Phonological awareness intervention research: A critical review of the experimental methodology. *Reading Research Quarterly, 34*, 28–52.

Valdez-Menchaca, M. C., & Whitehurst, G. J. (1992). Accelerating language development through picture-book reading: A systematic extension to Mexican day care. *Developmental Psychology, 28*, 1106–1114.

van Kleeck, A. (1995). Emphasizing form and meaning separately in prereading and early reading instruction. *Topics in Language Disorders, 16*(1), 27–49.

van Kleeck, A. (1998). Preliteracy domains and stages: Laying the foundations for beginning reading. *Journal of Children's Communication Development, 20*, 33–51.

van Kleeck, A. (2003). Research on book sharing: Another critical look. In A. van Kleeck, S. A. Stahl, & E. Bauer (Eds.), *On reading to children: Parents and teachers* (pp. 271–320). Mahwah, NJ: Erlbaum.

van Kleeck, A. (2004). On the road to reading fluently: Where is science in helping us balance meaning-oriented and skill-oriented approaches. *American Journal of Psychology, 117*, 300–316.

Weitzman, C., Roy, L., Walls, T., & Tomlin, R. (2004). More evidence for Reach Out and Read: A home-based study. *Pediatrics, 113*(5), 1248–1253.

Whitehurst, G., Arnold, D. S., Epstein, J. N., Angell, A. L., Smith, M., & Fischel, J. E. (1994). A picture book reading intervention in day care and home for children from low-income families. *Developmental Psychology, 30*, 679–689.

Whitehurst, G., Falco, F. L., Lonigan, C. J., Fischel, J. E., DeBaryshe, B. D., Valdez-Menchaca, M. C., et al. (1988). Accelerating language development through picture book reading. *Developmental Psychology, 24*, 552–559.

Whitehurst, G., & Fischel, J. (2000). A developmental model of reading and language impairments arising in conditions of economic poverty. In D. Bishop & L. Leonard (Eds.), *Speech and language impairment: From theory to practice* (pp. 53–71). East Sussex, UK: Psychology Press.

Whitehurst, G., Fischel, J., Lonigan, C., Valdez-Menchaca, M., Arnold, D., & Smith, M. (1991). Treatment of early expressive language delay: If, when. and how. *Topics in Language Disorders, 11*(4), 55–68.

Whitehurst, G., & Lonigan, C. (1998). Child development and emergent literacy. *Child Development, 69*, 848–872.

Whitehurst, G., & Lonigan, C. (2001). Emergent literacy: Development from prereaders to readers. In S. B. Neuman & D. K. Dickinson (Eds.), *Handbook of early literacy research* (pp. 11–29). New York: Guilford Press.

Whitehurst, G., Zevenbergen, A. A., Crone, D. A., Schultz, M. D., Velting, O. N., & Fischel, J. (1999). Outcomes of emergent literacy intervention from Head Start through second grade. *Journal of Educational Psychology, 91*, 261–272.

Yaden, D. B., Rowe, D., & MacGillivray, L. (2000). Emergent literacy: A matter (polyphony) of perspectives. In M. Kamil, P. Mosenthal, & P. Pearson (Eds.), *Handbook of reading research* (Vol. III, pp. 425–454). Mahwah, NJ: Erlbaum.

Yaden, D. B., Smolkin, L. B., & Conlon, A. (1989). Preschoolers' questions about pictures, print conventions, and story text during reading aloud at home. *Reading Research Quarterly, 24*, 188–214.

Yaden, D. B., Smolkin, L. B., & MacGillivray, L. (1993). A psychogenetic perspective on children's understanding about letter associations during alphabet book readings. *Journal of Reading Behavior, 25*, 43–68.

11

Language and Reading Development Reflect Dynamic Mixes of Learning Conditions

KEITH E. NELSON
MARNIE E. ARKENBERG

There is no question that human behavior is complex. Investigations ranging widely across phenomena, from how children learn to walk or sing or read, or to solve addition or balance beam problems or construct narratives suggest that most significant behavioral and cognitive advances result from the complex, dynamic interactions of multiple components. Dynamic systems perspectives are especially useful in investigating the complexities of childhood individual differences in a way that allows researchers to view the components and the results of the cooperating variables that underlie behavior.

In this chapter we first present key information on what components of developmental dynamic mixes contribute to display of current skills and to progress in learning new skills. The particular model we present, called the dynamic "tricky" mix (DTM) theory, is shown to have important implications for assessing children's skills and for providing innovations in teaching that may accelerate skills acquisition. We strongly emphasize prior studies and new possible studies in which close monitoring of mixes of learning conditions can lead to dramatic acceleration of a child's learning. Paradoxically, by keeping track of the genuine complexity of factors influencing performance and learning, "simpler" ways of boosting children's depth of engagement and their pace of learning emerge.

One value of any theory is its ability to foster new observations. DTM theory has led to some surprising and important observations on children's learning that we document here. We demonstrate that past learning rates of children with disabilities are not a good indicator of learning rates when care is taken to foster excellent, complex mixes of conditions that the children have previously rarely encountered. More broadly, this theory, and the observations already in hand, provide multiple reasons to be optimistic about future acceleration of children's progress in literacy, language, and other domains. To see how some future pathways to excellent learning might be laid out, it is necessary to examine theoretical details and supportive research findings.

DYNAMIC SYSTEMS THEORY

Dynamic systems theories stress the embeddedness of multiple, complex components within ongoing, real-time systems. Examples of dynamic systems include fluid dynamics, emergence of weather patterns, chemical reactions, protein synthesis, and embryological development, as well as childrens' and adults' behaviors. These systems are self-organizing in the sense that there is no overarching guideline for development, even though highly specific genetic, chemical, and physical structures comprise one kind of contributor. Rather, system behavior is the result of the ongoing convergence of many nonlinear components. Furthermore, human behavior is not determined solely based on internal or external influences, but through highly particular interactions between the here-and-now environment, past experiences, current activations, and anticipation of future experiences.

The example of young children learning to crawl and walk has been used to illustrate these dynamic system convergences of many factors in ongoing, convergent mixes. Thelen and Smith (2006) emphasize that crawling and walking behaviors, like all human behaviors, are assembled dynamically in real time in specific contexts. In their own words,

> Crawling is a coherent behavior that infants use to locomote when they have sufficient strength and coordination to assume a hands-and-knees posture, an environment to support it and to motivate self-movement, but a system not yet balanced and strong enough to walk upright. Crawling is a stable behavior for several months. But when infants learn to walk, the crawling behavior becomes destabilized by the patterns of standing and walking. There is no program for crawling assembled in the genes or wired in the nervous system. It self-organizes as a solution to a problem in a task

> context (move across the room), later to be replaced by a more efficient solution. (p. 281)

As another example, consider a 10-month-old who has stuffed giraffes at home but has no words for them. This child at a zoo may establish joint attention with a parent, then point excitedly to the zoo's baby giraffe. Child and adult then further participate in the emergent dance of parent–child gestures, visual attention, positive emotion, and words around giraffes and our human reactions to them. Whether the child achieves a successful mapping of *giraffe* as a word to important aspects of word meaning depends upon the dynamic interplay of these cognitive, language, and social exchange/engagement conditions in real-time episodes.

THE DYNAMIC "TRICKY" MIX THEORY OF DEVELOPMENT

Dynamic "Tricky" Mix theory or DTM is a relatively new example of a theory that makes use of the general framework of dynamic systems theories, while specifying in some detail the different components that contribute to children's learning (Nelson, 2000, 2001; Nelson et al., 2001, 2004). We suggest that learning is dependent upon a complex, tricky-to-achieve, converging set of conditions that must cooperate at high levels for high rates of learning to be achieved. The crux of the theory is this: Numerous social, emotional, motivational, cognitive, structural challenges and current neural *network* conditions must reach threshold levels of convergence to support any advance in learning and then increasingly high learning rates occur as above-threshold convergences intensify. Each contributing condition can in part be separately tracked, but also sits in relation to the other contributing components and the real-time, ongoing, emergent, interacting mix. The optimal convergence of the components that might contribute to children's highly accelerated learning is relatively rare for most children and most domains of learning—precisely because the complexity of needed interaction of conditions is so high, and because conditions sometimes detract from favorable mixes for learning. At the same time, and for the same theoretical process reasons, whenever a child experiences regular, repeated DTMs, then sustained levels of very powerful learning are seen across periods of months and years. This has occasionally been demonstrated in children with severe, multiple-year lags behind norms in reading or mathematics, or oral language, when they are placed in dramatically new mixes of conditions (Camarata, Nelson, & Camarata, 1994; Dickinson, McCabe, & Clark-Chiarelli, 2005; Lepper, Woolverton, Mumme, & Gurtner, 1993; Nelson, Welsh, Camarata, Heimann, & Tjus, 2001; Nelson, Craven, Xuan,

& Arkenberg, 2004; Nelson, Camarata, Welsh, Butkovsky, & Camarata, 1996; Nelson, Heimann, & Tjus, 1997; Torgeson, Wagner, & Rashotte, 1997). The potential for many more children to achieve such successes is high if theoretically guided interventions are more often provided, as discussed from several angles later in this chapter.

OVERVIEW OF RESEARCH DIRECTIONS FROM THE DYNAMIC TRICKY MIX PERSPECTIVE

From this Dynamic Tricky Mix perspective, convergent findings across naturalistic and experimental studies are stressed as being essential to refined understanding at the process level of children do and do not make progress. Research findings are integrated within this model from studies of children with no reading or language development disabilities; children with autism, language delay, dyslexia, and deafness; as well as at-risk children. For all these groups, it is argued that most theories, and most educational and clinical programs, systematically underestimate learning potentials in the reading and language development of children, because empirical research so seldom captures the accelerated learning rates observable when multiple converging conditions are highly favorable.

One implication is that we now know enough to create innovative, theoretically guided, excellent mixes of the complex conditions that support learning. This leads to the prediction that very strong accelerative effects will be created. At the same time, the same Dynamic Tricky Mix perspective implies that the success rates of educational and intervention programs will be further enhanced by tailoring of the overall mix of learning conditions to the constraints represented by the child's biological makeup. Rather than one-size-fits-all education, mixes should be set up, monitored, and revised to ensure that they accommodate individual, biologically based and experience-based differences.

In the context of this book, it is important to see that this theoretical framework accommodates multiple types of interactions that need to be understood to capture learning processes and to inform educational efforts; these interactions are explicated later.

A CLOSER LOOK AT DYNAMIC TRICKY MIXES AND LEARNING CONDITIONS

Learning occurs only when there is above-threshold positive convergence of some conditions from each of five components. We use the acronym *LEARN*: *Launchers* + *Enhancers* + *Adjustment* + *Readiness* + *Networks* =

LEARN. As convergence of these components is progressively enriched, the rate of learning is progressively accelerated. Even though definite overlaps between conditions make learning complex, as we discuss later in the section on centrality of interactions, the LEARN organization provides one way to generate a dynamic convergence accounting for already observed phenomena in children's learning, as well as to make useful predictions about possible future discoveries.

Figure 11.1A illustrates the very modest learning that occurs when the LEARN conditions barely converge. In contrast, when multiple, strong learning conditions converge in real time at high levels, the dynamic result is rapid, excellent learning, as illustrated in Figure 11.1B.

The Organization of LEARN

Launching Conditions

For children to acquire new information, structures, or skills, there must be an impetus and opening for that learning to begin. These are referred to as *launching* conditions. The idea behind launching conditions is that for children to learn new skills or information, there must be genuine challenges accompanied by some kind of processing attempts. Launching impetus may arise from a combination of beliefs, noticed challenges, active pursuit of a learning opportunity, modeling of learning by others, and expectancies.

Launching conditions thus must include challenges for the learner and

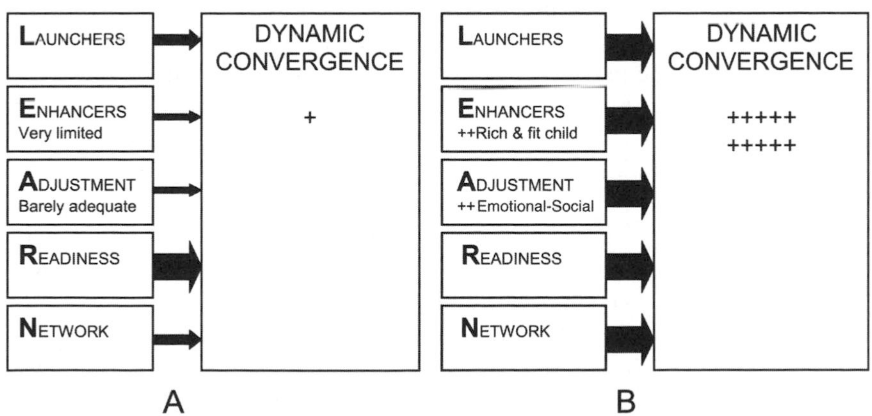

FIGURE 11.1. Dynamic tricky mix patterns of convergence shift from A to B. In A, Readiness is the one factor that is highly positive, and Enhancers and Adjustment are limited. Overall convergence is just barely adequate to support learning. In B, all five major factors are highly positive and converge strongly to support high rates of learning.

incorporate initial conditions of orientation and engagement. At the neural level, the early stages of one-trial, amygdala-mediated learning, as described by LeDoux (2000), fit extremely well here. This work shows that after establishment of such initial representations neurally, new and separate networks support long-term maintenance of acquired knowledge. Other conditions that contribute to the chances of getting a challenge noticed and into the initial launching steps toward long-term representation include priming of relevant neural *networks* and aspects of attention, interest, expectancy, belief, and arousal.

Enhancing Conditions

Enhancing conditions can be described as within-task strategy, processing, engagement, and awareness factors that bolster or augment learning. The role of *Enhancers* is to mediate the probability of successful learning through high attention and rapid pattern detection, and the rich and meaningful entry of new representations into long-term memory. Small shifts in this component, when the other four key conditions are favorably online, can have large consequences for learning.

The use of DTM to study children's behavior heuristically orients us toward different kinds of patterns of input–learner–context interactions rather than simply toward the questions of whether different components of a behavior may or may not contribute to that behavior. The next examples illustrate the important role of Enhancers in dynamic interaction with the other conditions of LEARN.

Metacognition serves nicely as one example of an enhancer. Several investigators have found support for the idea that metacognitive awareness can improve reading performance. For example, when Flavell (1979) examined metacognition in relation to reading comprehension, he found that older and better readers were more aware of the need to use strategies for comprehension. Similarly, Wagoner (1983) showed that poor readers often fail to recognize that reading requires self-monitoring. Similarly Johns (1979) provided evidence that beginning readers are oblivious of the need for helpful strategies in reading comprehension. Finally, de Sousa and Oakhill (1996) studied the relation among children's metacognition, their reading comprehension, and their level of interest. Two groups of good and poor comprehending 8- and 9-year-olds were matched on vocabulary and single-word reading. When children were asked to identify information from text they had read, a significant difference favoring the good readers emerged in terms of children's ability to assess their comprehension of material. However, when children were presented the same task in the context of a game, the poor comprehenders showed increased interest, increased metacognition, and increased performance. These results fit easily with the notion that relatively small shifts in procedure–context enhancement may perturb children away from poor overall dynamic mixes to mixes that engage their focus and motivation in real time and support higher levels of awareness and learning.

A second widely documented enhancer of children's progress in syntax is a particular kind of conversational responding by adults. The strategy of reflecting back a child's expressed meaning by "recasting" the sentence that carries the meaning has been shown experimentally to accelerate children's pace of syntactic growth (Fey, Cleave, & Long, 1997; Baker & Nelson, 1984; Camarata et al., 1994; Nelson, 2000). Recasts, such as "Yes, the cat was chased by that big black dog" as a reply to the child's "Doggie chase cat" illustrate this strategy.

Adjustment

The *A* in *LEARN* stands for *Adjustment* conditions. Adjustments that occur as learning episodes unfold cross the bridge between the traditionally dichotomized cognitive and social–emotional realms.

Consider the child who, after answering a basic reading comprehension question correctly in the classroom, reacts with a sense of ownership and pleasure. Contrast this with a child who has failed in this task. Whereas the child who answered correctly may feel pride and look forward to the next question, and to learning more of the material, the child who answered incorrectly may feel disappointment and embarrassment, and continue to ruminate about that failure. Both of these situations, if repeated, may set up classroom interaction spirals; however, the direction for the successful child may be positive, whereas that for the child who failed may be a downward spiral that moves the child toward a lack of interest, or toward fear.

Adjustment is not solely dependent upon the learner. Also involved might be a parent, teacher, peer, or sibling—those who are onlookers, partners, and potential teachers—who transactionally influences the ongoing social, emotional, and motivational states of the child during potential learning episodes (Nelson et al., 1997; Rogoff, Turkanis, & Bartlett, 2001).

One demonstration of Adjustment processes lies in Elliot and Dweck's work (1988). They showed that when late elementary school-age children were led to believe they had high or low ability, both children with learning goals (children who desire to learn the material because they value knowledge acquisition) and children with performance goals (children who desire to do well on the evaluation) were equally likely to learn new information when no strong challenges were presented. However, when confronted with difficulties, children who had learning goals were able to persist in learning across failures regardless of whether they were led to believe they had low or high ability. But for children with performance goals, only those who believed they had high ability also persevered. Those who believed they had low ability showed a decline in generation of useful strategies for solving a problem.

Thus, beliefs about oneself interact online to influence the child's dynamic Adjustment processes during instruction, with negative emotion and attributions contributing to poor activation of strategy resources (probable processing and learning Enhancers). These strategy resources otherwise would be available to the same child under more positive Adjustment conditions.

An excellent example of how favorable launching conditions (e.g., a theory or belief) may arise and then dynamically interact with Enhancer and Adjustment conditions comes from Dweck's work on how children's views about intelligence influence the way they approach a learning task (Dweck, 1999; Dweck & Leggett, 1988; Dweck, Mangels, & Good, 2004). Children who believe that intelligence is a fixed trait, that is, who hold an entity theory of intelligence, tend to be concerned with performance goals that demonstrate their intelligence. Thus, for these children, achievement is a way of looking smart. On the contrary, some children adhere to an incremental theory of intelligence, in which they view intelligence as the result of learning; therefore it can be increased by efforts that increase knowledge.

In a recent neurophysiological investigation, Butterfield, Mangels, 2003; Mangels, Butterfield Lamb, Good, and Dweck (2006) used event-related potentials (ERPs) to examine how students' theories of intelligence influence the allocation of attention to negative performance feedback, and how attention is directed toward subsequent feedback that could be used to repair errors in knowledge. ERPs measure electrical activity in the brain through recordings on the scalp. In contrast to continuous electroencephalography (EEG) signals, ERPs allow for an investigation into the time course and rough brain location of processes time-locked to different kinds of stimuli. Of particular interest to this investigation were two neurobehavioral correlates: (1) P3, a frontal positive-going amplitude that occurs around 300 msec poststimulus, which is thought to measure unpredictable, unlikely, or highly significant stimuli, where increases in amplitude are related to the level of significance; and (2) the amplitude and duration of negative-going activation in the left temporal region in response to learning-relevant feedback suggestive of the level of processing of corrective and related information relevant to later increased performance (Butterfield & Mangels, 2003).

In Mangels et al. (2006), students holding either entity theories or incremental theories of intelligence were asked to answer a series of general knowledge questions from varied domains, then to rate how confident they were of their answers. Two types of feedback then followed this task: (1)

performance-relevant feedback that indicated whether the student's answer was correct or incorrect; and (2) learning-relevant feedback that provided the correct answer regardless of whether the student's answer was correct or incorrect. At the end of the procedure was a surprise retest of those questions that the students had answered incorrectly.

The authors found that, compared to students with an incremental theory of intelligence, students who held entity theories of intelligence showed a greater anterior frontal P3 to negative feedback for answers that they had rated with either high or low confidence, suggesting that these students were more influenced by negative feedback of any kind than were students holding an incremental theory of intelligence. These results were coupled with differences in negative-going activation over the left temporal lobe for entity versus incremental theorists; students holding incremental theories exhibited greater left inferior temporal negativity at longer durations than did entity theorists, suggesting a difference in reactive control processes toward learning-relevant information. An increase in duration of activation in the left temporal lobe is thought to be indicative of activation of conceptual representations related to to-be-learned information that assists in enhancing memory of that information.

These results, together with behavioral results showing that incremental theorists performed significantly better on the retest portion of the experiment, suggest that how students react initially to negative feedback can influence later learning of new correct information. Thus there is neurophysiological evidence that students with different theories of learning are in contrasting ways dynamically adjusting their attention and their processing to the same steps in a learning/feedback procedure.

Readiness

Readiness conditions refer to the state of the child's already-established knowledge, emotion, and information-processing systems relative to the impending challenges. These conditions include working memory capacity, basic domain knowledge, planning skills, the capability to abstract patterns or to draw analogies, attentional and inhibitory control, perceptual skills, and emotion regulation mechanisms. Children's Readiness at any age can be expected to be highly variable and depends on their biological makeup, their current levels of maturation, and their prior histories of learning.

Neural Networks

Within each child there will be high fluctuations across learning episodes in terms of how easily and appropriately already-established neural Networks are activated. Current states and patterns of functional activation are crucial. Change simply cannot occur if the system is too far offline. There must be a minimal level of arousal or energy for the system to function, and core processes of attention, perception, abstraction, and memory must be online to provide any substantial potential for learning. Stronger activation of the functional Networks underlying these processes increases processing and learning speeds.

In addition, the degree of relevant parallel processing may also be a powerful catalyst toward the rate of learning. The successful abstraction and storage of new text and language structures may be boosted substantially by more working memory analytic buffers operating in parallel, and more parallel long-term memory retrieval–storage pathways, (cf. Calvin, 1990; Damasio, 1994; Elman et al., 1996; Nelson, 1987, 1989, 1998, 2000; Nelson et al., 2001, 2004).

More on the Interactions Dynamically of All LEARN Conditions

Unlike most variants on theories of learning, DTM suggests that learning emerges from the convergence of these multiple, complex underlying LEARN conditions. DTM theory is consistent with one earlier theory, Rare Event Learning Theory, which had less elaborated detail but also stressed that learning will be infrequent until mixes of complex supportive conditions come into place (e.g., Nelson, 2000). Whether learning occurs depends on whether the LEARN conditions meet threshold levels of activation. More and more dynamic convergence then leads to higher and higher rates of learning.

For learning to commence, children must be engaged, motivated, and focused. Furthermore, they must have the background knowledge and background experiences needed for the learning situation, as well as the emotional tone and regulation that support acquisition. For learning to proceed at near-optimal rates, multiple task-relevant Enhancers must be brought into the dynamic interplay of conditions. In everyday situations, the likelihood that these conditions will emerge in an optimal or near-optimal pattern is quite unlikely. Children often are in states of emotional dysregulation, are not paying attention, and do not have the relevant background knowledge or strategies.

Furthermore, preschool, school, and clinical situations that are structured specifically for learning to occur rarely take into account the ways that *individual children's* patterns of experiences, knowledge, abilities, personality, and level of interest and motivation interact in complex and dynamic ways with the social and cognitive patterns of teaching encounters. However, we can structure situations in theoretically guided ways, so that high or very high levels of convergence and rates of learning are more likely to occur. In such conditions we would expect learning in many instances to proceed in a dramatic way. The next section covers some empirical demonstrations of these kinds of shifts in learning rates when dynamic mixes shift.

ILLUSTRATIVE STUDIES OF RAPID LEARNING IN TYPICAL CHILDREN AS REFLECTING DYNAMIC MIXES

Vocabulary Growth

The National Reading Panel (2000) suggests that vocabulary is one component for reading success. Because vocabulary continuously expands across the lifetime, the potential for reading success may also be expanding similarly. For this reason, examining vocabulary rates and growth may be an essential component in understanding complex skills such as reading.

It is well known that at around 17–19 months of age, some children demonstrate explosive growth in their vocabularies, in the same period when other children are only creeping along in lexical growth (Dale & Fenson, 1996; Hart & Risley, 1999). As an example, Smith (1926) suggested that the average 18-month-old knows between 3 and 100 words. Others have been more optimistic in their analysis. Nelson and Bonvillian (1978) suggest that a vocabulary of approximately 600 words is more likely. In fact, Aitchison (2003) proposed that, by 2 age years, children may range in the terms of the number of words known from 6,000 to 14,0000 words. It is likely that these hugely variable estimates are neither correct nor incorrect. Rather, it may be that individual differences in vocabulary are this large, and that this variability reflects the patterns of transactions that have accumulated from the initial onset of vocabulary learning (Weizman & Snow, 2001).

Very low vocabulary levels may be indicative of children whose learning spirals have resulted in not only stalled learning but also an actual decrease in the tendency for LEARN components to converge in above threshold ways. In contrast, higher vocabulary levels represent the kind of learning that is possible when highly positive spirals of learning are created. However, the fundamental reasons for such huge individual differences have not been sorted out from naturalistic studies. From the DTM theory, it is predictable that many children have in place needed cognitive and language Readiness factors, but await the arrival of highly favorable interactive conditions that mix in processing supports, lexical challenges, and mutually high engagement with a caregiver, before their learning potential leads to a burst in vocabulary growth. At least two experimental studies support this contention.

Work by Smith, Jones, Landau, Gershkoff-Stowe, and Samuelson (2002) used causal experimental methodology to demonstrate how changing the dynamics of the learning situation could lead to dramatically increased learning rates. Matched groups of children received either no lexical training or lexical training for 8–9 weeks on nonsense words that mapped to clear, shape-based categories of objects. The key result was that children who were provided repeated exposures to unfamiliar objects that shared that same shape were able to generalize the name of the new objects based on shape. Smith et al. concluded that learning a coherent category structure allowed children to refine their attentional strategies, and that this refinement led to changes in vocabulary acquisition that could be seen outside the laboratory as well.

The DTM interpretation is that the lexically trained children were "perturbed" in their dynamic learning systems by the training experiences, leading to a vast acceleration of their lexical progress *outside* the experimental sessions. In each of the studies, the pace they showed outstripped the control, untrained children's vocabulary progress in home language use by 178–253% across 2 months.

Experimental studies, such as that by Arkenberg (2006), provide additional evidence of the high rates of learning that are possible when the dynamics of the learning situation are changed. In that study two groups of ten 4-year-olds were matched on vocabulary knowledge, awareness of print concepts, working memory, phonological awareness, attention, and ability to generalize. One group of children participated in a 12-week word-learning intervention, in which they were exposed to 450 unfamiliar animal names. In accordance with DTM theory, children were exposed to these new words under highly engaging, child-directed sessions in which the investigator followed the child's lead by allowing him or her to dictate the next animal to be learned, and by building into playful discussions at least eight tokens of each of the new lexical items. This scenario translated into a mix that we would expect to create high rates of learning. Launching conditions included children's interest in the material sparked by embedding the goal learning within the context of free play that the child directed; Enhancers such as numerous and varied visual and verbal tokens of the to-be-learned items were provided. Furthermore, children were rewarded with praise for remembering the animal names, and they were never provided with discouraging remarks if they did not remember. These contingencies provided an opportunity for increasingly positive Adjustments. Children's Readiness for the material was determined through the use of multiple cognitive assessments prior to the intervention. Finally, children's growing knowledge was assessed regularly through tailored interactions used to gauge children's Network conditions.

Results from the intervention portion of the experiment showed that when children were taught new lexical items during these intensive, rich, positive, and highly engaging episodes, they demonstrated exceptionally high rates of gain of up to 20 words per hour. By way of contrast, estimates of fairly typical naturalistic rates for 4-year-olds are much lower, at between 2 and 20 words per day (e.g. Anglin, 1993). A classic Matthew effect (Stanovich, 1986) was also observed, in which children's rate of learning in intervention increased by more than 10% across the 12-week period. That such a high rate of acquisition can occur suggests that children certainly have the capability to learn many new words when the conditions for learning are favorable. In addition, it appears that multiple cognitive gains contributed to these findings. Because we assessed cognitive ability in the two groups of children prior to, halfway through, and at the end of the intervention, we were able to compare changes in working memory, phonological awareness, attention, and generalization abilities for children who did and did not participate in the intervention. The children in both groups were well-matched on these cognitive abilities prior to the intervention; however, we saw significant cognitive gains across time only for children in the intervention group.

Experts in many fields routinely show the same kinds of cognitive and learning increases in both skills and knowledge seen in the studies we have presented. In fact, "expertise" is defined according to those benefits. To illustrate, Bedard and Chi (1992) compiled a list of characteristics experts typically show as the result of having learned a certain domain extensively:

- Experts, by definition, know a lot about their domain of expertise.
- Compared to individuals who do not know as much about a topic, experts show evidence of a highly cohesive and complex knowledge base (Gobbo & Chi, 1986; Johnson & Mervis, 1994).
- Experts show clear memory and perceptual advantages for information about their domain of expertise compared to novices (Chi & Koeske, 1983; Johnson & Mervis, 1998; Reingold, Charness, Schultetus, & Stampe, 2001).
- Experts use different processing strategies for domain-related information than do novices (Larkin, McDermott, Simon, & Simon, 1980).

Presumably these expertise advantages lead to the phenomenon that, compared to novices, experts more quickly learn new information in areas about which they already know a lot. It is interesting that children who are learning language show these same kinds of characteristics. Thus, although not typically described in this way, lexical acquisition can be thought of as the development of expertise. We might refer to this as the "Lexpertise" model of word learning. The main tenet of this model is that basic cognitive abilities not only set the stage for word learning to occur but also change in response to that learning, thus creating a dynamic upward spiral that promotes increasingly more efficient future word learning. We are not entirely alone in making the connection between expertise and linguistic proficiency: Wagner and Stanovich (1996) made similar claims with regard to learning to read. What is pertinent to this argument is that Dynamic "Tricky" Mix theory is as well-suited for explaining advances in normal word learning, syntax growth, and reading skills development as for explaining changes associated with expertise.

Syntactic Growth

In large-sample, naturalistic studies of syntax development, a remarkable phenomenon still awaits explanation. By about age 24 months, some children show complexity in syntax far beyond that of their agemates, and far beyond what most theoretical accounts encompass for that age. For example, in Fenson, Dale, Reznick, Bates, and Thal (1994), whereas the top 10% of children raced ahead in multiword combinations and syntactic constructions, the bottom 10% of children have barely progressed in syntax. How is that possible? *Readiness* constraints, which, the literature suggests, should prevent these levels of complex acquisition in the fastest 10% of children until 6 or more months later, are not operating to keep these children's language simple.

One possible solution to this conundrum might be to demonstrate that only those 24-month-old children whose levels of perception, motor planning, pattern detection, selective inhibition, goal-setting and monitoring, and working memory are at a 36-month level or higher can pull off complex syntax. This seems unlikely, however, and another straightforward interpretation is available: For most children, complex syntax foundations are in place long before the children encounter excellent Dynamic Tricky Mix conditions for syntax learning. Experimental, causative studies on syntax acquisition from multiple research groups support the same conclusion. It is the rich, well-specified mix that incorporates the high levels of joint attention, social–emotional engagement, scaffolding dialogue, and few demands for immediate response that propel ordinary 2- to 4-year-old children to learn with extreme rapidity syntactic structures (e.g., passives) that are far ahead of normative expectations (Akhtar & Tomasello, 1997; Baker & Nelson, 1984; Fey, Cleave, & Long, 1997; Nelson, 2000).

In summary, these studies show that remarkable acceleration of vocabulary and grammar acquisition rates can be achieved readily in ordinary 14- to 60-month-old children, across 2–3 month periods under optimal conditions of above-threshold convergences of learning conditions.

IMPLICATIONS FOR WORK WITH ATYPICAL CHILDREN

If we look to create new learning episodes that reflect insights from dynamic systems perspectives, there should be many opportunities to design curricula and interventions for both atypical children and typically developing children. In all cases, the particulars of the "mixes" of systems conditions can be expected to be critical.

In this section we look at the surprising gains made by school-age children with autism spectrum disorder. Both of the studies we briefly review here involved Swedish children who objectively had a history of slow to zero rates of gain over many preschool and early grade years in two communication modes—speech and text.

In these studies, fundamentally new mixes were created in which individual children again and again took the lead in using computer software to create messages. By selecting words from printed displays on the screen, children created text sentences, then the computer displayed sentence meaning through both visual animations and oral Swedish. In these new mixes the teacher's role shifted toward more close observation of the children's interests and communication, along with timely responsive recasts of what the children created, along with emotional and social positivity. The children's monthly rates of gain in literacy accelerated more than 5 times over baseline (control) rates. In Swedish speech, for which the new mixes provided fewer scaffolded challenges than they provided for text challenges, the children also made strong gains. The bottom line for these children with autism spectrum disorder is that after years of extremely slow progress, when new dynamic mixes differed dramatically from what they were already receiving, children demonstrated high potential for progressing at normative rates in both literacy and spoken language (Nelson et al., 1997; Nelson et al., 2001).

NEW, THEORETICALLY GUIDED DIRECTIONS IN SUPPORTING LANGUAGE AND READING DEVELOPMENT

Ideas from DTM theory set up an interesting set of teaching/learning possibilities for accelerating language learning in both typically and atypically developing children. Parents, teachers, aides, and clinicians who are striving to accelerate spoken language or literacy skills in both children without disabilities and those who are far behind in these domains would be wise to combine Launchers (i.e., challenges) that are appropriate for an individual child's Readiness. These Launchers should be mixed dynamically with Enhancers, Adjustment, and Networks conditions into small, ongoing episodes.

One possibility is for parents and practitioners to be aware of a particular child's initial and changing level of knowledge, skills, experience, and interest to create and maintain the most favorable *LEARN* conditions. By remaining committed to continual individual and frequent online assessment, adults can provide tailored, child-specific input that capitalizes on the child's knowledge, cognitive strengths, and interests. An expertise framework (discussed earlier, see Arkenberg, 2006) also may help in creating favorable Adjustment and Network activation, Enhancers, and related conditions by pointing toward contents of a domain in which a child is most expert. When those contents are activated for a child in learning episodes, working memory may quickly retrieve basic information, accompanied by clear organizers with rich associative links. Then, when challenges for potential learning enter working memory, these representations can be more efficiently used in comparison processes leading to detection–abstraction of the new challenging structures (cf. Case, 1998). As an example, consider a child who is interested in, and knows a lot about, dinosaurs as a domain of expertise. Introducing new, difficult syntactic forms in the context of playing with dinosaurs might aid in very rapid syntactic advances. Sentences with easily activated lexical items about dinosaurs would reduce overall processing load, allowing most of the child's online processing resources to be used in abstraction and encoding of new syntactic structures.

Leveraging Higher-Order Skills from One Domain to Support Other Domains

Once language and literacy skills are both framed in terms of expertise theories, it becomes natural to look outside those domains for expertise that a child may already possess that might somehow facilitate teaching of communication skills. The potential for interesting transfer would be especially high once a child has reached a level of expertise in which all the following hold true:

- Great depth of knowledge
- Rich and rapidly retrievable organizational schemes
- An extensive and flexible toolkit of strategies
- Higher-order planning and monitoring of plans

This package of characteristics is very similar to what Nelson and Nelson (1978) discussed as "Stage 5: Flexible Extension" for the acquisition of complex systems. These authors also stressed that strong individual differences in the relative pace of moving through varied domains, such as narrative, syntax, vocabulary, music, and mathematics, would set up the likelihood that one child might achieve powerful transfer from advanced levels in one domain that would be entirely different than the source of high transfer for another child.

How might such potential transfer be set up in school settings for children who are far behind in literacy, spoken language, or both? For a child with "incidental expertise"—incidental in the sense that it would not usually be brought into serious instructional planning, for example, in drawing or music—the most complex performance levels in the expert domain might be shared with the class or with just a dyadic teaching partner. Then the ways that the child narrates orally and in text could be demonstrated in relation to a drawing or musical sequence, providing a basis for teaching more complex reading, writing, and oral storytelling, with their accompanying lexical and syntactical complexities. Using and reflecting on the higher-order plans and monitoring the already-expert domain may guide and motivate aspects of the child's progress toward spoken and/or written language. This appears rarely to have been attempted in preschool or school settings.

Looking from another angle, the domain of oral language often may leverage literacy advances. Spira, Bracken, and Fischel (2005) provide one relevant set of data (cf. Scarborough, 2001). They show that there are strong Readiness differences in a broad range of oral language skills among children with significant reading disability (RD) at Grade 1, and that progress in overcoming reading disability by grade 4 is significantly associated with such language Readiness over and above grade 1 reading scores.

The Value of Exploring High Challenge in Dramatically New Tricky Mixes

Many of the studies we reviewed earlier showed that a variety of children were capable of learning complex challenges at remarkably high rates compared with their nil or low rates for seemingly simple challenges. Two-year-olds readily learn passives that 10-year-olds may more typically still be acquiring, but only when an experiment or a culture provides the younger children with meaningful, conversationally embedded, well-mixed social learning encounters (Allen & Crago, 1996; Nelson et al., 2004). These passive-competent 2-year-olds deliver multiple important and surprising conclusions:

- They demonstrate Readiness in terms of brain maturation, prior linguistic structures, memory, attention, processing speed, rapid speech processing, and other necessary cognitive systems to extract passive structures from ongoing receptive language, and subsequently incorporate them in their speech output.
- This high potential for processing and learning is mobilized effectively when social–emotional positive conditions and Enhancing dialogue accompany a wide range of passive sentences used by their conversational partners.

The same set of conclusions also applies to 6-year-olds with severe language impairments (language age of 3 years), who participated in 10–40 hours of newly-mixed, focused conversations designed to facilitate acquisition of passives, relative clauses, gerunds, and other complex syntactic structures (e.g., Nelson et al., 2001, 2004).

These examples should help motivate us as researchers, teachers, and clinicians to look skeptically at our typical assessments and insights for estimating the potential of children with and without disabilit,y and what "zones of challenge" may be within their processing reach. Once we try new challenging mixes with rich Enhancers and see a particular 2- or 10-year-old enjoying the process of moving rapidly ahead in reading, spelling, writing, speaking, or listening–comprehending, then our "playing field" of possible favorable learning procedures and contexts expands enormously.

High or low challenges in a mix no doubt interact in complex ways with the expectancies, emotions, and social processes that evolve over many episodes of potential engagement with a learning partner. A child who is learning over many episodes but realizes (as does the teacher) that she or he is creeping along may have a fairly low excitement and attention level. When a greater range of challenge levels is mixed in, and the child and the teacher come to recognize that the child is learning many of the most complex challenges easily, then motivation, anticipation, and enjoyment all may spiral upward in ways that make the online mix during instruction highly positive and convergent. Over weeks and months, this may result in learning that is dramatically greater than what we would have seen in a more traditional instructional scenario.

An implication of the "trickiness" of establishing a mix of learning conditions to support an individual child's development may be seen in the usual preschool conditions; that is, many children at different skills' levels have just one teacher and one aide. If the adults use a narrow set of strategies for interaction, with a narrow focus on a few skills considered interesting and appropriate, then it is extremely unlikely that very many children will receive optimal learning conditions. As Dickinson et al. (2005) observed relative to usual preschool settings, "Indications are that far too few children receive the type of support for language and literacy development that is associated with optimal growth" (p. 214).

In their own research with an intervention termed the Literacy Environment Enrichment Program, Dickinson et al. (2005) trained and coached teachers on an expanded set of strategies incorporating multiple challenge components. These components included phonological awareness, vocabulary, reading dialogues, and emergent writing. From the DTM perspective, within the expanded set of challenges and teacher strategies, teachers create new mixes of conditions, thus enhancing the probability that a particular child receives a mix that substantially impacts learning. Results indicated that, on average, over and above learning rates in comparison preschools, there were enhancements for children's vocabulary, phonological awareness, and early literacy. Similarly impressive gains in early academic skills, together with gains as well in social–emotional skills, have been shown by 4- to-5-year-old Head Start children in a project that trained teachers explicitly on strategies for facilitating language, literacy, and social–emotional skills (Bierman et al., 2007; in press). Beyond encouraging demonstrations of this kind, we believe that a further level of intervention effectiveness is likely when repeated rounds of coaching and monitoring more directly assess and try to perturb ongoing dynamic mixes. In the next section we discuss some possibilities.

Moving toward Optimal Mixes

A Scenario

Consider 20 different children in a grade 2 classroom, each of whom is 2 years behind norms in both reading and oral language. From dynamic systems perspectives, we can predict that many of the particular mixes of learning conditions include challenges that are productive for one child and a waste of time for other children, because they already know what is being presented, or because other conditions do not converge adequately to support processing of relevant challenges.

This kind of limitation holds true for the mapping of new text to existing vocabulary, for the learning of new vocabulary and syntax, and for the learning of new narrative and composition skills. Another limitation is that because expertise begets new knowledge, children who are already significantly behind in communication skills tend to have a disadvantage in learning rates compared to children already at or above norms. This is similar to the idea that the rich get richer and the poor get poorer—deemed the "Matthew effect" by Stanovich (1986).Together these considerations might lead one to an extremely pessimistic view concerning communicative progress for children with RD and/or language impairment. However, if traditional ways of teaching are transformed in multiple ways, the prognosis for such children becomes far more positive.

Mixes of Innovative Procedural Moves

To create online interactive dynamic mixes that contribute to rapid learning by children, a combination of procedural moves requires attention. Four of these moves are presented:

1. Better monitoring of what each child already knows is essential. This serves as a base for small- or large-group planning that minimizes "false-teaching" activities, in which all the targeted structures

are already known to all the children. Clearly, rich monitoring will also support 1-1 or 2-1 teaching episodes in which there is substantial tailoring of challenges in phonological awareness, vocabulary, syntax, and narrative to children's existing repertoires.

2. Mistrust any single way of teaching. Instead deploy exploration and effectiveness monitoring of at least two distinct ways of teaching toward the same challenges.
3. The choices of ways of teaching under trial also should include tailoring to what is known about the social, motivational, emotional, and cognitive conditions that have so far been monitored as being relatively high in supporting an individual child's engagement and learning. In this regard, new teaching research could build on findings such as those of Ladd, Birch, and Buhs (1999), who found that kindergarten achievement was influenced by teacher–child relationships, peer relationships, child participation patterns, and child cognitive maturity.
4. These tailorings, and the monitoring of their effectiveness, should evolve, so that what is least effective in Time 1 monitoring is replaced by new distinct mixes of conditions in Time 2 (e.g., the next month's teaching), and the majority of teaching practices in place are producing better learning than in the prior period.

When implemented, all of these innovations dramatically improve the likelihood that, over time, children's growth rates will accelerate. Moreover, to the extent that the convergent mix of learning conditions achieved in classrooms becomes as positive as those observed under favorable experimental conditions documented in the literature, it is predictable that despite poor prior histories of learning text and oral language, many children with communicative disabilities may learn at very high rates. Levels of 20–50 words per day for new oral and text vocabulary should be approached for 6- to 9-year-olds. These speculative rates are high compared with what has been observed to date in most classrooms, but the multiple theory-based innovations described would create learning mixes that would be new and powerful. Though less precisely anchored in prior literature, very high rates of learning for new syntactic and narrative structures, and fluent comprehension of connected text and oral discourse should also be achievable.

In summary, for children at high risk for, or already demonstrating, impairments in language or reading, there is a strong basis for expecting improvements in learning that lead many children into normative and above-normative rates of skills acquisition. This has been achieved and reported in short-term studies in the literature (Dickinson et al., 2005; Nelson et al., 1996, 2001, 2004; Torgeson et al., 1997). For broader-scale and longer-term successes, we argue that we have specified the foundation for theoretically guided multiple innovations. The goal is to bring far more children into learning contexts that provide a very high frequency of learning challenges, accompanied by all the other, needed interactive, dynamic conditions that support highly efficient and often-optimal processing and learning.

NEW THEORETICALLY GUIDED DIRECTIONS IN ASSESSMENT

In typical preschool and school settings, assessments before instruction begins are exceedingly thin. Only a few potentially relevant skills are examined at all, and these are only narrowly tested by a single examiner in a decontextualized fashion. Instruction in reading or oral language most often provides the same instructional episodes to all children in a class. When finer-grained instruction is arranged, it is based upon two or three levels of perceived skill in different subgroups of children who may receive different books, games, drills, or other activities, roughly dependent on their perceived skills levels. From a DTM perspective, this set of procedures is virtually guaranteed to lead to low probabilities of engaging very many children in instructional mixes that approach optimum motivational or learning efficiency characteristics.

The Nature of Assessments

Consider first the nature of assessments. Dynamic systems theories hold strongly that if a child "knows" and in one context can deploy some part of language, say, a noun phrase or a syllable, or a vocabulary item such as "unicorn," whether the child will be able to achieve online, timely, and appropriate use in a new context is a complex proposition. Thus, if a child passes an item on a language or reading subtest administered in standard, decontextualized fashion by a single tester, we should expect—particularly for recently acquired skills—high variability in deployment. Variables dynamically interacting to produce this variation are the dynamic systems variables we have so far discussed (e.g., Adjustment socially and emotionally, Enhancers, and current Neural Networks activation).

Other difficulties arise from assessments that indicate a lack of language or reading skills in a child. Based upon narrow assessment, a child may receive instruction on all skills not demonstrated in the assessment. However, this instructional effort may be wasted if most of the skills were already in place but just not demonstrated under the particular dynamic conditions of testing.

Assessment Mixes

Taken together, the inherent risks of either underestimating or overestimating the child's current skills repertoire from typical assessment procedures imply that multiple changes would work toward better learning opportunities for children with and without language and reading difficulties. Some recommendations follow:

1. Assessments should always be viewed as subject to dynamic conditions, and should be broadened to include sharply contrasting testing packages—different testers, physical and social contexts, and interactive patterns between the child and testers.
2. Instruction should continue to examine and to contrast, as argued elsewhere, different instructional packages that try to achieve positive dynamic mixes through different pathways.
3. Instructional phases should try to move new oral and text representations for a child from initial deployment in whatever context proves feasible to increasingly rapid, fluent, flexible deployment across multiple social partners, multimedia formats, and communicative goals.
4. It can be expected that the particular pathways to a child's achievement of such consolidated and flexible communicative skills will be dramatically different for many children in terms of how social–motivational engagement is achieved and what scaffolding activity patterns contribute efficiently to a child's progress. As a consequence, a necessity will be frequent monitoring and *Adjustment* of both social–emotional processes and specific, presumed cognitive-processing facilitators or *Enhancers* throughout instructional phases.

THE CENTRALITY OF INTERACTIONS

We have incorporated in the previous discussions the importance of interactions from a number of different theoretical and practical angles. Here it is appropriate to highlight and contrast seven types of interactions.

Biology by Experience

Biological makeup at every point in development interacts with experience. For children who are progressing well, and for children who are not, there is still a great deal to be learned about how individual differences in (partly) biologically based *Readiness* characteristics, such as attention, memory, pattern detection, and planning, interact with individuals' experience to produce development. In many instances, we have seen that for children with learning difficulties, however, when new experience in rich transactional, dynamic mixes was provided with some rigor, children's demonstrated bursts in learning rates forced a reappraisal of levels of biological *Readiness* that were already in place but underestimated prior to enriched intervention.

Dynamic Systems Frameworks of Interacting Conditions

Dynamic systems theories argue that systems for performance and learning are inherently dynamic interactions of multiple, complex, nonlinear factors that frequently move from chaotic states to structured states, and back again. Part of the emphasis provided by the variant on these theories we have presented, the Dynamic Tricky Mix theory, is on the "trickiness" of moving into and maintaining (with reasonable probability, but not certainty) well-structured positive mixes of conditions that support learning. To cross the *threshold* into learning, one crucial level of real-time interaction is to "mix" is enough convergence of social–emotional and cognitive–linguistic factors. Beyond that level, increasingly positive interactions, with highly favorable levels of many variables and well-timed dynamic convergences, can lead to increasingly high rates of learning. These rates may approach the *maximum*, optimal level achievable given the individual learner's current state of *Readiness*.

What is already in the child's head, as we have seen in many experimental demonstrations, is very often sufficient as a foundation of *Readiness* for progress in language or literacy, even for children with a poor history of progress that qualifies them for disability status in either or both of these areas. Multiple projects have shown that children far behind in communication do learn at normative rates, and sometimes even faster than matched comparison children with disabilities, when new learning mixes bring substantial challenges into episodes that also carry positive tone, social–emotional engagement, and scaffolds for processing. In *Readiness* terms, it has been demonstrated that children with deafness and autism, as well as those with dual deficits in language and literacy, can progress in literacy without waiting for new progress in vocabulary and syntax (Nelson et al., 1997, 2001). Similarly, children with specific language impairment progress under new, conversationally engaging mixes without first requiring any advances in their current auditory processing skills or working memory abilities (Nelson, 2000; Fey et al., 1997). Thus, applied progress can move in coordinated fashion with theoretical progress. By taking clues from very diverse methodologies and instructional frameworks, the field can use much more brainstorming of particular new mixes of learning conditions, with close monitoring of both engagement processes and learning advances.

Complex Perturbation Effects

DTM theory organizes learning conditions according to five categories (with some admitted overlap), each of which must contribute positively to produce any convergence that leads to learning. These five spell the acronym, LEARN (see Figure 11.1). The account given here and in other writings, however, needs some future elaboration along the lines of yet another kind of interaction pattern. As a potential learning episode unfolds, the five broad LEARN categories of functional activation—Launchers, Enhancers, Adjustment, Readiness, and Neural Networks—interact. As one category shifts level when a perturbation is encountered, it not only contributes differently to new rounds of online mixes with other conditions, but it also often indirectly influences better mixes by interacting with the levels of other factors. Let us say that an adept social, humorous move by a teacher impacts the child's Adjustment socially and emotionally toward greater positivity. This change may lead rapidly to new Network activations of long-term language representations that are most relevant to challenges being presented in reading by the teacher. So, in the next few minutes after the child's Adjustment level shifts, the Network activations also shift, and the overall dynamic mix of conditions is doubly "tricked" toward a higher probability that reading challenges will be processed and learned.

On the applied, practical side, it is of great interest to look for any innovations in teaching or context arrangement that may lead to double- or triple-"whammy" effects on multiple conditions and their overall convergence to support learning. Similarly, on the theoretical side, it is important to provide refined accounts of how these kinds of interactions are created, which of them have the most impact on learning, and which real-time neural mechanisms parallel and support them.

Learning Cycles across Many Learning Days

Another level of interactions occurs when we examine relationships between current episodes of learning encounters and either earlier episodes or those that follow by weeks or months. The possible dynamic mixes of conditions in current episodes interact with what mixes have occurred; what learning took place; and what attitudes, expectations, or emotions shifted in recent episodes in a similar context, with similar partners and learning challenges. The child as learner and social partner, and the teacher as instructor and social partner often shift patterns that tend to promote increasingly positive or increasingly negative probabilities of new episodes with a positive DTM.

We see the importance of monitored learning cycles across time in cases when children's biological readiness appears low in some important processing capacity. For instance, let us suppose that a particular child with significant language delay also displays definite impairments in working memory during language processing. An effective dynamic mix shifts other conditions during conversation, so that, despite the memory limitation, learning of new language structures occurs. The theory emphasizes that new mixes may be created in multiple ways, and that only monitoring can determine whether an attempted mix actually promotes learning for an individual child. Enhancers that could be tried would include "priming" already known language structures by redundancy in a short stretch of conversation. Within these priming stretches of conversation, presentation of challenging structures would also occur. Thus, the child's system potentially can more easily handle old meanings/structures using fewer memory resources, so that more memory resources are devoted to analyzing and encoding new language structures. For a particular child, however, this particular attempted enhancement might have no impact unless it is dynamically combined in the same stretches of conversation with high-interest topics and multiple recasts/paraphrases, and somewhat slower speech by the child's conversational partner. Monitoring variations along these lines, and their impact on engagement and learning by the child, are crucial to finding what mixes of new conditions interact productively with the child's current cognitive capacities.

Interactions across Domains and Subdomains of Expertise

Children's progress toward expert levels often shows highly uneven profiles for different domains. Similar unevenness is evident whenever close analysis is provided, as in microgenetic studies of levels of expertise in different subdomains, such as the lexicon, grammar, writing, reading, music, mathematics, chess, or art. Examination of learning from the point of both larger and smaller branches of many varied domains allows for increasing specificity, as well as generality in thinking about the mechanisms of development in areas such as vocabulary and reading. More work on cross-domain interactions and individual paths is needed, particularly for the higher levels of expertise within a domain. It is at these higher levels of domain mastery that one can see the greatest potential for powerful transfer processes concerning organization, mindfulness, strategies, planning, monitoring, and editing. Multiple theoretical ideas relevant to the discussion of these issues were provided by Nelson and Nelson (1978), who speculated:

> we have made clear for each of the systems separately, and also for the patterns among the systems of relative acceleration or delay (e.g., discourse rules far ahead, far behind, or on a par with sentence rules), that there are strong individual differences which eventually need explicit theoretical de-

> scription. The other kind of question that our account leads toward is the question of how the child uses available evidence to make the transitions between successive stage levels. Our theory implies that such processes of transition could look quite different for the child's different systems at any one point in general cognitive development, particularly if some systems have already reached the next-to-final stage when other systems are at one of the first two stages. (p. 275)

Complex Interactions of Foundational Cognitive and Emotional and Social Processes

In many respects the literature on correlates and apparent underpinnings of children's mastery of important developmental achievements in language and in literacy is "too good"; that is, there are so many reasonable, evidence-based variables that correlate with communicative progress when group designs and statistics are employed that designing interventions for children in developmental trouble or at risk for delay might seem very daunting. Intervening on all apparently relevant cognitive and language processes appears to be beyond the scope of anyone's resources, and choosing instead a small and feasible set of variables for intervention appears to require improved theoretical grounding to become an approach that might work for most or all children.

This set of circumstances leads us to return to the observation that children's demonstrated bursts in learning rates under multiple, theoretically guided causal experiments force a reappraisal of what levels of biological *Readiness* were already in place but underestimated prior to enriched intervention. This point requires some elaboration.

In the studies reviewed earlier demonstrating that children with a history of extremely poor progress in literacy and/or language do learn at or above normative rates with new dynamic mixes—child-focused challenges, together with social–emotional positivity and interactional processing supports relevant to the challenges—insight is provided into three levels of common misassumption about these children with "learning disabilities." First, without waiting for greater maturation or new cognitive skills, children can reach developmental levels that are substantially above levels at which they may have plateaued for months or years. Second, multiple assumed, possible prerequisites turn out not to be true prerequisites for progress, because many or most children proceed without those typically correlated cognitive or communicative skills in place. Third, the rate at which progress can occur is far beyond what was seen in the past for these children or expected by school or clinical plans.

Future research could build foundations for designing even better new mixes of conditions by directly addressing the social–emotional *Adjustment* processes. For example, more attention could be given to the work of Pianta and colleagues (e.g., Hamre & Pianta, 2001) and their overall finding that positive teacher–child relationships in the early school years are associated with children's academic gains across multiple years of school.

Contextual Savvy Interacting with All Other Learning Conditions

Children who possess more text skills, who feel more confident in a particular assessment or teaching context, and who have well-established, expert-level "context scripts" are more likely to display their current skills effectively in tests or to engage their current skills more effectively in active comparisons to new challenges in teaching episodes. It is important to see that the scripts children acquire about contexts will powerfully interact with other conditions to affect their performance.

An interesting demonstration of this phenomenon is provided by Gee (1997) for reading test contexts for undergraduates. Honors undergraduates showed how much they knew about the expected frameworks for reading comprehension passages and questions when they were given the Educational Testing Service (ETS) multiple-choice questions, without glance at the relevant text passage. They correctly sorted out most of the answers based upon general scripts! There is little doubt that, at every level from kindergarten on, there is rich opportunity for such context scripts sometimes to conceal what has really been comprehended or learned. Yet with explicit attention to such scripts, there may also be many occasions when new learning may be facilitated by emphasizing how new challenges fit within an already familiar framework.

CONCLUSIONS

Oral, written, and sign communication are inherently complex and dynamic, integrating a rich variety of social, emotional, motivational, cultural, attitudinal, linguistic, and cognitive–information-processing components. Understanding how typically and atypically developing children proceed through the stages of acquisition in language and literacy requires that these more complex, dynamic, real-time processes be more richly documented than they have been in prior literature. However, we have shown that we already know enough to enrich theoretical accounts and innovations in education.

Research has demonstrated that by rearranging the mixes of conditions present in child–adult interactions, some startling accelerations of children's progress in language and literacy often can occur, without waiting for the acquisition of presumably prerequisite skills levels in cognition. Children—whether typically developing children or those with language delay, autism, deafness, or motor difficulties—often can "do more with less"; that is, they can achieve excellent rates of progress in language or reading or writing, with less memory, attention, or other skills than are assumed necessary by much theory and educational practice.

The DTM model calls attention to complex issues in assessing children's skills. In test-taking contexts, there is a high risk of a child demonstrating less complex performance than his or her current skills set could support under different contextual conditions.

A third strand of emphasis is that much can be gained by looking at communication domains in terms of the acquisition of expertise. Doing so helps to shift preschool and school curriculum goals away from possibly arbitrary educational objectives, toward flexible skills in language production and comprehension, and in reading and writing. This "expertise" perspective invites the implementation of some high standards of communication skills that would have to be assessed in real-time communication performance. In addition, the perspective raises expectations. Put bluntly, may we dare to expect that by adolescence, all, or nearly all, children are capable of reaching high expertise levels in all the above domains for first language and also in at least one second language?

Fortunately, the feasibility of future achievement for these kinds of expert levels appears much enhanced by findings discussed within the DTM theoretical perspective. It is fully predictable from this theory that with a one-teacher, one-curriculum approach for language or literacy for 30 children in a class, there will be extensive portions of a day when each child will encounter no mixes of learning conditions that reach a needed threshold for learning to begin. Furthermore, it is predictable that even when learning does occur, the mixes present will be far below optimal for a child most of the time. From the DTM perspective it appears unlikely that any strong shift toward optimal learning rates will be achieved by trying to refine testing of cognitive and language components in decontextualized, brief procedures and to couple such test results to any one-size-fits-all curriculum that presents step-by-step, small incremental challenges in language or literacy. Instead, moving more children toward excellent skills levels in all modes of communication will require assessment, initial teaching attempts, and continued monitoring and revision of teaching–learning procedures that jointly take into account individual differences in children and teachers, and the power of theoretical models, such as "expertise" and dynamic systems, to frame innovations.

CURRENT LIMITATIONS AND FUTURE DIRECTIONS

Every theory has its limitations and the DTM theoretical perspective is no exception. Current challenges include the need for researchers and practitioners more often to take seriously the claim that individual, frequent, online assessment of engagement, coupled with individualized and frequently adjusted lessons/scaffolds that capitalize on a child's interests, talents, and readiness, may be keys to achieving optimal or near-optimal communicative growth. We agree that this often is a daunting task even for an individual working with one child, let alone a classroom full of children. At the same time, in future work, there are potentially very high payoffs from this approach. By identifying which episodes of teaching are not highly effective, and why, then the same resources can then be applied to create substantially more positive impacts on motivation, initial learning, and generalized flexible use of knowledge and skills.

Further possibilities arise, particularly relative to which dynamic assessments and adjustments occur. Continual improvements in computerized technology provide headway toward allowing intensive assessments of learning progress and minute-by-minute adjustments in teaching/presentation strategies. Yet everyday teaching practice seldom employs these tools, and it almost never links this kind of information dynamically to how motivation, learner attitudes and theories, and social–emotional adjustment converge, or fail to converge, with presented challenges to the learner.

As mentioned earlier, the DTM theory is not without limitations. DTM is a general theory of learning, yet it has been applied to a relatively small set of populations and, within those populations, to relatively few participants. Thus far, systematic investigations have focused on small groups of middle-income, developmentally normal preschoolers; children with specific language impairment; or children with autism spectrum disorders. With only a few studies that attempt to test the limits of DTM, the ability to generalize to other populations, including children living in poverty, is still quite limited. In addition, investigation of DTM has been limited to specific aspects of literacy and language acquisition, such as early stages of reading, lexical learning, and the acquisition of specifically targeted syntactic structures. To demonstrate DTM is a widely useful explanatory theory, investigations into more varied linguistic and nonlinguistic domains need to be undertaken. In addition, DTM is still in development, and LEARN components are sometimes underspecified in any particular study. For example, Adjustment conditions may be interpreted as applying to how a child is regulating emotions during a learning episode, or to changes in how a child feels about the learning material, yet individual studies have not yet monitored both of these possibilities. One strength is that DTM attempts to explain learning and to describe the components that factor dynamically into that learning, and this heuristically has led to monitoring of multiple conditions as the learning itself is occurring within episodes. This same strength of drawing attention to components and their measurement dynamically could also be extended to how favorable convergences of learning conditions occur across cycles of many learning episodes. However, this strength also places restrictions on the type and extent of investigation that can feasibly be performed in particular everyday contexts. Investigation of multiple online conditions may be difficult or impossible to study on the time scale that DTM proposes, because either the methods and tools of assessment are difficult to employ in usual learning scenarios, or the time it would take for teachers and investigators to assess each component at enough moments in time is simply unrealistic when average learning, rather than individual child performance, is the primary focus.

Despite these limitations, experiments that have addressed multiple LEARN components as part of their methods have shown dramatic results in terms of children's learning capacities. These high learning rates suggest that although DTM theory may not yet be fully elaborated or complete, it has the potential to make important contributions to advances in learning.

REFERENCES

Aitchison, J. (2003). *Words in the mind: An introduction to the mental lexicon* (3rd ed.). Cambridge, MA: Blackwell.

Akhtar, N., & Tomasello, M. (1997). Young children's productivity with word order and verb morphology. *Developmental Psychology, 33*, 952–965.

Allen, S., & Crago, M. (1996). Early passive acquisition in Inuktitut. *Journal of Child Language, 23*, 952–965.

Anglin, J. M. (1993). Knowing versus learning words. *Monographs of the Society for Research in Child Development, 58*, 176–186.

Arkenberg, M. E. (2006). *Children's lexical expertise*. Unpublished doctoral dissertation, University Park, PA: Pennsylvania State University.

Baker, N. D., & Nelson, K. E. (1984). Recasting and related conversational techniques for triggering syntactic advances by young children. *First Language, 5*, 3–22.

Bedard, J., & Chi, M. T. H. (1992). Expertise. *Current Directions in Psychological Science, 1*, 135–139.

Bierman, K. L., Domitrovich, C. E., Gest, S. D., Welsh, J. A., Nix, R. L., Greenberg, M. T., et al. (2007, April). *Promoting school readiness among economically disadvantaged preschoolers: Initial outcomes of Head Start REDI*. Paper presented at the Society for Research in Child Development, Boston, MA.

Bierman, K. L., Domitrovich, C. E., Gest, S. D., Welsh, J. A., Nix, R. L., Greenberg, M. T., Blair, C., Nelson, K. E., & Gill, S., et al. (in press). *Child development*.

Butterfield, B., & Mangels, J. A. (2003). Neural correlates of error detection and correction in a semantic retrieval task. *Cognitive Brain Research, 17*, 793–817.

Calvin, W. H. (1990). *The cerebral symphony*. New York: Bantam.

Camarata, S., Nelson, K. E., & Camarata, M. (1994). A comparison of conversation based to imitation based procedures for training grammatical structures in specifically language impaired children. *Journal of Speech and Hearing Research, 37*, 1414–1423.

Case, R. (1998). The development of conceptual structures. In D. Kuhn & R. S. Siegler (Eds.), *Handbook of child psychology: Vol. 2. Cognition, perception, and language* (5th ed., pp. 745–800). New York: Wiley.

Chi, M. T. H., & Koeske, R. D. (1983). Network representation of a child's dinosaur knowledge. *Developmental Psychology, 19*, 29–39.

Dale, P. S., & Fenson, L. (1996). Lexical development norms for young children. *Behavior Research Methods, Instruments, and Computers, 28*, 125–127.

Damasio, A. (1994). *Descartes' error: Emotion, reason and the human brain.* New York: Putnam.

de Sousa, I., & Oakhill, J. (1996). Do levels of interest have an effect on children's comprehension monitoring performance? *British Journal of Educational Psychology, 66*, 471–482.

Dickinson, D. K., McCabe, A., Clark-Chiarelli, N. (2004). Preschool-based prevention of reading disability: Realities versus possibilities. In C. A. Stone & E. R. Silliman (Eds.), *Handbook of language and literacy: Development and disorders* (pp. 209–227). Mahwah, NJ: Erlbaum.

Dweck, C. S. (1999). *Self-theories: Their role in motivation, personality, and development.* Philadelphia: Taylor & Francis/Psychology Press.

Dweck, C. S., & Leggett, E. L. (1988). A social-cognitive approach to motivation and personality. *Psychological Review, 95*, 256–273.

Dweck, C. S., Mangels, J. A., & Good, C. (2004). Motivational effects on attention, cognition, and performance. In D. Y. Dai & R. J. Sternberg (Eds.), *Motivation, emotion, and cognition: Integrative perspectives on intellectual functioning and development.* Mahwah, NJ: Erlbaum.

Elliot, E. S., & Dweck, C. S. (1988). Goals: An approach to motivation and achievement. *Journal of Personality and Social Psychology, 54*, 5–12.

Elman, J. L., Bates, E. A., Johnson, M. H., Karmiloff-Smith, A., Parisi, D., & Plunkett, K. (1996). *Rethinking innateness: A connectionist perspective on development.* Cambridge, MA: MIT Press.

Fenson, L., Dale, P. A., Reznick, J. S., Bates, E., & Thal, D. (1994). Variability in early communicative development. *Monographs of the Society for Research in Child Development, 58.*

Fey, M., Cleave, P., & Long, S. (1997). Two models of grammar facilitation in children with language impairments: Phase 2. *Journal of Speech, Language, and Hearing Research, 40*, 5–19.

Flavell, J. H. (1979). Metacognition and comprehension monitoring: A new area of cognitive–developmental inquiry. *American Psychologist, 34*, 906–911.

Hamre, B. K., & Pianta, R. C. (2001). Early teacher–child relationships and the trajectory of children's school outcomes through eight grade. *Child Development, 72*, 625–638.

Hart, B., & Risley, T. R. (1999). *The social world of children: Learning to talk.* Baltimore: Brookes.

Johns, J. L. (1979). The growth of children's knowledge about spoken words. *Reading Psychology, 1*, 103–110.

Johnson, K. E., & Mervis, C. B. (1994). Microgenetic analysis of first steps in children's acquisition of expertise on shorebirds. *Developmental Psychology, 30*, 418–435.

Johnson, K. E., & Mervis, C. B. (1998). Impact on intuitive theories on feature recruitment throughout the continuum of expertise. *Memory and Cognition, 26*, 382–401.

Ladd, G. W., Birch, S. H., & Buhs, E. S. (1999). Children's social and scholastic lives in kindergarten: Related spheres of influence? *Child Development, 70*, 1373–1400.

Larkin, J., McDermott, J., Simon, D. P., & Simon, H. A. (1980). Expert and novice performance in solving physics problems. *Science, 208*, 1335–1342.

LeDoux, J. E. (2000). Emotion circuits in the brain. *Annual Review of Neuroscience, 23*, 155–184.

Lepper, M., Woolverton, M., Mumme, D. L., & Gurtner, J. L. (1993). Motivational techniques of expert human tutors: Lessons for the design of computer-based tutors. In S. P. Lajoie & S. J. Derry (Eds.), *Computers as cognitive tools* (pp. 75–105). Hillsdale, NJ: Erlbaum.

Mangels, J. A., Butterfield, B., Lamb, J., Good, C., & Dweck, C. S. (2006). Why do beliefs about intelligence influence learning success? A social cognitive neuroscience model. *Social Cognitive and Affective Neuroscience, 1*, 75–86.

National Reading Panel. (2000). *Report of the National Reading Panel: Teaching children to read: Reports of the subgroup*. Washington, DC: National Institute of Child Health and Human Development.

Nelson, K. E. (1987). Some observations from the perspective of the rare event cognitive comparison theory of language acquisition. In K. E. Nelson (Ed.), *Children's language* (Vol. 6, pp. 289–331). Hillsdale, NJ: Erlbaum.

Nelson, K. E. (1989). Strategies for first language teaching. In M. Rice & R. Schiefelbusch (Eds.), *The teachability of language* (pp. 263–310). Baltimore: Brookes.

Nelson, K. E. (1998). Toward a differentiated account of facilitators of literacy development and ASL in deaf children. *Topics in Language Disorders, 18*, 73–88.

Nelson, K. E. (2000). Methods for stimulating and measuring lexical and syntactic advances: Why Fiffins and lobsters can tag along with other recast friends. In L. Menn & N. B. Ratner (Eds.), *Methods for studying language production* (pp. 115–148). Hillsdale, NJ: Erlbaum.

Nelson, K. E. (2001). Dynamic Tricky Mix theory suggests multiple analyzed pathways (MAPS) as an intervention approach for children with autism and other language delays. In S. von Tetzchner & J. Clibbens (Eds.), *Understanding the theoretical and methodological bases of augmentative and alternative communication* (pp. 141–159). Toronto: International Society for Augmentative and Alternative Communication.

Nelson, K. E., & Bonvillian, J. D. (1978). Early language development: Conceptual growth and related processes between 2 and 4½ years of age. In K. E. Nelson (Ed.), *Children's language* (Vol. 1, pp. 467–556). New York: Gardner Press.

Nelson, K. E., Camarata, S. M., Welsh, J., Butkovsky, L., & Camarata, M. (1996). Effects of imitative and conversational recasting treatment on the acquisition of grammar in children with specific language impairment and younger language-normal children. *Journal of Speech and Hearing Research, 39*, 850–859.

Nelson, K. E., Craven, P. L., Xuan, Y., & Arkenberg, M. E. (2004). Acquiring art, spoken language, sign language, text, and other symbolic systems: Developmental and evolutionary observations from a Dynamic Tricky Mix theoretical perspective. In J. M. Lucariello, J. A. Harris, R. Fivush, & P. J. Bauer (Eds.), *The development of the mediated mind: Sociocultural context and cognitive development* (pp. 175–222). Mahwah, NJ: Erlbaum.

Nelson, K. E., Heimann, M., & Tjus, T. (1997). Theoretical and applied insights from multimedia facilitation of communication skills in children with autism, deaf children, and children with motor or learning disabilities. In L. B. Adamson & M. A. Romski (Eds.), *Research on communication and language disorders: Contributions to theories of language development* (pp. 296–325). Baltimore: Brookes.

Nelson, K. E., & Nelson, K. (1978). Cognitive pendulums and their linguistic realization. In K. E. Nelson (Ed.), *Children's language* (Vol. 1, pp. 223–286). Hillsdale, NJ: Erlbaum.

Nelson, K. E., Welsh, J., Camarata, S., Heimann, M. & Tjus, T. (2001). A rare event transactional dynamic model of tricky mix conditions contributing to language acquisition and varied communicative delays. In K. E. Nelson, A. Koc, & C. Johnson (Eds.), *Children's language* (Vol. 11, pp. 165–195). Hillsdale, NJ: Erlbaum.

Reingold, E. M., Charness, N., Schultetus, R. S., & Stampe, D. M. (2001). Perceptual automaticity in expert chess players: Parallel encoding. *Psychonomic Bulletin and Review, 8*, 504–510.

Rogoff, B., Turkanis, C. G., & Bartlett, L. (2001). *Learning together: Children and adults in a school community.* New York: Oxford University Press.

Scarborough, H. (2001). Connecting early language and literacy to later reading (dis)abilities: Evidence, theory, and practice. In S. B. Neuman & D. K. Dickinson (Eds.), *Handbook of early literacy research* (pp. 97–110). New York: Guilford Press.

Smith, L. B., Jones, S., S, Landau, B., Gershkoff-Stowe, L., & Samuelson, L. (2002). Object name learning provides on-the-job training for attention. *Psychological Science, 13*, 13–19.

Smith, M. E. (1926). An investigation of the development of the sentence and the extent of vocabulary in young children. *University of Iowa Studies in Child Welfare, 3*(5), 92.

Spira, E. G., Bracken, S. S., & Fischel, J. E. (2005). Predicting improvement after first-grade reading difficulties: The effects of oral language, emergent literacy, and behavior skills. *Developmental Psychology, 41*, 225–234.

Stanovich, K. E. (1986). Matthew effects in reading: Some consequences for individual differences in the acquisition of literacy. *Reading Research Quarterly, 21*, 360–406.

Thelen, E., & Smith, L. B. (2006). Dynamic systems theories. In R. M. Lerner (Ed.), *Handbook of child psychology. Volume I. Theoretical models of human development* (pp. 258–312). New York: Wiley.

Torgeson, J. K., Wagner, R. K., & Rashotte, C. A. (1997). Foundations of reading acquisition and dyslexia: Implications for early intervention. In B. A. Blachman (Ed.), *Foundations of reading acquisition and dyslexia: Implications for intervention*. Mahwah, NJ: Erlbaum.

Wagner, R. K., & Stanovich, K. E. (1996). Expertise in reading. In K. A. Ericsson (Ed.), *The road to excellence: The acquisition of expert performance in the arts and sciences, sports and games*. Mahwah, NJ: Erlbaum.

Weizman, Z. O., & Snow, C. E. (2001) Lexical output as related to children's vocabulary acquisition: Effects of sophisticated exposure and support for meaning. *Developmental Psychology, 37*, 265–279.

12

Individual Differences in Oral Language and Reading

It's a Matter of Experience

ELAINE R. SILLIMAN
MARIA MODY

Kelly,[1] 10½ years old and midway through grade 4, does not have a history of delayed language development. She also does not have a family history of dyslexia; however, her 7-year-old sister is currently receiving intervention for an articulation problem. At the beginning of the school year, Kelly tested below the basic level in reading and, according to her mother, needed to work harder than normal to maintain decent grades. She enjoys math but dislikes reading. In addition, Kelly still has difficulty with time concepts. Based on school monitoring data, Kelly is struggling with text comprehension, especially inferencing. Expository text is especially difficult for her. In comparison to her classmates' performance on reading comprehension, Kelly's scores place her at the 19th percentile. Teacher comments on her written work indicate that Kelly has significant problems with spelling and punctuation, and with producing more complex sentence structure and selecting more complex vocabulary.

Caren, also 10 years old and midway through grade 4, has a family history of dyslexia. Her father was diagnosed with dyslexia as a teenager. Caren was evaluated for dyslexia in grade 2 by a licensed psychologist. Results indicated a marked gap between her intellectual level (a nonverbal IQ of 130) and her decoding abilities, attributed to working memory limitations. Caren began receiving private tutoring that focused on improving her skills in oral reading accuracy and fluency. Moreover, in addition to her decoding problems, Caren experienced problems in the classroom in rapidly and accurately processing the language of instruction. Her grade 4 teacher reports that Caren has a tendency not to attend well when she has to engage in two actions simultaneously and requires "quiet to listen and really hear what is being said." In contrast, Caren's parents did not find a comparable problem at home (an audiological evaluation revealed that Caren's hearing levels were within normal limits). On the other hand, Caren's parents, in addition to being concerned about her reading and spelling problems since grade 1, are uneasy about her poor written sentence structure, including her inconsistency in producing appropriate subject–verb agreement, especially in her writing of expository texts.

Kelly and Caren illustrate a major issue for the comprehensive understanding of oral language–reading relationships. This question involves explaining those aspects of their development trajectories that are constrained by neurobiological and genetic factors, and those facets that may differ on the basis of variations in individual experience (Kovas & Plomin, 2007; Pennington, Snyder, & Roberts, 2007). This is no easy task. As the developmental psychologist Jerome Kagan (2008) points out, "It is difficult to predict a psychological reaction from a brain profile (because) each person's history influences the brain's reaction to a particular event" (p. 6) at any given point in time.

MAIN THEMES

What Is a Language Impairment?

Our purpose in this final chapter is twofold: to examine the role of three crucial building blocks in children's development of an oral language register and to relate these foundations to individual variations in experience and their potential effects on oral language–reading relationships. We are especially interested in those students, similar to Kelly and Caren, who may be classified as having language impairment or dyslexia and/or as struggling with the academic language demands of instruction. Unlike the consensus on the clinical identification of dyslexia (see Chapters 8 and 9, this volume by Shaywitz, Gruen, & Shaywitz, and Byrne, Shankweiler, & Hine, respectively), there is no "gold standard" for identifying oral language impairment (for a full discussion, see Silliman & Scott, 2006). This reality is reflected in the array of labels found in the literature that refers to oral language problems, including specific language impairment (SLI), language impairment (LI), nonspecific language impairment, primary language impairment, and language learning disability (LLD), among other descriptors.

The disparity in characterizations is due to principled differences in conceptual perspectives. One framework, the domain-specific perspective, deems disruptions in spoken language development as specific to the linguistic system, typically in underspecified grammatical representations or, alternatively, in slower rates of processing language that suggest limitations in phonological, or verbal, working memory. The alternative conceptual stance, the domain-general point of view, initially looks to connections among more general purpose, cognitive or perceptual mechanisms that serve as the infrastructure for oral language (Lum & Bavin, 2007; Norrix, Plante, Vance, & Boliek, 2007; Ullman & Pierpont, 2005; Windsor & Kohnert, Chapter 5, this volume). These disconnections in the infrastructure then constrain the developmental specialization of other systems that also unfold with experience, such as the oral language system (see Chapter 2 by Evans, this volume). The absence of agreement on "what a language impairment is" impacts not only the measures that practitioners and researchers select for assessing oral language impairment but also how best to examine its relationship to reading outcomes and how intervention decisions may be made.

Understanding Individual Differences from a Usage-Based Perspective

Given the lack of accord on the nature of oral language impairment, our perspective, like that of Kagan (2008; and several authors in this volume), is that understanding the oral language–reading relationships depends on recognizing that connections between these two language systems are dynamic events framed by the social context in which individual students are participating. Because there is general consensus that oral language experiences during the preschool years serve as the foundation for emerging literacy abilities (Catts, Fey, Zhang, & Tomblin, 1999; Dickinson & Tabors, 2001; Dickinson, McCabe, Anastasopoulos, Peisner-Feinberg, & Poe, 2003; Foorman, Anthony, Seals, & Mouzaki, 2002; Scarborough, 2001, 2005; Wise, Sevcik, Morris, Lovett, & Wolf, 2007), our purpose is to highlight individual differences in the use of the oral language register.

To achieve this objective, we explore the nature of social-interactional experiences modulating individual differences in the developing oral language register from a usage-based perspective, including development within and outside of "normal variation." Usage-based models of oral language acquisition are functional. A shared premise is that linguistic structure materializes from actual language use. What is learned about language and how it is learned cannot be separated from the patterns children identify through repeated, but varied, encounters with their social and linguistic worlds (see Figure 12.1). Moreover, the frequency of patterns in a language, from its phonology to its discourse genres, drives brain organization and development, biasing them toward linguistic and discourse experiences that are consistent with the particular language. At the same time, pattern frequency also characterizes individual child experiences and varies within a language community, if not within families in that language community, in ways that culminate in individual differences. It should be noted that usage-based descriptions have not yet been applied, except in a general way, either to language delay or LI.

The chapter is organized into sections that examine three critical building blocks of the oral language register: speech perception, word learning, and the construction of syntax. In each section, the developmental pathway of the domain is described first, followed by patterns associated with oral language impairment. Where feasible, we illuminate individual differences through a usage-based lens.

SPEECH PERCEPTION AND THE HOME LANGUAGE PHONETIC INVENTORY: THE FIRST CRITICAL BUILDING BLOCK

The contributions of oral language experience to individual language profiles begin as early as age 6–7 months. This is the period when infants start to show a distinct, language-specific preference for the phonetic contrasts of their native language versus non-native contrasts.

The Developmental Trajectory

According to Kuhl (2007), infants' experience with the sounds of their language "commits the brain's neural circuitry to the properties of native-like speech" (p. 111) and their subsequent development of native language phonetic categories. In turn, the acquisition of a language-specific sound repertoire paves the way for learning more complex utterances whose patterns resemble the phonetic structure of the native language.

In short, based on the nature and quality of their social interactions with caregivers and others, infants as young as age 6 months already demonstrate sensitivity to the distributional frequencies, or statistical patterns, of the sounds and words comprising their native language. This sensitivity is evident in their speech perception and speech production abilities (Boysson-Bardies, 2001; Goldstein, King, & West, 2003; Kuhl, 2007; Saffran, 2001; Saffran & Theissen, 2007). Bruer (Chapter 3, this volume) notes that it may be the prolonged exposure to these home oral language

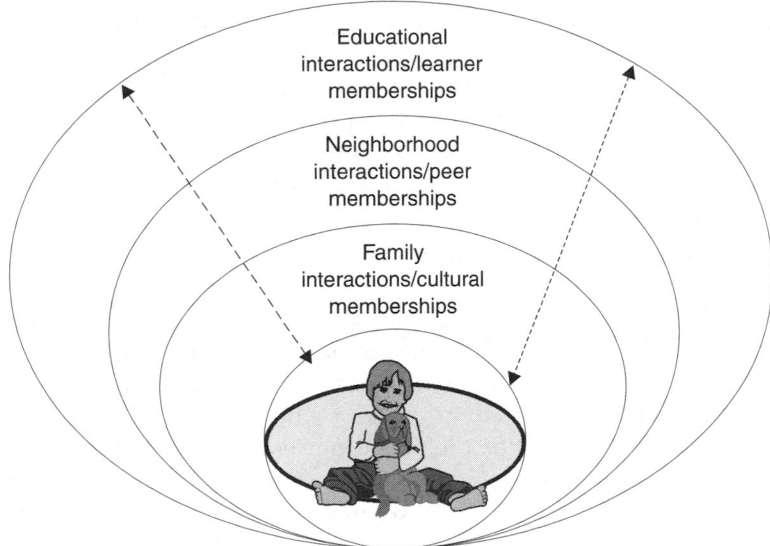

FIGURE 12.1. The multidimensional social world. The different patterned arrows reflect variations in experience (interactions) with particular social dimension.

influences that accounts for an apparent reduction in sensitivity, or resistance to influences from a new language.

Onset of Two-Word Combinations and Early Speech Processing as Predictors of Later Variation in Oral Language Profiles

The usage-based work described earlier leads to two central questions for early identification of oral language impairment: First, are there predictors for delayed onset of oral language development? Second, can infants at risk for later oral language impairment be identified by means of their responses to speech stimuli? Both of these questions have been addressed by longitudinal studies.

Delayed Onset of Oral Language

The first question, that of predictors of late talking, has been the subject of several longitudinal investigations that vary in length, sample size, assessment methods, cutoff criteria for late talking, and statistical power. Two of the larger studies are highlighted here.

The first study (Thal, Bates, Goodman, & Jahn-Samilo, 1997) combined prospective and retrospective procedures to explore the continuity of language development in 402 middle-class children who participated in the original norming of the MacArthur Communicative Development Inventory (CDI; Fenson et al., 1994), a parent self-report inventory. In the prospective study, 185 children were followed over 6-month spans, from 20 to 26 months. At initial assessment (Time 1, 20 months), 13% fell at or below the 10th percentile of the CDI Toddler form, which indicated late-talking status relative to vocabulary size and sentence use. Six months later (at Time 2, 26 months), 60% of the late talking group at Time 1 "stayed late" (Thal et al., 1997, p. 248) at higher than chance levels based on the same Toddler form. The retrospective study, using CDI data from 217 children to examine stability between 13 months and 20 months, again found continuity in late-talker status for the group as a whole. Demographic variables, such as socioeconomic status (SES), did not emerge as significant predictors, nor did measures of gestural production and early vocabulary comprehension and production. Moreover, whereas strong evidence for continuity in late talking at the group level was found, predictive ability across a 6-month time span for individual children was poor. These results suggest caution on a clinical level. The prediction of greater than chance risk for atypical language learning in children under the age of 3 years continues as a vexing prognostic problem, because individual differences in the rate of language development mask the forecasting of who will be a late bloomer (Ellis Weismer, 2007).

Predictors of late talking were also investigated in a large-scale, prospective epidemiological study of 1,766 primarily white toddlers, all single births, from middle-class, monolingual English-speaking families in Western Australia (Zubrick, Taylor, Rice, & Slegers, 2007). This group of developmentally typical children was followed from birth to 8 years old, with an explicit focus on "late language emergence" (LLE) at age 24 months, defined syntactically as not combining two to three words.[2] A 13.4% prevalence rate of LLE was determined relative to children falling at the lower end of the distribution based on parent self-report measures of early oral language emergence. Similar to results in Thal et al. (1997), the Zubrick et al. results indicated that LLE was not associated with traditional predictors, such as family characteristics or SES. Instead, a complex of neurobiological and genetic factors was the best predictor of LLE membership at 24 months: (1) gender (male toddlers had three times the risk compared to female toddlers), (2) less than 85% of optimal fetal birthweight or birth at less than 37 weeks' gestation (twice the risk), and (3) a positive family history of LLE.

A follow-up study at age 7 years of 128 children with LLE and 109 children with a normal history of language emergence applied a growth curve analysis to outcomes (Rice, Taylor, & Zubrick, 2008). Among the findings were that (1) gender disparities found at age 24 months for children with LLE did not persist, suggesting a faster acceleration rate in language acquisition for males than females; (2) most LLE children did "catch up" by age 7 years in the morphosyntactic areas assessed; (3) for 10–13% of the LLE group, a delay in combining words at 24 words was reflected in a "clinical level of performance" (p. 405) in the morphosyntactic marking of third-person singular *-s* and past tense *-ed*, which has been interpreted as evidence for a domain-specific, selective impairment of the linguistic system (Rice, 2007); and (4) 23% of the LLE group met clinical criteria for their grammatical awareness of morphosyntactic relationships.

Of some interest, the oral language battery that Rice et al. (2008) administered to children at age 7 years tended toward heavy loading in the morphosyntactic domain. Other aspects of oral language knowledge, such as levels of phonological awareness, were not included. As a consequence, the concept of selective (morphosyntactic) impairment remains conditional. Evidence from the grammatical awareness measures showing that nearly one-fourth of the children with LLE were lagging behind their age peers in this area, despite not having production problems with morphosyntactic inflections, was not further related to the broader domain of metalinguistic aptitude. Both phonological and grammatical awareness are subsets of this larger meta-umbrella.

To recapitulate, as of yet, there is no consensus on the predictive relationships that forecast linkages between LLE at 24 months and later oral language impairment, an issue compounded by the fact that a large majority of toddlers with LLE go on to develop oral language registers that fall within the normal range of variation. Also unidentified is how individual variations in children's social worlds beyond 24 months, including the richness of emergent literacy experiences during the preschool years, may either negate or enhance the predictive power of LLE for subsequent language and learning problems. As Scarborough (2005) points out, different early oral language skills predict future beginning reading levels at different preschool ages. Whereas syntactic abilities may be predictors at ages 2½–3 years, by age 5 years vocabulary and phonological awareness, "but not syntax" (Scarborough, 2005, p. 8) is prognostic.

Early Segmentation of the Speech Input

The second question pertains to early speech processing as a potential risk indicator of oral language impairment. This topic was addressed in a retrospective longitudinal study of 412 infants from monolingual English-speaking homes (Newman, Ratner, Jusczyk, Jusczyk, & Dow, 2006). These infants initially participated in a series of six laboratory experiments that examined their sensitivity to word segments in a speech stream beginning at age 5 months and continuing through age 12 months (e.g., attending to short passages with a familiar word, such as *cup*, vs. passages without the familiar word). At 24 months, parents of the 412 children completed a questionnaire about vocabulary development, and the top and bottom 15% in vocabulary development were then identified, resulting in 22 children. At ages 4–6 years, a battery of oral language and cognitive measures was administered to a representative subset with high and low production vocabularies at 24 months. Results indicated that children who were more successful at segmenting the speech stream as infants (i.e., they displayed obvious social attention) and had larger production vocabularies at age 24 months evidenced more advanced language skills at ages 4–6 years.

From a neurobiological perspective, there is the suggestion that a common neural substrate, the superior temporal sulcus, may serve both early speech perception and social functions, such as engaging in joint attention and following the gaze paths of caregivers (Redcay, 2008). Pending further empirical verification, it may be the case that the social emergence of relatively coordinated joint attention is necessary for the emergence of sustained attention to the caregiver's speech stream, a possibility that might contribute to LLE as well (Zubrick et al., 2007).

For example, in the Newman et al. (2006) study, those children who were less successful at segmentation as infants had small production vocabularies at age 24 months, a finding that appears consistent with other longitudinal studies focusing on late talkers (Lee & Rescorla, 2008). They were also less advanced in their overall language skills at ages 4–6 years, although they still scored within ±1 standard deviation on the oral language measure. Newman et al. (2006) interpreted these findings to suggest that a degree of continuity exists in language ability "from 7 months of age through the preschool years" (p. 651). Further support for this notion comes from research linking: (1) phonetic preference patterns in babbling to first words (Vihman, Macken, Miller, Simmons & Miller, 1985), (2) early speech perception experience to later phonological memory (Mody, Schwartz, Gravel, & Ruben, 1999), (3) the increasing relationship between the efficiency of online speech processing and vocabulary growth from ages 15 to 25 months (Fernald, Perfors, & Marchman, 2006), and (4) first signed words to prelinguistic gestures in deaf infants (Cheek, Cormier, Repp, & Meier, 2001).

Finally, Newman et al. (2006) outlined a number of study limitations that must be dealt with in future longitudinal work on the feasibility of infant risk predictors for subsequent LLE and oral language impairment. Among their recommendations was to incorporate into prospective infant studies sensitivity to phonotactic probabilities in the speech stream as a concept that may reliably predict individual differences in infant responsiveness. "Phonotactic probabilities" are also a distributional notion. The term refers to the likelihood that specific segments, whether defined as syllables, onsets and rimes, or phonemes, will occur in a particular position within the words of a language (Vitevitch, Luce, Pisoni, & Auer, 1999). A related sublexical process is "phonotactic regularity," the patterns regulating the ordering of these elements within words (Brea-Spahn & Silliman, in press). Both phonotactic probability and regularity affect spoken word recognition (Vitevitch et al., 1999).

The Role of Experience in the Development of Speech Perception Strategies

It is worth noting that despite the importance of the frequency and consistency of the phonetic input to a developing language system, the language-acquiring child has an extraordinary capacity to extract consistencies from an inconsistent speech signal. This is evident in his or her abilities to form phonological categories, the building blocks for vocabulary growth and later reading development, in the face of context- and speaker-related phonetic variations (Mody, 2003; Studdert-Kennedy, 1986). However, these building blocks appear influenced by the nature of early language experience. For example, Nittrouer (2002) found that the quality of early language experience influences the perceptual strategies by which children progressively sharpen their acoustic processing of the speech signal that eventually allows them to extract the phonetic structure of their language. In other words, in the transition to beginning reading, children must learn "what information to extract from the acoustic speech signal and how to organize that information in order to access phonetic structure" (Nittrouer, 2002, p. 248).

In summary, a missing piece in the infant risk predictor research similar to the longitudinal research on LLE (e.g., Rice et al., 2008; Thal et al., 1997; Zubrick et al., 2007) is acknowledging how variations in the nature and quality of the infant's early interactional experiences, may (1) influence the infant's sharpened attention to probable phonotactic patterns in the speech stream and (2) contribute to individual profile differences in vocabulary learning at age 24 months and beyond that constitute an essential component of the oral language register. As noted by Byrne and colleagues (see Chapter 9, this volume) and van Kleeck and Norlander (Chapter 10, this volume), vocabulary and early print experiences are largely determined by the preschool home milieu, including the quality of language experiences. In turn, the nature of caregivers' cultural priorities, values, and expectations about oral language–literacy relationships predict later reading outcomes. As such, "the diversity of the vocabulary parents use reflects the scope of the knowledge base the parents are putting in place" (Hart & Risley, 1995, p. 99). As a result, young children's early experiences with spoken language vocabulary interact with literacy activities on the path to reading, contributing to the development of the oral and academic language registers.

WORD LEARNING: THE SECOND CRITICAL BUILDING BLOCK

The Developmental Trajectory

Phonotactic Probability and Neighborhood Density

A consistent finding about distributional patterns at the phonotactic level is that high-frequency words are more likely than low-frequency words to overlap in their phoneme segments. These phonologically similar segments are known as "neighborhoods," defined as "the number of real words that can be created by adding, deleting, or changing one sound in a real target word" (Munson, Swenson, & Manthei, 2005, p. 108). Dense neighborhoods have multiple overlapping segments that include semantic, morphosyntactic, and phonological similarities. For example, in high-frequency words, phonemes often overlap as in word-initial /s/ in *seat, sat, sun, said*, and *safe*, as do adjacent phonemes, such as the /si/ in *sing, sick*, and *sill* (Storkel & Morrisette, 2002). In contrast, sparse neighborhoods have fewer overlapped segments, such as the word *choice*, which has a restricted set of neighbors, such as *voice* and *chase* (Munson, Swenson, & Manthei, 2005). Hence, positive correlations exist between phonotactic probability and neighborhood density (Vitevitch et al., 1999), and between word familiarity (also referred to as "vocabulary breadth") and phonological familiarity, although less is known about the latter relationship (Garlock, Walley, & Metsala, 2001).

Furthermore, these two relationships hold for the rate and precision of spoken word recognition. According to the neighborhood activation model (Vitevitch et al., 1999), when neighborhoods are dense, increased lexical competition occurs for activation, which can result in slower (and, perhaps, less accurate) recognition. In effect, high neighborhood density can hinder the speed of word recognition. Conversely, the sparser the neighborhoods, the less lexical competition occurs. Here, speed and access of spoken words likely increase.

However, there is a developmental aspect to lexical competition and word neighborhoods. Garlock et al. (2001), in a study that controlled word frequency and neighborhood density, and estimated age of word acquisition (early vs. late), found that the competition effect emerged around age 5½ years for words from sparse neighborhoods, compared to age 7 years for words from dense neighborhoods (Munson, Swenson, & Manthei, 2005). In other words, contrary to expectations, lexical competition was activated "for words with more robust representations and few competitors" (Garlock et al., 2001, p. 484) or highly familiar words that were acquired earlier. Comparable findings were reported in a separate study that employed repetition of monosyllabic words that varied either in neighborhood density or phonotactic probability (Munson, Swenson, & Manthei, 2005). Children with a mean age of 4 years, 3 months did not evidence a neighborhood density effect for real-word repetition, whereas older children with a mean age of 7 years, 2 months showed this effect.

The implication for vocabulary learning and the emergence of phonological awareness is a powerful one. Lexical competition is an indicator of the restructuring of lexical representations from a more holistic organization to a more segmental organization that then supports growth in neighborhood density. The relationship between vocabulary size and degree of phonological awareness is accentuated by the point that "the more words children know, the more likely they are to be analytic in their representation of the sounds of those words" (Nagy, 2005, p. 36).

That a wide range of individual differences exists for the onset of this restructuring process seems plausible. For example, young children with large production vocabularies (approximately 600 words at age 2 years) are likely candidates to become more efficient fast mappers. Fast mapping, sometimes referred to as "incidental learning," is a process by which minimal exposure to a novel meaning results in at least partial storage of the meaning. One speculation is that fast mappers seem more sensitive to retaining situationally specific word cues (McGregor, Sheng, & Smith, 2005), which then allows the building of neighborhoods having greater phonological similarities. Furthermore, the existence of preestablished neighborhoods may then prime young children's fast acquisition and retention of new conceptual links, and their semantic and lexical representations (Gershkoff-Stowe & Hahn, 2007). A similar effect of neighborhood density on adults' fast mapping has also been found (Storkel, Armbruster, & Hogan, 2006). We now shift to how variations in language experience may factor into fast-mapping ability.

The Role of Experience on the Fast Mapping of New Word Learning

In a seminal home-based study, Hart and Risley (1995) followed the vocabulary learning of 42 infants/toddlers from ages 12–36 months, whose families were distributed across the SES spectrum. This work brought attention to the magnitude of variations in the individual richness of early vocabulary experiences. As Hart and Risley (1995, p. 155) note, "The greater the amount of Language Diversity in parent talk, the more opportunities the child has for observational learning about how words refer and how they are used in relation to other words."

Other studies with preschool and kindergarten samples also yield converging evidence about the critical importance of young children's exposure to vocabulary diversity, especially cognitive state meanings, such as *think, know, understand, believe, discover*, and so on. These meanings are associated with an emerging theory of mind. The quality and diversity of these interactions extend across a wide domain of experience. These include routine home talk with parents (Jenkins, Turrell, Kogushi, Lollis, & Ross, 2003), oral picture book reading (Adrian, Clemente, & Villanueva, 2007; Vernon-Feagans et al., in press), peer talk (Hughes & Dunn, 1998), caregiver–child play interactions (Nixon, 2005), and the explicit teaching of cognitive state verbs during kindergarten picture book reading as a way to support children's understanding that text interpretation is always an active construction of the mind (Peskin & Astington, 2004). One conclusion about these findings from a usage-based perspective is that frequency of experience with a varied range of more literate word meanings in real-world "informative contexts" (McGregor, Sheng, & Ball, 2007, p. 361) is an influential factor in new word learning through the fast-mapping mechanism. However, a major unresolved issue concerns knowing what a word means.

Knowing a Word

Word learning, whether it takes place in the oral or written domain, always represents a continuum of "knowing." This continuum ranges from "I don't know it" to "I've heard or seen it, but I don't know what it means," to "I know it, can define it, and use it appropriately" (Dale, 1965). As previously mentioned, incidental word learning is often referred to as "fast mapping," whereas "slow mapping" entails increasing the semantic depth (richness and precision) of meanings through the process of semantic elaboration. The fast–slow mapping distinction is illustrated in the following example from a child's first birthday party (McGregor et al., 2007):

> Mom says, "Let me light the candle"; a few seconds later, Dad says, "Let's blow out the candle." The child has heard the lexical form [candle] twice while seeing the referent and witnessing some relevant events (lighting, blowing). What he has actually learned about the word *candle* at this point in time is minimal. . . . Over time as he has more encounters with candles, he will learn to label them himself. He will come to know that they are hot, that they come in various colors and sizes, and that they are made of wax. In this sense, the learning of the word *candle* on his birthday is just the initial step in an extended process. (p. 353; emphasis in original).

The integration of new word learning into comprehension depends on the strength of overlapping linkages among the conceptual, semantic, and lexical domains. These interconnections were originally proposed as a set of hypotheses to account for why larger vocabularies and more proficient reading comprehension are highly correlated (Nagy, 2005, 2007; Stahl & Nagy, 2006). It seems reasonable, however, that similar linkages exist to varying degrees to support new word learning in the oral domain (Verhoeven & Van Leeuwe, 2008).

1. *Conceptual (topic) knowledge*, including *world knowledge*, is expressed through the bidirectional semantic mapping of meanings to their word forms (individual lexical items) and the lexical mapping of the word forms to their meanings. The strength of these bidirectional connections likely contributes to the scope or breadth of meanings in the lexicon and their depth (elaborated meanings, including multiple meanings). For example, consider the 8-year-old child who learns a "child-friendly" definition of a *sphinx* (its pronounced form) as a make-believe creature with a lion's body and human head usually carved of stone (the concept/referent) (McGregor et al., 2007, p. 364). Can we then interpret that the child "knows" the meaning of this concept across situations of its use?

Later on, the same child, when shown a picture of a sphinx, cannot recall its name. Does this then imply that the child does not know the meaning? McGregor et al. (2007) consider this kind of pattern not unusual in the 8-year-olds of mixed ethnicity whom they studied, when recall, rather than recognition, is required. What this pattern implies is a dissociation phase characterized by the relatively independent development of semantic and lexical aspects of new word learning; that is, the underlying semantic knowledge is fast-mapped into the lexicon, but the linkages between the conceptual–semantic and lexical levels of meaning have not yet become sufficiently bidirectional to "own the meaning." Alt and Plante (2006) depict this dissociation as "I know the word, but not what it means" (a conceptual–semantic gap) or "I know what the word means but can't think of its name" (a lexical gap).

2. *Metalinguistic aptitude*. Individuals vary in their word consciousness or their skill to talk and think about word meanings in explicit ways regardless of "whether this information is provided by context, by explanations, or by definitions" (Nagy, 2007, p. 55). The ability to employ greater precision and specificity of word use in appropriate contexts, for example, meanings such as *vicissitudes* and *assuage*, reflect the accessibility of a more flexible and elaborated semantic network, as well as lexical depth.

The causal linkages of metalinguistic awareness to vocabulary and reading comprehension remain undetermined, however. Stahl and Nagy (2006) identify two contenders that likely act in concert. One arises from the metalinguistic awareness of derivational morphology (prefixes and suffixes), which integrates form and meaning in the generation of new word learning (Carlisle, 2004). Derivational knowledge is related to reading achievement by grade 3 (Carlisle, 2000) and contributes to the rate of word reading at both elementary and secondary levels (Carlisle & Stone, 2005). By grades 4 and 5, derivational knowledge influences reading comprehension independently of reading vocabulary (Nagy, Berninger, & Abbott, 2006). Of some note, given the strong relationships between derivational knowledge and reading comprehension outcomes, there have been few experimental studies on whether the explicit teaching of derivational structure (i.e., word roots, prefixes, and suffixes) through morphological analysis impacts on the reading vocabulary of students with comprehension problems (Reed, 2008).

A second, interrelated candidate that Stahl and Nagy (2006) cite is sensitivity to multiple meanings (or "polysemy"). An elaborated semantic network of multiple meanings allows rapid adjustment to subtle shifts in shades of meaning as a function of the discourse or text context, and supports understanding of the varied forms of figurative language. Achieving this level of word learning can become a "gargantuan task" (Snow & Kim, 2007, p. 136) when students do not read beyond school-required tasks or when they are confronted with text comprehension problems.

3. *Reciprocity between reading comprehension and new word learning*. As just mentioned, more proficient readers generally have richer semantic networks, perhaps because they read more. Longitudinal data on the development of Dutch children's reading comprehension from grades 1 to 6 (Verhoeven & Leeuwe, 2008) suggest that children who have greater semantic depth to draw on initially are more likely to benefit from new word learning opportunities over time through the texts they read. This reciprocity, and the fact that "the rich get richer" over time as a consequence of the magnitude of their reading experience, strongly suggests that explicit vocabulary instruction should begin in preschool (Nagy, 2005; Snow & Kim, 2007).

An unresolved question is how sensitivity to phonotactic patterns of spoken language evolves as a function of the quality of early language experiences. One speculation is that sensitivity permits young children to become more attuned to those acoustic properties of the speech signal that "count" relative to extraction of the phonetic structure underlying new meanings (Nittrouer, 2002; Nittrouer & Lowenstein, 2007). On the other hand, it may be the case that children described as having "poorer" vocabularies and less sensitivity to phonological units (e.g., onset and rime) when they enter school are less responsive to fast-mapping experiences of novel meanings, because they apply less efficient perceptual strategies for organizing the speech signal so that phonetic structure and phonotactic patterns can emerge. One outcome may be that minimal lexical competition is activated. A different possibility is that, even if these fine-grained distributional properties are organized into phonetic patterns and lexical competition is activated at appropriate levels, these children may be more affected by interference from the lexical competition process. Children with oral language impairment afford opportunities to pursue these questions in the context of their oral language register development.

The New Word Learning of Children with Oral Language Impairment

Three related topics are considered in this segment. These are fast-mapping ability; facility in managing the intertwined lexical processes of inhibition and competition, as suggested by gating tasks; and how variations in interactional experiences may affect individual profiles of late language emergence. In the past, neither usage-based theories nor individual differences have been characteristic of the fast-mapping and gating research strands. However, shifts in theoretical frameworks are beginning to appear.

Fast-Mapping Performance

Few studies have explicitly investigated relationships between phonotactic probability and neighborhood density in the fast mapping of children with known oral language impairment. Instead, efforts to understand the dynamics of fast mapping in children with LI have typically involved nonword repetition (NWR) tasks to illuminate relationships between vocabulary and the accuracy of repetition performance. Gathercole and Baddeley (1989) initially proposed a linkage between NWR and word learning. The premise was that both new word and nonword learning shared a corresponding process; that is, both types of words must be identified and held for production in phonological memory, a component of working memory; hence, the argument that the phonological memory mechanism functions identically in real word and nonword learning. Our interest in this section is not the relationship between NWR and word learning in children with oral language impairment, but in children's ability to engage in activities that have been explicitly identified as fast-mapping tasks. These fast mapping tasks may also employ nonwords. The important point is that in creating nonword tasks, at a minimum, the phonotactic probabilities of the syllabic or multisyllabic structures must be determined, because a preponderance of either high- or low-frequency phoneme sequences can bias results (Brea-Spahn & Silliman, in press; Storkel & Morrisette, 2002).

Only a few studies have been conducted with the explicit purpose of assessing the fast-mapping skills of children with LI. In one study, Gray (2006) utilized nonword fast mapping for familiar and unfamiliar object names with 53 children with LI, ages 3 to 6 years old, and 53 controls matched for gender and age. Results were ambivalent because the fast-mapping outcomes for the two groups did not differ except at age 5 years. Gray attributed the absence of significant findings to the possibility that phonotactic probability, as well as neighborhood density, was not controlled in the selection of nonwords for the fast-mapping task.

In the second fast-mapping investigation, Alt and Plante (2006) did control for the phonotactic probability and neighborhood density of nonwords, which were either monosyllabic or bisyllabic. Following extensive training, 46 preschool children, 23 with language impairment and 23 controls matched for age and gender, were presented via computer display with a semantic features task (attributes of objects) and a lexical task (names of objects) in phonotactically frequent and infrequent conditions. The manner of presentation was also varied within conditions, including a vocal prompt accompanying presentation, nonspeech noise (e.g., a telephone ringing), and silence. One pattern of findings indicated that the children with LI were less successful than the control children in determining the lexical labels in both the phonotactically frequent and infrequent conditions. The better performance of the control children across the phonotactic conditions was interpreted to indicate that they had at least formed partial phonological representations of the target labels via fast mapping.

In a second pattern of outcomes, the participants with LI fast-mapped fewer semantic features in both the phonotactically infrequent and silent (nonverbal) conditions in comparison to the control group. However, children's LI did not impede their fast mapping of high-frequency phonotactic features across linguistic, nonlinguistic, and silent conditions, but appeared to do so when low phonotactic probability co-occurred in the silent condition. Alt and Plante (2006) put forward one explanation for this seemingly counterintuitive finding. The low-probability, silent condition made heavier demands on children's allocation of their cognitive and linguistic resources for the fast mapping of phonological representations. Alternately, a high-demand processing condition may adversely affect the timing and integration of interactions among existing phonological, lexical, and semantic representations in some unknown way. Disruptions in coordination would then limit how rapidly and adequately novel meaning can be encoded, thus contributing to protracted development of neighborhood density and the emergence of lexical competition. This option receives some support from a reading comprehension study by Ricketts, Bishop, and Nation (2008), who found that poor comprehenders encountered difficulty in maintaining long-lasting semantic representations for novel meanings. Insufficient lexical competition due to lower quality neighborhood density would also suggest weaker bidirectional linkages between the conceptual–semantic and lexical domains (McGregor et al., 2007), as well as limited word consciousness (Nagy, 2007).

Performance on Gating Tasks

In a gating task (Mainela-Arnold, Evans, & Coady, 2008), fragments of a word are presented (gated), with the acoustic units increasing in size until the participant recognizes the word. The sample in this study comprised 16 children with LI, ages 8 years, 5 months to 12 years, 3 months, and 16 chronological and nonverbal, IQ-matched peers. They listened to 48 gated monosyllabic words balanced in terms of word frequency, neighborhood density, and initial sounds. Findings indicated that the two groups were not differentially impacted by the three variables indexing distributional regularity. The authors attributed the outcome partially to the possibility that selection criteria for word frequency and neighborhood density may have not have been appropriate for the sample's age range.

However, group differences did emerge at the point of acceptance, which is "the gate after which the children did not alter the once-identified word" (Mainela-Arnold et al., 2008, p. 389). Children with LI vacillated about possible candidate choices, more so than their peers, and were more likely to select words having no phonological relationship to the target words. Two hypotheses were proposed to guide future research on the dual-lexical processes of inhibition and competition. One speculation is that children with LI may be more vulnerable to interference from lexical competition effects when new words are weakly represented. Vulnerability could then result in greater difficulty in suppressing competition, a prospect that has garnered preliminary support from other studies on oral language impairment (Norbury, 2005; Tomblin, Mainela-Arnold, & Zhang, 2007). Another likelihood is more susceptibility to the effects of interference when what has just been said is followed by a new word whose "activation strength would have to compete with the activation of the word the child has just spoken" (Mainela-Arnold et al., 2008, p. 390). Either of these alternatives would restrict the child's ability to infer plausible choices. Finally, a third option has yet to be ruled out. General language aptitude, and not competitive or inhibitory processes, may account for individual variations in word learning ability, even at the level of the oral language register (Munson, Kurtz, & Windsor, 2005).

The Role of Experience in New Word Learning in Children with Late Language Emergence

Minimal research has been conducted on the process of word learning in the context of caregiver–child interactions, when the child has LLE. Recall the Zubrick et al. (2007) longitudinal study on general neurobiological and genetic predictors of LLE at 24 months. In the behavioral realm, Rescorla and colleagues (Lee & Rescorla 2002, 2008; Rescorla, 2002, 2005; Rescorla, Dahlsgaard, & Roberts, 2000) have conducted the only longitudinal investigation on late talkers that also followed the development of mental state meanings. The specific focus was the frequency and type of mental state meanings that mothers and their late-talking preschoolers produced during 30 minutes of videotaped play interactions at ages 3, 4, and 5 years. A total of 30 middle- to upper-middle-class white children, all late talkers, were matched at the initial intake on age, SES, and nonverbal ability to 15 typically developing children (Lee & Rescorla, 2008). When first identified during the 24- to 31-month period, the late talkers had a mean production vocabulary of 20 words, compared to a 226-word mean production vocabulary in the typically developing children (Lee & Rescorla, 2002).

The mental state meanings examined included the less developmentally complex physiological states (*hot, hurt, awake,* and *asleep*), affective states (*happy, sad, upset, worried,* and *mad*), and desires/motivations (*want, need,* and *like*), as well as the more developmentally and semantically complex cognitive states, such as *think, know, pretend, understand,* and *remember* (Lee & Rescorla, 2008, p. 37). By age 5 years, the two groups did not differ in their frequencies of the physiological, affective, and desire categories. A significant difference occurred only for the cognitive state verbs. The comparison group more frequently produced this category than did the late talker group. Moreover, whereas the cognitive verbs *know, think,* and *pretend* were used the most often by both groups, only the comparison group consistently embedded these verbs within a sentential complement explicitly marked by *that.* An example of sentential complementation is "I thought that the policeman was riding a motorcycle" (typically developing child, age 4 years), in contrast to the less syntactically complex clause "I'm just pretending, Mom" (late talker, age 5 years; p. 33). Furthermore, sentential complements were just beginning to emerge in 55% of the late talkers at age 5 years, suggesting that wide variation still existed among this group, whereas all of the comparison children produced complementation by age 5 years.

These longitudinal results are generally consistent with findings from a cross-sectional, usage-based study with a sample of forty 4-year-olds selected from a large, diverse sample. Nixon (2005) found that cognitive state verbs were strongly correlated with sentential complements in 4-year-olds, although sentential complements were less frequently produced than simple clauses with other mental states, such as "She is funny" (p. 21).

A second major question asked by Lee and Rescorla (2008) concerned whether the four categories produced by the children and their mothers were referentially related. A pattern similar to the child comparisons ensued. Mothers of late talkers did not differ in their production of physiological, affective, or desire terms at any of the three ages. The pertinent finding was that whereas the comparison group mothers did not increase their frequency of cognitive state verbs over 3 years, mothers of the late talkers did so, although the frequency of their reference was less than that of the mothers in the comparison group children at age 3 years. Mothers' use of cognitive state terms with children at age 3 years was also significantly correlated with their children's frequency of use at ages 4 and 5 years. The authors note that the nature of the correlational data did not allow disaggregating whether the mothers of late talkers were responding to their expectations about what children could understand, or whether children's reduced usage of cognitive verbs reflected their less diverse experiences with how mothers fashioned input.

An important detail about these cognitive state findings not explicitly addressed in the results is that cognitive verbs represent belief concepts, but not all belief expressions are equally complex. For example, belief verbs denoting relative certainty ("I *know* where my shoes are") are easier for young children to use appropriately than are belief verbs encoding degrees of relative uncertainty (Nixon, 2005), such as "I *think* my shoes are under the bed." Data were not provided for either the late talker or for comparison dyads in the frequency of their use of relative certainty versus relative uncertainty.

What of the long-term outcomes for this group of late talkers given their home and educational experiences? Rescorla (2002, 2005) reported on the status of the late talkers and members of the comparison group at ages 6, 9, and 13 years, taking an assessment stance that differed substantively from that of Rice et al. (2008). By age 6 years, about 6% of the late talkers evidenced oral language impairment (Rescorla, 2002), a percentage less than that determined in children at age 7 years by Rice et al. (2008). Approximately 33% received some type of speech–language intervention for a period of time; two children were placed in special education during the elementary years. Several children in the comparison group also received speech–language or reading intervention. Based on a comprehensive, individually administered battery of oral language and academic tests at age 13 years (Rescorla, 2005), findings indicated, first, that the magnitude of differences between the two groups was largest for both vocabulary knowledge (e.g., the resolution of multiple meanings; see also Norbury, 2005) and reading comprehension (at age 6–7 years). There were no significant differences between the two groups in decoding and oral reading fluency (Rescorla, 2002). Second, children's vocabulary performance at ages 24–31 months was a strong predictor of vocabulary and reading comprehension scores at age 13 years.

The slower and less robust word learning of the late talkers, first evident by age 9 years (Rescorla, 2002), and its noteworthy impact on reading comprehension has a major implication for future research on individual differences. A primary consideration is the potential substantive distinction between oral language impairment, with associated literacy learning problems as a categorical characterization, and "a language endowment spectrum" (Ellis Weismer, 2007, p. 95) that appears to distinguish many late talkers and may lead to some children being identified as having a distinct reading comprehension problem in grade 4 onward (e.g., Cain & Oakhill, 2006, 2007; Catts, Adlof, & Weismer, 2006; Nation & Snowling, 2004; Ricketts et al., 2008). In fact, Rescorla (2005) agrees with the speculation about a language endowment spectrum (see also Munson, Kurtz, & Windsor, 2005). Along this continuum, children with the most problems in language functions might be more severely impaired, whereas those with more functional, albeit weak, systems, such as late talkers, may have milder impairments.

From a wide perspective, Perfetti's (2007) "lexical quality hypothesis" speaks to relationships between word learning and comprehension in both the oral and reading comprehension realms in children with oral language impairment or even late talkers. The lexical quality hypothesis explains high-quality lexical representations for reading comprehension as an amalgam of well-specified orthographic, phonological, and grammatical representations combined with more generalized and less context-bound meanings that are all tightly bound together as a unit.[3] This fusion of linguistic units promotes *stability* in rapid word retrieval, *synchrony* between the activation of word identity constituents and their actual identification, and the *integration* of meanings for constructing comprehension. Low-quality lexical representations, in contrast, comprise less well-specified linguistic units that are not tightly bound with more variable consequences for the stability, synchrony, and integration of word identification and constructive comprehension. Most critically, Perfetti, consistent with Nagy (2005, 2007), makes the strong case that lexical quality "is acquired through effective experience with words" (p. 365), through oral language and literacy experiences. Therefore, the social experience (the effective teaching) of word learning provides a window into understanding the learning of children as speakers and as readers who differ in their comprehension skill. In effect, how, when, and where one "knows" a word is a function of the grading of lexical quality "across words for a given individual and across individuals for a given word" (Perfetti, 2007, p. 380).

CONSTRUCTING SYNTAX: THE THIRD CRITICAL BUILDING BLOCK

The Developmental Trajectory

Finding Patterns in the Input

As with speech perception and word learning, statistical patterning appears to play a major role in the early development of syntax. Applying a usage-based model, Tomasello (2000, 2007) builds the cross-linguistic case that, contrary to the nativist account of a genetically determined grammatical mechanism, young children first construct their syntax on the basis of the cultural learning that socializes them into a collaborative frame of mind. This cooperative mind-set supports emerging language learners as they learn how to share intentions with others. At the same time, they begin to differentiate between their own perspective (e.g., first-person "me") and the perspectives of others (e.g., third-person "them"), followed by the spoken production of situationally specific lexical items (Tomasello, 2000, 2007). These early word approximations vary based on children's individual interactional experiences with what they see, hear, and say.

Building Connections from Distributional Patterns

Once children can attend to and discern patterns in the language they hear, they then begin the gradual communication process of generating more abstract grammatical constructions, perhaps through analogical comparisons (Gentner & Namy, 2006). For example, regardless of the specific words used in utterances, sooner or later children must be able to infer through comparison the structural (subject–verb–object) and functional (agent–action–patient) similarities among "I hit Jeffrey," "You hug Mommy," and "Jamie kicking ball" (Tomasello, 2000, p. 161).

Others (e.g., Thompson & Newport, 2007) consider statistical learning of early syntax to be children's ability to work with transitional probability patterns as a function of the input they hear. In this context, "transitional probability" means the predictability of neighboring linguistic elements, such as that between adjacent words as an organizing framework for parsing phrases (Thompson & Newport, 2007). An example of the relationship between transitional probability patterns and phrase parsing would be the resolution of ambiguity in the utterance "They were [drinking glasses]" versus the more ambiguous "They were drinking [glasses]."

Statistical patterns of regularity also emerged in a home-based longitudinal study of the speech of 50 caregivers directed to their young children, who were followed from ages 14 months to 30 months (Huttenlocher, Vasilyeva, Waterfall, Vevea, & Hedges, 2007). Individual caregiver differences were maintained over the 16-month study, in that their syntactic complexity and diversity varied as a function of education and not income level. More educated caregivers generated increased proportions of multiclausal combinations, as well as noun phrases per utterance, for example, "The lady got the book that had a beautiful binding at Barnes & Noble last week" (Huttenlocher et al., 2007, p. 1080) versus a less complex, one-clause utterance such as "The lady got the book." Two conclusions surface from this study. First, in terms of oral language comprehension, young children who repeatedly experience more complex, multiclausal utterances from caregivers across a variety of situations, such as the object–relative clause complement in the preceding example, likely build a stronger cognitive scaffold for broadening their capacity to attend to, process, parse, and comprehend what is being said.

Second, as Huttenlocher et al. (2007) suggest, repeated experience also influences the probability of children producing more complex clausal structures increasingly on their own. Further production evidence comes from a cross-linguistic and cross-sectional experimental study of English-speaking (n = 57) and German-speaking (n = 60) children, ages 3 and 4 years old, which explored their ability to produce sentences with object–relative clauses via sentence repetition (Kidd, Brandt, Lieven, & Tomasello, 2007). The case is made that, similar to adults, preschool children are already sensitive to the distributional patterns (the forms and functions) of relative clauses in their home language. Moreover, Kidd et al. propose that "a distributional learning mechanism" (p. 890) serves as a linguistic means for identifying these frequency patterns. Others refer to an identity relations mechanism that guides young children in discerning when different levels of phonological and syntactic representations "can be matched to each other" (Mehler, Endress, Gervain, & Nespor, 2008, p. 209). What remains at issue is how young children determine in a relatively unconscious manner which patterns are sufficiently significant that they attend to certain distributional relations and not to others.

We next examine two areas with different theoretical lenses on the behavioral profiles of oral language impairment. One is the domain-specific viewpoint, with a particular emphasis on relationships between phonotactic probabilities and breakdowns in morphosyntactic learning, as mentioned earlier. The other is a domain-general viewpoint on possible associations between atypical functioning of procedural memory and nonlinguistic pattern learning.

The Morphosyntactic Learning of Children with Language Impairment as a Function of Phonotactic Probabilities

Agreement–Tense Omission Perspective

The prevailing domain-specific view of language impairment is one characterized by a "notable disruption in the linguistic system of affected children for the grammatical function of finiteness marking" (Rice, 2007, p. 419) in clauses in which tense and agreement are obligatory.[4] This depiction is known as the agreement–tense omission model (ATOM; Pine, Conti-Ramsden, Joseph, Lieven, & Serratrice, 2008). For example, in simple main clauses, such as "Jenny kissed Harry" and "My big red dog licked his bowl," only the verb position mandates past-tense inflection. Rice suggests that this obligatory tense property is found in languages, such as English, in which explicit subjects are required. Some preschool children in the LI category appear to treat finiteness marking as optional, for example, "My dog lick the bowl," and maintain variable use beyond the expected developmental period (age 4–5 years), sometimes up to age 8 years (Rice, 2004), when optional marking of the past-tense form may reappear in writing (Windsor, Scott, & Street, 2000). This inconsistency in the verb morphology of grammatical tense marking in the oral domain, including use of past-tense inflections, is attributed to inadequate and protracted development of underlying morphosyntactic representations (Rice, 2007; Rice et al., 2008). Rice (2004) describes this profile as a clinical signature of specific (or grammatical) LI, suggesting that it may be a less severe form of LI because it is restricted to agreement–tense relations.

Role of Phonotactic Probabilities in Tense–Agreement Marking

Others within the domain-specific perspective challenge the sufficiency of Rice's linguistic representation account of specific language impairment. In this alternative view, attention is given to relationships between phonotactic probabilities and the past-tense inflection *-ed*. However, two recent studies that explored this relationship in children with oral language impairment were neither rooted in usage-based theory nor did they directly consider individual differences.

One investigation included 10 preschool-age children (Leonard, Davis, & Deevy, 2007). The other involved 14 preadolescent children (Marshall & van der Lely, 2006) described as having grammatical-specific language impairment (G-SLI). As opposed to SLI, G-SLI is defined as a persistent and homogeneous type of language impairment, because it is a "relatively pure grammatical impairment . . . [involving] syntax, morphology, and . . . phonology" (Marinis & van der Lely, 2007, p. 559). A key term is "persistent." In this framework, children do not qualify for a G-SLI designation until they are at least 9 years of age (Marshall, Marinis, & van der Lely, 2007).

Control groups in the two studies were matched on linguistic and age criteria. The collective premise of both studies was that the frequency of phonotactic sequences (i.e., their regularity) "in a language as a whole . . . predict which regular forms are marked for tense, (and) not frequency within the past tense domain" (Marshall & van der Lely, 2006, p. 308). However, the two studies differed in their methodology along two critical dimensions. One variation involved the selection of verb types, for example, real words (Marshall & van der Lely, 2006) versus nonword verbs (Leonard et al., 2007). With nonwords, including nonword verbs, a premise is that children need to engage in incidental learning or fast mapping to store temporarily at least a partial lexical schema of an unfamiliar word in working memory, then access it rapidly for oral reproduction (Brea-Spahn & Silliman, in press). Nonword repetition tasks are increasingly common in the identification of child LI (for meta-analyses of nonword tasks, see Coady & Evans, 2008; Graf Estes, Evans, & Else-Quest, 2007). The other dimension of difference involved the nature of the phonotactic analyses conducted to select target items. In one case, the frequency of spoken English past-tense forms was examined in the context of single-syllable verb stems and verb-end clusters (e.g., *yelled*/yeld/ and *buzzed*/bΔzd/[5]; Marshall & van der Lely, 2006). In the other instance, the analysis entailed the positional phoneme and biphone[6] frequencies to determine high (e.g., *rith–rithed*) and low (e.g., *jith–jithed*) phonotactic probabilities of single-syllable nonword verb stems and inflected forms (Leonard et al., 2007).

Despite the age differences of the two samples, results were somewhat similar, although interpretations significantly diverged. In the Leonard et al. (2007) inquiry, preschool-age children with LI marked past tense less frequently, but more so with verb stems of low phonotactic probability in comparison to controls matched on either mean length of utterance or age. The negative effects of low phonotactic probability on past-tense inflection were not attributed to barriers in retaining information in working memory. Instead, the case is made that prolonged dependence on high phonotactic probability patterns for tense marking may suppress sensitivity to low phonotactic probability patterns of tense inflection.

Bruer (see Chapter 3, this volume) provides a similar rationale for the concept of "entrenchment," which is the reduction of neural network plasticity caused by effectively learning a task and not challenging oneself with new task learning. This constrained flexibility then makes new learning more difficult. To state this point in another way, some preschool-age children with LI may be generally less attuned to the obligatory nature of tense–agreement in finite clauses; for them, the phonotactic probability cues for past-tense marking may be less transparent, thereby heightening the possibility that they will fail to parse and infer patterns of regularity adequately in lower phonotactic probability contexts. Hence, fast-mapping abilities of children with LI may be constrained in these situations, which then restrict new word learning.

In contrast, Marshall and van der Lely (2006) ascribed the difficulties that their school-age sample had with real-word verb stem clusters associated with lower frequency factors to a specific limitation in morphological segmentation. This restraint is speculated to arise from a qualitatively different phonotactic parsing mechanism for the construction of verb stem + inflectional structures. As a consequence, children with G-SLI have lower-quality representations of stem + inflection, which in turn restricts their ability to take advantage of lower frequency phonotactic probability cues in the speech streams surrounding them for the purpose of constructing more complex morphological structures (Marshall et al., 2007).

Which hypothesis—entrenchment or a qualitatively different morphological parser—holds more merit for a better understanding of the oral language registers of children with LIs can only be resolved through future research. Of some note, both entrenchment and parsing issues play a role in a domain-general model that focuses on procedural learning in spoken language impairment.

Procedural Memory Effects on Pattern Learning in Language Impairment

The procedural deficit model (Ullman, 2001; Ullman & Pierpont, 2005) represents a domain-general description of LI in contrast to the domain-specific accounts discussed earlier (e.g., Marshall & van der Lely, 2006; Rice, 2007). By "domain-general" Ullman and Pierpont mean that "specific" LI actually reflects a broader dissociation of the brain structures supporting the procedural memory system from the declarative memory system, which serves semantic memory. In this dual-system framework, the procedural system is a general learning mechanism responsible for the implicit learning and eventual automaticity of complex sequential skills, from driving a car to certain sequential aspects of grammatical patterns. For example, the rapid parsing or segmenting of grammatical phrases for interpretative purposes based on language-specific distributional patterns may be considered a sequential function.

The procedural memory system also shares neural functions with the declarative memory system, which, according to Ullman (2001), subserves lexical–semantic access, among other functions. Because of these shared neural functions, Ullman and Pierpont (2005) propose that individuals with

LI draw on the declarative memory system as a compensatory strategy. As a consequence, they are susceptible to problems in new word learning when (1) meaning can only be inferred through the analysis of grammatical structure, (2) it is necessary to hold actively large amounts of information in working memory, and (3) new information is presented quickly, as it is in real-world fast mapping or incidental word learning. Hence, the atypical functioning of the procedural memory system impacts on the functions of the declarative memory system. For example, lexical recognition tasks, such as pointing to the name of a picture, should pose fewer difficulties than the lexical retrieval of items that require rapid recall, a serial function (see also McGregor et al., 2007). In brief, Ullman and Pierpont (2005) build the case that a general purpose, nonlinguistic mechanism, the procedural memory system, can better explain the "range and variation of the particular impaired linguistic and non-linguistic functions" (p. 400) that occurs across and within individuals than can other accounts, including domain-specific explanations.

It should be noted, however, that the Ullman and Pierpont (2005) application of procedural knowledge to "nonintentional" (implicit) learning substantially differs from the applications in the metacognitive and reading instruction literature to intentional (or explicit) learning. From the perspective of learning science, procedural knowledge is aligned with metacognition or "the ability to recognize the limits of one's current knowledge, then take steps to remedy the situation" (Bransford, Brown, & Cocking, 1999, p. 35). From the standpoint of reading instruction research, "procedural knowledge" is having metacognition about comprehension strategies or knowing what, when, and how to apply strategies consistent with one's purpose for reading (e.g., Pressley, 2002).

The Entrenchment Issue

Tomblin, Mainela-Arnold, and Zhang (2007) were the first to apply the procedural memory framework to the nonlinguistic pattern learning of 85 adolescents in grade 8 (mean age, 15 years) who were initially identified with spoken language impairment in kindergarten (mean age, 5 years, 9 months) (see Tomblin et al., 1997) and 47 of their classmates in grade 8 (mean age, 14 years, 7 months). The two groups were matched for nonverbal IQ; however, Tomblin et al. elected to use the kindergarten language composite measures obtained on the two groups rather than grade 8 measures, because of the assumption that a greater number of individual differences in grammatical and lexical learning would be more apparent in kindergarten than in grade 8.[7] A blocked-design serial response time task, a visual–spatial activity, combined with a growth curve analysis, was used to assess whether the shape of the learning curves of adolescents with LI differed from those of their typically developing peers in sequential pattern learning.

Results indicated that the two groups differed only in the pattern (sequence-specific) phases of the task, not in the random (nonpatterned) phases, which led Tomblin et al. (2007) to the interpretation that the group with LI encountered greater difficulty in suppressing competing patterns for rapid response selection than did their peers. Of interest, the growth curve analysis revealed that "this excess competition emerges only after the initial formation of candidate statistical representations" (p. 287). In other words, the adolescents with LI were able to generate a template of possible patterns but took longer to refine the template into a matching model, another prospective example of entrenchment.

The Parsing Issue

Another question addressed whether individual differences in grammatical and vocabulary performance in kindergarten were associated with procedural learning variations. Sequential processing was associated only with the composite grammar measures and not the composite lexical measures. The absence of a relationship between the adolescents' sequential learning and kindergarten performance on the vocabulary composites may reflect an underestimation of the complexity of word learning over the school-age years.

Tomblin et al. (2007) explain the grammatical association on the basis of a sequential learning system that fails to chunk or parse grammatical sequences systematically from the input. They also point out that if findings are replicated across other sequential learning domains, then the use of the term "specific language impairment" would be an unsuitable description of a domain-general problem. Given the novelty of this research area, an intriguing hypothesis for future investigation is that when parsing analyses are insufficient, one outcome may be a reduction in detecting the very regularities that are necessary for synchronization and integration with larger grammatical units, as well as the subsequent generation of richer grammatical representations. Insufficient discovery of regularities from candidate distributional patterns and resulting low-quality grammatical representations may result in underconnectivity, depending on the nature of individual experience. "Underconnectivity" appears functionally similar to Bruer's (see Chapter 3, this volume) concept of entrenchment. It is the less than optimal synchronization of the integrative neural circuitry that operates, either on an interregional or interhemispheric basis, when a rapid shift in strategy is crucial for problem solving or a new plan, including strategies, must be formulated for problem solving (Just, Cherkassky, Keller, & Minshew, 2004). The Just et al. description is also consistent with Perfetti's

(2007) description of the linguistic processes governing high-quality comprehension, and parallels as well the metacognitive literature's concept of procedural knowledge in contrast to the more implicit notion that Ullman and Pierpont (2005) express.

A significant question merits future exploration. Fast-mapping and gating studies, at least on a preliminary basis, indirectly suggest that children with oral language impairment might have prolonged problems with the stability, synchrony, and integration of their word learning. If these patterns continue to be found, they may challenge the Ullman and Pierpont (2005) proposition that the declarative memory system, described as responsible for lexical–semantic retrieval, remains intact in this group.

CONCLUSION

Throughout this final chapter, we have attempted to show that usage-based models are practical in the weight they give to what is linguistically likely (Chater & Manning, 2006). By "practical," we mean that usage-based models can provide a more transparent view of how variations in children's experiences over time with the multidimensional social world contribute in important ways to their language-specific knowledge of speech perception, word learning, and syntax—the foundations of the oral language register. In this framework, the social world functions as the mediator through which children capitalize on the frequency and regularity of the perceptual, lexical, and grammatical patterns that they continuously, but differentially, experience to infer and modify the structures and uses of the oral language register.

However, although frequency contributes to the building of children's expectations for pattern similarity, it cannot fully account for the language-learning process. As Diessel (2007) points out, frequency works in tandem with brain and learning mechanisms, such as information processing and inferencing, to support the representation of language knowledge in memory that "in turn influences . . . activation and interpretation in language use" (p. 123). This returns us to the issue posed about Kelly and Caren at the beginning of the chapter—how to explain individual differences in their behavioral profiles given the variable effects of frequency of experience on language and literacy learning combined with variations in neurocognitive responses to the social and linguistic worlds. The search for answers does not necessarily begin and end with the genetic code. For example, genetic studies of reading disability report that in 68% of identical twins, when one twin has a reading disability, the other also has a reading difficulty (Light & DeFries, 1995). The lack of a 100% co-occurrence in identical twins indicates that genes cannot tell it all; so, we are back to acknowledging the role of experience in accounting for individual differences. One possibility is to pursue the notion of differentiated continuity in oral language and literacy learning experiences.

A Differentiated Continuity Perspective

What appears to be missing from the standard nature versus nurture debate is the notion of a continuum of oral language and reading ability. This concept was highlighted in discussions of early speech perception and speech segmentation abilities (Fernald et al., 2006; Newman et al., 2006; Mody et al., 1999; Vihman et al., 1985), of late talkers (Ellis Weismer, 2007; Lee & Rescorla, 2008), of word learning (Munson, Swenson, & Manthei, 2005; Nagy, 2005; Perfetti, 2007; Stahl & Nagy, 2006), of difficulties with the construction of morphosyntax in the early years or as a persistent phenomenon (Marinis & van der Lely, 2007; Rice, 2007; Rice et al., 2008), and of variations in reading comprehension skill (Verhoeven & Van Leeuwe, 2008). Clearly, such a continuum opens up a wide playing field on which variations in the nature and frequency of experience may act. Why might this be so?

Perhaps one reason is that genes code individual predispositions for different outcomes in the form of a continuum that then interacts with the frequency and quality of experience. The resulting varied and complex outcomes should then come as no surprise. To illustrate this point, the inherited infrastructure of children with language and/or reading impairment may be poorly differentiated, as seen in language studies with at-risk infants (Been & Zwarts, 2003; Molfese, Molfese & Modgline, 2001; Richardson, Leppänen, Leiwo, & Lyytinen, 2003). Moreover, the patterns of differentiation may vary not only from child to child but also fluctuate in their degree of responsiveness to the real-time "dynamic tricky mixes" of internal and external influences that Nelson and Arkenberg describe (see Chapter 11, this volume). Such fluctuations are known to mediate individual responses to reading intervention as well (see Berninger, Chapter 4, this volume).

As a consequence, the nature and quality of the social and linguistic input combined with the responsiveness of the individual child's cognitive system influence whether outcomes are positive or negative. For example, applying the Bruer (see Chapter 3, this volume) and Just et al. (2004) points of view, a language-impaired system that is deeply "entrenched" or experiencing underconnectivity may be less pliable, which could be manifested as reduced sensitivity to the salient frequency patterns of the language input. Less pliability would also mean less attention to pattern similarity, the likelihood of lower-quality lexical and grammatical representations, and greater discontinuities in children's developmental trajectories in oral language and reading.

Neuroimaging research may provide some interesting insights in this regard. These methods have the potential to show differences in brain activation between groups despite similarity in the groups' behavioral responses. Using magnetoencephalography (MEG; see Simos, Sarkari, & Papanicolaou, Chapter 7, this volume, for a description of MEG), Wehner, Ahlfors, and Mody (2007) found significant differences in brain activity in children with and without reading impairment, despite the lack of a predicted behavioral difference on a phonologically demanding discrimination task involving subtle speech contrasts. Similarly, functional magnetic resonance imaging (fMRI) and diffusion tensor imaging (DTI; see Weber & Gaillard, Chapter 6, this volume, for further detail) have the potential to test a differentiated continuity hypothesis by examining the strength of structural and functional connections between various brain areas engaged in language activities in children who have LI compared to age- and performance-matched controls, using systematic and careful stimulus manipulations.

Intervention Implications

Students, like Kelly and Caren are symbolic of the many students who tussle day after day with the language of instruction. This daily struggle is made even more difficult by the fact that language serves as both the medium and content of instruction. The intervention implications of a differentiated continuity perspective are relatively straightforward. The oral language register is the bridge to the instructional language register. To a great extent, the Kellys and Carens, who are the real focus of this volume, are attempting to apply their oral language registers in a less than effective way to the demands of the instructional register.

As such, we suggest, pending further research, that the intertwined processes of entrenchment and underconnectivity may be factors differentially affecting the degree of mental flexibility necessary to adapt to and to apply strategically new language learning that then results in improved responsiveness to reading and writing instruction. In the best of all possible worlds, speech–language pathologists and other educational staff will design individualized interventions that meet two goals. First, intervention plans must link directly to curricular content and the language of instruction. Second, to intensify metalinguistic and metacognitive knowledge, intervention plans should systematically and explicitly assist students like Kelly and Caren to (1) identify lexical–semantic and syntactic patterns that are only partially familiar to them, (2) understand these patterns in a deeper manner through multiple opportunities for comparison and contrast, and (3) then make decisions about how to relate these patterns in an integrated way to real classroom reading and writing.

In conclusion, we have emphasized that varied distributional patterns arise from the inputs with which young children have experience. These patterns are associated with the construction of the early oral language register at the phonetic, vocabulary, and syntactic levels, which in turn influence their instructional language register. It is the quality and integrity of the oral language register that contributes to children's multiple memberships and sense of nested identity within the family, the neighborhood, and the school.

NOTES

1. All names are pseudonyms.
2. Others, such as Rescorla (2005), describe late talkers as "children identified under the age of 3 with expressive language delay" (p. 459).
3. In oral comprehension, the orthographic component would not be involved (Perfetti, 2007).
4. Finite clauses carry tense (denoting time of action), for example, "John kicked the ball to Mary." Nonfinite clauses do not carry tense, such as "*Turning around quickly* makes you dizzy." Nonfinite clauses convey aspect; that is, their time of action remains unmarked.
5. Parentheses indicate the phonetic symbols that index actual pronunciation. The verb-end clusters are underlined.
6. A biphone is a segment of speech that comprises two adjacent distinct phonemes in a word or phrase. For example, in *yelled*, there are two biphone units: ye-eld.
7. In this epidemiological study, students identified with LI in kindergarten or a subsequent reading disability were reassessed in grades 2, 4, and 8 (see Catts et al., 2006). The kindergarten composite language measures comprised comprehension, expression, vocabulary, grammar, and narrative (Tomblin, Records, & Zhang, 1996).

REFERENCES

Adrian, J. E., Clemente, R. A., & Villanueva, L. (2007). Mothers' use of cognitive state verbs in picture-book reading and the development of children's understanding of mind: A longitudinal study. *Child Development, 78*(4), 1052–1067.

Alt, M., & Plante, E. (2006). Factors that influence lexical and semantic fast mapping of young children with specific language impairment. *Journal of Speech, Language, and Hearing Research, 49*(5), 941–954.

Been, P. H., & Zwarts, F. (2003). Developmental dyslexia and discrimination in speech perception: A dynamic model study. *Brain and Language, 86*(3), 395–412.

Boysson-Bardies, B. (2001). *How language comes to children*. Cambridge, MA: MIT Press.

Bransford, J. D., Brown, A. L., & Cocking, R. R. (1999). *How people learn: Brain, mind, experience, and school.* Washington, DC: National Academy Press.

Brea-Spahn, M. R., & Silliman, E. R. (in press). Tuning into language-specific patterns: Nonword repetition and the big picture of bilingual vocabulary learning. In A. Y. Durgunoglu (Ed.), *Language learners: Their development and assessment in oral and written language.* New York: Guilford Press.

Cain, K., & Oakhill, J. (2006). Profiles of children with specific reading comprehension difficulties. *British Journal of Educational Psychology, 76*(4), 683–696.

Cain, K., & Oakhill, J. (2007). Reading comprehension difficulties: Correlates, causes, and consequences. In *Children's comprehension problems in oral and written language: A cognitive perspective* (pp. 41–75). New York: Guilford Press.

Carlisle, J. F. (2000). Awareness of the structure and meaning of morphologically complex words: Impact on reading. *Reading and Writing, 12*(3), 169–190.

Carlisle, J. F. (2004). Morphological processes that influence learning to read. In C. A. Stone, E. R. Silliman, B. J. Ehren, & K. Apel (Eds.), *Handbook of language and literacy: Development and disorders* (pp. 318–339). New York: Guilford Press.

Carlisle, J. F., & Stone, C. A. (2005). Exploring the role of morphemes in word reading. *Reading Research Quarterly, 40*(4), 428–449.

Catts, H. W., Adlof, S., & Weismer, S. E. (2006). Language deficits in poor comprehenders: A case for the simple view of reading. *Journal of Speech, Language, and Hearing Research, 49, 278–293.*

Catts, H. W., Fey, M. E., Zhang, X., & Tomblin, J. B. (1999). Language basis of reading and reading disabilities: Evidence from a longitudinal investigation. *Scientific Studies of Reading, 3*, 331–361.

Chater, N., & Manning, C. D. (2006). Probabilistic models of language processing and acquisition. *Trends in Cognitive Sciences, 10*(7), 335–344.

Cheek, A., Cormier, K., Repp, A., & Meier, R. (2001). Prelinguistic gesture predicts mastery and error in the production of early signs. *Language, 77*(2), 292–323.

Coady, J., & Evans, J. F. (2008). The uses and interpretations of nonword repetition tasks in children with and without specific language impairments. *International Journal of Language and Communication Disorders, 43*(1), 1–40.

Dale, E. (1965). Vocabulary measurement: Techniques and major findings. *Elementary English, 42*, 895–948.

Dickinson, D., McCabe, A., Anastasopoulos, L., Peisner-Feinberg, E. S., & Poe, M. D. (2003). The comprehensive language approach to early literacy: The interrelationships among vocabulary, phonological sensitivity, and print knowledge among preschool-aged children. *Journal of Educational Psychology, 95*(3), 465–481.

Dickinson, D. K., & Tabors, P. O. (Eds.). (2001). *Beginning literacy with language.* Baltimore: Brookes.

Diessel, H. (2007). Frequency effects in language acquisition, language use, and diachronic change. *New Ideas in Psychology, 25*, 108–127.

Ellis Weismer, S. (2007). Typical talkers, late talkers, and children with specific language impairment: A language endowment spectrum? In R. Paul (Ed.), *Language disorders from a developmental perspective: Essays in honor of Robin S. Chapman* (pp. 83–101). Mahwah, NJ: Erlbaum.

Fenson, L., Dale, P., Reznick, J. S., Bates, E., Thal, D., & Pethick, S. (1994). Variability in early communicative development. *Monographs of the Society for Research in Child Development, 59*(5, Serial No. 242).

Fernald, A., Perfors, A., & Marchman, V. A. (2006). Picking up speed in understanding: Speech processing efficiency and vocabulary growth across the 2nd year. *Developmental Psychology, 42*(1), 98–116.

Foorman, B. R., Anthony, J., Seals, L., & Mouzaki, A. (2002). Language development and emergent literacy in preschool. *Seminars in Pediatric Neurology, 9*(3), 173–184.

Garlock, V. M., Walley, A. C., & Metsala, J. L. (2001). Age-of-acquisition, word frequency, and neighborhood density effects on spoken word recognition by children and adults. *Journal of Memory and Language, 45*, 468–492.

Gathercole, S. E., & Baddeley, A. D. (1989). Evaluation of the role of phonological STM in the development of vocabulary in children: A longitudinal study. *Journal of Memory and Language, 28*, 200–213.

Gentner, D., & Namy, L. L. (2006). Analogical processes in language learning. *Current Directions in Psychological Science, 15*(6), 297–301.

Gershkoff-Stowe, L., & Hahn, E. R. (2007). Fast mapping skills in the developing lexicon. *Journal of Speech, Language, and Hearing Research, 50*(3), 682–697.

Goldstein, M. H., King, A. P., & West, M. J. (2003). Social interaction shapes babbling: Testing parallels between birdsong and speech. *Proceedings of the National Academy of Sciences USA, 100*, 8030–8035.

Graf Estes, K., Evans, J. L., & Else-Quest, N. M. (2007). Differences in the nonword repetition performance of children with and without specific language impairment: A meta-analysis. *Journal of Speech, Language, and Hearing Research, 50*(1), 177–195.

Gray, S. (2006). The relationship between phonological memory, receptive vocabulary, and fast mapping in young children with specific language impairment. *Journal of Speech, Language, and Hearing Research, 49*(5), 955–969.

Hart, B., & Risley, T. R. (1995). *Meaningful differences in the everyday experiences of young American children.* Baltimore: Brookes.

Hughes, C., & Dunn, J. (1998). Understanding mind and emotion: Longitudinal associations with mental-state talk between young friends. *Developmental Psychology, 34*, 1026–1037.

Huttenlocher, J., Vasilyeva, M., Waterfall, H. R., Vevea, J. L., & Hedges, L. V. (2007). The varieties of speech to young children. *Developmental Psychology, 43*(5), 1062–1083.

Jenkins, J. M., Turrell, S. L., Kogushi, Y., Lollis, S., & Ross, H. S. (2003). A longitudinal investigation of the dynamics of mental state talk in families. *Child Development, 74*, 905–920.

Just, M. A., Cherkassky, V. L., Keller, T. A., & Minshew, N. J. (2004). Cortical activation and synchronization during sentence comprehension in high-functioning autism: Evidence of underconnectivity. *Brain, 127*(8), 1811–1821.

Kagan, J. (2008). Using the proper vocabulary. *Developmental Psychobiology, 50*(1), 4–8.

Kidd, E., Brandt, S., Lieven, E., & Tomasello, M. (2007). Object relatives made easy: A cross-linguistic comparison of the constraints influencing young children's processing of relative clauses. *Language and Cognitive Processes, 22*(6), 860–897.

Kovas, Y., & Plomin, R. (2007). Learning abilities and disabilities: Generalist genes, specialist environments. *Current Directions in Psychological Science, 16*(5), 284–288.

Kuhl, P. K. (2007). Is speech learning "gated" by the social brain? *Developmental Science, 10*(1), 110–120.

Lee, E. C., & Rescorla, L. (2002). The use of psychological state terms by late talkers at age 3. *Applied Psycholinguistics, 23*, 623–641.

Lee, E. C., & Rescorla, L. (2008). The use of psychological state words by late talkers at ages 3, 4, and 5 years. *Applied Psycholinguistics, 29*(1), 21–39.

Leonard, L. B., Davis, J., & Deevy, P. (2007). Phonotactic probability and past tense use by children with specific language impairment and their typically developing peers. *Clinical Linguistics and Phonetics, 21*(10), 747–758.

Light, J. G., & DeFries, J. C. (1995). Comorbidity of reading and mathematics disabilities: Genetic and environmental etiologies. *Journal of Learning Disabilities, 28*, 96–106.

Lum, J. A. G., & Bavin, E. L. (2007). Analysis and control in children with SLI. *Journal of Speech, Language, and Hearing Research, 50*(6), 1618–1630.

Mainela-Arnold, E., Evans, J. L., & Coady, J. A. (2008). Lexical representations in children with SLI: Evidence from a frequency-manipulated gating task. *Journal of Speech, Language, and Hearing Research, 51*(2), 381–393.

Marinis, T., & van der Lely, H. K. J. (2007). On-line processing of wh-questions in children with G-SLI and typically developing children. *International Journal of Language and Communication Disorders, 42*(5), 557–582.

Marshall, C., Marinis, T., & van der Lely, H. (2007). Passive verb morphology: The effect of phonotactics on passive comprehension in typically developing and grammatical-SLI children. *Lingua, 117*(8), 1434–1447.

Marshall, C. R., & van der Lely, H. K.J. (2006). A challenge to current models of past tense inflection: The impact of phonotactics. *Cognition, 100*, 302–320.

McGregor, K. K., Sheng, L., & Ball, T. (2007). Complexities of expressive word learning over time. *Language, Speech, and Hearing Services in Schools, 38*(4), 353–364.

McGregor, K. K., Sheng, L., & Smith, B. (2005). The precocious two-year-old: Status of the lexicon and links to the grammar. *Journal of Child Language, 32*(3), 563–585.

Mehler, J., Endress, A., Gervain, J., & Nespor, N. (2008). From perception to grammar. In A. D. Friederici & G. Thierry (Eds.), *Early language development* (pp. 191–213). Philadelphia: Benjamins.

Mody, M. (2003). Phonological basis in reading disability: A review and analysis of the evidence. *Reading and Writing: An Interdisciplinary Journal, 16*, 21–39.

Mody, M., Schwartz, R. G., Gravel, J. S., & Ruben, R. J. (1999). Speech perception and verbal memory in children with and without histories of otitis media. *Journal of Speech, Language, and Hearing Research, 42*, 1069–1079.

Molfese, V. J., Molfese, D. L., & Modgline, A. (2001). Newborn and preschool predictors of second-grade reading scores. *Journal of Learning Disabilities, 34*(6), 545–554.

Munson, B., Kurtz, B. A., & Windsor, J. (2005). The influence of vocabulary size, phonotactic probability, and wordlikeness on nonword repetitions of children with and without specific language impairment. *Journal of Speech, Language, and Hearing Research, 48*(5), 1033–1047.

Munson, B., Swenson, C. L., & Manthei, S. C. (2005). Lexical and phonological organization in children: Evidence from repetition tasks. *Journal of Speech, Language, and Hearing Research, 48*, 108–124.

Nagy, W. (2005). Why vocabulary instruction needs to be long-term and comprehensive. In E. H. Hiebert & M. L. Kamil (Eds.), *Teaching and learning vocabulary: Bringing research to practice* (pp. 27–44). Mahwah, NJ: Erlbaum.

Nagy, W. (2007). Metalinguistic awareness and the vocabulary–comprehension connection. In R. K. Wagner, A. E. Muse, & K. R. Tannenbaum (Eds.), *Vocabulary acquisition: Implications for reading comprehension* (pp. 52–77). New York: Guilford Press.

Nagy, W., Berninger, V. W., & Abbott, R. D. (2006). Contributions of morphology beyond phonology to literacy outcomes of upper elementary and middle-school students. *Journal of Educational Psychology, 98*(1), 134–147.

Nation, K., & Snowling, M. J. (2004). Beyond phonological skills: Broader language skills contribute to the development of reading. *Journal of Research in Reading, 27*, 342–356.

Newman, R., Ratner, N. B., Jusczyk, A. M., Jusczyk, P. W., & Dow, K. A. (2006). Infants' early ability to segment the conversational speech signal predicts later language development: A retrospective analysis. *Developmental Psychology, 42*(4), 643–655.

Nittrouer, S. (2002). From ear to cortex: A perspective on what clinicians need to understand about speech perception and language processing. *Language, Speech, and Hearing Services in Schools, 33*(4), 237–252.

Nittrouer, S., & Lowenstein, J. H. (2007). Children's weighting strategies for word-final stop voicing are not explained by auditory sensitivities. *Journal of Speech, Language, and Hearing Research, 50*(1), 58–73.

Nixon, S. M. (2005). Mental state verb production and sentential complements in four-year-old children. *First Language, 25*, 19–37.

Norbury, C. F. (2005). Barking up the wrong tree?: Lexical ambiguity resolution in children with language impairments and autistic spectrum disorders. *Journal of Experimental Child Psychology, 90*(2), 142–171.

Norrix, L. W., Plante, E., Vance, R., & Boliek, C. A. (2007). Auditory–visual integration for speech by children with and without specific language impairment. *Journal of Speech, Language, and Hearing Research, 50*(6), 1639–1651.

Pennington, B. F., Snyder, K. A., & Roberts, R. J., Jr. (2007). Developmental cognitive neuroscience: Origins, issues, and prospects. *Developmental Review, 27*(3), 428–441.

Perfetti, C. (2007). Reading ability: Lexical quality to comprehension. *Scientific Studies of Reading, 11*(4), 357–383.

Peskin, J., & Astington, J. W. (2004). The effects of adding metacognitive language to story texts. *Cognitive Development, 19*, 253–273.

Pine, J. M., Conti-Ramsden, G., Joseph, K. L., Lieven, E. V., & Serratrice, L. (2008). Tense over time: Testing the agreement/tense omission model as an account of the pattern of tense-marking provision in early child English. *Journal of Child Language, 35*(1), 55–75.

Pressley, M. (2002). *Reading instruction that works: The case for balanced teaching* (2nd ed.). New York: Guilford Press.

Redcay, E. (2008). The superior temporal sulcus performs a common function for social and speech perception: Implications for the emergence of autism. *Neuroscience and Biobehavioral Reviews, 32*(1), 123–142.

Reed, D. K. (2008). A synthesis of morphology interventions and effects on reading outcomes for students in grades K–12. *Learning Disabilities Research and Practice, 23*(1), 36–49.

Rescorla, L. (2002). Language and reading outcomes to age 9 in late-talking toddlers. *Journal of Speech, Language, and Hearing Research, 45*(2), 360–371.

Rescorla, L. (2005). Age 13 language and reading outcomes in late-talking toddlers. *Journal of Speech, Language, and Hearing Research, 48*(2), 459–472.

Rescorla, L., Dahlsgaard, K., & Roberts, J. (2000). Late-talking toddlers: MLU and IPSyn outcomes at 3.0 and 4.0. *Journal of Child Language, 27*(3), 643–664.

Rice, M. L. (2004). Growth models of developmental language disorders. In M. L. Rice & S. F. Warren (Eds.), *Developmental language disorders: From phenotypes to etiologies* (pp. 207–240). Mahwah, NJ: Erlbaum.

Rice, M. L. (2007). Children with specific language impairment: Bridging the genetic and developmental perspectives. In E. Hoff & M. Shatz (Eds.), *Blackwell handbook of language development* (pp. 411–431). Malden, MA: Blackwell.

Rice, M. L., Taylor, C. L., & Zubrick, S. R. (2008). Language outcomes of 7-year-old children with or without a history of late language emergence at 24 months. *Journal of Speech, Language, and Hearing Research, 51*(2), 394–407.

Richardson, U., Leppänen, P., Leiwo, M., & Lyytinen, H. (2003). Speech perception of infants with high familial risk for dyslexia differ at the age of 6 months. *Developmental Neuropsychology, 23*(3), 385–397.

Ricketts, J., Bishop, D. V. M., & Nation, K. (2008). Investigating orthographic and semantic aspects of word learning in poor comprehenders. *Journal of Research in Reading, 31*(1), 117–135.

Saffran, J. R. (2001). Words in a sea of sounds: The output of infant statistical learning. *Cognition, 81*(2), 149–169.

Saffran, J. R., & Thiessen, E. D. (2007). Domain-general learning capacities. In E. Hoff & M. Shatz (Eds.), *Blackwell handbook of language development* (pp. 68–86). Malden, MA: Blackwell.

Scarborough, H. S. (2001). Connecting early language and literacy to later reading (dis)abilities: Evidence, theory, and practice. In S. B. Neuman & D. K. Dickinson (Eds.), *Handbook of early literacy research* (pp. 97–125). New York: Guilford Press.

Scarborough, H. S. (2005). Developmental relationships between language and reading: Reconciling a beautiful hypothesis with some ugly facts. In H. W. Catts & A. G. Kamhi (Eds.), *The connections between language and reading abilities* (pp. 3–24). Mahwah, NJ: Erlbaum.

Silliman, E. R., & Scott, C. M. (2006). Language impairment and reading disability: Connections and complexities. *Learning Disabilities Research and Practice, 21*(1), 1–7.

Snow, C. E., & & Kim, Y-S. (2007). Large problem spaces: The challenge of vocabulary for English language learners. In R. K. Wagner, A. E. Muse, & K. R. Tannenbaum (Eds.), *Vocabulary acquisition: Implications for reading comprehension* (pp. 123–139). New York: Guilford Press.

Stahl, S. A., & Nagy, W. E. (2006). *Teaching word meanings*. Mahwah, NJ: Erlbaum.

Storkel, H. L., Armbruster, J., & Hogan, T. P. (2006). Differentiating phonotactic probability and neighborhood density in adult word learning. *Journal of Speech, Language, and Hearing Research, 49*(6), 1175–1192.

Storkel, H. L., & Morrisette, M. L. (2002). The lexicon and phonology: Interactions in language acquisition. *Language, Speech, and Hearing Services in Schools, 33*, 24–37.

Studdert-Kennedy, M. (1986). Sources of variability in early speech development. In J. Perkell, & D. H. Klatt (Eds.), *Invariance and variability in speech processes* (pp. 58–76). Hillsdale, NJ: Erlbaum.

Thal, D. J., Bates, E., Goodman, J., & Jahn-Samilo, J. (1997). Continuity of language abilities: An exploratory study of late-and early-talking toddlers. *Developmental Neuropsychology, 13*(3), 239–273.

Thompson, S. P., & Newport, E. L. (2007). Statistical learning of syntax: The role of transitional probability. *Language Learning and Development, 3*(1), 1–42.

Tomasello, M. (2000). The item-based nature of children's early syntactic development. *Trends in Cognitive Science, 4*(4), 156–163.

Tomasello, M. (2007). Cooperation and communication in the 2nd year of life. *Child Development Perspectives, 1*(1), 8–12.

Tomblin, J. B., Mainela-Arnold, E., & Zhang, X. (2007). Procedural learning in adolescents with and without specific language impairment. *Language Learning and Development, 3*(4), 269–293.

Tomblin, J. B., Records, N. L., Buckwalter, P., Zhang, X., Smith, E., & O'Brien, M. (1997). Prevalence of specific language impairment in kindergarten children. *Journal of Speech, Language, and Hearing Research, 40*(6), 1245–1260.

Tomblin, J. B., Records, N. L., & Zhang, X. (1996). A system for the diagnosis of specific language impairment in kindergarten children. *Journal of Speech and Hearing Research, 39*(6), 1284–1294.

Ullman, M. T. (2001). A neurocognitive perspective on language: The declarative/procedural model. *Nature Reviews: Neuroscience, 2*(10), 717–726.

Ullman, M. T., & Pierpont, E. I. (2005). Specific language impairment is not specific to language: The procedural deficit hypothesis. *Cortex, 41*, 399–433.

Verhoeven, L., & Van Leeuwe, J. (2008). Prediction and the development of reading comprehension: A longitudinal study. *Applied Cognitive Psychology, 22*, 407–423.

Vernon-Feagans, L., Pancsofar, N., Willoughby, M., Odom, E., Quade, A., & Cox, M. (in press). Predictors of maternal language to infants during a picture book task in the home: Family SES, child characteristics and the parenting environment. *Journal of Applied Developmental Psychology.*

Vihman, M. M., Macken, M. A., Miller, R., Simmons, H., & Miller, J. (1985). From babbling to speech: A re-assessment of the continuity issue. *Language, 61*, 397–445.

Vitevitch, M. S., Luce, P. A., Pisoni, D. B., & Auer, E. T. (1999). Phonotactics, neighborhood activation, and lexical access for spoken words. *Brain and Language, 68*, 306–311.

Wehner, D., Ahlfors, S., & Mody, M. (2007). Effects of phonological contrast on auditory word discrimination in children with and without reading disability: A magnetoencephalography (MEG) study. *Neuropsychologia, 45*(14), 3251–3262.

Windsor, J., Scott, C., & Street, C. (2000). Verb and noun morphology in the spoken and written language of children with language learning disabilities. *Journal of Speech, Language, and Hearing Research, 43*, 1322–1336.

Wise, J. C., Sevcik, R. A., Morris, R. D., Lovett, M. W., & Wolf, M. (2007). The relationship among receptive and expressive vocabulary, listening comprehension, pre-reading skills, word identification skills, and reading comprehension by children with reading disabilities. *Journal of Speech, Language, and Hearing Research, 50*(4), 1093–1109.

Zubrick, S. R., Taylor, C. L., Rice, M. L., & Slegers, D. W. (2007). Late language emergence at 24 months: An epidemiological study of prevalence, predictors, and covariates. *Journal of Speech, Language, and Hearing Research, 50*(6), 1562–1592.

Index

Page numbers followed by an *f*, *n*, or *t* indicate figures, notes, or tables.

P